PROPHECY IN CARTHAGE

Prophecy in Carthage
Perpetua, Tertullian, and Cyprian

CECIL M. ROBECK, JR.

THE PILGRIM PRESS
CLEVELAND, OHIO

The Pilgrim Press, Cleveland, Ohio 44115
© 1992 by The Pilgrim Press

The following publishers have generously given permission to use extended
quotations from copyrighted works: from *The Acts of the Christian Martyrs*, by
Herbert Musurillo, © 1972, reprinted by permission of Oxford University Press;
from *The Letters of St. Cyprian*, vols. 1–5, by G. W. Clarke, © 1984, 1986, and
1989, reprinted by permission of the Paulist Press

Printed in the United States of America
The paper used in this publication is acid free and meets the minimum
requirements of American National Standard for Information Sciences-
Permanence of Paper for Printed Library Materials, ANSI Z39.48–1984

97 96 95 94 93 92   5 4 3 2 1

Library of Congress Cataloging-in-Publication Data
Robeck, Cecil M.
Prophecy in Carthage : Perpetua, Tertullian, and Cyprian / Cecil M. Robeck, Jr.
p.   cm.
Includes bibliographical references and index.
ISBN 0-8298-0924-4 (alk. paper)
1. Prophecy—Christianity—History of doctrines—Early church, ca. 30-600.
2. Prophets—Tunisia—Carthage (Extinct city) 3. Passio SS. Perpetuae et
Felicitatis. 4. Perpetua, Saint, d.203. 5. Tertullian, ca. 160-ca. 230.
6. Cyprian, Saint, Bishop of Carthage. 7. Carthage (Extinct city)—Church
history. I. Title.
BR195.P74R63   1992
234'.13—dc20   92-28622
CIP

FOR PATSY

Contents

PREFACE

The gift of prophecy has long played an important role in the history of the people of God. The prophets were important to Israel, proclaiming the revelations of Yahweh in many and diverse situations. The early church saw the benefits of both prophet and prophecy. The Apostle Paul highlighted this gift when he tried to correct certain excesses among the Corinthian Christians. He saw it as a useful tool in the body of Christ, sovereignly bestowed by the Spirit of God upon certain individuals in order to provide edification, encouragement, and/or comfort to the body.

With the long history of prophetic phenomena, including dreams, visions, oracles, even words uttered in another tongue under inspiration of God's Spirit, it would seem that the problems of definition would have been ironed out long ago. But understandings differ. Definitions sometimes exclude one another. And prophetic phenomena seem not to be confined to the church or even to Israel out of which the church sprung.

Christianity was spawned in an empire both pagan and antagonistic. Early Christians were forced to contend with claims of prophetic activity in cults, such as Delphi, that they condemned. Growing up as it did in the midst of the various philosophies of the day, the early church had to deal with assorted marginal and heretical claims to divine inspiration. Viewing the church as the New Israel and, in many cases, wishing to engage in productive dialogue with Jewish leaders, many patristic writers analyzed the work of the Old Testament prophets and studied Jewish expectations and prophetic claims. Providing as it did new freedom for entire segments of previously oppressed humanity, the church was required to assess not only questions of discernment between genuine and spurious prophetic claims but also issues of order such as those posed by the Corinthians and the enthusiasts of the New Prophecy. As time passed on and the original apostles died out, concerns to preserve the apostolic faith and tradition, while at the same time allowing the church freedom to listen to the voice of the Spirit, rose to the surface.

Throughout this period, the church was yet finding out who it was. At times it experienced persecution, at other times some toleration, even acceptance. Calls for renewal and other primitivistic impulses were raised at times. Expectations varied, conditioned in part by time and place and the personalities involved. Regional factors came into play. New contexts and settings required different understandings. The church was in a state of flux as it moved to ever-expanding regions of the empire.

On many occasions, the church's understanding of the prophetic phenomena has also differed. The Reformers, for instance, tended to view this gift as exegetical or expository in nature, often equating it with the task of preaching. The Roman church saw the charisma move steadily from the possession of enthusiasts to the pronouncements of bishops to the infallible statements of the prelate of Rome. Liberal Protestants have often argued it is the voice of social protest, a voice that speaks out against certain moral, social, and political ills in contemporary society. Pentecostals and charismatic Christians have tended to view this charisma in relatively privatized terms of spontaneously uttered oracles, inspired by the Holy Spirit and spoken in a specific situation. A brief survey of the canonical prophets will go far to demonstrate the truth inherent in each of these positions.

In a sense, the church today is little different from the preceding church. It is still confronted by pagan and occult religious and prophetic claims around the world. It is still confronted by the presence of a Jewish people who continue to probe the meaning of their prophetic books, looking for a messianic figure who will be a prophet like Moses. The roots of Christianity still lie deeply within the religion of Israel. To understand itself, therefore, the church must continue to search the writings of the Old Testament, where it, too, is confronted with prophetic phenomena from a very early stage. Whole segments of society are finding liberation in Jesus Christ, a phenomenon that continues to provoke questions about prophetic voices and order alike. Self-proclaimed "prophets," from Simon Kimbangu to those in contemporary Kansas City still need appropriate attention and adequate testing. And the authority of the apostolic faith as it is found in creed and canon is one that is yet hotly debated in some circles of the church. Is continuing revelation really a threat to a fixed canon?

As a lifelong Pentecostal, I have struggled with many of these questions. As a church historian, I have also observed many parallels between contemporary claims regarding prophetic phenomena and the claims of

Christians through the centuries. As I reflected on the subject, I have explored the gift of prophecy in the Old and New Testaments, looked at the *Didache*, the *Shepherd of Hermas*, the works of Justin Martyr and Irenaeus, Clement, Hippolytus, Origen, and others like them. I have struggled with the advocates of the New Prophecy and the bishops whose leadership those advocates so hotly contested. It was this study that led inevitably to North Africa, where there were sufficient sources in place to see how prophetic phenomena manifest themselves over an extended period of time—about three generations. Perpetua, Tertullian, and Cyprian were quite different, yet they shared many of the same concerns. I have been urged on, not only by the claims of my own tradition but also by the renewed study of prophetic phenomena during the past decade. A study of the role and function of prophetic gifts at Carthage should have some relevance for the whole church. It may help to balance enthusiasts, broaden fundamentalists, narrow those who view prophetic activity too broadly, and challenge those who have overlooked an important charisma of the church. It may raise to a new level of appreciation the place that this gift might have among oppressed people, while calling to account those who engage in oppression.

In order to facilitate the use of this volume, I have relied on the following standard translations of the texts throughout, unless otherwise noted. For *The Passion of Perpetua and Felicitas*, I have used Herbert Musurillo's excellent translation from *The Acts of the Christian Martyrs*, ed. Henry Chadwick, Oxford: The Clarendon Press, 1972. In order to have an English translation of Tertullian's many works that are gathered in a readily available form, I have used the recent reprints of Alexander Roberts and James Donaldson, eds., *The Ante-Nicene Fathers*, rev. ed. by A. Cleveland Coxe, vols. 3 and 4, Grand Rapids: William B. Eerdmans Publishing Company, 1973 and 1972. For the works of Cyprian, I have employed the exhaustive work of G. W. Clarke, *The Letters of St. Cyprian*, Ancient Christian Writers Series, vols. 43, 44, 46, and 47, New York: Newman Press, 1984, 1986, 1989. I wish to thank Oxford University Press and Paulist Press for permission to quote the works of Musurillo and Clarke, respectively. I wish also to thank the National Council of the Churches of Christ in the U.S.A. for permission to quote the RSV.

A study of this magnitude could not be undertaken without the love, prayers, support, and time made possible by friends and family who have prodded me along. To mention all of them would be impossible. To mention any runs the risk of overlooking some important contributors. There are some, however, to whom I am deeply indebted. Many secretaries have played a tangible role through the years, among them Sandy Wheatley, Ann Lausch, Diane Woods, Betty Means, Elaine Stewart,

Barbara Kempthorne, and Jennifer Stock. A special word of thanks is due to the staff of the word processing office at Fuller Theological Seminary. Janet Gathright typed the first draft, Dave Sielaff did the final one. In between, Anne White and Susan Carlson Wood made significant contributions. A challenge from James D. G. Dunn; a stimulating assignment from George E. Ladd; gentle encouragement and prodding by Glenn W. Barker, Russell P. Spittler, and Robert P. Meye; instructive comments from Geoffrey W. Bromiley, Robert C. Gregg, Richard A. Norris, and David M. Scholer; the congenial interaction of colleagues Donald A. Hagner, James E. Bradley and Richard A. Muller; the generosity of William Tabbernee; the enthusiastic advocacy of Gerald T. Sheppard; and the patient understanding of my editors, Barbara Withers and Marjorie Pon, at The Pilgrim Press have all become part of this project. Where it has not lived up to expectations, I must bear sole responsibility.

I would be remiss not to mention my family here as well. My parents, Cecil M. and Berdetta M. Robeck, were instrumental in my own spiritual formation and in the development of my critical loyalty to the Pentecostal tradition. Each of my four sons, Jason Lloyd, John Mark, Peter Scott, and Nathan Eric, has contributed enormously to the completion of this work. The fact that almost all of this work has been completed on their time, evenings, weekends, even vacations, means that they have given generously of their time with dad to see it through. My wife, Patsy, has had to be even more understanding, for in my many absences, she has had to fill my role too. Without her complicity in the vision we share, none of this would have ever happened.

Finally, I wish to acknowledge the strength the Lord has granted me to endure the demands of the past few years. It is to God's glory that I write, that the church, my sisters and brothers, might look at previous generations of our fellow believers and learn from their experiences and be edified. To some extent, then, I share the same concerns and hopes expressed by the redactor of *The Passion of Perpetua and Felicitas*.

CHAPTER ONE

Introduction

THE UNIQUENESS OF "PROPHETIC GIFTS" AT CARTHAGE

The literature that came forth from Carthage, especially in the first six decades of the third century, provides an important watershed of information on how prophecy and prophetic gifts such as visions functioned and what role they played for that community. By "function" is meant their interpretation, application, and effect on members of the church or the congregation as a whole. By "role" is meant the extent of their presence in the North African church and the place they were given in the church.

During the roughly six decades, A.D. 202–258, the church at Carthage underwent several selective persecutions. Some were aimed at the new converts with the hope that their public example would deter others who were contemplating a conversion to Christianity. Such was the persecution of A.D. 202/3 by Severus, in which Perpetua and Saturus suffered and died. Other persecutions, notably those under Decius (A.D. 251) and Valerian (A.D. 257–258) were aimed at the clergy, with the expectation that the church could not continue to grow without their leadership. It was in the Valerian persecution that Cyprian lost his life.

In Carthage during these years, there were those who recorded experiences that described or illustrated the various functions and the role which prophetic gifts played in the North African church of their day. Perpetua, a twenty-two-year-old layperson and catechumen, and Saturus, one of her fellow prisoners, both left diaries in which they recorded several of their visions together with the interpretation and/or application of them as they occurred in their original setting. In turn, these accounts were incorporated into a larger work by an unnamed redactor who attempted to demonstrate that in his or her own day (circa A.D. 206/7) the Spirit continued to distribute such charismata as prophecy and visions according to the promise of Acts 2:17–18 (cf. Joel 2:28–29).[1]

Tertullian, possibly a presbyter in the church at Carthage, but certainly an important theologian-writer there, was a contemporary of Perpetua, Saturus, and this unnamed redactor. His earliest writings have extremely little to say on the subject of prophecy, although he does allow that it was a gift he expected would continue in the church until the consummation.[2] Therefore, Perpetua is treated first in this study, since her own visions predate Tertullian's keen interest in visions and prophecies.

By the beginning of the second decade of the third century, Tertullian had aligned himself with what became known as the New Prophecy, or Montanism. It was a prophetic movement through and through which made the claim that the Paraclete was speaking anew in and through its prophets. A number of Tertullian's works mention clearly his affinities with this group, particularly those written from about A.D. 207 and onward.[3] Included in some of these writings are his perspectives on the subject of ecstasy as it relates to prophecy, and in various arguments he records and uses several oracles and visions to support some theological point. Furthermore, he provides an extended apology for the continuing role of the Paraclete in the church.

By midcentury, Tertullian had died at a very old age[4] and the influence of Montanism within the North African church had begun to subside. Cyprian was declared bishop of Carthage and, in a sense, a new era was begun. Yet, in Cyprian's epistles and treatises are found numerous references to visions. Of course, some of his epistles are those he received from others, but they, too, mention visions and prophecies. Indeed, from Cyprian's writings, one may conclude that such phenomena were not at all unusual nor were they unexpected among Christians of mid-third-century Carthage. They were sufficiently common as to be readily expected. They were a normal part of the Christian life.

This study is based on these three sets of documents and these writers. Several articles have been addressed specifically to the subject of Perpetua's visions and to the vision of Saturus.[5] A few more have covered the subject of Tertullian, especially as he has been related to Montanist prophecy.[6] Yet, fewer have been written on the subject of prophecy and/or visions as they appear in the writings of Cyprian.[7] To date, no one has treated the subject as it has unfolded from A.D. 202 to 258 in Carthage.[8]

The relationship of psychology to the study of these individuals has been applied in some cases quite extensively. Marie-Louise von Franz has written the longest study to date on the visions of Perpetua, interpreting them in light of the dream symbolism developed by psychologist C. G. Jung.[9] Mary Lefkowitz has attempted to write a short bit of psychohistory based at least in part on Perpetua's visions.[10] Through the analysis of two of Perpetua's visions, Peter Dronke has attempted to establish the extent of Perpetua's "self-awareness" by evaluating the integrity of the outer and inner parts of Perpetua and her context as they are portrayed in her diary.[11]

The most significant study of Cyprian's use of visions is by Adolf von Harnack, who concludes that they record Cyprian's personal political attempts at the psychological manipulation of his congregation while he was an absentee bishop.[12] For purposes of the present study, an in-depth psychological evaluation of Perpetua, Tertullian, and Cyprian will not be attempted. However, reference will be made to aspects of these existing psychological studies when relevant. The visions and prophecies of these individuals will be examined primarily by looking at them historically and theologically to determine what factors gave rise to them, to their symbolism, and to their interpretations and applications.

At first glance, Perpetua's visions appear to have had essentially a personal focus, and those of Saturus an ecclesiastical one. Yet the redactor apparently saw a more universal use for them, unlimited by time or space. Tertullian appealed to visions and prophecies to support his own theological arguments, whereas Cyprian moved in some ways beyond theology and back into the realm of personal practice. He claimed the authority of his visions in making appointments to ecclesiastical office, providing comfort to the confessors, seeking personal guidance, and exhorting his congregation to unity.

WHAT IS MEANT BY "PROPHETIC GIFTS"?

Before we begin our foray into the literature of the third-century congregation at Carthage, it is important to define certain terms. "The gift of prophecy," or as Paul called it, simply, "prophecy,"[13] is a phenomenon with a long tradition among the people of God. Israel had its prophets, and the church has had hers. But simple and workable definitions of this phenomenon have been difficult to isolate. The Reformers, for instance, tended to view this gift as exegetical and/or expository, often equating it with the task of preaching or teaching.[14] Others have understood it to be a voice raised against certain moral, social, or political ills of their day.[15] Still others, particularly within Pentecostalism or within the more recent charismatic renewal, have generally understood the gift of prophecy to include a spontaneously inspired utterance given on behalf of God.[16]

Recent New Testament scholarship has struggled with definition as well. David Hill summarized this struggle especially as it related to the ongoing Society of Biblical Literature seminar on the subject in the early seventies. In 1973, M. E. Boring offered a definition of "prophet" that was modified a year later to apply specifically to the Christian prophet. David Aune offered a further revised definition that Hill found to be more acceptable.[17] While acknowledging his indebtedness both to Boring and to Aune, David Hill included a concern of J. Lindblom that took seriously the idea of a prophetic class of persons. "A Christian prophet," Hill maintained, is a Christian who functions within the Church, occasionally or regularly, as a divinely called and divinely inspired speaker who receives intelligible and authoritative revelations or messages which he is impelled to deliver publicly, in oral or written form, to Christian individuals and/or to the Christian community.[18]

By such a definition, Perpetua, Saturus, and Cyprian would be prophets in third-century Carthage, along with a number of others named in Tertullian's treatises and Cyprian's letters and epistles. By this same definition, Tertullian, Firmilian, and the redactor of *The Passion of Perpetua and Felicitas* would not be prophets. Their role would be that of reporters and/or eyewitnesses of such activity. David Aune has criticized Hill's definition as making it difficult to distinguish between prophets, preachers, and teachers by his inclusion of the words "divinely called and inspired."[19]

Aune's own definition includes the words that "The Christian who functions in the prophetic role . . . believes that he receives divine revelations in propositional form."[20] The verb "believes" subjectifies the definition by moving it toward the category of the psychological. The claim "I believe" is in need of testing, and if the person making the claim speaks forth a truly prophetic word, such as in the case of a prediction that is fulfilled, the claim is upheld. This definition, then, provides a clear role for testing or discernment.

Including the phrase "in propositional form," however, a phrase that Boring also finds acceptable,[21] is a bit more problematic. Is a "propositional statement" another term for oracle? If, for instance, a vision does not come equipped with a "propositional statement" (e.g., a clear oracular utterance), then the question must be raised as to whether it is a genuine *prophetic* vision. If, however, the interpretation granted to the vision by the seer of the vision is understood as the propositional statement, then the vision is understood to be prophetic.

For our purposes, emphasis will be placed on the prophetic function rather than the prophetic person. The definition provided by David Hill will be rewritten so that prophecy may be understood as a "divine revelation received by a Christian who functions in the prophetic role on an occasional, regular, or temporary basis, which is then shared in an oral or written form with other Christians."[22] The form this revelation takes *may* be described as a vision that is then interpreted in a propositional format, or this revelation *may* take a strictly oracular form. The behavior of the person receiving such a revelation at the time the revelation is received *may* be described as being in a state of "ecstasy," although there *may not* be any such language used. And, the effect of the revelation *may* be to bring upbuilding, encouragement, or consolation to those Christians who hear or read it (1 Cor. 14:3). It may, however, also provide guidance in specific circumstances (see Acts 11:28; 13:1–3; 20:22–23; 21:4, 9–14).

The term "prophetic gifts" has been chosen to include visions and even certain dreams within the context of what is understood to be prophecy. In the Old Testament, prophets were first called seers,[23] a designation which seems to indicate that a prophet was sometimes visually stimulated. The prophet *saw* perhaps visions, perhaps dreams that God had revealed.

Further evidence of the relationship between visions and prophets may be found in such Old Testament passages as Hos. 12:10, in which Yahweh spoke and by implication revealed the prophetic word through oral or spoken messages, through visions, and through parables:

> I spoke to the prophets;
> it was I who multiplied visions
> and through the prophets gave parables. (RSV)

On numerous occasions the prophets from early to late spoke of visions as the source of some of their prophetic oracles.[24] The New Testament has references to such phenomena, although their clear connection to the prophet is less apparent.[25] Thus, it appears to be appropriate to discuss the subject of visions as one "prophetic gift," especially if we accept James Ash's thesis that by Cyprian's time the charisma of prophecy was no longer *called* prophecy, even though it functioned in that way.[26] Clearly, for the church in third-century Carthage, "visions" picked up where "prophecy" left off.

THE STUDY OF PROPHECY IN THE ANTE-NICENE CHURCH

The history of the church at Carthage has been well documented by two major French studies released almost simultaneously at the turn of the century. Paul Monceaux's seven-volume study on the literary history of African Christianity documented the church's thought as it developed from its beginnings until the Arab invasion.[27] The second study was authored by Dom H. Leclercq in 1904. It covered the background and origin of the church in Africa from its beginnings to the eighth century. Its focus was less on the literature and the literary thought of the church than that of Monceaux's work and more on the events which occurred in the societal context.[28] Both studies, however, make clear the archaeological and literary wealth of the North African church.

Within the past two decades, the study of the gift of prophecy has come into its own. No fewer than a dozen major works have been published on the subject.[29] Some of these (Boring, Dautzenberg, Ellis, Grudem, Müller) address the subject solely within the New Testament, whereas others move beyond the bounds of the canonical literature and include at least a chapter that addresses the subject into the second century (Aune, Cothenet, Hill, Panagopoulos). Reiling's monograph focuses largely on this later material. His work covers the subject as it appears in a single chapter of the *Shepherd of Hermas*. Ronald Heine provides a valuable collection and translation of many oracles that surfaced in the Montanist movement, but without assessment.

The gift of prophecy has received a great deal of attention in scholarly journals as well. Articles abound on the gift of prophecy in the New Testament, especially those which focus on the creative role of early Christian prophets and the genuine logia of Jesus. By comparison, the number of articles on prophecy in the postcanonical and Ante-Nicene materials are relatively few in number.[30] There are a few older, important articles that have bearing on the subject as well,[31] but it is clear that the surface of what is available in the Ante-Nicene literature has merely been scratched. As late as 1981, Howard Clark Kee, professor of biblical studies at Boston University, noted in a review of David Hill's then recently published work, *New Testament Prophecy*, that this gift of prophecy was "an important, neglected phenomenon of Christian origins."[32]

During that same year John Panagopoulos, who himself had authored the most substantial treatment of the gift of prophecy to date and had edited a second volume on the subject as the result of a consultation held at the Ecumenical Institute in Bossey, Switzerland, in 1975, laid out a four-fold agenda for future research in Christian prophecy in his own review of David Hill's book. It included:

(1) the examination of the relations between the several forms and functions of prophecy in the different early Christian writers and the historical process of development that the phenomenon underwent;

(2) knowledge of the historical and theological factors that determined this development, particularly in the second century;

(3) the investigation not only of the distinctive elements but also the constants in early Christian prophecy despite (or because of) its variety in form, content, and purpose; and

(4) the attempt to build up a historical picture of the prophetic phenomenon throughout the relevant Christian writings up to Montanism.[33]

Only on the basis of such work, Panagopoulos argued, would it be possible for us to understand adequately "the permanent significance of prophecy for the life and mission of the Church today."[34]

It is clearly the case that the subject of prophets and prophecy was of critical importance for the early church, especially up to and during the second century. With the competing claims of the orthodox,[35] the Gnostic,[36] and the Montanist,[37] each of whom claimed a genuine prophetic tradition, the role of teaching became increasingly important. Decisions had to be rendered regarding who these prophets were, what it was they were saying, and how they were exercising their alleged prophetic gifts. Both discernment and definition were critical.[38]

Nevertheless, amid this crucible of competing prophetic claims, many scholars have noted a general decline in the appearance of prophetic gifts in the patristic period. There have been at least four basic theses set forth to explain this decline. Adolf von Harnack believed that this decline was in some way related to the formation of the canon: "Its [the canon's] creation very speedily resulted in the opinion that the time of divine revelation had gone past and was exhausted in the Apostles, that is, in the records left by them." Harnack went on to qualify this remark by saying that "We cannot prove with certainty that the canon was formed to confirm this opinion." Nevertheless, he argued, "The New Testament, though not all at once, put an end to a situation where it was possible for any Christian under the inspiration of the Spirit to give authoritative disclosures and instructions."[39]

Related to this in part, but coming at it from another perspective is the position shared by David Hill and David Aune. David Hill linked the so-called decline of prophecy to the repudiation of Montanism and the concomitant rise of those "catechists, preachers, scholars, and theologians" who brought more "rational and didactic forms of spiritual utterance" into the church.[40] Aune especially affirmed the conclusion that the rise of theologians and teachers displaced prophecy.[41]

Hans von Campenhausen proposed a similar, yet more general solution to the problem, suggesting that the decline of prophecy is related to the official transmission of the apostolic tradition or, to use his words, "traditional apostolic truth." It was not a clear case of opposing schools—the official "ecclesiastical" versus the "charismatic"—for those in ecclesiastical offices possessed the Spirit and those who might be described as "charismatic" or pneumatic received their power to teach from that traditional apostolic truth. But when those who proclaimed spontaneous oracles became rare, or became identified with schism or heresy, it was an "objective and dogmatic" reality that led to the intensifying of official ecclesiastical authority because of its accompanying safeguards.[42]

James Ash has in some ways built upon the position of von Campenhausen, yet he is strikingly dissimilar in his conclusion. His contention is that it was neither canon, nor heresy, nor even the concern for "traditional apostolic truth" *per se* that led to the ultimate decline of prophetic gifts. Rather, it was that "the charisma of prophecy was captured by the monarchial episcopate, used in its defense, and left to die an unnoticed death when true episcopal stability rendered it a superfluous tool." Thus, by Cyprian's day, one might say that "traces of the charisma remained," and Ash contends that although there was a phenomenon which still functioned in the same way the gift of prophecy had functioned, "The charisma was no longer called prophecy."[43]

While there are elements of truth in each of these positions and there was a decline in prophecy elsewhere during the second century, the role of prophetic gifts in third-century North Africa provides an exception to these general facts. But this raises a number of questions. Why, for instance, were such phenomena on a decline elsewhere during the late second century, but in many ways appear to be still on their ascendancy in Carthage through Cyprian's tenure as bishop, if not into the Donatist period that followed? Was there any connection between the presence of such phenomena and ecclesiastical expectations or between these phenomena and the repeated persecutions that wrought havoc on the third-century Christian community in Carthage? In what ways (both in form and in function) did these phenomena differ from or in what ways were they like those that had appeared in the church during the previous two centuries? Is it possible to understand what factors may have contributed to their presence in Carthage? Is it possible to determine what factors may have influenced how they were understood, interpreted, and applied in the Christian community there? It is on these and other questions that attention will be focused. Although Panagopoulos has outlined a set of proposals for the future study of prophecy that is aimed primarily at studies in the second century, most of these same concerns also point us toward a study of third-century prophetic gifts in Carthage and their unique place in the thought of the early church. I propose to work with these suggestions to provide an understanding of the role and function of prophetic gifts for the church at Carthage from the captivity of Perpetua to the death of Cyprian. The long-term role and function of the gift of prophecy can be studied at Carthage like few other places in the early church.

PART ONE

PROPHETIC VISIONS IN
THE PASSION OF PERPETUA AND FELICITAS

CHAPTER TWO

INTRODUCTION TO *THE PASSION*

Life for new converts to Christianity became insufferable in North Africa following the edict of Septimius Severus about A.D. 200. He is said to have forbidden all conversions to Judaism and Christianity, and promised stiff penalties to those who chose to violate his edict.[1] The edict itself is lost, but W. H. C. Frend has supplied "three independent pieces of evidence that point to some form of imperial intervention in this period."[2] They include (1) a quotation from Eusebius, *Ecclesiastical History*, 6.1, which indicates that intense persecution took place under Severus, (2) a quotation from Hippolytus, *Commentary on Daniel*, 1.20.2–3, that points to the intimidation which Christians underwent at the hands of pagans, and (3) a quotation from the questionable Spartian, *Vita Severi*, 17.1, which states that under Severus an edict or decree was made which indicated that those who practiced Judaism and Christianity would suffer "grave penalties."[3] Thus, while no such formal edict has been located, it seems highly probable that it did exist.

Following the decree, the government sought out and arrested selected individuals from among those who had been newly converted to the faith.[4] If this edict of A.D. 202/3 was enforced in the same way as were later edicts aimed at Christianity, the use of torture was excessive.

Writing some ten years later to Scapula, the proconsular governor of North Africa, Tertullian noted that Severus had ordered simple condemnation for those who confessed their guilt and torture for those who denied it.[5] Yet, because of the discretionary powers given to the magistrates, the enforcement of Severus's edict was not uniform. Some magistrates tortured those who had willingly confessed their Christian faith.[6] Such was the situation surrounding the events described in one of the earliest acts of the martyrs, events that allegedly took place during the persecution of A.D. 202/3. *The Passion of Perpetua and Felicitas* describes the events leading up to and including the executions of several catechumens of whom two were men, Saturninus and Revocatus, and two were young women, Vibia Perpetua and Felicitas, her slave. Saturus, their leader, was not with them at the time of their arrest, but soon joined them voluntarily.[7]

THE TEXT

The Passion of Perpetua and Felicitas is one of the earliest and most influential of the accounts of the martyrs. Critical editions of the various texts are to be found in many sources,[8] and several English translations of the work are available as well.[9] *The Passion* divides easily into four parts. The first part (1.1–2.3), written in third-person narrative style, may be ascribed to the hand of a final editor or redactor. In this section the purpose for which the work in its present form has been written is explained.[10] A brief introduction of the major characters is also made. The redactor introduces the second section (3.1–10.15) as a narrative originally recorded by Perpetua, its primary character.

The second part of *The Passion* is written in the first person, a fact that lends credibility to the redactor's introduction, since the style employed in the section attributed to Perpetua, when compared to that used by the final redactor, has led Shewring to conclude that "her rhythms are sufficiently different from the redactor's to make it reasonably certain that her narrative was never revised by him."[11] This conclusion has been upheld in the more recent study by Åke Fridh, based on the Latin text,[12] although his study of the Greek text has led him to conclude that the work attributed to the redactor and the work attributed to Perpetua may be from the same hand, while the vision of Saturus is by another person.

This portion of the work includes three visions embedded within an account of Perpetua's experiences from the time of her capture and imprisonment until shortly before her martyrdom. It is, in fact, a brief diary of her imprisonment, purportedly left by her own hand.

The third part of *The Passion* (11.1–13.7) very briefly introduced by the redactor, contains the record of a vision attributed to one of the male catechumens, Saturus. The introductory line is in the third person, but in a manner similar to that found in Perpetua's section, Saturus's vision is retold in the first person. Once again, credibility is given to the redactor's statements regarding the use of original source material.

Part four (14.1–21.11) returns once again to the third person. It consists largely of a narrative of the passion of these and other martyrs. It seems to have been written by an eyewitness to the acts of the martyrdoms that are described in the document,[13] quite possibly by the redactor.

This work survives in three different forms: a shorter and a longer Latin manuscript, and a Greek manuscript.[14] Careful study of the relationship between these respective manuscripts leads generally to the conclusion that the longer Latin manuscript takes priority. This fact has been amply demonstrated by Robinson and others,[15] although Harris and Gifford argue for the priority of the Greek text.[16] More recently, Fridh has attempted through metrical analysis of *The Passion* to show that the vision attributed to Saturus was originally written in Greek, while the remainder of the text was originally Latin. These separate accounts were then brought together in a bilingual format. The second step saw the Greek section translated into Latin, and a third step saw the Latin portions translated into Greek. Thus, it is the second step, the Latin version, on which we must rely.[17] Clearly, this is a hypothetical reconstruction, and although it is an interesting suggestion, it holds little importance for the present study since the full Latin text is the earliest extant one. Perhaps it is sufficient to note the statement of Gustav Bardy that "In the milieu of the third century, the African Church is always a Latin Church."[18]

THE DATE OF THE PASSION

A number of factors work together to help establish 7 March 202/203 as the date when the martyrs of *The Passion* gave their lives. From the document itself, for instance, there is mention of the birthday of Geta the Caesar, son of Septimius Severus.[19] Timothy Barnes has clearly set forth the case for Geta's birthday at the beginning of March.[20]

The redactor of *The Passion* seems also to have expected that among the readers would be those who were witnesses to the events set forth (1.6).[21] Thus, *The Passion* itself must have been put into its final form shortly after the incidents described within it took place.[22] The fact that Tertullian mentions *The Passion* in his work *On the Soul*, which can be dated about A.D. 207, surely points to the fact that the work was already known among his readers.[23]

In addition to these facts, the evidence provided by W. H. C. Frend[24] seems to point to a date of about A.D. 202/203 as when the events recorded in *The Passion* occurred. Eusebius outlines events that took place in Alexandria during the tenth year (A.D. 202/2 or 202/203) of the reign of Severus, including a persecution of Christianity which sought out new converts.[25] Other external evidence pointing to 7 March 202/203 appears in a variety of sources.[26]

MONTANISM AS POSSIBLE BACKGROUND

That the events described in *The Passion* took place in North Africa is quite clear. The Greek and shorter Latin versions mention Thuburbo minus, a town about thirty-five miles southwest of Carthage, as the place in which the martyrs were arrested.[27] Mention of this town may well be based on an early confusion that identified the present group of martyrs with another group of Thuburbitan martyrs,[28] or the arrests took place in

Thuburbo minus, and the imprisonment, trial, and executions took place in Carthage.[29] In A.D. 202/203, Carthage was the capital of the province, "the seat of the civil and military government, [w]here dwelt the Proconsul, the Magister Militum and numberless subordinate officials of every grade and title, and each day justice, supported by the irresistible authority of arbitrary power, was administered in the Forum."[30]

The longer Latin manuscript, which presents *The Passion* in its most original form, makes no mention of any city, but the identification of this work with Carthage seems to rest on several hints within and without the work. Some of the language in the prologue and conclusion of the work in its present form is also reminiscent of an enthusiastic expression of faith, and certain scholars have taken this to be indicative that the work had reached its final form at the hand of a Montanist Christian.

Montanism arose in Asia Minor about A.D. 172[31] and spread to Rome sometime prior to the time Victor became bishop (A.D. 189),[32] for it seems to have been discussed in Rome quite early during the period when Eleutherus was Bishop (circa A.D. 174–189).[33]

From A.D. 200–207, during which time the martyrdom of Perpetua and her friends took place and *The Passion* was recorded in its final Latin form, it was a period when a proto-Montanism was present in Carthage. This was probably no more than an enthusiastic form of the Christian faith whose adherents were cognizant of the role of the Holy Spirit in daily life and who expected miraculous charismata to be present among them as a matter of course.[34] Yet, somewhere along the line, the authority of Montanus, Prisc[ill]a, and Maximilla was acknowledged by certain Carthaginian Christians.[35]

Carthage was important to Rome because of the vast quantity of grain produced there and shipped throughout the empire.[36] It is probable, then, that Montanist teachings came to North Africa via the frequent traffic between Rome and Carthage. These teachings were accepted by some within the congregation at Carthage, most notably among whom was Tertullian himself. Yet, Montanism did not immediately become a separate and distinct movement in North Africa, but rather emerged *within* the community of faith as a supplement to the existing expression of faith. Events described by Tertullian that fit our understanding of Montanist practices, for example, took place in the ordinary congregational meeting. Those who were so inclined stayed after the meeting in order to benefit from the exposition of certain revelatory gifts in addition to the sermon that had already been preached.[37]

John de Soyres has argued that Perpetua and Felicitas themselves are to be numbered among the Montanists[38] and that "the redactor's language is precisely that of the Montanists."[39] Bardy is more tentative in his observation, arguing that at least the Preface and Conclusion display elements that are echoed in Montanism.[40] Timothy Barnes, however, argues most stridently that not only was the redactor a Montanist but also the martyrs were too, for he claims, "the theological character of the *Passion* is Montanist through and through."[41] As evidence of the redactor's Montanism, Barnes points to the use of Joel 2:28 in the Preface (1.4–5), the commendation of the ecstatic state (20.3), and the repetition of the redactor's introductory themes in the Conclusion of the work (21.5).[42]

Barnes has also set forth three arguments that he believes point to the Montanism of the martyrs. First, from Perpetua's dreams of her brother Dinocrates, he infers that a martyr "can effect the release of a soul from hell and secure its admittance to heaven,"[43] a belief he attributes to Montanism. Second, from the dream of Saturus, he observes that the martyrs manifest a "subversive attitude towards the clergy" implying that "[the clergy's] only hope lies in the martyrs at whose feet they fell."[44] Finally, Barnes points to "the assistance afforded by the martyrs to the persecutors," which in the case of Perpetua he labels as coming near "to suicide."[45]

The other side of the Montanist argument, however, seems to be a more convincing one. Pierre de Labriolle, whose work on the Montanists in 1913 is yet to be surpassed, notes that there is nothing *unique* to Montanism in *The Passion*.[46] In addition, Weinrich has provided some forceful arguments against those articulated by Barnes. Against Barnes's contention that the martyr has special petitionary powers in Montanist thought, Weinrich mentions the study by F. Dölger which shows that the background to Perpetua's vision may be explained "on the basis of popular pagan conceptions concerning the condition of those who have died violently or prematurely"[47] and, thus, entirely apart from any Montanist influence.

Secondly, Weinrich argues that the martyrs in Saturus's vision, rather than taking a stance that subverts the clergy, are surprised by the deference with which they are treated by the bishop Optatus and the presbyter Aspasius. Furthermore, the words with which the martyrs address the bishop, particularly "*papa,*" clearly imply "that the martyrs recognized the bishop's authority."[48]

Thirdly, Weinrich quotes the words of Perpetua in 4.5 that the reason for Saturus's voluntary surrender was that "a sense of continuing responsibility toward the imprisoned group" motivated Saturus.[49] In the case of Perpetua, Weinrich notes that her action "is not different from that of Bishop Pionius, who placed himself on the gibbet so that the nails could be driven in (*Mart. Pion.* 21.2)."[50]

Weinrich is quick to conclude that the martyrs were in fact "orthodox,

Catholic Christians," and he has produced two substantial arguments favoring this assertion. First, Tertullian never mentioned Perpetua as a member of the New Prophecy, even when it would have been appropriate and useful for him to do so. Second, in the fourth century, a church was dedicated in Carthage to the memory of these martyrs. Such an honor would probably never have happened had they been "sectarian martyrs."[51]

THE REDACTOR

With the question of Montanist activity on the part of the martyrs more or less settled in favor of orthodoxy, we are still left with the possibility of such an activity on the part of the final redactor. Attempts to link the final form to a known author of the time center largely on Tertullian.

The most notable exception to this position was taken by R. Braune in a meeting of the Faculty of Letters in Strasbourg on 26 March 1955. His response suggests that the deacon Pomponius mentioned by Perpetua (1.2) is the redactor. His decision not to accept Tertullian as the redactor centers on (1) his inability to find Tertullian's brash and vigorous style in the document, a position shared by Weinrich, and (2) his judgment that alleged philological similarities between Tertullian's known writings and those found in *The Passion* are "pressed and peremptory."[52]

Weinrich adds to Braune's first argument a second one that he considers to be important not only in dismissing Tertullian as the redactor but also in dismissing any Montanist leanings in the redactor. This consists of "the disparity between Tertullian's severe attitude toward pregnancy and children in the light of 'imminent distresses'[53] and the simple, unconscious narrative of Felicitas' child-bearing in prison."[54]

Another who contests Tertullian as the redactor of *The Passion* is Fridh who advances the theory that the redactor was a contemporary of Tertullian.[55] Campos claims more convincingly that "if the Passion is not by Tertullian it must be argued as belonging to a disciple who was very well versed in the ideas and literary style of the great African master."[56] David Scholer has suggested that the redactor was "very possibly a woman," but provides no rationale for this suggestion.[57] This suggestion merits further consideration in light of the feminist concerns of Perpetua, the obvious leadership role she is granted in the vision of Saturus, and the redactor's own personal interest to convey the story of this young woman so vividly.

Among the proponents of the view that Tertullian was the most probable redactor of *The Passion*,[58] d'Ales has presented the most articulate and comprehensive series of arguments in his favor.[59] The fiery Tertullian was present and active in congregational life of Carthage at the time of Perpetua's martyrdom. His *Apology* had been published in A.D. 197, and this important work had undoubtedly placed him at the center of things within the congregation at Carthage. It should come as no surprise, then, that when he was a presbyter within the congregation at Carthage[60] he knew of Perpetua. Indeed, between A.D. 212–213, Tertullian wrote of her as "the most heroic martyr."[61] The fact that she was known and so highly regarded by Tertullian just a few short years following her martyrdom suggests that she was martyred at Carthage. The congregational leadership at Carthage had played a significant role in the visitation and support of the martyrs while they were yet in prison (3.7; 6.7; 16.4), and contact between Tertullian and Perpetua, while not recorded, is not an impossibility.

d'Ales has observed that the redactor addressed his readers as "brothers and little children" (1.6). This paternalistic salutation, he argues, would have been appropriate only for a bishop or a priest.[62] Since Tertullian may have been a presbyter at Carthage, it would have been appropriate for him to address his readers in this way, the more so because of his fame as an established author.

The evidence that the redaction of *The Passion* is the work of Tertullian may be summarized briefly. Tertullian was probably a presbyter at Carthage during the persecution of A.D. 202/203. He could easily be described as a religious enthusiast who had already been impressed by the faith of martyrs, as may be evidenced in his composition *To the Martyrs*, written about A.D. 197.[63] The similarities of style and language between *To the Martyrs* and *The Passion* are significant, and Robinson has amassed many expressions for which he has found parallels in a variety of Tertullian's other works.[64] In addition, Tertullian was, like the redactor, literate in both Greek and Latin.

Although the evidence appears to point in the direction of Tertullian as the author/redactor of *The Passion of Perpetua and Felicitas*, the case is not without its problems. First, to name Tertullian as the redactor is to argue from silence. The redactor did not autograph *The Passion*, and, at best, the case is built on circumstantial evidence.[65] Second, when Tertullian wrote of Perpetua's passion in his treatise *On the Soul* some years later, he erred in ascribing the vision to Perpetua when it was Saturus's in which the events he cites took place.[66] Third, the concern expressed by R. Braune over the fact that previous philological studies undertaken to examine both *The Passion of Perpetua and Felicitas* and other known writings of Tertullian were "pressed," needs to be taken seriously.[67] To be sure, there are similarities, but more study is necessary in order to ascribe the authorship of *The Passion* to Tertullian with any finality.

Regardless of the inability to determine precisely who the final author/redactor of *The Passion* was, the work does betray something of the mind and situation of the congregation at Carthage shortly after the turn of the third century. The church was embroiled in a period of intense persecution. It was also a time of social ferment as well as a time in which some Christians believed that they were required to take seriously their call to become martyrs for the sake of their Lord. It was a time of faith and of great expectations and, as such, certain members of the congregation expected God to be revealed to them in miraculous ways. The redactor was one such person. She or he believed that the acts of these five martyrs should be recorded for posterity as evidence of God's power in the ongoing life of the church in the last days (1.1–6). In recording *The Passion of Perpetua and Felicitas*, the redactor undoubtedly encouraged the persecuted congregation, and some members received such edification from this record that they ascribed to it almost a canonical status.[68] At a later date Augustine, himself, preached several sermons/homilies based on *The Passion of Perpetua and Felicitas* after the account had been read to the congregation.[69]

Among the events depicted in *The Passion* are a series of visions.[70] It is to these that we now turn. My purpose is to study the features of these visions, so that we might understand their function and purpose, first, for the recipients of the visions and, finally, for the church at Carthage. The first three of these visions have been ascribed to Perpetua. Each of her visions will be studied separately. This evaluation will be followed by an analysis of Saturus's vision, and this section will conclude with an evaluation of the redactor's purpose in providing both the narrative material and the visions in their present form.

CHAPTER THREE

THE VISION OF PERPETUA'S PASSION

At the time of her arrest Perpetua was a recent and committed convert to Christianity. Although she had undergone some systematic training in spiritual things, she was still unbaptized. Early in her imprisonment, Perpetua's father came to her, seeking to persuade her to renounce her new faith. When she refused to do so, he threatened her, then left her, apparently in order to allow her time to reconsider her decision.[1]

Perpetua was baptized shortly after her initial discussion with her father, but before she entered the dungeon for an extended period of time. She wrote of her baptism that "the Spirit indicated that from the water nothing was to be sought except bodily endurance."[2]

What Perpetua means by this is not entirely clear, but there may be a clue in what, just prior to A.D. 200, Tertullian had written to those about to be baptized. He instructed them that as they ascended from the sacred font of baptism with arms extended their first request of the Lord should be that "peculiarities of grace and distributions of charismata might to supplied to them."[3] Perpetua, newly baptized, may have been making reference to these same instructions. Thus, it may be by means of a particular charisma (martyrdom?) that Perpetua is able to confess her faith, endure persecution, and ultimately be martyred.

That Perpetua wrote these words only after she had been sentenced to death may indicate they were her personal reflection on the single most pressing need she had, the need to make her confession sure even in the face of torture. Yet, she says that this need was revealed to her by the Spirit during her reflection.[4]

Apparently this recognition came after her baptism. As yet, Perpetua was still unaware of her future. She had been arrested as a confessor, but her trial and sentence still lay ahead. Her only living brother, also a Christian, although not among those who had been arrested, only later suggested that she ask the Lord for a vision in order to provide some certainty of her future.[5] This suggests that even after her baptism, Perpetua did not know to what extent she would need "bodily endurance." She would surely need some endurance to survive in prison, but this need would pale into insignificance next to her need for endurance in the arena.

Perpetua's time in prison was, clearly, unpleasant. She was kept in a hot, dark dungeon most of the time, and at first she was very anxious for the welfare of her infant son. If it had not been for the resourcefulness of two deacons, Tertius and Pomponius, who bribed the guards, Perpetua and the others would probably have languished in the oppressive heat and darkness of the dungeon until their trial and execution. Apparently as a result of such bribes, however, the prisoners were allowed some measure of freedom within the prison for one day. Visitors, including Perpetua's son, her mother, and her brother came to see her in an area of the prison that was less oppressive, and when Perpetua was returned to the dungeon, she was allowed to take her newborn son with her. According to her own testimony, she spent many days (3.9) in the dungeon with her son, and his presence with her did much to relieve her anxiety.

THE OCCASION

Perpetua's first vision was occasioned after the visit of her brother, some days following her imprisonment. He suggested that she ask for a vision because she was already "greatly privileged."[6] The purpose of such a request would be so that Perpetua and her family might know whether she would be martyred or released as a result of her upcoming trial. Perpetua believed that she was one "who could speak with the Lord whose great blessings [she] had come to experience,"[7] and as a result, she agreed to ask for a vision. She promised her brother that she would tell him the results of her request the next day.

Exactly what Perpetua meant when she said she believed she could converse with the Lord is difficult to say. It may mean no more than that she agreed with her brother's assessment. As a confessor she had somehow, by virtue of that confession, been given a place of honor before the Lord, and, therefore, she believed that the Lord would honor her request. This explanation seems inadequate, however, since her formal confession before the procurator was yet to come. More likely, Perpetua's statement indicates that conversing with the Lord was something to which she was already regularly accustomed.[8] It also seems to indicate that in some way there was a two-way dialogue; that is, the idea of conversing indicates that what she meant included more than her own speaking to the Lord. If Perpetua's case is similar to that of Tertullian's anonymous sister who was a member of the congregation at Carthage, Perpetua at times conversed with the Lord while "in the Spirit."

It is not possible to know whether the vision occurred during the day or during the evening hours. Perpetua's words are simply, "And I asked, and this was shown to me."[9] That Perpetua asked her brother to wait until the next day for the results suggests the vision came at night, although since Perpetua requested such a vision and it came as a result of the request, that would seem to indicate it came, not as a dream, but in a time of prayer, perhaps prayer "in the Spirit." Still, it may be the case that Perpetua prayed before retiring for the night and the vision came in the form of a dream. Regardless of which form it took, Perpetua was "awakened" (4.10) or aroused from a dream or a trancelike state with full recollection of what had transpired in the vision, and it has been preserved in writing.

The vision itself is an interesting study in prophetic and apocalyptic exegesis. Its chief characters are Perpetua, a dragon, Saturus (a prisoner with Perpetua), and an old man dressed as a shepherd. Also of significance in the vision is a ladder up which first Saturus and then Perpetua climb. (See appendix A for the text of the vision.)

The detail of the vision is lucid. Perpetua saw a golden or bronze ladder that reached toward heaven. It was so narrow that only one person at a time could ascend. It was bounded on each side by a range of torture devices designed to claim all who ascended the ladder except those who did so intently and expeditiously. At the base of the ladder lay an immense dragon who attempted to frighten away all who would climb it.

In the vision, Saturus preceded Perpetua up the ladder and, upon completion of his climb, summoned Perpetua to follow, with specific instructions for her to beware of the dragon at its base. Perpetua followed, invoking the name of the Lord Jesus Christ for protection. Stepping on the head of the dragon, she began her climb to a garden in which an old shepherd milked his sheep and around whom a multitude of white-robed beings stood. Upon seeing her, the old man welcomed her and gave her a piece of cheese made from the milk of his sheep. She ate it. The vision ends abruptly as Perpetua awakened at the sound of voices.

THE IMPORTANCE OF BACKGROUND TO INTERPRETATION

Although each character and element of the vision held some significant meaning for her, Perpetua did not choose to leave in writing either the basis for her understanding of these elements or her interpretation of these elements. She wrote simply what she believed to be the ultimate message of her vision. When she discussed the vision with her brother, they both "realized that we would have to suffer."[10] The result of their discussion reveals that they gave up any hope for escape, acquittal, or dismissal of Perpetua's case. Neither she nor her brother expected anything other than the death penalty to be imposed on her as a result of refusing to renounce her confession of faith.

In order to understand how Perpetua came to this conclusion based on the vision she received, it is important to recognize the various cultural and religious factors that certainly must have played a role in the life of many Christians at the beginning of the third century in Carthage.[11] Carthage had enjoyed a long and distinguished history as a city formerly founded by the Phoenicians, possibly as early as the ninth century B.C.[12] The city had played an important role as it interacted with the empire of Greece, but it was finally conquered by the Roman general Scipio Aemilianus in 146 B.C.[13] Later it was razed, but the Phoenician influence lingered throughout North Africa, particularly in neighboring Numidia.

During the reign of Caesar Augustus (27 B.C.–A.D. 14) a new Carthage, a Roman Carthage, was founded on the old site. It was in this Carthage that Perpetua received her vision. Although Carthage in A.D. 202 was a Roman colony in which the dominant language was Latin, many spoke Punic, and some Libyan. A few of the more educated seem to have spoken Greek as well, but "Greek had never gained much foothold; it had only lingered as the speech of polite society."[14] Vibia Perpetua, a woman of respectable birth, liberal education, and noble marriage,[15] spoke the Greek language according to her fellow martyr, Saturus.[16] Her ability to do so surely opened another cultural world to her. Thus, from a cultural setting, Perpetua may have drawn from parallels in her experience that were Phoenician, Latin/Roman (such as Virgil), and also Greek.[17]

An additional fact: Perpetua was a Christian. As recent as her conversion might have been, she had undoubtedly received instruction from Scripture as a catechumen, possibly from a Greek text, more likely from an early Latin text.[18] Her spiritual life was probably immersed in the teachings of the law, the prophets, Jesus, and the apostles as well as in the traditions of the church in North Africa. It seems also to have included extensive introduction to Jewish apocalyptic elements.[19] Thus, in addition to the secular factors that could have provided parallels, Perpetua was surely affected also by the Christian instruction she had received, Christian instruction drawing from its Jewish heritage as well as from early Christian writings, among which may have appeared the *Shepherd of Hermas,* the *Apocalypse of Peter,*[20] and possibly the *Gospel of Thomas.*

The experience of other Christians in Carthage may have been important to Perpetua's spiritual upbringing as well. About the time of her birth, twelve Christians from Scillium were tried and executed in Carthage because of their Christian confessions.[21] It is difficult to believe that other Christians at Carthage would not have kept this memory alive among them and done so as a source of encouragement and exhortation for new converts.

THE DRAGON

With these factors in mind, I turn our attention to the various elements of Perpetua's vision. We are drawn immediately to the dragon/serpent lying at the base of the ladder. Perpetua's description of this character is: "At the foot of the ladder lay a dragon/snake (*draco*) of enormous size, and it would attack those who tried to climb up and try to terrify them from doing so."

Saturus preceded Perpetua up the ladder, and when he had reached the top, he turned to her, saying, "Perpetua, I am waiting for you. But take care; do not let the dragon bite you." Perpetua's diary tells in her own words what transpired next. " 'He will not harm me,' I said, 'In the name of Christ Jesus,' Slowly, as though he were afraid of me, the dragon stuck his head out from beneath the ladder. Then, using my first step, I trod on his head and went up" (4.7).

Several important factors that contribute to our understanding of this vision may be discovered through the analysis of certain words and phrases connected with the dragon/serpent. First among these is the identification of the *draco* itself. The term commonly refers to a serpentlike dragon or a sea monster.[22] Jewish canonical literature abounds with references to serpents and dragons. They come under a variety of names, sometimes mentioned merely as serpents[23] or dragons,[24] and on other occasions they are called Leviathan,[25] Rahab,[26] or Behemoth.[27] In almost all instances, these terms refer to a created being that acts as an evil force to keep humanity from relying upon God, thereby taking to itself divine prerogative. It is a being which at times must do God's bidding, but because of its inherently evil nature, it must ultimately be destroyed by the hand of God.

Jewish Apocryphal literature[28] and Jewish apocalyptic literature, both Apocryphal and pseudepigraphic, provide numerous examples of dragon-like beings, particularly under the name of Leviathan or Behemoth.[29] Christian apocalyptic, like its Jewish counterpart, portrayed evil in serpent and dragon figures, but in the end the dragon is identified as Satan.[30] The clearest statement to this effect has been left by John the apostle who wrote in Rev. 20:2 that an angel "seized the dragon, that ancient serpent, who is the Devil and Satan, and bound him for a thousand years."[31] Other early Christian writers have given their assent to this identification by employing it throughout their own writings.[32] Of particular interest among those who used this language shortly after the death of Perpetua is Cyprian, bishop of Carthage between A.D. 252 and 258.

In one place, Cyprian identifies the serpent with the pioneer Antichrist, undoubtedly meant to be understood as Decius.[33] In his *Epistle* 33, Cyprian addressed the presbyters, deacons, and the congregation at Carthage concerning Celerinus. His hope was that as a result of a vision which he had received, they should accept Celerinus into the office of reader. Part of his introduction of Celerinus included the statement that Celerinus had undergone tortures for his faith, yet he had proven to be an overcomer. In Cyprian's words, "although his [Celerinus's] feet were bound on the rack, yet the serpent was trodden on and ground down and vanquished."[34] Once again, the image of the serpent is linked at the least to persecution and potentially to martyrdom as well.

It would seem from this brief survey of the dragon as symbol that, within Christian circles at least, the dragon was understood to be Satan. The tradition of the dragon as an evil creature, an enemy of God, was a long one, but its personification as Satan had become clear in the revelation of John over a century before Perpetua's martyrdom. It seems also clear that at least portions of the New Testament "were first rendered into Latin during the last quarter of the second century in North Africa."[35] Thus, Perpetua's use of *draco* in the record of her vision would seem to point to Satan as the one who would attempt to keep her from making a positive public confession of faith and thereby keep her from being martyred.

Perpetua's appeal to the name of Jesus Christ for protection from the dragon should be noted here, too. Appealing to the name of a deity or the name of a noted authority or ruler to obtain authority has a long history in both Jewish and Christian circles. Moses was given the name of God (Exod. 3:13–14) to indicate to the captive Israelites the authority by which he spoke to them and to Pharaoh. Josephus seems to indicate that some exorcists in his day appealed to Solomon's name for the authority to exorcize demons.[36]

In the words of Jesus himself, many will come to him at the end, claiming to have prophesied, cast out demons, and performed wondrous deeds, all in his name.[37] The experience of the early church was such that healings (Acts 3:6, 16) and exorcisms (Acts 16:18) were accomplished in or with the name of Jesus Christ. A variety of patristic sources also show that the name of Jesus Christ was invoked most frequently in adjurations associated with exorcisms.[38] In effect, the name of Jesus was invoked as a symbol of the Christian's authority over the demonic realm.[39] The history of how the phrase, "in the name of Jesus Christ," was used in the early church sheds light on Perpetua's understanding of the dragon as Satan. Her adjuration, although appearing in the indicative rather than the imperative, seems to have been efficacious in that the dragon apparently feared her from that time onward, and she was able to overcome the dragon. Her adjuration or invocation would then be consistent with what appears to have been widespread Christian practice at the time.

The personification of the state or of a state leader as a dragon is important to note here also. Nebuchadnezzar was likened to a *draco* in Jer. 51:34; Pharaoh was the water-dwelling dragon of Ezek. 29:3; 32:2; and the Roman general Pompey was the proud dragon of *Psalms of Solomon* 2:29. Dölger has also noted that the portraying of states or heads of states in the form of a dragon or serpent overcome by Caesar became a tradition which found clear articulation in the coinage of the Roman empire throughout the fifth century.[40] For hundreds of years, then, the identification of evil kings and emperors with the dragon/serpent theme was a common one. In Perpetua's case, it may also imply a link between the state as persecutor of Christians and Satan. The dragon of Perpetua's vision could be interpreted as referring to Severus, the personification of evil or of Satan, as responsible for the tribulation and persecution of the church by the state. A profound similarity exists here between Perpetua's vision and one recorded by Hermas.

In the *Shepherd of Hermas*, an encounter between Hermas and a whale-like beast is described.[41] The description of this beast makes it clear that it was *not* a whale Hermas saw, but rather that it was *like* ($\dot{\omega}\sigma\epsilon\iota$) a whale. It was to be understood as a monster that stirred up the dust, something a whale would not have done.[42] Hermas's approach toward this monster clearly unnerved him, for, by his own confession, he began to weep and call upon the Lord to rescue him.[43] His concern for his personal safety brought with it a recollection that he was not to doubt; and this enabled him, by faith in God, to face the beast.

Parallels between Perpetua's experience with the dragon and Hermas's with the beast are numerous. Both were initially unnerved by their confrontation with the beast.[44] Similarly, both were encouraged to move forward.[45] Perpetua says that she relied on the name of the Lord Jesus Christ that the dragon would not hurt her (4.6). Hermas, too, seems to have done this. His words describing his approach do not say this specifically, but rather, "Clothed . . . with faith in the Lord, and remembering the great things which He had taught me, I boldly faced the beast."[46] However, when he had passed the beast and related the incident to a white-haired woman, typifying the church, she told him that he had survived "because you cast your care on God, and opened your heart to the Lord, believing that you can be saved by no other than by His great and glorious name."[47] Perpetua and Hermas both overcame the monster by relying on the name of the Lord.[48]

A final, yet striking, parallel between Perpetua's meeting of the dragon and Hermas's confrontation with the whalelike monster needs to be noted. In the words of the old woman Hermas met after passing the monster, he identified the beast as a "type of the great tribulation that is coming."[49] If, indeed, Perpetua's dragon is to be understood as the person-ification of Satan and evil through Severus and his persecution of the church, then it would seem that both Hermas and Perpetua had an inter-est in, perhaps even an imminent expectation of, the coming *eschaton*.

The image presented to us of Perpetua conquering the dragon by placing her foot on it is one with broad historical significance as well. The act of placing one's foot on the head or neck of the enemy is commonly found in Scripture. Perhaps the clearest example is found in Josh. 10:22–27. In this passage, Joshua captured five kings who were hidden in a cave: the kings of Jerusalem, Hebron, Jarmuth, Lachish, and Eglon. He then summoned his troops forward and ordered them to "Put your feet on the necks of these kings." Joshua spoke to his army, encouraging them to be strong, "for thus the Lord will do to all the enemies against whom you fight."

The idea conveyed by this act, is one of conquest and subordination. It seems to lie behind Ps. 110:1, in which the Lord instructs David's Lord to "Sit at my right hand until I make your enemies your footstool."[50] Dölger has set forth a series of examples from history, including the picture of Caesar Valentian on Roman coinage with his right foot on the human head of a serpent.[51]

Finally, in Luke 10:19–20, Jesus himself gave authority for the seventy to "tread on snakes and scorpions . . . and over all the power of the enemy." Perpetua had much from which she could have drawn to interpret her action, particularly from Scripture. Gen. 3:15 may be the basic text here, but Rom. 16:20, or Ps. 110:1, or Luke 10:19–20 were also available to help her interpret the act of placing her foot on the dragon's head and thereby understand that act to be one symbolic of her success over Satan, who was personified in the Roman government.

THE LADDER

The second symbol in Perpetua's vision that needs interpretation is the image of the ladder. Perpetua wrote of it:

> I saw a bronze ladder of extraordinary height extending all the way to heaven, and [it was so] narrow that it was not possible to climb except alone: and on the sides of the ladder were fixed all kinds of iron imple-ments. There were swords, lances, hooks, [and] daggers there: so that if anyone went up negligently or without attentively looking upwards, she/he would be mangled and her/his flesh would adhere to the iron im-plements. (4.3; translation mine)

Several scholars have proposed that the key to understanding the ladder symbol in this vision lies with the parallel provided in Jacob's dream at Bethel.[52] This idea is unconvincing, however, since closer examination demonstrates that the differences are at least as important as the similarities. The two basic similarities are (1) that a very high ladder bridged the gulf between earth and heaven and (2) at the top of the ladder was someone who spoke to the recipient of the dream or vision. In Jacob's dream, the speaker was identified as the Lord (יהוה), whereas in Perpetua's vision, it was an old man garbed in shepherd's clothing.

The differences between the two pictures are far more numerous and no less significant than the similarities. First, Jacob saw no dragon/serpent guarding the ladder; Perpetua did. Second, Perpetua's ladder was extremely narrow allowing for only one person at a time to climb it; Jacob saw angels both ascending and descending the ladder. Third, Jacob made no mention of instruments of torture fastened to his ladder; Perpetua saw a variety of such instruments, including swords both long and short, lances or light spears, and hooks or barbs intended to frighten if not to destroy all who would attempt to climb the ladder. Fourth, but not least, Perpetua was summoned to the top of her ladder, where she was addressed by the old shepherd; Jacob was addressed by Yahweh, who stood above the ladder while Jacob lay sleeping at its base.

If the differences between Jacob's vision and Perpetua's outweigh the similarities, the fact remains that even in the pagan mind of the day, the concept of a ladder which reached from earth to heaven was not unknown. Quasten has pointed to the parallels in ancient Egyptian papyri and in the cult of Mithras that demonstrate this fact.[53] Similarly, the idea appears in other places within the Jewish tradition. The pseudepigraphic *Ascension of Isaiah* may provide a parallel for the ascent of the soul through successive steps from earth to heaven, and Philo's *De somniis* provides a full explanation of the meaning of Jacob's ladder as a figure of the atmosphere, the abode of incorporeal souls.[54] In light of Perpetua's conclusion that she would face martyrdom, the ladder becomes a symbol of transition from life on earth to life in heaven.[55] Yet, it is more than that, for at least two other characteristics of importance are attached to the ladder. It is both narrow, and it is lined with instruments of torture.

In recognition of the role of the dragon (Satan) to frighten all who would attempt to climb the ladder, the ladder could also be described as a symbol of the Christian life itself. The idea of the "two ways" is a common one within the biblical tradition as a whole. In the Old Testament the idea emerges repeatedly. In Deut. 30:19, for instance, the choice of life and blessing is set over against the choice of death and cursing. In Ps. 1:6, the way of the righteous is known by the Lord, whereas the way of the wicked is marked for death. In Jer. 21:8, the way of life is the way of surrender, whereas the way of death is typified by resistance.

The intertestamental period saw the continued development of this theme. At Qumran, the *Manual of Discipline* clearly outlined the two ways.[56] Similarly, *The Testament of Asher*, 1:3–9, set forth the two ways of life. Those who attempted to follow both ways were described as "double-faced" and, thus, they served not God but Beliar.[57]

In his discussion of the two ways, the writer of *4 Ezra*, used language similar to that of Perpetua's. In a passage that allegedly records the words of the archangel Uriel spoken to Ezra concerning the way or portion of Israel within the present age, the language is particularly noteworthy:

> There is a builded city which lies on level ground, and it is full of all good things; but its entrance is narrow and lies on a steep [incline], having fire on the right hand and deep water on the left, and there is one only path lying between them both, that is between the fire and the water, (and so small) is this path, that it can contain only one man's footstep at once.[58]

Similarities exist between Ezra's "level ground" and Perpetua's "immense extent of garden"; between Ezra's path on a steep incline and Perpetua's ladder; and between Ezra's fire and water, which were meant to be perilous to the traveler, and Perpetua's torture implements of iron. But, perhaps most noteworthy is that in both Ezra's account and Perpetua's vision, the way of the path or of the ladder is so narrow as to allow only one individual at a time to negotiate it, and both the path and the ladder lead from the present situation on earth to heaven or the Age to Come. The traffic pattern in both cases is only one way—up.

A distinctively Christian interpretation of the narrow ladder in Perpetua's vision may also have in its background the words of Jesus, who taught that the gate was narrow and the way hard which leads to life.[59] The narrowness of Perpetua's ladder may parallel the narrow gate about which Jesus spoke, while the difficulty of the way may correspond to Perpetua's torture instruments.

The parallels that exist in other early Christian literature cannot be overlooked either. The theology of the "two ways" is intrinsic to the significance and the message of the *Didache*.[60] It appears again in the *Epistle of Barnabas*.[61] Jean Daniélou has noted, too, that the themes of the "narrow way" and the ladder have been combined in the fourth-century work of Pseudo-Hippolytus, the *Pascal Homily*, 51.[62]

With the possibility that the tradition of the "two ways" lies behind Perpetua's interpretation of the vision, the narrow ladder would be symbolic of the "narrow way." The purpose of the dragon would be to divert attention from the narrow way to the tangible things around. Those who would walk the narrow way must keep their eyes focused on the goal at the top of the ladder rather than direct their attention to those things around them.

The instruments of torture are important to this interpretation as well. In a sense, they could be interpreted symbolically as indicative of the various trials in the Christian life that appear from time to time. It is true that some trials can deter Christians from keeping their eyes on the goal of the narrow way. However, the specific naming of the various torture implements, the swords, lances, hooks, and daggers mentioned by Perpetua, suggest that she saw them as the real articles of execution for Christians of her day. She could not have been unaware of the capital nature of her offense against the edict of Severus nor would she have been unaware of the means whereby Roman justice was normally enforced. A literal interpretation of these iron implements is all that would be essential to the overall understanding of the vision. Yet, the recognition once again of the spiritual dimension of her vision seems to indicate that, to her mind, the fear of torture and execution at the hands of Roman soldiers would be sufficient to deter all but the most dedicated from reaching the top of the ladder.[63] Satan, and the Roman government could be understood as being in collusion to keep all aspiring climbers from succeeding in their walk along the "narrow way."

The actual passage up the ladder by Perpetua is described in the most meagre of terms. "I ascended," wrote Perpetua quite simply. From her first step on the head of the dragon to her emergence into the garden, the link is simply "ascend." From this fact, it should be noted that her vision was actually focused on two different planes and not on the passage between them. The first dealt with the battle in which she was engaged when she received the vision. It revealed to her the complexity and the reality of her situation. She was participating in a spiritual battle. In its outward trappings, it was personified by the Roman state and by the various means through which the state sought to force her to renounce her Christian faith. Its inner significance, however, lay in the fact that Satan himself, the immense dragon who wished to frighten those who would climb the narrow ladder, was behind the persecution and torment under which she was suffering.

Perpetua's ascension, the link between her torment at the base of the ladder and her entry into the garden at the top of it, makes two things clear. First, her faith was in Jesus Christ, as is evidenced by her appeal to his name as she stepped on the dragon. That faith enabled her to tread on the dragon with no ill effects, allowing her to overcome the dragon. Second, her eyes were apparently focused on "the prize that was set before her" in that she suffered no harm in the ascent itself. Perpetua had stated that this was possible only for those who climbed the ladder with care and with their attention on the top of the ladder rather than on the threats around them as they climbed.

THE SHEPHERD

The second plane on which Perpetua's vision was focused was that of the garden. Its concern lay in the outcome of her ascent up the ladder. It is with reference to this level or plane that we meet the third element of the vision, which now needs illumination. It comes in the figure of the man Perpetua met at the top of the ladder. Her successful ascent up the ladder led her to a scene described in her words in the following manner:

> And I ascended [the ladder], and I saw an immense tract of garden, and sitting in the midst [of it] was an aged (white-haired) man in the dress of a shepherd, large (in stature), milking sheep: and many thousands of white-clothed ones were standing around [him]. And he raised his head and looked at me and said to me: "[It is] well [that] you came, daughter." And he called me and from the cheese on which account he was milking he gave to me a morsel; and I accepted with hands folded, and ate; and altogether those standing around said "Amen." (4.7b–9; translation mine)

If it was the serpent/dragon that occupied our attention at the base of the ladder, it is equally the aged shepherd who occupies it at the top of the ladder. It would seem that the interpretation of her vision must rely ultimately on the proper identification of the man and an understanding of the various statements that are made concerning the meeting which took place in her vision between Perpetua and the aged man.

The person Perpetua first saw at the top of the ladder was (1) a tall, aged man, (2) sitting, (3) dressed as a shepherd, and (4) performing an ordinary task of a shepherd, the milking of his sheep. While not all of these details hold equal value in our attempt to identify and understand the significance of this individual, some of them are significant. Once again, it is appropriate to review potential resources on which Perpetua could have drawn that might have informed her understanding of such imagery.

Jewish apocalyptic literature provides a striking example in Dan. 7:9–10 with a description of the "Ancient of Days." It reads:

> As I watched,
> thrones were set in place,
> and an Ancient One took his throne,

his clothing was white as snow,
   and the hair of his head like pure wool;
his throne was fiery flames,
   and its wheels were burning fire.
A stream of fire issued
   and flowed out from his presence.
A thousand thousands served him,
   and ten thousand times ten
   thousand stood attending him.
The court sat in judgment,
   and the books were opened.

This scene described by Daniel portrays the events that occurred in one of his dreams (Dan. 7:1). There are several details in it that could conceivably provide a background to the symbolism of Perpetua's vision. The first is the figure himself. He is described as one who was "ancient," a fact most probably linked to the presence of hair "like pure wool." Perpetua's shepherd is said to be "white-haired," hence, aged. Second, the posture of the "Ancient One" is a sitting one. Perpetua's description of the shepherd includes the fact that he was sitting. Third, the "Ancient One" is surrounded by literally thousands who stand before him to serve him and many more who stand before him apparently waiting for a court of judgment to be convened. In Perpetua's vision, the shepherd is surrounded by thousands of "white-clothed ones." Finally, the one who is described as the "Ancient One" in Daniel's dream appears to be acting as a judge about to render some decisions on behalf of those who stand before him, decisions based on the books he has before him. He is clearly an authority figure. While Perpetua's vision lacks any formal statement regarding a judgment scene for the multitudes, her reception by the shepherd is a solitary judgment rendered in her favor. The shepherd's designation of Perpetua as "daughter" clearly points to the shepherd's authority in the situation, as does her response to his request. At the very least, the "Ancient One" and the "shepherd" could easily pass for some type of divine figure. This is especially true in the case of Daniel's figure, since the passage goes on to indicate that the "Ancient One" gave to one "like a human being [son of man]" an authority which was limitless (Dan. 7:11–14).

As we move on into early Christian literature, we are confronted by a number of incidents in which a bright light, a man with a shining countenance, a young man, or a man sometimes dressed as a shepherd is seen in visionary experiences. Paul saw a bright light in his encounter with Jesus during his journey along the Damascus Road (Acts 9:3–6; 22:6–11; 26:13–18), but nothing in these passages indicates his actually having seen Jesus. Rather, he says that he alone heard Jesus speak to him (Acts 22:9). Still, in 1 Cor. 15:8, he claims that the risen Christ appeared to him as one untimely born.

John's account in Rev. 1:10–18 depicts one who is said to be "like the Son of Man" in typically apocalyptic language. This account is clearly reminiscent of, yet distinct from, Daniel's dream account. John describes this visionary individual as

> clothed with a long robe and with a golden sash across his chest. His head and his hair were white as white wool, white as snow; his eyes were like a flame of fire; his feet were like burnished bronze, refined as in a fur-nace; and his voice was like the sound of many waters. In his right hand he held seven stars, and from his mouth came a sharp two-edged sword, and his face was like the sun shining with full strength.[64]

The only parallel readily apparent between John's likeness of the "son of man," and Perpetua's shepherd is the white hair. However, it provides a second encounter with a "son of man" figure alongside that of Daniel's, but in contrast to Daniel's. In contrast to Daniel's figure, John's "son of man," not the "Ancient One," is described as having white hair. Thus, Daniel's dream may still provide the most suitable background to Per-petua's vision.

The analysis of a third "son of man" passage, however, provides another interesting possibility. Stephen, the first Christian martyr found in Acts, received a vision just prior to his martyrdom at the hands of the Jews in Jerusalem. In this vision he saw "the Son of Man [Jesus] standing at the right hand of God" (Acts 7:56).

C. H. Dodd analyzed a number of canonical passages which record both visionary and nonvisionary appearances of the risen Christ and concluded that there are two types of postresurrection appearances to be found in the New Testament: those which he labels "concise" and those which are "circumstantial."[65] The "concise" pericopes are thought to originate in the corporate memory of the Christian community, and they "tell us nothing which is not absolutely essential to a bare report of what hap-pened or what was said."[66] The "circumstantial" accounts, however, "allow more room for the taste and ability of the individual narrator,"[67] and are free narratives that do not originate in the corporate memory of the church. They originate with individuals or small groups.

Elaine Pagels, following the lead of J. Lindblom,[68] rightly identifies the Stephen vision as belonging to the "circumstantial" type of appearance narrative since, occurring after Pentecost, it reveals the risen Jesus against the backdrop of God's glory and lends itself to an interpretation through an "inner eye."[69] Unlike the resurrection narratives of the Gospels, it emphasizes the continuing presence of the risen Jesus with those who follow Him and provides the opportunity for Luke "to share the revelations that he [Jesus] communicates to the elect."[70]

In the vision of Stephen, no words are said nor revelations given by the risen and ascended Jesus, but Stephen's description, in which he indicates that he saw "the heavens opened and the Son of man standing at the right hand of God" (Acts 7:56), seems to communicate that Jesus is standing to act as vindicator of Stephen, to receive Stephen, or in ready eagerness to return.[71]

That Stephen also saw the glory of God when he saw Jesus standing at God's right hand seems, as in Paul's Damascus Road account, to link a bright light with a visionary encounter with Jesus.[72] By the time of Cyprian (A.D. 252), such a linkage appears even in the countenance of the young man who appeared in the vision of a dying priest.[73]

The image of the shepherd is exceedingly helpful in attempting to understand what potential factors contributed to Perpetua's own interpretation of her vision. Scripture carries many statements concerning shepherds, a number of which identify deity in terms of shepherd imagery. Several of the prophets clearly identified Yahweh as a shepherd who feeds a flock (Isa. 40:10–11; Jer. 31:10; Ezek. 34:6–31). The Psalmist, too, held this perspective when he wrote, "Yahweh is my shepherd," but in this instance, the Psalmist considered the relationship personal and individual rather than strictly corporate (Ps. 23:1). The apocryphal work, Sirach, also characterized Yahweh as a shepherd, saying that "He [Yahweh] rebukes and trains and teaches them [all living beings], and turns them back as a shepherd to his flock" (Sirach 18.13b).

The metaphorical application of "shepherd" was not limited to Yahweh, however. The term was also applied to the spiritual leadership of Israel (Ezek. 34:1–10; Zech. 10:3). In I Enoch, the term "shepherd" may also have been used to describe seventy angels who had been given charge over Yahweh's sheep (Israel), angels who were charged to "pasture" them.[74]

The metaphor of the "good shepherd" was also appropriated by Jesus to describe his own ministry (John 10:11, 14). He pictured himself as a shepherd who, in fulfillment of a prophecy, would be struck and whose sheep would be scattered (Matt. 26:31; cf. Zech. 13:7). He also likened the Son of Man to a shepherd who would one day separate the sheep from the goats, inviting the sheep first to his right hand and finally to participate in his kingdom (Matt. 25:31–46, esp. vv. 32–33). The writer to the Hebrews also described Jesus as the "great shepherd of the sheep" (Heb. 13:20; see also 1 Pet. 2:25; 5:4).

The identification of Christian leaders as shepherds in the early church, then, should come as no surprise. The New Testament contains no references that employ the term "shepherd" when referring to Christian leaders, but the reference to pastors in Eph. 4:11 is suggestive of shepherd imagery. The imagery is again present in Paul's address to the elders of the congregation at Ephesus, where he portrays the congregation as a flock of sheep to be guarded and fed by their elders (Acts 20:17–35, esp. vv. 28–31; cf. 1 Pet. 5:2–4).

Ignatius, writing *To the Philadelphians* near the close of the first century, encouraged the congregation, which he described as sheep, to follow the shepherd, by which he meant the bishop.[75] Perhaps of most significance, once again, is the appearance of the shepherd motif in the *Shepherd of Hermas*, dating from the first half of the second century.[76]

Hermas claims to have been given a series of visions. Within the fifth vision, he was confronted by "a man of glorious aspect, dressed like a shepherd, with a white goat's skin, a wallet on his shoulders, and a rod in his hand."[77] This figure described himself as the "angel of repentance,"[78] who was sent to Hermas to make him strong in his faith. By way of contrast, this shepherd showed Hermas two other "shepherds," one of whom he identified as the "angel of luxury and deceit," the other as the "angel of punishment."[79] At the least, then, this "shepherd" is to be understood as "the epiphany of a divine being."[80]

Our search of the literature, then, points to the probability that at the very least the shepherd of Perpetua's vision can be described similarly as an epiphany of a divine being. Indeed, it may be indicative of Hermas's angel of repentance, the "Son of Man," or even Daniel's "Ancient One." It remains to be seen whether other factors in her description of meeting with him will clarify exactly who that divine being is. The various factors which appear to be helpful in this regard include (1) that he welcomes her as "my child," (2) that he gives her some cheese which Perpetua accepts in a reverent posture, and (3) that he is seated in a large garden surrounded by thousands who are dressed in white garments and who seem to participate in worship.

The first, and indeed, the only recorded exchange of words between the shepherd and Perpetua are those the aged shepherd addressed to Perpetua. "I am glad you have come, my child," he said as he observed her from a distance. Then he summoned her to him.

The designation "child" is a Greek appellation in an otherwise Latin text. Its anomalous presence tends to point to its genuineness. The designation, too, places the two primary figures of the vision, the aged shepherd and the young Perpetua, in a clear relationship to one another. The shepherd, it should be understood, is the figure of prominence, exercising control in the encounter. Perpetua has passed from the domain

FIGURE 1

Introductory Formula:	I saw . . . a grey-haired man . . . in shepherd's garb. . . . He raised his head, looked at me, and said:
Admonition: Address and command to come with assurance	"I am glad you have come, my child." He called me over to him
Promise: of eternal life?	and gave me, as it were, a mouthful of the milk he was drawing; and I took it into my cupped hands and consumed it.

of the dragon into that of the shepherd. Moreover, she has been welcomed into the presence of the shepherd as a daughter.

Her welcome by the shepherd consists of a two-part acknowledgment of her presence in the garden: first, through a verbal affirmation ("I am glad you have come") with its accompanying statement of their respective relationships ("my child") and, second, through the granting of sustenance in the form of milk, or more likely, a morsel of cheese.

The oracle itself might best be understood in Aune's terminology as an "oracle of assurance."[81] In Perpetua's vision, a supernatural being appeared in the form of a shepherd and delivered a message in word and deed, in essence, an oracle. The encounter, using Aune's categories might be described as shown in Figure 1.

The verbal affirmation of Perpetua's presence communicates the fact that *she* has taken initiative in their meeting. She has, in fact, come to the shepherd. This statement itself could refer back to the fact that Perpetua had asked for the vision. Thus, it could be argued that the shepherd is none other than the Lord from whom Perpetua had requested the vision (4.1). Her interpretation of the vision that she would be executed for her faith would then come from her understanding of the reception of the cheese from the shepherd, events described at the end of the vision.

More probable, however, is the interpretation that would have these words be a simple acknowledgment of her presence after her successful encounter with the dragon and her equally successful negotiation of the torturous ladder. The interpretation of the vision that recognizes an imminent martyrdom would be tied up in the whole of the vision, each component having its own significance. As such, the shepherd could be the "Lord," but other factors would yet need to be studied.

Once again, then, the designation "child" could be significant in that it is a term used with reference to the father/child relationship between God and God's children.[82] This identification is undercut, however, by noting that the term is also a form of familiar address often from an older person (the aged shepherd) to a younger one (Perpetua),[83] but sometimes from a person of renown to one of lesser prominence.[84]

Perhaps of more help, but certainly no less problematic, is the giving of the cheese to Perpetua. The use of cheese in this instance, the mention of folded hands, and the "amen" of those who stood around have all given rise to the idea that some form of Eucharistic practice is in mind here. Epiphanius noted that the Montanists, because of their use of bread and cheese in the Eucharist, were called "Artotyrites."[85] This statement has since led some to argue that Perpetua held membership in the sect of the Montanists and that her reception of the cheese indicates that she was engaged in an act of Montanist piety.[86]

It has now been sufficiently demonstrated that although the Montanists and Artotyrites both arose in Asia Minor, the Montanists were not Artotyrites. In fact, the Artotyrites were unknown prior to the fourth century. Since this is so, Perpetua could not have been an Artotyrite; and by the reverse logic of Epiphanius, in all probability she was not engaged in an act of Montanist Eucharistic piety.[87] Yet it does remain for us to gain some understanding of the significance of the giving and receiving of the morsel of cheese.

To help in this regard, Herbert Musurillo, in his recent edition has translated the Latin term for "cheese" (*caseo*) as "milk," which was "consumed" rather than "eaten" (*manducavi*), and the hands, which are generally translated as being "folded" (*iumctis*) he has rendered as "cupped."[88] It is true that such a translation is possible if secondary meanings, and these quite rare in some cases, are adopted. The verb *manducavi* generally means "to chew," "to eat," "to consume." The verb *iungo* means "to join," "to unite," "to connect," and thus could be interpreted in the sense that Musurillo has given it. It is, however, most difficult to translate *caseo* as other than "cheese." Yet its connection with milk goes without saying, although Dodds has more convincingly suggested that we have a conversion from milk to milk solids, curds so to speak, brought about by a "sort of time-compression which is common in dreams."[89]

Whether the term *caseo* should be translated as "milk," its connection with milk, albeit in a solid form, may be the real significance of this element of the vision. In no case does the term "cheese" have a "spiritual" meaning or relate to a real figure in a "symbolic" way in Scripture. It appears nowhere in the New Testament, and only rarely in the Old. Where it does occur, it has a very literal meaning. David brought cheese to his brothers (1 Sam. 17:18). He also carried cheese to eat (2 Sam.

17:29). In Job 10:10, the term appears in a question asked of God by Job, "Did you not pour me out like milk and curdle me like cheese?" This is the only other place in which the term appears in Scripture, and it has here a figurative sense, but it carries no specific spiritual significance.

The term "milk" on the other hand has an extensive symbolic usage, not only throughout Scripture but also in secular experience and mystery cults alike.[90] It is symbolic throughout Scripture in its connection with honey as a plentiful drink of the Promised Land.[91] It is thought to be the food of the new convert,[92] providing the basic building block toward spiritual maturity. Indeed, milk became an important symbol to the early Christian community as a drink of eternal life.

The *Epistle of Barnabas*, 6:16–17, explains the meaning of the drink of milk and honey through the analogy, "As the infant is kept alive first by honey, and then by milk, so also we [Christians], being quickened and kept alive by the faith of the promise and by the word, shall live ruling over the earth." Meslin has shown that the origin of a milk drink administered to neophytes is present in Alexandria from the time of Hippolytus, noting that according to the *Canons of Hippolytus*, following the communion of the faithful, "the priests and deacons take the cup of milk and honey and present them to the neophytes after which these latter ones may have communion with bread and chalice, *in memoriam saeculi futuri et suavitatis bonorum in eo fruendorum.*"[93]

That such a practice was also present in the church at Carthage is acknowledged by Tertullian as well. His work on *The Chaplet* carries the description of this practice. He writes that immediately following baptism, "we are taken up (as new-born children), we taste first of all a mixture of milk and honey."[94] Tertullian alludes to this practice as one generally found within the church when he chides Marcion in *Against Marcion*, 1.14.3. Thus, it was a practice within the church at Carthage at least as early as A.D. 207 when the first book of *Against Marcion* was published, and from the way Tertullian speaks of it, it appears that the practice predates his remarks considerably.

In light of this data, it is not impossible that what Perpetua saw in her vision was understood as Meslin has described it, as the eschatological act in which Perpetua received milk curds or cheese as "nourriture d'éternité."[95] This suggestion seems to be especially appropriate in light of Perpetua's very recent baptism while in prison. If the church at Carthage practiced this rite in conjunction with baptism, there is no reason not to expect Perpetua to have participated only recently in this rite herself. Moreover, the connection of this symbolism to the act of martyrdom may have already been fixed in her mind, in that by her own hand she noted that in the water of baptism "the Spirit prescribed that . . . nothing else was to be sought for than bodily endurance" (3.5). Thus, the vision given to Perpetua may have been informed at this point by a common Christian practice of the day, reinforced in Perpetua's case by her own recent experience.

Perpetua's participation in the reception of cheese as symbolic of eternal life points once again back to the shepherd figure as the one who gave it to her. Perpetua was, to be sure, an active participant in the ongoing account, having faced the dragon, ascended the ladder, entered the garden, and gone to the shepherd. But, in this instance, her role seems to be a passive one in which the shepherd gives her the cheese, which she receives with hands folded. In short, then, the shepherd is surely to be understood as the giver of eternal life and, as such, the shepherd would seem to be Jesus. It has already been noted that there is biblical precedent for identifying Jesus with the shepherd motif, but this imagery was also present in the North African church, for Tertullian writes that the shepherd motif was to be found on cups and even on various communion chalices in the church.[96] In the latter case, he even connects the "flavor of the ewe" with the chalice.

Finally, the garden is important for two reasons. First, it is the place where the shepherd is, at the top of the ladder, and second, it is a place where thousands of white-robed individuals are also present. The most obvious interpretation of this garden spot is that which identifies it as heaven, the dwelling place of the righteous dead.[97]

Such an interpretation, too, stands within a long tradition, once again involving the apocalyptic, although not exclusively so. Generally, heaven is linked to the idea of a paradise. Jesus' comment to the thief who asked for mercy on the cross promised their mutual presence in paradise that very day (Luke 23:43). Paul wrote of a man, possibly himself, who was caught up perhaps in visionary fashion into the third heaven, a paradise.[98] It should be noted, too, that John the Revelator in his apocalypse described the paradise of God as being the place where those who would be conquerors would be granted the privilege of eating from the tree of life (Rev. 2:7).

That the concepts of "paradise" and "garden" are to be understood as equivalents is observable from the way the translators of the Septuagint used the term "paradise" ($\pi\alpha\rho\acute{\alpha}\delta\epsilon\iota\sigma\sigma$) at times to translate the Hebrew term "garden" (גן).[99] Thus, it is not surprising to find the Garden of Eden described by the term $\pi\alpha\rho\acute{\alpha}\delta\epsilon\iota\sigma\sigma$, nor is it surprising to find the term put to use in pseudepigraphic sources of the apocalyptic genera. The *Testament of Levi*, 18:10–11, for instance, identifies the Garden of Eden with the future paradise to be opened by a new priest raised up by Yahweh when the writer of this work wrote:

And he shall open the gates of paradise,
And he shall remove the threatening sword from Adam
And he shall give to the saints to eat from the tree of life,
And the spirit of holiness shall be on them.

Similarly, 4 Ezra 7:36 mentions the furnace of Gehenna as an eschatological pit of torment over against the paradise of delight, the eschatological
place of refreshment. 1 Enoch 60.8 and 61.12 see the dwelling place of the
righteous as an expansive garden, whereas 2 Enoch 8:1–8A, 8:1–3, 5, and
8B describe the garden in detail, including the fact that it flows with
honey and milk.

In the early patristic era the idea was prominent that the righteous
dead dwelt in paradise, at least as an intermediate step following their
deaths.[100] Writing after the death of Perpetua, Tertullian spoke of paradise
on two occasions as the abode of martyrs only.[101] In his latter citation he
used the vision of Saturus, which he erroneously attributed to Perpetua, in
addition to Rev. 6:9–11, to substantiate his claim (13.8). In any event,
while Tertullian's work certainly had no influence on Perpetua's interpretation of the vision, she could have relied on other sources such as
those already cited in order to have reached the conclusion that she
reached regarding the vision.

In summary, then, this first vision recorded in The Passion played a
significant role in Perpetua's life. She had been arrested as a relatively
young Christian during a period of persecution in North Africa ordered
shortly after A.D. 200 by Septimius Severus. His target was the catechumens, with the anticipated outcome of breaking the will of those arrested
for this capital offense, while at the same time dissuading any other
conversions.

While awaiting her hearing on the charges, Perpetua, a well-educated
daughter of an influential family, asked the Lord for a vision that would
reveal the outcome of the hearing. She received a vision and concluded
from it that she was to be martyred. In resolute fashion, she prepared
herself psychologically to endure the anticipated persecution. In effect,
the vision seems to have been sought for clarification of God's will, for
guidance; and it seems to have strengthened her resolve to endure hard-
ship to the end.

Although it is not immediately obvious how Perpetua came to the
understanding she did of what her vision meant, an analysis of the various
components of her vision indicates that the interpretation was obvious
given her background and training. It also gives a fair indication of the
type of education she had received at the hands of her Christian mentors
during the less than a year in which she had been a Christian. From the

symbolism involved in the vision, she seems to have undergone training, which was clearly influenced by works of an apocalyptic nature such as Daniel, Ezekiel, Revelation, 1 and 2 Esdras, *4 Ezra, 1 Enoch,* and the *Shepherd of Hermas.* She may also have been exposed to some extent to the Psalms, Isaiah, Jeremiah, the Pentateuch, and John.

Her interpretation of the vision seems also to have been influenced by practices and concepts to be found within the North African Christian community. Among these was the use of a milk and honey mixture served to the newly baptized, and the reliance on the name of Jesus Christ in overcoming the demonic realm. In like manner, from her secular experience would have come her understanding of the executioner's tools and her recognition of the psychological element of her confrontation with her father and the state.

Perpetua's first vision is, easily interpreted if (1) the dragon is in the broad spectrum of things understood to be Satan, at times personified by the state and the Severi, at times by Perpetua's pleading father; (2) the ladder is seen as the transition from life on earth to life in the garden/paradise/heaven marked by martyrdom; (3) the various instruments of torture are understood to be the executioner's tools designed to discourage anyone from a successful pursuit of martyrdom; (4) the shepherd is understood to be the Lord, who welcomes her and gives to her (5) the cheese, indicative of the nourishment of eternal life. The presence of those dressed in white robes who say "Amen" when Perpetua eats the cheese adds a final bit of authenticity to the vision as well as a confirmatory word of witness[102] that Perpetua has been called to and accepted the role of martyr.

In the midst of this portion of the vision, Perpetua is aroused once again to her real surroundings. At the sound of the white-robed multitude saying essentially, "So be it," she is jarred to her senses, still tasting a sweetness in her mouth. She has, in effect, heard a prophetic word through her vision and has in the reception of the cheese which she yet tastes, as well as with the audible and arousing confirmatory word, "Amen," had an experience that for her connects the realm of the visionary to the real world. As a result, Perpetua shared her vision with her brother and together they interpreted it and applied it to her future as an indication of her impending passion. Thus, both Perpetua and her brother seem to have accepted the vision as a prophetic word and had no further expectations for her in the present life.[103]

Only a few days after her experience with the first vision, Perpetua was once again confronted by an impassioned plea from her father to renounce her Christian faith. Her response to him was to fall back on what she believed to be God's will, which would be revealed in the dock. With the words addressed to her father, "we are all in his [God's] power."[104] Perpetua assured her father that her faith commitment was not merely the whim of a confused mind, but rather was symbolic of a personal relationship being borne out in her life.

Shortly after her father's visit, Perpetua's hearing took place before the recently appointed local governor, Hilarianus. Her father appeared once again in the courtroom trying to dissuade her from her faith. Seizing the opportunity, Hilarianus attempted to convince Perpetua even more force-fully by having her father beaten before her eyes. She refused to recant, although not without personal concern for her father's welfare. As a result of her resolve to confess publicly her Christian commitment, she was sentenced to die by exposure to beasts. She was deprived of any further contact with her child, and returned to prison to await the day of execution.[105]

During this waiting period, Perpetua experienced the second and third of her four visions. These two visions seem to constitute a single unit of thought, both involving her brother Dinocrates, and they will thus be treated together as two parts of a single experience.

PERPETUA'S DINOCRATES VISIONS

Perpetua had been sentenced to death for the crime of being a new convert to Christianity. Hilarianus had prescribed that she and her fellow prisoners be condemned to die by exposure to wild beasts.[1] Their scheduled date of execution was to be the upcoming birthday of Geta Caesar (7.9). In the interim, the condemned prisoners were returned to the dungeon of the prison to await their execution.

During their final period of imprisonment, the confessors were apparently kept together. They were able to communicate regularly with one another, and they were allowed the privilege of praying together. Following one such time of community prayer Perpetua wrote, "while praying I spoke out and uttered the name Dinocrates" (7.1; see appendix B). From what Perpetua tells us, this experience was out of the ordinary. She was surprised by the intrusion of the thought of Dinocrates into her prayer.

THE OCCASION

In this, the first mention of Dinocrates in *The Passion*, we are told all that we really know about him. Perpetua explains that she had had a brother, Dinocrates, who at the age of seven had died of a cancerous growth on the face. His suffering had been intense and his outward appearance grotesque (7.5).

Perpetua's emotional response to the sudden remembrance of Dinocrates suggests that a fairly extended period of time had transpired since his death. She had not thought of him previously during her imprisonment, and was surprised at the suddenness with which his name came to her. Following her surprise came grief, as once again the reality of his suffering and death came to her mind (7.1).

It is clear that Perpetua was concerned for the ultimate spiritual welfare of her deceased brother. Such a concern would seem to be a very natural one, increasingly so, as she moved forward toward her own imminent death. This fact, however, has given rise to speculation that her visions of Dinocrates may have been nothing more than a stress-induced form of wishful thinking.[2] Yet, it must be noted that the visions of Perpetua and

Saturus have been treated by the church as genuine since earliest times.[3] In light of its ancient acceptance as a genuine vision, Perpetua's Dinocrates vision will be taken at face value unless it becomes apparent through analysis of its content that it is not possible to accept it as such.

In any case, Perpetua understood herself "to be in a worthy state," and as such she was bound to pray "on his behalf" (7.2). Her recognition of her own worthiness seems to have been a direct result of what she considered to be an unexpected recollection of her brother Dinocrates.[4]

Precisely what Perpetua meant by describing herself as being in a "worthy state" is not totally clear. Prior to her first vision, her living brother had said that she was "greatly privileged" (4.1). He encouraged her to ask for a vision that would reveal the outcome of her imprisonment. Acting on his encouragement she had both asked for and received such a vision, for she believed herself able to speak to the Lord and expected him to answer (4.2). Thus, on the one hand, her "worthy state" may refer to nothing more than that as a Christian she had access to the Lord, who at times responded to her requests by means of visions. Furthermore, she may have thought herself as proven "worthy" in that she had already been rewarded with one vision. On the other hand, her "worthy state" may have taken its meaning from her recent confession and sentencing. Confessors and martyrs of that day were thought to have a unique position before the Lord to ask for certain things and to expect their requests to be granted,[5] and there is no apparent reason why Perpetua would not have been aware of such an idea.

In response to her sense of "worthiness," Perpetua began to pray for Dinocrates and to sigh deeply for him before the Lord (7.2). The emotional nature of Perpetua's prayer is not to be overlooked. It conveys a genuine concern for some assurance or knowledge of her brother's eternal state. Nor can the parallel that exists between Perpetua's experience and Paul's words in Rom. 8:26b be ignored.[6] While there is a remote possibility that we find here a reference to praying in tongues, the context seems merely to indicate that Perpetua "prayed her heart out" on the subject of her brother to the point that she ultimately expressed her concerns through sighs of a deeply emotional nature.

That night she had the first of two visions of Dinocrates:

> I saw Dinocrates coming out of a dark hole, where there were many others with him, very hot and thirsty, pale and dirty. On his face was the wound he had when he died. . . . There was a great abyss between us: neither could approach the other. Where Dinocrates stood there was a pool full of water; and its rim was higher than the child's height, so that Dinocrates had to stretch himself up to drink. (7.4, 6b–7)

Perpetua goes on to tell what she felt when she saw her brother. "I was sorry that, though the pool had water in it, Dinocrates could not drink because of the height of the rim" (7.8). On the basis of this nocturnal "vision" or "revelation," when she woke up, Perpetua concluded that her "brother was suffering" (7.9).

Perpetua's interpretation of the first vision, in turn, motivated her to further action. She became confident that she could help Dinocrates in his suffering and, as a result, made him a subject of daily prayer. How many days her prayers continued is not known, but her language is clear enough to indicate that a considerable length of time transpired between her first vision of Dinocrates and her second one. During the interim, Perpetua and her fellow prisoners were transferred to the local military prison. "And," she wrote, "I prayed for my brother day and night with tears and sighs that this favour might be granted me" (7.10).

At some point in her confinement at the military prison, Perpetua and her fellow prisoners were put in chains. Her mention of this fact seems to indicate that this was not normal practice but something which took place on a particular day. It was on this particular day, when the prisoners were kept chained, that Perpetua experienced her second vision of Dinocrates (8.1). Although the passage under consideration gives no further data on the circumstances surrounding her having this vision, Perpetua mentions at the end of it that she awoke. She uses the same terminology she had used in her earlier Dinocrates vision, so that the process of revelation was probably identical in both cases (8.4). This cannot be verified, of course, and there is no mention of what time of day the second vision took place. The description of her second Dinocrates vision picks up at the place where the first one left off and is as follows:

> I saw the same spot that I had seen before, but there was Dinocrates all clean, well dressed, and refreshed. I saw a scar where the wound had been; and that pool that I had seen before now had its rim lowered to the level of the child's waist. And Dinocrates kept drinking water from it, and there above the rim was a golden bowl full of water. And Dinocrates drew close and began to drink from it, and yet the bowl remained full. And when he had drunk enough of the water he began to play as children do. (8.1b–4a)

Perpetua's conclusion as to the meaning of this second Dinocrates vision was: "I realized that he had been delivered from his suffering" (8.4b).

Undoubtedly, but without further comment from Perpetua, the reader is left to conclude that Perpetua's prayers were efficacious on behalf of her brother Dinocrates.

DINOCRATES

In order to determine how Perpetua came to the conclusions that she has set forth for us concerning these two parts of what in reality is a single narrative, we need to look once again at what cultural and religious factors might have contributed to this complicated set of events. It will be necessary to look briefly at Dinocrates, the chief character of the visions, the dark place in which he suffers, the fountain or pool of water, which at first is too high for his reach but which later is not only within reach but also has on its rim a golden bowl from which to drink, the significance, if any, of Dinocrates' healing and entering into normal childlike activity. Perpetua has noted what she believed were the interpretations to these visions, but has not told us how they functioned (how she arrived at her conclusions) nor what role they played in her own life (in what way they were significant to her). Through our analysis it is anticipated that we will be able to determine some of the answers to these questions.

The first issue to be settled concerns Dinocrates. I have already noted that the explicit information regarding him is meagre. Dinocrates, one of Perpetua's two brothers, had died at the age of seven from a cancer that Perpetua described as "a source of loathing to everyone" (7.5). Apparently, an extended period of time had passed between the time Dinocrates had died and when Perpetua thought of him while imprisoned. Weighing against this implication, of course, might be Perpetua's own preoccupation with events surrounding her arrest, trial, and imprisonment as well as the welfare of her own infant son. She could have been so concerned and anxious over these things that she had let any previous concern for Dinocrates slip away. It was, bear in mind, only after she notes that her anxiety over her own child was settled that the first vision of Dinocrates took place (6.8). The surprise that Perpetua expresses at the intrusion of thoughts concerning Dinocrates into her time of prayer, however, coupled with her explanation that "the name had never entered my mind until that moment," tend to support quite strongly the implication that Dinocrates' death was something in the distant past. She had not thought of him in a great while (7.1).

What we are not told in any explicit way is whether Dinocrates had been a baptized Christian at the time of his death. What we are told is that on the basis of her initial vision of Dinocrates in which he was unable to get relief for his thirst because of the fountain's height, Perpetua concluded that he was in a place of suffering. Furthermore, on the basis of her second vision, she concluded that Dinocrates was no longer suffering, with the implication being that her prayers had made the difference.

Two centuries after Perpetua's death, what little material we have on Dinocrates was taken in two opposite directions. A man whom Augustine described as "my much-loved son Victor,"[7] who had taken the name Vincentius Victor, had left the Rogatist schism of the Donatist Church to join the Catholics. Augustine was pleased to note Victor's conversion, but he was concerned that Victor's books were introducing heretical teaching into the church. One such teaching was that "infants which are forestalled by death before they are baptized may yet attain to forgiveness of their original sins."[8] In reply, Augustine interacted with the two examples that Victor had cited in support of this position: the thief on the cross who was promised entrance into Paradise and Dinocrates.

Victor had argued that Dinocrates was not baptized at the time of death, but as a result of his sister's prayer had been "given the remission of sins and an abode with the blessed,"[9] which would in turn give way to a reward of a place in "the kingdom of heaven" at the resurrection.[10] As a result of this theory, Victor is said to have written, "In their [the unbaptized infant dead] behalf I most certainly decide that constant oblations and incessant sacrifices must be offered upon the part of the holy priests."[11]

Augustine's critique of Victor's position is of help if for no other reason than to make it clear that Victor's argument is an argument *ex silencio,* and therefore, where no corollary evidence is present, a weak argument. Furthermore, Augustine noted that the mention of Dinocrates "does not occur in the canon of Holy Scripture whence in all questions of this kind our proofs ought always to be drawn."[12] Thus, Augustine implies that while Perpetua's vision may be legitimate, Victor's appeal to a noncanonical source is wrongly placed. Besides, Victor's interpretation and the inference that he drew from it for the theology and practice of the church were heretical.

Instead, Augustine offered an explanation of the facts himself. He made it clear that in his own reading of the visions of Perpetua, in no case did "the saint herself, or whoever it was that wrote the account, say that the boy . . . died without baptism."[13] Augustine's own interpretation is set forward in the following manner:

> As for Dinocrates, he was a child of seven years of age; and as children who are baptized so old as that can now recite the creed and answer for themselves in the usual examination, I know not why he may not be supposed after his baptism to have been recalled by his unbelieving father to the sacrilege and profanity of heathen worship, and for this reason to have been condemned to the pains from which he was liberated at his sister's intercession.[14]

The question of whether Dinocrates had been baptized cannot, however, be easily nor finally settled with such an explanation. If Augustine believes that Victor's argument has been weakened because it is based on silence, his own argument is equally subject to this same fault.[15] Indeed, what little evidence is available would generally speak against the conclusion that Dinocrates had been baptized prior to his death. Robinson's argument is powerful, though itself based on probability. It does seem improbable that the seven-year-old son of a pagan would have received Christian baptism even if his sister was a catechumen when he died.[16] The improbability increases even more if Dinocrates' death occurred prior to Perpetua's conversion.

Neither Augustine's assessment of Dinocrates as the baptized seven-year-old son of a pagan father, who was forced by the father to engage in idolatry and who died in that state, thereby incurring "mortal condemnation,"[17] nor the reconstruction by Vincentius Victor that Dinocrates had died unbaptized can be proven from the text. Yet, it may be possible to gain some further insight and understanding of Perpetua's thinking by noting some of the beliefs regarding the state of the dead in her day.

IDEAS OF AFTERLIFE AS BACKGROUND

It is logical that as a Christian, newly converted within a climate conducive both to persecution and to possible martyrdom, Perpetua would have become somewhat conversant with the Christian understanding of the afterlife. The Christian perspective on the afterlife was linked in its origin to the concept of life and death prevalent in Israel's understanding, an understanding that had evolved through the centuries as Israel's inspired writers reflected on God's dealings with humanity.

In the Old Testament, the abode of all the dead was originally thought to be a land of darkness and confusion in the nether world, where persons were described as "shades" or ghostlike characters.[18] It was a world patterned after that of the living, at least in its social relationships, but it was a world of the dead. R. H. Charles has noted, and I think rightfully so, that at its earliest, this land called Sheol שְׁאוֹל did "not differ essentially from the Homeric Hades."[19] Only in the later biblical writings did there come to be the anticipation of a separation of the righteous from the unrighteous in death and the development of a concept of a resurrection for the righteous.[20]

The earliest understanding of שְׁאוֹל, almost invariably rendered as ᾅδης in the LXX, stood for centuries, although it underwent modification, especially during the intertestamental period, when in accommodation to morality, it came to include a separate existence for the righteous and the unrighteous in the nether world (*1 Enoch* 22:8–13). It is suggested, again by Charles, that this view gained acceptance, even prominence, as the concept of the resurrection of the just and righteous entered into the Jewish understanding of things.[21] No longer was Sheol to be considered the eternal abode of all humanity who had passed through the portal of death; for some it would be merely an intermediate state from which they would "be removed in the resurrection to share in the glories of the Messianic Kingdom or to receive due punishments for their sins."[22]

In Jesus' day, the separation of the righteous from those who were evil was given credibility through his reference to an unnamed rich man and Lazarus in Luke 16:19–31: "The poor man died and was carried away by the angels to be with Abraham. The rich man also died and was buried. In Hades, where he was tormented, he looked up and saw Abraham far away with Lazarus by his side."[23] As the story progresses, the rich man asks Abraham to send Lazarus to him with a drop of water. His request is refused because the tables have been righted. Lazarus who had suffered in life was comforted in death, while the rich man who had enjoyed the "good life" but did not share it was now expected to endure anguish. To ensure that they remained apart, an uncrossable chasm had been fixed between them (Luke 16:26).

By the time of the New Testament, the conception of Sheol or Hades had undergone a further change and "no longer signified the intermediate state of the righteous and of the wicked, but came to be used of the abode of the wicked only . . . the wicked simply remained in Sheol, which thus practically became hell or Gehenna."[24]

In light of this brief survey of the biblical data it is clear that few real parallels exist between Perpetua's description of the abode of Dinocrates and the view of Hades portrayed in Scripture. In Luke 16:26 there is mention of a great chasm fixed between Lazarus and the rich man. In her vision, Perpetua noted that "between me [Perpetua] and him [Dinocrates] was a great abyss: neither was able to approach the other" (7.6). Yet, even here the difference is as significant as the similarity, since Perpetua was not yet dead and was only able to see her brother's state through a visionary process.[25]

Perpetua's depiction of the realm in which she saw Dinocrates was at points consistent with the biblical data of the Old Testament, for she described it as a "dark [or gloomy] place." Furthermore, Dinocrates' countenance and those who were with him were described as showing discomfort. He was portrayed as "intensely hot and parched, dirty and pale" and was said to carry on his face the cancerous wound from which he had died

(7.4). Perpetua's immediate conclusion was that Dinocrates was "suffering" (7.9).

Again, we are plagued by inconsistency with the biblical record as she prays for her brother and apparently, as a result, Dinocrates' situation is changed so that he is transformed into a clean, well dressed, and cool or refreshed child. Furthermore, his wound has been healed and he plays as a child would play (8). Such a thought is foreign to the message of Scripture. Even the majority of pseudepigrapha did not allow for change after life has ended or intercession by the righteous on behalf of the dead.[26] If there are inconsistencies between Perpetua's depiction of the afterlife and that portrayed by the canonical literature, more help may be attained by looking at such depictions as were to be found in the popular secular literature of Perpetua's day, especially if, as Dölger has pointed out, the Christians of that day had difficulty in separating their Christian teachings from the deeply rooted perceptions of the pagan folk literature.[27]

The popular mind at the beginning of the third century A.D. was greatly influenced by pagan thought. Centuries before, the Greeks had posited an abode for the dead spirits or shades in an underworld ruled by the god Hades and his dreaded goddess queen Persephone.[28] Persons such as "brides, and unwedded youths, and toil-worn old men, and tender maidens with hearts yet new to sorrow, and many, too, that had been wounded with bronze-tipped spears, men slain in fight, wearing their blood-stained armour," at death were said to come first to Erebus, a part of this underworld in the higher region of Hades.[29] Yet, it was already a place described by Homer as lying "beneath the murky darkness,"[30] a place where few persons were said to have gone and returned to the living. It was a place tormented by memory and the frustration produced when those who inhabited the region were not allowed to right the wrongs done against them during their lifetimes. It was in Erebus that the newly dead were expected to get all in order before formally entering Hades, the place where they must temporarily reside until this was done.

In the lower regions of Hades was Tartarus, a place considered to be the source of everything gloomy, misty, unfruitful, loathsome, and dank.[31] Of particular significance is Hesiod's description of Tartarus as a "great gulf," the abode of the Titan gods.[32] The corpus of Homer containing the *Hymn to Hermes* mentions a threat made by Apollo against Hermes, a threat to cast him even as a young child "into dusky Tartarus and awful hopeless darkness, and neither your mother nor your father shall free you or bring you up again to the light, but you will wander under the earth and be the leader amongst little folk."[33] This comment gives rise to the suggestion that infants or small children who died prematurely were thought to have occupied a particular place within Hades.[34]

From Greek thought on the afterlife, several points may be noted. First, those who died were said to become disembodied spirits or shades who inhabited a region in the underworld ruled by Hades. This region was the house of Hades, or simply referred to as Hades. It was divided into several subregions for housing various types of persons, among whom were those whose crimes were particularly heinous and those who had died untimely deaths. When a spirit entered Hades, it was not allowed to leave.[35] That spirit remained in whatever state it had entered. Thus, children remained children in the underworld, a concept to which the writer of the *Hymn to Hermes* referred.[36]

The Romans held similar views of the afterlife, having adopted much of the Greek Pantheon and assumed many of its mythologies. Particularly helpful to our understanding from the Roman perspective is an extended description of the afterlife found in Virgil's *Aeneid*.[37] In the Roman Pantheon, the god Hades was renamed Pluto, but his position was the same as that of Hades since he acted as the king of the underworld. Erebus was replaced by the bank of the river Styx over which the buried dead were ferried by the dreaded boatman, Charon. The rest remained there to await a proper funeral, their ashes to be covered with earth.[38]

Virgil's primary character, Aeneas, although yet living was allowed to go with Charon across the river Styx because he possessed a golden branch, a gift to be given to Proserpina, the Roman counterpart to Persephone, queen of the underworld. Upon his crossing of the Styx, Aeneas was confronted by the sound of crying. Virgil remarks that "At once are heard voices and wailing sore—the souls of infants weeping, whom, on the very threshold of the sweet life they shared not, torn from the breast, the black day swept off and plunged into bitter death."[39] Such a citation gives rise to the idea that babies and small children who had died while young remained in the state in which they had lived—as children, even suffering children, as denoted by their cries.

Further on, Aeneas spoke of finding the Fields of Mourning. There he met Deiphobus, "his whole frame mangled, his face cruelly torn—his face and either hand—ears wrenched from despoiled brows, and his nostrils lopped by a shameful wound. Scarce, indeed, did he know the quivering form that would hide its awful punishments."[40]

Tartarus remained the same as that found in Greek mythology. Virgil described it as a place that "yawns sheer down, stretching into the gloom twice as far as in yon sky's upward view to heavenly Olympus. Here the ancient sons of Earth, the Titan's brood, hurled down by the thunderbolt, writhe in the lowest abyss."[41]

Finally, Virgil described the Elysian Fields as the abode of heroes, warriors and poets, the good and the pure, those who discovered truth and made life nobler, and those who served others.[42] Articulating a doctrine of the transmigration of souls, Virgil noted that many spirits "at the water of Lethe's steam . . . [in the Elysian Fields] drink the soothing draught and long forgetfulness."[43] Once done, these souls were said to be willing once more to enter mortal bodies.[44]

In summary, then, Roman religion treated the afterlife in much the same way that Greek religion had. Those souls that had died were separated from their mortal bodies to become wandering shades in the netherworld ruled by Pluto. Morality played a significant role in this afterlife, with evil rewarded by evil and good with good.[45] In Roman thought, those who died prematurely, such as children who had died from disease, were treated separately within Hades since they had no posterity to care for their remains.[46] In addition, those who died with wounds continued, as did Deiphobus, to carry their wounds in Hades.[47]

Several points of comparison exist between Greek and Roman perceptions of Hades, of those persons who inhabit it, and the description that Perpetua has left in her diary concerning Dinocrates. Among the elements to be compared are: (1) the dead go to a place of gloom or darkness; (2) the dead retain their identity and appearance, carrying even the wounds and scars inflicted on their bodies during their life on earth; (3) the dead often, but not necessarily always, suffer in Hades at least temporarily; (4) the living can have an effect on the status of the dead, enabling them to move from a state of anguish and torment to a state in which suffering has ceased;[48] and (5) the dead may be allowed to drink from a liquid that quenches thirst or may aid in the process of forgetting the past, in either case bringing about a state of refreshment and the potential for new life.

With this survey of ideas on the afterlife common in Perpetua's day, ideas originating in the Hebrew/Christian tradition, as well as in both Greek and Roman traditions, we begin to catch a glimpse of some of the factors that may have been present in Perpetua's thought process when she received her visions of Dinocrates. Yet, one final source might provide even more specific help in the solution of her interpretation process. The *Apocalypse of Peter*, which dates from the first half of the second century, contains a section devoted to the "untimely dead," specifically in the form of children who had died at the hands of abortionists who had expired, or from exposure:[49]

> And near this flame [used to burn adulterers] there is a great and very deep pit and into it there flow all kinds of things from everywhere: . . . and the women (are) swallowed up (by this) to their necks and are punished with great pain. . . . Opposite them is another place where the children sit, but both alive, and they cry to God. . . . Other men and

women stand above them naked. And their children stand opposite to them in a place of delight. And they sigh and cry to God because of their parents . . . [who] killed their children. And the children shall be given to the angel Temlakos.[50]

It is obvious from this quotation that these children did not die the type of death Dinocrates did, but there are some points to be made by looking at this passage as instructive of some Christian thought, at least in Egypt,[51] if not in Carthage itself, during the period in question. Of great significance to the present study are the notion of the abyss, the presence of punishment for sin, and, most important, the note that children were understood to remain as children who sat as a group similarly betrayed, crying out to God for their vindication. Ultimately they were said to be given over to the safekeeping of an angel.

At least one modern Roman Catholic writer has argued that "with the text of the *Martyrdom of Perpetua and Felicitas* (c. 203) we are at the beginning of Western ideas of Purgatory."[52] Reference is made to Perpetua's prayers on behalf of Dinocrates, which were judged to be efficacious since Dinocrates was delivered from his suffering. But, once again, we have been brought remarkably close, even in Christian literature, to the point of pagan perceptions of the afterlife,[53] perceptions that posit an abyss where justice is meted out.

The fountain or pool of water and, even more specifically, the golden bowl from which Dinocrates drank are significant in the interpretation of Perpetua's vision as well. Once again, Perpetua's training and background may be called upon to provide possible explanations of how she came to understand these symbols.

In Scripture, the symbols of bowls, cups, and fountains occur repeatedly. Yahweh is known as the "fountain of living waters" (Jer. 2:13, cf. Ps. 36:9). Indeed, water was clearly the symbol for life (Isa. 44:3; 55:1; 58:11; Joel 3:18), whereas the pitcher broken at the fountain was used by Qoheleth to depict death (Eccles. 12:6). Jesus spoke of the living water he could give, a drink of which would be eternally satisfying (John 4:10, 13–14; cf. John 7:37–38).

Perhaps it is the Revelation, though, that provides the closest parallel from the canonical writings to what we find depicted in the vision of Perpetua. John recorded the words spoken by the One sitting upon the throne: "I am the Alpha and the Omega, the beginning and the end. To the thirsty I will give water as a gift from the spring of the water of life" (Rev. 21:6). The final invitation to the reader of the Revelation goes on to reaffirm that statement in the form of a promise that the water of life will be given without price to those who desire it (Rev. 22:17).

References to cups are frequent throughout Scripture, but in most cases they are involved with symbolic representations. They do not represent utensils from which life-giving drinks are taken, but containers out of which Yahweh's fury and/or judgment is poured.[54] The symbolic idea was personified in one instance as the nation of Babylon, which became "a golden cup in the Lord's hand, making all the nations drunken" (Jer. 51:7).

From the pagan background of Perpetua's day, Meslin has noted the existence of scenes on Dionysian sarcophagi in which infants are depicted as attempting to become intoxicated in the "cratère d'immortalité."[55] To be noted also is the parallel provided in the drink from the Lethe stream in the Elysian Fields of the Aeneid which, in effect, provided each shade with the ability once again to enter into mortality by wiping out any remembrance of previous existence.[56]

INTERPRETATIONS OF THE DINOCRATES VISIONS

It has already been noted that Vincentius Victor and Augustine understood Perpetua's Dinocrates visions as supporting their own theological biases. Vincentius Victor had presupposed that Dinocrates was unbaptized at death, whereas Augustine had presupposed him to have been baptized prior to his death. Both of these scholars believe Perpetua's prayers to have been efficacious on behalf of Dinocrates.

The details of the visions were used in stressing certain allegorical features. Augustine, for instance, noted that the wound which had appeared on the face of Dinocrates also appeared on his soul, a soul with corporeal parameters. It was this suffering, perhaps symbolic of original sin, from which Perpetua's prayers rescued Dinocrates' soul.[57]

The work of Marie-Louise von Franz, employing Jungian psychological principles does not seem to be too far from this allegorical format. In her chapter on the second and third visions of Perpetua, von Franz views Dinocrates, in part, as the personification or the anima of Perpetua herself.[58] It is she who has the longing for the baptismal font. Drawing from the hermetic literature, von Franz notes parallels that view God as providing a container to those in the afterlife, filled with νοῦς, into which those who have died immerse themselves.[59]

Yet, in keeping with Jungian psychology, von Franz notes that the water that Dinocrates drinks is to be understood as "Spirit." In keeping with Perpetua's confession, then, "the water of the basin is here, by way of suggestion a kind of baptismal water, as a symbol of Christ or of the Holy Spirit."[60] Thus, when Perpetua engaged in a conscious quest for the reality of her own baptism, she realized the inner resource of power that enabled her to move with resolve toward her own martyrdom.[61]

More recently, Eugenio Corsini has offered another theological interpretation to Perpetua's visions of Dinocrates and, specifically, of the
significance of the water and font. He argues that the water is symbolic of
baptism. Dinocrates is in a place that corresponds to the Christian concept of hell. Moreover, like Augustine, he argues that Dinocrates' disfigurement is "a symbol of a moral malady, namely of a sin."[62]

Corsini criticizes Meslin's attempt to find in the so-called *boissons
d'éternité* of secular literature parallels to what is found in the case of
Dinocrates. Instead, Corsini suggests that what lies behind the imagery of
Perpetua's vision are "two baptisms." The first baptism is her baptism with
water, the second her baptism of martyrdom. Thus, in Corsini's interpretation, the cup of gold that lies on the rim of the basin "reestablishes
the New Testament connection between the first baptism and the other,
of passion, as Jesus recalled in the metaphor of the drink of the cup."[63]

In this way, then, Corsini translates Perpetua's martyrdom into an
efficacious act on behalf of her brother Dinocrates. But it is efficacious
because God is omnipotent and sovereign. He points out that Dinocrates
is not enabled to climb up to get the water, but, rather, the fountain is
lowered so that he might partake. Furthermore, he contends that the
voice which speaks through Perpetua when she unexpectedly remembers
Dinocrates is none other than the "voice of the Spirit," and it was by this
means that Perpetua was "in possession of a gift of grace" that enabled
Dinocrates to be relieved of his suffering.[64]

Perpetua's prayer, then, was narrowly prescribed by her "*dignatio*" and
her baptism. Perpetua's prayer, life, and death must be understood, as
Corsini puts it, "in the light of a mystical-sacramental conception of
baptism."[65] This concept of baptism is, as Corsini has attempted to show, a
Pauline-based conception in which death is understood to be a mystical
burial with or in Christ's own death and resurrection. Perpetua's baptism
of martyrdom unites her with Christ, thus forming a "single body" through
which Perpetua and Christ work out the salvation of her brother.[66]

While Corsini's interpretation is very interesting, its complexity as a
theory belies its truthfulness. In light of this survey of Perpetua's visions of
her deceased brother, several conclusions can be drawn. First, undoubtedly Perpetua's anxiety level was high as she sat on death row. It may have
been that in her situation she was prone toward receiving visions.

Second, Perpetua did remember her brother Dinocrates. The psychological factors affecting her were surely real. They should neither be
denied nor underestimated. As such, her own anxiety level may have
been raised even more as she contemplated the horrid nature of her young
brother's death, since it was probable she would face an even worse
physical disfigurement.

Third, as a relatively new convert, Perpetua had apparently received her baptism prematurely due to her imprisonment and her imminent death. As such, she probably did not possess a high level of theological sophistication. Her Christian training was probably not extensive, although, as has been demonstrated thus far, it certainly employed apocalyptic imagery. She seems also to have had some understanding of death and the afterlife, particularly on the existence of heaven and hell.

Fourth, because Perpetua had been reared in a Roman setting by a pagan father, it seems much more likely that she was still greatly influenced by the thinking of her secular society on the subject of death and the unfortunate state of those who died prematurely. Her brother had died some time previously, probably prior to her own conversion. So her thoughts of him as one of those who died before his time would tend to be thoughts in which she would imagine him as suffering the fate of the untimely dead. Her most significant and natural response would be to pray for him.

If each of these statements is true, as would seem to be indicated by our study, we need not look for elaborate theological doctrines such as mystical-sacramental views of martyrdom as baptism or intermediate states of suffering such as purgatory. In light of contemporary religious imagery common in her culture, the visions may be taken at face value as perceptions of afterlife that are consistent with Perpetua's personal anxiety with respect to her own death and her sudden remembrance of her brother's demise. Is it possible, then, that what we have in the Dinocrates vision is nothing more than a word of comfort, a prophecy *per se*, which follows the guideline that Paul set forth in 1 Cor. 14:3 ("those who prophesy build up the church")?

Perpetua, upon remembering and, indeed, dwelling on the subject of her brother's death, could easily have become anxious concerning his eternal state, especially if she had not been a Christian at the time of his death. But now with her personal commitment to confess Christ about to be tested even by death, she may have become more anxious. Yet, because of her inexperience as a Christian and the limited nature of her formal Christian teaching on the subject of death and the afterlife, it is possible that the first vision in which she saw Dinocrates suffering was nothing more than preparatory. She received it, in effect, to bring about a crisis in which her anxiety would be relieved and her faith enhanced.

The second vision of Dinocrates could, then, be understood as providing the resolution to Perpetua's anxiety. She prayed, pouring out her heart with tears and sighs, being confident that some resolution would be forthcoming. When she "awoke" she had a knowledge that Dinocrates was not suffering.

To assume that he had been "delivered" as a direct result of her prayers takes the argument too far. Perpetua may have believed that her prayers had delivered him from his suffering, but we have seen that she was probably greatly influenced at this point by her pagan past, which was undoubtedly fostered by the social milieu that was Carthage, and she had probably very little formal teaching along these lines from the church. Thus, it is more likely that the revelation which occurred for her was one designed to lower her anxiety in the face of her own imminent death. She had no reason to worry either for her brother's eternal state or for her own.

CHAPTER FIVE

The Vision of the Egyptian (10.1–14)

By the time Perpetua experienced the last of her visionary encounters, she had very little time left before her execution. Perpetua saw this final vision on the day immediately prior to her death.[1] Her recording of it for posterity must have been one of the last acts performed while she was in prison.

Since her vision of Dinocrates, a number of days had passed. During the interim, Perpetua notes, an adjutant whose duty it was to act as prison supervisor, was touched by the spiritual strength to which these captives bore witness. As a result, he allowed for increased visitation rights to the mutual benefit of the condemned and those who came to see them (9.1).

Among those who came to visit Perpetua was, of course, her pagan father, who made his final attempts to persuade her not to continue in her confession. His appeal, like those he had previously made, was filled with pathos, heart-wrenching to all but the most recalcitrant. Perpetua, though moved by the fact that her father would be unhappy in his declining years, remained nonetheless firm in her decision to undergo martyrdom (9.2, 3).

THE OCCASION

On the day before her fight with the beasts in the local amphitheater, Perpetua says that she saw a vision (10.1; see appendix C) that she recorded. Unlike the first vision for which she had asked (4.2) or the second one that appears to have resulted from Perpetua's concern for Dinocrates after his name had intruded into her prayers (7.1), reference to this third vision is made without a significant context. Perpetua simply notes that she saw the vision about to be described. The most significant contextual statement made was that it occurred the day before she was to die.

The vision itself is composed of three major components. In the first portion of the vision, a man named Pomponius, a deacon, came knocking at the prison doors. Perpetua answered his knocks, opening the prison gates herself. Pomponius then instructed Perpetua to come with him because there were those who were waiting for her. Hand-in-hand, the two went through "rough and broken" country until they arrived at the amphitheater. On their arrival, Pomponius encouraged Perpetua with the words, "Do not be afraid. I am here, struggling with you" (10.1b–4). When he had finished saying this, Pomponius left her.

The second scene occurs at the amphitheater itself. After Pomponius left her, Perpetua was met by two individuals of importance to her vision and its message. In the first, she came face to face with her opponent, an Egyptian of vicious appearance. As she was being prepared for her fight with this Egyptian, Perpetua noted that suddenly she was transformed into a man. While she was being rubbed down with oil in preparation for the wrestling match, the Egyptian began to roll in the dust (10.4–7).

The second person that Perpetua met was described as a man of "marvelous stature"; indeed, so tall was he that he stood above the amphitheater. Perpetua described him as though he were an athletic trainer. When he spoke, all were compelled to listen, and his oracle included what might be described as the terms of the fight, or the challenge. If the Egyptian were to win, Perpetua must die by the sword. If Perpetua were to win, she would receive a branch. Following his words, he like Pomponius, left her to finish the task (10.8–10a).

With the third scene, the vision built to a climax. What began as a fist fight between the sexually transformed Perpetua and the vicious Egyptian developed into a life-and-death struggle with no holds barred. Perpetua fought with hands and feet until she subdued the Egyptian, face in the dirt, and she stepped on his head. With her victory, the crowd went wild. The "trainer" reentered, kissing Perpetua and speaking to her, this time a word of peace to his "daughter." She received the victory branch and left the amphitheater through the Sanavivarian gate, or the Gate of Life (10.10b–13).

Perpetua's conclusion as she interpreted this vision was twofold. First, she understood that her fight with the wild beasts, which was scheduled for the morrow, would be merely the form the real fight would take. The fight was not so much with beasts; it was with the devil. Second, she knew that she would be victorious in the confrontation (10.14).

In keeping with our attempt to determine how these visions functioned for Perpetua and how she arrived at the interpretation she did, it is necessary once again to analyze some of the cultural and religious factors that probably influenced Perpetua when she attempted to interpret and apply her visions. In this particular vision, then, it will be necessary to give closer attention to Pomponius, to the vicious Egyptian, to the man of marvelous height, to the fight itself, and to all oracles that occur within the vision.

POMPONIUS

Several features of Perpetua's third vision seem to have direct correspondence with her real situation. First among them is Perpetua herself.
She understood herself to be the principal performer in the vision and is
even called by name. Second is the prison. She had been in prison for
some months. Now, on the day before her death, in the beginning of her
account she recognizes her true location. Third was the amphitheater.
She had been condemned to die at the fury of wild beasts, and the
traditional place where such events took place was the amphitheater.
There is clearly a note of reality in her account that is evident through
these facts.

An additional feature that carries the same potential for a direct correspondence with reality, but which is more obscure, is her mention of
Pomponius. Perpetua calls him a deacon, a designation that may again
provide a link to reality. She knew him and he knew her as well. She does
not appear to have been at all reticent to go with him in her vision when
he took her by the hand, and he called her by name.

As already noted, R. Braune has suggested that Pomponius is the
probable redactor of *The Passion of Perpetua and Felicitas*.[2] Thus, he was
likely a friend of Perpetua and the others who were put to death alongside
her and an eyewitness to the execution (16.1–21.11). Also, he would
have had a heart for Christian strugglers and martyrs of a future age in
light of his concern to preserve Perpetua's visions and Christian witness for
them (1.5).

The fact that Pomponius does not seem to be the most likely candidate
for redactor of this work, however, need not detract from the possibility
that he was a close friend of Perpetua. He could have been both a close
friend and a member of her own congregation. He could have been
responsible for meeting many of her personal needs in prison, the deacon
whose task it was to care for those who had been arrested in Carthage and
jailed for their faith. Perpetua indicates that it was in this latter capacity
that Pomponius served so well. It was he and his fellow-deacon, Tertius,
who had successfully bribed the guards so that Perpetua and the others
might move outside the dungeon proper to a nicer part of the prison where
they might be able to get some exercise. It was Pomponius and Tertius
who, in Perpetua's words, "ministered to us" (2.7).[3] Thus, Perpetua designated these two men as blessed.

The significance of Pomponius's dress, the unbelted white tunic and
elaborate sandals, is not at all clear. They may merely be present in the
description to provide detail to Perpetua's recollection of the vision, a

point that speaks generally in favor of its legitimacy. The dress of Pomponius, and especially Perpetua's description of his elaborate sandals, taken together with Perpetua's other references to feet in this vision, have enabled psychohistorian Mary Lefkowitz to reach the conclusion that this detail is actually related to her desire to overcome certain threatening male figures, especially her own father.[4]

Pomponius's garb, however, may hold a certain significance in and of itself. The unbelted white tunic may refer to Pomponius in a more or less "glorified form."[5] It may be reminiscent of the white-robed ones in Perpetua's first vision. In Rev. 6:11, those who had been martyred and lay under the altar were clothed with white robes. Ultimately, this attire was granted to a wide range of individuals from every tribe who stood before the Lamb (Rev. 7:9, 13, 14), those who had come through the great tribulation. Such clothing, whether it be linked in its imagery to the martyred or whether it be seen as having parallels in angelic beings and therefore messengers, may communicate a linkage in the mind of Perpetua that is related to messages of things to come.

The shoes Pomponius wore may also be significant. They may be made of gold and silver, as some manuscripts imply, or they may be white.[6] In either case, they again may remind Perpetua of a picture derived from the *Shepherd of Hermas.* Hermas was confronted by the white-haired virgin whom he identified with the church. This took place shortly after his confrontation with the monster that he overcame. In his description, the virgin wore white sandals.[7] In this case, then, Pomponius may be reminiscent of the church that will watch as Perpetua meets the Egyptian.

In Perpetua's vision, it was Pomponius's task to take her from the prison and bring her to the amphitheater. He did this by commanding her, "Perpetua, come; we are waiting for you" (10.3). The "we" to whom Pomponius made reference is unnamed, but it may have included the already gathered crowd at the amphitheater or it may have had reference to those Christians who were not imprisoned. In either case, it may also have been a subtle reference to the "cloud of witnesses" to whom the writer to the Hebrews referred.[8]

Pomponius led Perpetua by the hand along a rugged path to the amphitheater. There he left her. But as he left her, he exhorted her not to be afraid, but rather to take solace in the fact that he, Pomponius, would vicariously struggle with her even as she struggled with the beasts.[9]

Once again, Aune's category of "oracle of assurance" comes into play. In this vision, Pomponius the deacon brings this second oracle, which may be diagrammed in the following manner:

Introductory Formula:	Then he told me
Admonition:	"Do not be afraid
Promise:	I am here, struggling with you."[10]

The significance of these first two oracles at least on the surface is that they were meant (1) to encourage her not to back out of her confession of faith at the last moment, but rather to make it secure in her act of martyrdom; (2) to lower the fear and anxiety level of Perpetua as she faced her imminent death; and (3) to assure her that she would not be alone when she suffered and died. Yet, there may be more here than first meets the eye.

Robinson has pointed to a parallel between Pomponius's message to Perpetua in her vision and the words of Hermas's Angel of Repentance.[11] The parallel is striking, for the Angel of Repentance, in essence, says the same three words to Hermas. His first word of encouragement is an exhortative: "Return, ye who walk in the commandments of the devil, in hard and bitter and wild licentiousness."[12] The second word, "fear not the devil,"[13] is explicit on two counts. First, it is an admonition exhorting the subjects not to fear. Second, and perhaps more important, it provided an exhortation that told the subjects *who* it was they were not to fear: namely, the devil. The third statement had to do with the promise of divine presence, for the Angel of Repentance promised that there was a reason the fear of the devil was superfluous. The devil had no power over those to whom the Angel was speaking, for "I will be with you."[14]

The idea of this "oracle of assurance" can be diagrammed as shown in Figure 2.

As striking as this parallel is in its wording when it is compared with Pomponius's message, it is even more so when the larger context, a wrestling match, is kept in mind. Hermas reminded the Angel of Repentance that the devil was a formidable foe nonetheless. But the Angel assured him that the devil does not hold sway over the servants of God who place all their hope in Him. Indeed, "The devil can wrestle against these, overthrow them he cannot."[15]

The message in both instances is the same, but in Perpetua's case, Pomponius does not mention the devil. Yet, if one assumes that these words are genuine prophetic oracles from the same source—for they come in visions to Hermas and to Perpetua—then they take on a new significance. First, in Perpetua's case they need to be understood as "first-person" proph-

FIGURE 2

Introductory Formula:	"Return, ye who walk in the commandments of the devil, in hard and bitter and wild licentiousness."
Admonition:	"Fear not the devil."
Promise:	"I will be with you."

ecies in which Pomponius takes a passive role, the role of a messenger, speaking only what he is to speak. In many biblical accounts, the messages are often preceded by what appears to take the place of a "messenger formula" such as "Thus saith the Lord." The substitute here is "Fear not" or "Do not be afraid."[16] Thus, the words that follow, in this case, "I am here, struggling with you," take on added significance, for they must then be understood as a word from the Lord himself, given through Pomponius.

Such an assurance of Jesus' presence with his disciples was a word of security given on occasion by Jesus himself. He promised his presence with them to the close of the age (Matt. 28:20). He also promised help for them through the Spirit when they had been taken captive because they were Christians (Matt. 10:16–22).

THE EGYPTIAN

In the second portion of this vision, Perpetua becomes aware of an enormous crowd in the amphitheater. They were said to be astonished, probably at the fact that now stood before them a young, well-bred woman. Perpetua also exhibited some surprise. Her own expectations had not been met. She had been condemned "to the beasts" (6.6; 10.5), yet there were no beasts present. What appeared in their place was a vicious-looking Egyptian together with his seconds and assistants. Who is this Egyptian? What does he represent? Perpetua identifies him as the devil, yet how she reaches that conclusion is not immediately obvious.

The most promising line can probably be found in the parallels that exist in this figure and a figure mentioned in the *Epistle of Barnabas*. In this early Christian work, most probably originating in Rome, the Greek text refers to the devil as the "Black One."[17] It would seem logical that what Perpetua saw in the Egyptian which made it possible for her to identify him as the devil was his dark skin. Thus, the otherwise vicious human figure took on the color of the personified adversary. Van Beek has noted that such an identification was common among Roman and Carthaginian

Christians since the early Christians imagined a black devil in keeping with the Way of Darkness.[18]

The subject of Egypt and the Egyptians as well as Pharaoh, their leader, is a common one in both Jewish and Christian writings. Scripture reveals that it was to Egypt that the people of God fled when they were in difficulty. Abram went there with Sarai when he failed to trust God for his provision in the land that God had given to him (Gen. 12:10–20). When famine struck again, Joseph's brothers went to Egypt to live. In Egypt, the Pharaoh, who knew not Joseph, eventually placed the sons and daughters of Israel into the bondage (Exod. 1:8–14) from which Yahweh had to deliver them.[19] Also, without consulting Yahweh, Israel made treaties with Egypt for protection—a protection that would not be forthcoming since Zion itself came under the judgment of Yahweh (Isa. 30:1–2). A search of the Jewish intertestamental literature yields nothing new on these accounts, merely a repetition of the biblical data.

In the Apocalypse, John used the term "Egypt" allegorically to refer to the city of Jerusalem, in which the two prophets would be killed in the end times. That the term is used in a pejorative sense here is apparent because Egypt is linked with Sodom.[20]

Egypt's king, the Pharaoh, was also depicted in negative terms. We have already noted that Pharaoh was depicted by Ezekiel as the dragon of the Nile whom God would destroy.[21] Quite probably the crocodile cult in Egypt that flourished in Perpetua's day derived from the worship of Pharaoh. The people of Egypt constructed a sacred pool at Arsinoe that became a major tourist attraction for Greeks and Romans alike where the fascinated populace could watch the priests feed the crocodile and then be consulted as the local oracle.[22] The image of Pharaoh as a crocodile dragon, when compared with the image of the dragon found in Perpetua's first vision, may also have supplied a link in her thought between the dragon of her first vision and the Egyptian. In any case, Perpetua identified both the dragon and the Egyptian as the devil.

There is one further note of interest that Perpetua recorded in her description of the Egyptian before the wrestling match. She notes that it was the custom before such matches for the contestants to receive a rubdown with oil.[23] The Egyptian, however, did not receive such a rubdown, but rather rolled himself in the dust. This activity may once again be related to an event recorded in the *Shepherd of Hermas*. When Hermas met the monster, it was busy stirring up the dust.[24] One cannot help but recollect the probable background to each of these events that may be played by Gen. 3:14, where the serpent was cursed and told that he would eat dust all the days of his life.

GENDER TRANSFORMATION

If the Egyptian motif is intriguing, Perpetua herself is equally so. She noted that she received the customary rubdown by her assistants. However, when she was stripped, she "became a man" (10.7).[25] This bizarre turn of events has no clear precedent in Scripture. The closest type of comment to be found is that of Paul when he wrote to the Galatians, "There is no longer Jew or Greek, there is no longer slave or free, there is no longer male and female; for all of you are one in Christ" (3:28). Yet even Paul's comment does not speak of changing females into males, but rather of the inherent equality of persons who are in Christ Jesus. In Christ, such arbitrary differences as race, social standing, and gender are meaningless.

The pseudepigraphic *4 Maccabees* provides what may be a first-century account of gender transformation.[26] The philosopher-rhetorician author of this work tells the story of a Jewish woman whose seven sons are commanded by Antiochus under penalty of torture and death to eat certain unclean foods, thereby violating their faith. Each, in turn, refuses to obey, and each, in turn is put to death. Antiochus pleads with the mother of these boys, but even as she watches them die, she will not intervene (*4 Maccabees* 8:1–12:19). The writer goes on to praise the steadfast conviction and "pious reason" of the mother who, in spite of great personal tragedy and the natural "passionate feelings," nevertheless evidenced a "manly courage" that enabled her to move beyond the limits of "a mother's love" (*4 Maccabees* 15:23). "More noble than men in fortitude and stronger than heroes in endurance," the author declared her (*4 Maccabees* 15:30). Men have conquered human passions, he went on, but here, "even a woman despised the greatest torments" (*4 Maccabees* 16:2). This mother succeeded by suppressing her normal feminine quality of "passionate feelings" for her sons and adopting the masculine quality of "courage."

Two Gnostic works also speak of transformation of women into men.[27] The *Gospel of Mary* introduces Mary as encouraging the disciples of Jesus to go out and preach the gospel of the kingdom. The disciples worry about whether they will be spared, since their Lord was not spared. Her words of encouragement exhort them to "praise his greatness, for he has prepared us (and) made us into men."[28] From this comment it appears that Mary included herself among those who had been transformed into males.

Similarly, the *Gospel of Thomas* contains two passages that speak of gender. The first one, Logion 22, seems to communicate the same basic idea as Paul's comment to the Galatians. However, it goes beyond Galatians, doing away with gender altogether.[29] Logion 114, however, is much closer to the statement made by Perpetua than is Logion 22. Jesus is reported to have had a conversation with Simon Peter regarding Mary's worthiness of life. Peter said, "Let Mary leave us, for women are not worthy of life. Jesus said, 'I myself shall lead her in order to make her male, so that she too may become a living spirit resembling you males. For every woman who will make herself male will enter the Kingdom of Heaven.' "[30]

What influence there might have been in Carthage from these early documents is not easily ascertained. Elaine Pagels has suggested that the symbolism of the *Gospel of Thomas*, Logion 114, is derived from everyday experiences. Thus, "what is merely human (therefore *female*) must be transformed into what is divine (the 'living spirit' the *male*)."[31] In other terms, she asserts, "this simply states what religious rhetoric assumes: that the men form the legitimate body of the community, while women are allowed to participate only when they assimilate themselves to men."[32] It is clear also from 4 *Maccabees* that a patriarchal perspective is understood to be the norm.

Frend has suggested that the influence might be Pythagorean in nature,[33] yet this climax in Thomas's theology, as it were, is the more plausible parallel since the *Gospel of Thomas* was found in Egypt prior to the third century.[34] Its movement to Carthage would not have been difficult, and the esoteric nature of the gnosticism in this document *may* have had some early influence in Carthaginian Christianity. The *Gospel of Thomas* looked beyond gender differences to an equality that played a significant role in Perpetua's continuation in her own confession. She may have seen in the renunciation of paganism and the embrace of Christianity a capitulation to "self-fulfillment," as Frend puts it,[35] or a "political act against her environment" with her attachment to the more "a-sexual fraternal relationships between men and women" available to her in Christianity.[36]

David Scholer is even more helpful when he suggests that, through gender transformation, Perpetua may be viewed as a "positive example of women's empowerment in the early church."[37] Needless to say, in a patriarchal society such as that which existed in Carthage during Perpetua's lifetime, the vision in which she was transformed into a man could enable her leadership to be accepted by hers and future generations through her courageous example as confessor and martyr, even if these congregations were patriarchal.[38]

THE MAN OF MARVELOUS STATURE

The second figure with whom Perpetua was confronted when she arrived at the amphitheater was the man of marvelous stature. His height was such that he rose above the top of the amphitheater. His identity is not made explicit, but she describes him as a "trainer," presumably a trainer of wrestlers.

It has already been demonstrated that Christians from the New Testament onward regularly received visions of men, sometimes young, sometimes old, sometimes readily identifiable, sometimes not, who would address them.[39] In this particular case the figure is imposing, not only to Perpetua, but seemingly also to the crowd. He asks for silence and apparently gets it.

The *Gospel of Peter*, known by Serapion of Antioch to have been in existence prior to A.D. 200, contains a passage that describes Christ in immense proportions. This Gnostic work described the resurrection scene in the following language. The soldiers watched as the stone covering the tomb rolled itself away. Two men entered the tomb and three men came out, two sustaining the other. ". . . and the heads of the two [were] reaching to heaven, but that of him who was led of them by the hand overpassing the heavens."[40] While Perpetua need not have relied on the *Gospel of Peter* for her imagery, such imagery was at least consistent with her own experiences, for she seems to have identified the trainer in some way as the Christ figure of the vision.[41]

The clothing of the man is described in detail. It is said that he wears a beltless purple tunic (*discincatatus, purpuram*) with two stripes running down the middle of his chest (*inter duos clavos per medium pectus habeus*). W. H. Shewring disagrees with this translation, asserting rather that what this figure wore was "two different robes—a beltless tunic with *clavi*, then an underlying vestment, the *purpura*, which allows itself to be seen between the *clavi* of the tunic." This he suggests is the costume of the trainer of gladiators.[42]

In addition to the purple and white tunic(s), this imposing figure wore shoes, once again described as wondrously made, but in this instance his shoes are described as being gold and silver. It may be this latter description that accounts for some of the manuscripts mentioning gold and silver shoes on the feet of the Egyptian.

In the hands of the trainer was the wand or rod that was a tool of the athletic trainer. But he also held a "green branch on which there were golden apples" (10.8). Daniélou has posited that a parallel exists between Perpetua's green branch with the golden apples and "the '*ethrôgh*,' the 'choice fruits,' and the *lûlâbh*, the 'palm tree branches, boughs of leafy trees and willows' of the Feast of Tabernacles (see Lv. 23:40)."[43]

Apple trees are mentioned repeatedly in the Song of Solomon in positive terms.[44] The term "apple" is used on several occasions in a figurative sense in the phrase "apple of the eye," again in a positive use of the term.[45] It also occurs in Prov. 25:11: "A word fitly spoken is like apples of gold in a setting of silver." Yet, even with this, the significance of the golden apples that Perpetua describes cannot be fully recaptured. It is appreciated to some extent, however, when the oracle that this trainer delivers is analyzed.

The oracle given by this supernatural figure could possibly be titled "The Charge" or "The Challenge." In short, it is an oracle that outlines the terms of the ensuing contest. For Perpetua, the battle is a life-and-death battle. "If this Egyptian defeats her," says the trainer, "he will slay her with the sword." However, "if she defeats him, she will receive this [presumably the green branch with the golden apples] branch" (10.9).[46] At the conclusion of his oracular utterance, this imposing figure withdrew, apparently to watch the outcome of the battle.

In an analysis of the oracle, it is readily apparent that it is Perpetua whose life is at stake. She has everything to lose, but she may also win the branch. As such, the branch appears to be a highly desired victor's branch, not unlike the laurel wreath presented to the victor in various games. Such a wreath appeared in many illustrations throughout the New Testament.[47] For Perpetua, then, the branch is a symbol of life.

The oracle itself brings to mind several passages of Scripture, but principally those found in Rev. 2 and 3, which speak of the one who "conquers" or "overcomes." In these passages several parallels exist with Perpetua's vision. There is a tree of life (Rev. 2:7); perhaps the branch of golden apples becomes symbolic of this. Mention is made that overcomers will not face the second death (Rev. 2:11). Perpetua's trophy would be a life spared in addition to the branch of golden apples. It is the overcomer who is clad in white garments (Rev. 3:5), perhaps a passage having a bearing on Pomponius's dress. In short, the oracle that comes by way of the giant trainer may have a background once again in the Apocalypse. What the Spirit said in John's day was being reapplied in Perpetua's new situation. She had at all costs to avoid the Egyptian's sword and, thereby, death.

But again, the *Shepherd of Hermas* may also provide a clue to our understanding. In *Similitude* 8, Hermas watches a tall angel distribute cuttings from the branches of a willow tree. When this operation has been completed, each person who had received a branch is asked to return it. The branches are returned, some green and with fruit, others withered, eaten by insects, or cracked. As these persons return their branches, they are separated. Those who return green branches with fruit are granted a seal, white clothing, and a crown.[48] They are also allowed to enter the walled city. These people are the overcomers.

The primary difference between Hermas's vision and that of Perpetua is the type of tree. Hermas's willow produces fruit of an unnamed variety. Perpetua's branch is green with golden apples. But both trees seem to indicate who are the genuine Christians. Hence, in Hermas the branches may be exchanged for life and in Perpetua the branch is conferred upon her as she goes toward the Gate of Life.

THE FIGHT AND ITS MEANING

With the third scene in the vision comes the battle itself. What has previously appeared as a metaphor now becomes reality, for the martyr becomes the athlete.[49] Perpetua describes the vision in terms reminiscent of a genuine gladiatorial match.

First, the contestants sized one another up, and then they let their fists fly. The Egyptian went for Perpetua's feet, but Perpetua used her upright position to her advantage and began to kick her opponent in the face with her heels. Next, she found herself lifted up into the air. Whether this is to be considered a form of levitation or merely the sensation received in the vision is not easily ascertained. What resulted from this, however, was of further advantage to Perpetua. She continued to "pummel" her foe.

Following a brief lull in the battle, Perpetua linked the fingers of her hands with each other and grabbed the head of the Egyptian. Pulled off balance, he fell on the ground, and she triumphantly announced, "I stepped on his head" (10.11). With this imagery, we are brought face-to-face once again with the imagery found in Perpetua's first vision. The act of standing on the foe's head was a sign of victory over that foe. The dragon had been conquered,[50] and now the Egyptian lay crumpled beneath Perpetua's feet. The Egyptian was defeated and Perpetua was victorious. While the defeat of the dragon held political overtones—Perpetua defeating the Roman government at its own game through her imminent martyrdom—her vision of the defeated Egyptian seems to take on spiritual symbolism here. Undoubtedly, the Egyptian's defeat at the heels of the transformed female Perpetua is intended to convey anew the fulfillment of God's promise in Gen. 3:15 in the martyrdom of Perpetua.[51]

With the defeat of the Egyptian apparent, the crowd in the amphitheater responded by shouting. Perpetua's assistants could be heard singing psalms. The mood was clearly a festive one as Perpetua walked toward the trainer figure and took the victory branch. The trainer kissed her, and gave the last of the three oracles in this vision, "Peace be with you, my daughter!" he uttered (10.13).

In one sense, the words spoken by the trainer can be favorably compared with the welcome Perpetua received from the old shepherd in her first vision: "I am glad you have come, my child." In both cases, the greeting is one of acceptance. While the shepherd used the Greek designation τέκνον to greet Perpetua, the trainer used the Latin term *filia*, which is more precise with respect to gender, but no less condescending. That is, in the cases of both the shepherd and the trainer, Perpetua is treated as a child of affection. The greeting conveys the inherent superiority of the figure who speaks.

The oracle here, however, provides a word of comfort in a time of stress. It acknowledges the outcome of the fight in Perpetua's favor, and it blesses her with peace. Thus, it fulfills once again a key function of a prophetic oracle according to 1 Cor. 14:3. It brings a word of peace and comfort to the distressed. With this word of comfort, Perpetua walked in triumph toward the Sanavivariam gate.

At this point in Perpetua's narrative, she awoke. Her remembrance of the vision brought with it the dawning of a realization—her conclusion. "I realized," she wrote, "that it was not wild animals that I would fight but the Devil, but I knew that I would win the victory" (10.14). Thus, her conclusion was twofold. First, while she knew that the death sentence imposed on her was one in which she was sentenced to be killed by certain wild animals, she looked to the spiritual significance of the event; and beyond the animals, she saw the devil as the one who would be attacking her in the process. Thus, Perpetua identified the dragon of her first vision and the Egyptian of the third vision with the animals, the state's tool for her execution. She perceived that the power of the devil lay behind this execution.

Perpetua's second insight was that she would not merely be put to death but, rather, that she would be victorious in her martyrdom. This vision seems to have been "directly related to her own immediate concerns."[52] Would she die in vain? No. She would overcome the devil and move on into eternal life. Thus, she awoke with the confidence that she could move toward her martyrdom in a state of expectancy.

CHAPTER SIX

THE VISION OF SATURUS

With the conclusion of Perpetua's vision of the Egyptian comes also the conclusion of Perpetua's literary contribution to *The Passion*. It is now convenient for the redactor to step in briefly and introduce the next component of *The Passion*. The transition is accomplished with the words, "But the blessed Saturus has also made known his own vision and he has written it out with his own hand."[1] Our attention is diverted from the experiences of Perpetua immediately prior to her martyrdom and refocused on the experience of a man named Saturus.

Saturus was not one of those young catechumens who had been arrested with Perpetua (2.1). Rather, he was absent when the others were arrested, but subsequently surrendered himself voluntarily to the Roman authorities (4.5). Whether he was himself a catechumen is difficult to say, for he seems to have taken positions of leadership in each of the places he is mentioned. In Perpetua's vision of the ladder, she waited at the base while he ascended. He then encouraged her ascension up the ladder while directing her movement past the dragon (4.5). In his own vision, Saturus gives the words of assurance that they had received the Lord's promise (11.4). It is also Saturus who addresses the mob the day prior to their execution, causing some to be amazed and others to become believers (17.2–3). Finally, Saturus, on the day of their execution, is the first to be martyred (21.8). It is thus quite possible that Saturus was the instructor of these new converts, although that position may also have been occupied by the teaching presbyter, Aspasius.[2]

THE OCCASION

The occasion for Saturus's vision and the circumstances immediately surrounding its onset are completely lacking. The vision does conclude with the words, "And then I woke up happy."[3] The term ἐξυπνίσθην in the Greek text is the same as that employed by Perpetua in each instance in which she received a vision (cf. 4.10; 7.9; 8.4; 10.13), so the phenomenon experienced by Saturus appears to be of the same order as that which Perpetua had experienced.

The vision itself falls into three sections. The first of them (11.2–10) begins with the assumption that both he and Perpetua have been put to death. It describes the events that transpire from the moment of their death until they arrive in a heavenly garden. There, they are summoned by certain angels to "greet the Lord."

In the second section of the vision (12.1–7), actually a continuation of the first, Saturus and Perpetua enter a place whose walls are light. There they see angels dressed in white robes and they hear a choir of voices chanting the Trisagion in unison. They are greeted by "an aged man with white hair and a youthful face," and they note the presence of elders.

In the final section of the vision (13.1–7), the scene shifts as it depicts their exit from the encounter with their aged yet youthful host. Outside the walled place they meet a bishop, Optatus, and a presbyter, Aspasius, who have been feuding. These two approach Saturus and Perpetua, asking for help to settle their quarrel. In the midst of their discussion, however, angels intervene, scolding the two church leaders and telling Optatus what he must do. Saturus and Perpetua once again enter the walled area, where they meet many of their fellow martyrs. There they are sustained by a very pleasant odor.

Notably absent from Saturus's account is any explicit interpretation of the vision. His account ends abruptly with the summary note that he awoke "happy." One may, then, assume that any "interpretation" as such would have been positive in nature, but questions would still remain: What did the vision mean? How did it function on behalf of the prisoners? What role might it have played for the church?

Our task, once again, will be to look at a variety of features in this vision that may shed light on its role and function in its original context. To help in this quest, it will be once again necessary to look at some of the cultural and religious factors on which, in this case, Saturus could have relied. In this analysis, attention will be paid to the various characters who appear in the vision, among them Saturus and Perpetua, the four angels, the ancient yet youthful man, and the elders as well as Optatus and Aspasius. In addition, the garden, including its location, the means of the martyrs' transportation to it, and the walls of light will be studied.

THE ASCENT

The first scene opens with the statement "we had died." (See appendix D.) From the outset, then, the vision has a futuristic focus, for Saturus and Perpetua are still very much alive. The vision involves the foretelling aspect of prophetic revelation. As the vision unfolds, it becomes readily apparent that Saturus has made direct reference to the death of Perpetua and his own. What follows this simple statement announcing their death, then, provides a cameo of what Saturus may have expected to occur following their execution. In any event, Saturus proceeds to describe the impact of their death by employing a clearly platonic clause, "we . . . had put off the flesh," as synonymous to the idea of death.[4]

At this point there is introduced a new set of characters: four angels who, without touching the martyrs with their hands,[5] nonetheless carried them toward the east. Saturus adds that he and Perpetua were not moved along or transported on their backs but that they were carried in a semierect posture "as though we were climbing up a gentle hill" (11.3).

During this journey, Saturus describes what might be called a point of transition in which he and Perpetua were said to be "free of the world," at which time they observed an intense light. At this juncture, Saturus turned to Perpetua and said the first words that were spoken in the vision. "This is what the Lord promised us," he assured her. "We have received his promise" (11.4).

Even as Saturus spoke, he and Perpetua continued to be borne along by the angels until they came to a garden in which were such plants as rose bushes and a large number of unnamed flowers as well as a number of trees. These trees were described as being "as tall as cypresses," and their leaves were said to be "constantly falling" (11.6).

Present in the midst of the flora Saturus describes were four angels even "more splendid" than the four who had brought them to the garden. These angels began to pay homage to the martyrs exclaiming, "Why, they are here! They are here!" At this point, the first four angels were observed to grow fearful, and they set the martyrs down. The martyrs then walked along a road to an open area, perhaps a meadow, where they met four other martyrs whom they knew. All of them were described as having been martyred in the same persecution: Jucundus, Saturninus, and Artaxius, by burning at the stake, and Quintas, most probably through torture while he was yet in prison. Saturus and Perpetua, on meeting these martyrs, asked them where they had been, but their conversation was interrupted, for the angels who had greeted them summoned them to follow with the words, "First come and enter and greet the Lord" (11.10).

In this first scene, several interesting issues arise, which, when probed, may yield some information that would be helpful in our attempt to understand what role this vision played for the martyrs. From the outset, it is clear that some of the elements of the vision are anchored in the reality of the historical scene. Among these are the anticipated deaths of Perpetua and Saturus. Related also to historical reality must surely be the identities of the four martyrs, Jucundus, Saturninus, Artaxius, and Quintas. These names undoubtedly were the names of four actual individuals about whom Saturus and Perpetua were aware. Whether all six had known each other prior to the deaths of the four is not known. But Saturus knew them by name as well as the fate of each, which is specifically described in this scene. Three had died by burning, one while yet in prison, and Saturus linked each individual by name with the type of death he had suffered.

That Saturus and Perpetua knew the other four in life is certainly not improbable. Saturus is careful to note that all six of them suffered their martyrdom in the same persecution. Thus, the reference seems clear that the four, like Saturus and Perpetua, were martyred in the persecution of Septimius Severus about A.D. 202. Furthermore, although the persecution was present in Egypt and in Rome for a relatively brief period, it was particularly pressing in North Africa. Hence, it is probable that the four, like Saturus and Perpetua, died in Carthage. If this was the case, these four, like Perpetua, would probably have been recent converts as well, although this cannot be known for certain.

Of interest in this scene, but not rooted in any literal way in historical reality, is Saturus's description of the angels and the garden. This is the first mention of angels in this *passio,* but their appearance in their present context suggests a Jewish or Christian influence.

The canonical literature of Israel speaks of angels or heavenly messengers on numerous occasions.[6] Yet, it is in the postexilic writings that Israel's understanding of angels becomes specialized. The book of *1 Enoch,* for instance, demonstrates a fully developed angelology, with seven archangels, each with a specific area of responsibility.[7]

Jesus himself seems to suggest that a prevalent idea of his day included the assignment of angels to carry the dead to paradise. In Luke 16:22, he noted that "The poor man died and was carried by angels to Abraham's bosom." The idea is also present in the pseudepigraphic *Testament of Abraham,* which dates from the end of the first century or the beginning of the second.[8]

In his treatise, *On the Soul,* Tertullian used language quite reminiscent of the passage under discussion. Such words as "flesh," "angel," "freedom," and "light" are all present in a single paragraph. In describing death, Tertullian wrote:

> when the soul . . . is released from its concretion with the flesh, it . . . is . . . certain that it escapes the veil of the flesh into open space, to its clear, and pure, and intrinsic light; and then finds itself enjoying its enfranchisement from matter, and by virtue of its liberty it recovers its divinity, as one who awakes out of sleep passes from images to verities. Then it tells out what it sees; then it exults or it fears, according as it finds what lodging is prepared for it, as soon as it sees the very angel's face, that arraigner of souls.[9]

While it is clear that Tertullian penned his *On the Soul* between A.D. 210 and 213 and, therefore, about a decade after Saturus was executed, the similarity of language and imagery between the two works at this particular point is remarkable. It may be merely that Tertullian was thinking of Saturus's vision when he penned this passage, a possibility that becomes the more credible when it is noted that he mistakenly refers to this vision as that of Perpetua, two chapters later in 55.4. It may equally have been the case that both Tertullian and Saturus owed such ideas to a common teaching present in the Carthaginian congregation, a teaching that represented a compilation of ideas drawn from either a Platonic source or a Jewish source with Greek "corrections."

Whatever the source of Saturus's imagery might have been, it is clear that he understood the imagery and his participation in the visionary world to be consistent with what he believed to be the Lord's promise. Hence, he assured Perpetua of this fact, claiming, "This is what the Lord promised us. We have received his promise" (11.4).

Whether these words constitute any prophetic oracle as such or they constitute nothing more than a simple observation is not immediately clear. In one sense, they function as an oracle, for they reiterate a word of comfort or assurance—to Perpetua at least—that she and Saturus have been and, therefore, will be (in the sense of a kind of historic future) successful in their martyrdom.

What promise it is that Saturus has in mind here is equally obscure. Petraglio has suggested that the promise fulfilled here is Jesus' promise in John 8:12 that "I am the light of the world; whoever follows me . . . will have the light of life." His reason for setting forth this suggestion is that John 8:12 is the only New Testament text where the "light" is promised.[10] If the light Saturus saw in his vision was that to which he referred when speaking to Perpetua of the fulfilled promise, then John 8:12 would, indeed, appear to be an appropriate background to his comment. But there are other solutions that may provide equally good explanations to his comment.

As early as *1 Enoch*, reference was made to the righteous dead being brought forth "in shining light."[11] This reference may have as its theme a light that surrounds the righteous, or it may emanate from the righteous. If it is the former, it is conceivable that in *The Passion* we have a picture of light which is quite similar. In a sense, Saturus and Perpetua, freed from the flesh and the world, have entered into a realm of light. Such an idea seems to parallel ideas available in Zoroastrian, Platonic, and Gnostic dualism.[12]

The language of Saturus provides an even more satisfactory explanation as he describes his visionary journey. As he and Perpetua are carried toward the east by four angels, their ultimate destination is a place whose walls are seemingly "constructed of light" (12.1). Before they reach this place, they must put off their flesh, break free from the world, pass through a large open space to a garden/orchard, and move through another open space along a broad road. Saturus's language indicates that when they broke free from the world, they "first saw an intense light" (11.4).

The image presented, then, need not mean that they were overcome by, or that they had entered into, a realm of dazzling light. Saturus's account may provide at this point nothing more than a comment that parallels the observation made by many a nighttime traveler. It may be nothing more than a vague description of the (soon to be described in detail) walls of light. The light from the city, if it may be so called, appears before the city itself comes clearly into focus. But, as the traveler nears the source of the light—the city, or in this case the walls—the total picture becomes focused, enabling the traveler to give a more ample description of the light that at first appeared as an energy intensive spot in the distance. If Saturus's comment that "This is what the Lord promised us" refers to the walls of light, a suitable parallel may be found in Rev. 21:23.[13]

In other respects, the promise to which Saturus refers need have no relation to the light at all, but only to the journey upon which he and Perpetua have embarked. Perpetua's initial vision found both of them successfully negotiating the ladder that connected earth with heaven. Perpetua had interpreted it to mean she would face martyrdom and, in light of her vision of the Egyptian, a successful one. Her successful negotiation of the act of martyrdom carried with it the promise of the green branch with apples of gold, a symbol of life. Might it not be the case that Perpetua's visions could have been construed by her as well as by Saturus as a promise of life that would be given even on the occasion of their deaths? If this is so, then Saturus's reference to the fulfilled promise comes as he breaks his last tie with the flesh and the world. Their journey up the gentle hill might be compared with their reaching the top of the ladder.[14] Their continuing journey to the place surrounded by the wall of light marks the continuation of a fulfilled "promise."

The direction in which the angels carried the martyrs as well as the location of the walled place are of equal interest. The direction is east, and the location of the walled place is at least two levels removed from earth. In the Old Testament, the direction "east" seems to carry no particular eschatological relevance. It is in the intertestamental period that it begins to convey this meaning. In 1 Enoch, for instance, Enoch claims to have crossed "far towards the east" in order to arrive at the Garden of Righteousness in which were growing many tall and fragrant trees.[15] Furthermore, Paradise is thought to exist in the third heaven.[16]

Robinson has noted similarities between Saturus's vision and the first vision in the *Shepherd of Hermas* that bear mentioning again.[17] These similarities revolve around an old woman who is revealed to be the church. Hermas wrote that "she rose from her chair, and four young men came and carried off the chair and went away to the east." Later, "two men appeared and raised her on their shoulders, and they went to where the chair was in the east."[18] In his third vision, Hermas is finally told that the young men he keeps seeing in his visions are "The Holy angels of God."[19] Thus, Robinson would call attention, first, to the fact that angels *carried* the church away and, second, that the woman was not lying prone, but rather was taken "by the arms,"[20] both details described in language similar to that used by Saturus.

THE GARDEN

The first place to which Saturus came in his visionary flight was a gardenlike spot, planted with a range of flora, including specifically mentioned rosebushes and cypress-high trees whose leaves were constantly falling. Sometimes described as a park,[21] the idea of paradise as a garden is a common one in Old Testament and apocalyptic literature.[22] But the idea of a tree whose leaves continually fall[23] is unknown. Petraglio has studied the Apocalypse for evidence of similarities between Saturus's plants and trees and finds, at best, an allusion to the imagery. After all, the Apocalypse speaks of the presence of the "tree of life which is in the paradise of God (Rev. 2:7)."[24] Yet, he has noted two differences between the imagery and words of Saturus and those of Revelation. Working from the Greek text of *The Passion*, he notes that Saturus consistently uses the term δένδρον to refer to the trees in the garden, whereas the Apocalypse uses the term ξύλον when it speaks of the tree of life. Furthermore, it is the "right" of the redeemed to eat of the fruit of the tree of life, but in Saturus's vision no such imagery exists.[25]

Robinson has looked most carefully at the trees whose leaves are continually shed. Although the Apocalypse notes that the leaves of the tree of life were "for the healing of the nations (Rev. 22:2)," no mention is made as to what use the leaves are put in Saturus's garden. Robinson's concern, however, centers on the Latin text and, in particular, on the verb *cadebant*.[26] He recommends that the verb be emended to read *canebant*. Thus, the trees in this garden spot are always "singing" rather than "falling." His emendation, adopted by several other scholars since,[27] is defended on four grounds.

First, the concept of trees that sing is not at all foreign to the Hebrew mind. Such language is to be found throughout the Old Testament.[28]

Second, the *Testament of Abraham*, a late first- or early second-century work to which reference has already been made provides a fascinating possibility when a cypress tree, at the command of God, "cried out in a human voice and said, 'Holy, holy, holy is the Lord God.' "[29] "It is at the least a strange coincidence," as Robinson puts it, "that the singing trees of Saturus' Vision grew '*in modum cypressi*'; and also that later on he hears '*vocem unitam dicentem: Ἅγιος, Ἅγιος, Ἅγιος: sine cessatione.*' "[30] Third, the term "without cessation" occurs not only in conjunction with the activity of the leaves that either fall or sing without ceasing but also with the voices that chant endlessly the Trisagion. Fourth, other passages, although dating from a much later time, provide suggestive parallels.[31] The support Robinson has set forth for the reading *canebant* seems to be quite adequate to make the emendation a plausible one. Yet, no clear textual evidence can be adduced other than the minority-reading *ardebant* that occurs in Codex Salisburgensis, but which itself cannot be original.

In the garden, Saturus and Perpetua met four other angels, described as "more splendid" than those who had transported the martyrs to this point. The two types of angels represented in Saturus's vision have been described by Daniélou as "the angels of earth and the angels of heaven."[32] It is the task of the first group to carry the soul of the dead through its journey. It is the task of the second group to welcome it. This is precisely what these splendid angels do with the words, "Why, they are here! They are here!" Saturus describes their activity as one of admiration for the martyrs (11.7).

The reaction of the four angels who had transported Saturus and Perpetua is bewildering, for at the voices of the four "heavenly" angels the text says they became "fearful," a term that denotes great fear or intense dread. One can only guess at why this would be the case, but perhaps their own task of transporting the dead from earth to the garden, their lack of brilliance when compared with the angels of the garden, or even their place of assignment may have had something to do with their reaction. In Saturus's eyes, the angels of the garden "outranked" those who had brought the martyrs there. It is also possible that the first set of angels responded in fear to the thought of their passengers when they saw those who "outranked" them admiring the martyrs so enthusiastically. Whatever the reason for their fear, the heavenly angels immediately set the agenda for the martyrs with the words, "First come and enter and greet the Lord" (11.10).

INSIDE THE WALLS OF LIGHT

At this point in the vision, the transfer from earth to the walls of light is complete. The journey as such is over. It is the words of the angels to the martyrs, the anticipation of meeting and greeting the Lord that moves the vision into the second scene. As Saturus and Perpetua proceed forward, they come to the place whose walls appeared to be constructed of light (12.1). Within it, they would meet face-to-face the Lord for whom they had suffered. But before they entered the gate, they met four more angels who may, as Rowland has suggested, have acted "as guardians of the celestial palace."[33] At the approach of the martyrs, the angels entered the gate and donned white robes.[34] It is possible that the white robes were placed on the martyrs, but the Latin text is decidedly vague at this point. In any case, it was only after the donning of the white robes by whomever, that Saturus and Perpetua enter the place surrounded by walls.

Saturus's account describes a bit of the ambiance of the scene within the walls. The senses of the martyrs are acute, taking in all that is there. From the time they enter the celestial gate (cf. Rev. 4:1), they hear the sound of voices chanting endlessly the Greek words recorded even in this otherwise Latin text, " Ἅγιος, Ἅγιος, Ἅγιος." Scripture provides at least two examples of the singing of the Trisagion; and in each case, their appearance recognizes the presence of the Lord upon his throne (Isa. 6:1–3; Rev. 4:6b–8).

The central figure within the walls is described as "an aged man with white hair and youthful face" (12.3). Saturus notes that neither he nor Perpetua could see the feet of this figure.[35] He was sitting on a throne flanked on his right and his left by "four elders, and behind him were standing other aged men." When Saturus and Perpetua came before him, they stood before a throne, and four angels lifted them up so that they could kiss the aged man (12:4–5).

The identity of the aged yet youthful white-haired being is quite obvious. The martyrs were invited within the walls with the sole purpose of greeting the "Lord." On entering his presence, the martyrs were lifted by four angels so that they might kiss him. He in turn passed his hand over their faces. No words of any sort were exchanged between the martyrs and this aged yet youthful figure, and they were excused from his presence immediately following this encounter. Thus, the figure depicted is clearly to be identified as the Lord.

In Perpetua's first vision, she saw the divine figure as an aged shepherd. The term *hominem canum* was used to describe him there, just as it is used here to depict Saturus's visionary figure (4.8; 11.3). It has already been pointed out that such imagery may well have its foundation in the Jewish apocalyptic of Dan. 7:9–10[36] or in Rev. 1:13b–16. Rowland argues that if there is purely a Jewish influence at this point, Rev. 4:1 may lie behind the idea here conveyed. But he takes the argument one step further. Building his case from John 12:41, with its allusion to Isa. 6:1, and supplementing it with Justin Martyr's citations of "certain Old Testament theophanies as visions of the pre-existent Christ," Rowland has concluded that the figure's youthful countenance is probably best understood as providing evidence that here is depicted a christophany.[37]

Still, it is possible that the description which appears in Saturus's vision again has as its background some imagery present in one of Hermas's visions. In his third vision, Hermas speaks at least twice of an aged woman who is symbolic of the church. She has a youthful face, but her skin and hair give the appearance of age.[38]

Even if the *Shepherd of Hermas* might provide the immediate imagery here, there is a recurring theme of "four" that may have an apocalyptic value in this vision. The martyrs are transported from earth to the garden by four angels. There, four more angels accompany Saturus and Perpetua to the walls of light, whose gate is guarded by four additional angels. As they enter the gate, they notice two sets of four elders, one to the right of the throne, the other to the left of it, as well as many others (adding up to 24?). Finally there are four angels in that place who lift Saturus and Perpetua up so they are able to kiss the ancient yet youthful figure before them. The final significance of the number four is not totally clear, but it may be the case that its significance is related to its use in the Apocalypse.

Petraglio has made a detailed study of the relationship between this portion of Saturus's vision and the Apocalypse. Like Rowland, although more clearly, he has demonstrated the similarities that exist between these two works. In addition to such allusions as may exist between the Son of Man vision of Rev. 1:13–14, Petraglio has noted several similarities between the central portion of Saturus's vision and Rev. 4. Indeed, it appears that Rev. 4 emerges as providing the focus for virtually every figure found within the wall of light. The heavenly gate (Rev. 4:1), the throne (Rev. 4:2–6, 9–10), and the presence of the elders around it (Rev. 4:4, 10) are very clearly present in both visions. Furthermore, the four living beings (Rev. 4:6b–9) may be equated with Saturus's four angels who stand before the throne.[39] Similarly, the Trisagion is present in Rev. 4:8 and in the vision under consideration. If the white robes were placed on the martyrs rather than on the angels, as would be logical in Saturus's vision— although this is not supported by the best textual evidence in the Latin manuscripts—there is yet another feature that may have a parallel in Rev. 4:4.

In the presence of their Lord, Perpetua and Saturus heard the unison chanting of the Trisagion and they were elevated to a state of "wonder." In the midst of this beatific vision, they were lifted up by four angels. In this elevated position, Saturus remarks that they kissed the aged man who in turn touched their faces with his hand. Their kisses were undoubtedly meant to be an act of worship or love. It seems equally certain that the figure's response included the acceptance of their admiration and acted as a greeting to the two martyrs. The passing of his hand across the faces of the martyrs is somewhat enigmatic, but Robinson has provided a plausible solution by proposing that this description may have been suggested by the act of God who, according to Rev. 7:17, "will wipe away every tear" from the eyes of those who stand before his throne.[40]

At the conclusion of their exchange of greetings, the pair of martyrs were addressed by the elders with the words "Let us rise." The text states that they obediently did as the elders said and gave the kiss of peace. The presence of this reference to the kiss of peace has been taken by Gifford and Harris as a Montanist tendency, one that was indicative of a major theological debate at the time of Saturus's death. Their citation of Tertullian's concern with this question is their most significant piece of evidence supporting its link to Montanism,[41] but in light of the purpose of Tertullian's work *On Prayer*, which was written for catechetical rather than apologetic purposes and which clearly dates from Tertullian's so-called pre-Montanist period, the suggestion of a Montanist connection here can probably be ignored.

Of more interest and certainly with other parallels is the second statement of the elders, which commanded the martyrs after their initial encounter with the Lord to "Go and play (*ludite*)." It should be observed that the word *ludite* appears more than once to be descriptive of the activity in which the righteous would be engaged in heaven. The same term was employed in Perpetua's second vision of Dinocrates where, after he was refreshed at the pool, "he began to play (*ludere*) as children do" (8.4). There may also be a parallel image in the *Shepherd of Hermas* that is used of Hermas himself.[42]

Barnes, however, following the lead of Dölger, has suggested that this command may in fact be an early liturgical formula.[43] In this case, it is the Greek text which reads "$\pi o \rho \epsilon \acute{\upsilon} \epsilon \sigma \theta \epsilon \ \kappa \alpha \grave{\iota} \ \chi \alpha \acute{\iota} \rho \epsilon \sigma \theta \epsilon$" that is followed. Hence, the translation is "Go and rejoice." Whereas Rev. 19:7 contains one reference to the rejoicing of the multitudes in heaven, Petraglio has pointed out that it is from Paul and his emphasis on rejoicing that the source of Saturus's imagery may be derived.[44]

The final portion of this scene within the walls of light is played out in a very brief conversation between Saturus and Perpetua. Saturus said to Perpetua following the command of the elders, "Your wish is granted," to which she replied, "Thanks be to God that I am happier here now than I was in the flesh" (12.7).

In this exchange, her wish is not explicitly stated. It may stem from her own vision of the shepherd. She had seen the shepherd; and in the intervening time, she had looked forward in anticipation to the time when she could personally greet the Lord. This now being done, she was happy—indeed, happier than she had been during her life on earth. The vision to this point, then, may be understood as providing both Saturus and Perpetua with a word of comfort during their imprisonment. Their witness would not be in vain, for after leaving off their flesh they would greet the Lord. They would enjoy the benefits of the righteous dead. In Perpetua's case, the vision that Saturus experienced could in part be interpreted as providing both a word of comfort and of confirmation to the validity of her own visions. She would, indeed, suffer a successful martyr-dom. But, the vision does not stop at this point.

THE PROBLEM TO BE SETTLED

The third scene of Saturus's vision moves the couple back outside the gate. There they meet two men, one named Optatus, described as a bishop who was standing to the right of the gate as they exited, and the other, Aspasius, a presbyter and teacher, or perhaps more appropriately a teaching presbyter, who stood to the left. Their general demeanor was described as sorrowful, and they stood far apart (13.1).

That these figures had a basis in the historical situation at Carthage during the persecution of A.D. 202 is generally acknowledged. It is, therefore, quite probable that Optatus was the bishop at Carthage and Aspasius a presbyter there, although no external evidence exists that would confirm this fact. The way Saturus describes them in such a matter-of-fact manner would suggest that those who read Saturus's account would also know them. Saturus simply wrote, "We saw bishop Optatus and the teaching presbyter Aspasius." Furthermore, Saturus implied a familiarity with Optatus and Aspasius and they with him and Perpetua when he asked whether they were not their bishop and their presbyter (13.3).

If it may be assumed that these figures were actual leaders in the church at Carthage during the persecution that led to the deaths of Perpetua and Saturus, then it is not difficult also to accept the probability that, based on their description in Saturus's vision, they were embroiled in an argument just prior to the martyrs' death. Indeed, the effect of the argument was major, causing disruption and contention within the church there. It was a real source of confusion and disunity. When Saturus and Perpetua came from the immediate presence of the Lord, they were confronted by these two men, who together threw themselves at the martyrs' feet with the request, "Make peace between us." Their reason for accosting the martyrs was that the martyrs, on their deaths, had left these leaders with whatever was at issue unresolved (13.2).

The effect the request had upon Saturus and Perpetua was, first of all, one of puzzlement. Together, Saturus and Perpetua responded by asking two questions. The first appears to have been a question arising out of their astonishment: "Are you not our bishop [obviously addressed to Optatus], and are you [Aspasius] not our presbyter?" Their second question presupposes that their assumptions in the first question were correct. It, too, was based on incredulity. The question was simply, "How can you fall at our feet?" The implication is that it was not the place of bishops and presbyters to be submitting themselves to laypersons in this manner.

The incredulity of the martyrs seems to have given way to expressions of emotion based on the magnitude of the situation. Saturus recalls that he and Perpetua were "moved" as they rushed to embrace the quarreling leaders. Perpetua then proceeded to address these leaders, as Saturus says, "in Greek" (an allusion to the language of heaven?), and the four of them, apparently at the initiation of the martyrs, went aside to a rose arbor for them to continue their discussion.

This passage has been problematic for many, giving rise to the explanation that this is proof that the martyrs were Montanists. De Soyres notes that "the object of the vision was to suggest a pacific solution [to a problem] on the basis of a certain concession to Montanistic scruples."[45] Barnes has also employed this vision in his arguments to demonstrate the Montanist nature of *The Passion*. His judgment is that Saturus's "dream manifests a subversive attitude towards the clergy."[46] His argument is based on the fact that the bishop and presbyter are outside the walls of light and therefore the presence of God, whereas the martyrs have been allowed inside. Furthermore, their sadness and isolation suggest by implication that their hope lies in the martyrs alone. Thus, they fall at the feet of the martyrs.

Weinrich has provided a sound rejoinder to Barnes's argument at this point. While it is possible to argue that Montanism exhibited a low opinion of the clergy on a variety of occasions,[47] the vision of Saturus seems to "support and reinforce" the clergy rather than subvert it.[48] This point is supported by at least three pieces of data. First, the martyrs were surprised, perhaps even shocked, to have their bishop as well as their teaching presbyter fall at their feet. Second, they addressed Optatus, their bishop, with the question, "Are you not our bishop?" and they used the deferential term *papa*. In short, by implication, they continued to recognize the bishop's authority in their use of this term. Third, when the angels came out to the rose arbor and scolded the bishop and the presbyter for bothering the martyrs, "the implication is that what had been asked of Perpetua and Saturus was beyond their competence"; that is, "Reconciling quarreling parties was not the function and prerogative of martyrs."[49]

However, Klawiter has attempted to make precisely this point in his article on the priestly authority of women. His contention is that "Whatever the full meaning of the episode, it seems to imply at least that one destined for martyrdom [whether male or female] has the power of the keys and can utilize it to bestow peace on other Christians."[50] He is willing to interpret this portion of the vision to mean that confessors, once martyred, are not to be bothered with the problems of the church, but he continues, arguing that even this position assumes that "while alive the destined martyr has the priestly power of the keys."[51]

On closer examination, such a teaching may not be as clearly present in the account as Klawiter might think. Weinrich's point that the martyrs were surprised at the approach of these church leaders is still a telling critique. So is the fact that the angels scolded these church leaders, telling them to allow the martyrs the opportunity to rest or be refreshed and to settle whatever quarrels they had among themselves. Thus, the appropriate interpretation of the vision would seem more clearly to lie in the alternative solution Klawiter concedes is possible: "This episode could be interpreted as teaching that once put to death, the martyr can no longer bestow peace (through the power of the keys) on Christians who have fallen out of fellowship because of sin. Christians are to work out their own problems and not pray to martyrs."[52]

The words of the angels to Optatus and Aspasius were such that these church leaders not only were separated from the martyrs but also were "put to confusion" (13.6). Thus, clear direction for Optatus and Aspasius was necessary in order to end not only their confusion but also their dispute.

At first glance, the third scene of Saturus's vision seems to be unrelated in any substantial way to the previous two scenes. This has been noted by Petraglio, yet in a different way. Scene one is rooted in the reality of imminent martyrdom. Scene three is also rooted in reality, the reality of a church in dispute. Thus, the second scene appears almost as an intrusion into reality, a kind of evasion of reality, and yet it is in a logical sequence with the first scene.[53]

RESOLUTION

It seems that resolution of the significance of the entire vision for the martyrs rests, not so much in its word of comfort for the martyrs themselves, but in the message directed to Optatus by the angels in the third scene. In short, it may be the case that their words to Optatus are to be understood as the significant oracular utterance, the message of the vision. The words to Optatus are:

You must scold your flock. They approach you as though they have come from the games, quarrelling about the different teams (13.6).

This understanding would suggest a scenario that responds favorably to the martyrs' real-life situation. It may be, as Klawiter has suggested, that the church in Carthage believed the confessors had, by reason of their confession and their imminent martyrdom, some special grace whereby they could be consulted by others for divine guidance or, as Klawiter has also suggested, the use of the keys for the resolution of problems. Such an idea does appear in Tertullian's address *To the Martyrs* written sometime prior to or concurrent with the martyrdom of Saturus.[54] It may also lie behind Perpetua's acknowledgment that she was "worthy" of receiving a vision (4.7; 7.2).

If such an idea was as widely accepted in Carthage as Tertullian seems to indicate, it is not improbable that Optatus and/or Aspasius had either visited the martyrs in prison, or sent word to them, asking for help in the resolution of their differences. Such a request may in fact lie behind Saturus's vision. It would also explain the surprise of these martyrs at the appearance of their bishop and presbyter, for these young catechumens had moved rapidly from the position of neophytes to ones who were being asked for help in the resolution of a major ecclesiastical or pastoral issue. Assured that they could help, Saturus could have prayed for a word of direction from the Lord, a word that would settle the dispute. This word came in the form of an oracle directed toward Optatus, exhorting him to provide resolution to the pastoral problem at Carthage by exercising more forcefully his ecclesiastical power. Thus, as Rowland has stated, the vision offers the solution to a real situation from "the standpoint of heaven."[55]

In this way, too, Petraglio has spoken to the so-called parenthetical nature of the second scene in which the martyrs fulfilled the command at the close of the first scene to enter and greet the Lord. The second scene is not parenthetical at all. It is "the ideal to which the situation of the earthly church ought to conform even now."[56] It stands in stark contrast to the sorrowful church leaders who do not participate directly in the events within the wall because their church is divided. Repentance is necessary, but so is direct action by the bishop, to whom the oracle is directed.

The oracle itself is a word of direction. It contains a command, "Put straight your people," and the reason for this command, "because they assemble before you as if they were returning from the games while yet disputing over the various teams." The action to be taken and the reason for its necessity are clear. There is disunity within the church at Carthage, a problem that will still be present when Cyprian becomes bishop.[57] The focus of their disunity at this time is not known, but a clear word has been spoken that exhorts the bishop to exercise some measure of control and leadership in a very disorderly situation. Rather than subverting the bishop, it strengthens his hand by divine command.

The vision moves toward its conclusion with the recognition that the martyrs had no other role in the settling of the dispute between Optatus and Aspasius and that the angels appeared anxious to close the gates of the wall. At this point, Saturus notes that he and Perpetua began to recognize many of their brethren and martyrs.[58]

Everyone present in that location was said to be sustained or nourished by an indescribable odor which satisfied them. Thus, in this final description of the heavenly realm, Saturus has moved from the sights and sounds of the place to its smell. Here again, his description seems to parallel that of Jewish and Christian apocalyptic. In *1 Enoch*, Enoch was very aware of aromatic trees on his journey toward the east.[59] As he entered the Garden of Righteousness he noted more trees, large trees of "goodly fragrance."[60]

Although no such description of paradise or of heaven appears in the canonical literature, a similar idea appears in the *Apocalypse of Peter*. In this work, the description of a great open garden included the fact that "(It was) full of fair trees and blessed fruits, full of the fragrance of perfume. Its fragrance was beautiful and the fragrance reached to us."[61]

Whether Saturus drew from these passages in his repertoire of ideas, it is not possible to determine. There are significant similarities, especially between Saturus's account and that of the *Apocalypse of Peter,* as has been noted by Frend.[62] But the significant difference is that when Saturus described the trees he did not note their smell, only their "falling" or "singing" leaves. Furthermore, his mention of the odor is without context as to its source. It is simply noted that the smell exists and it satisfyingly nourishes those who smell it.

One other possibility does exist to explain that smell, although its likeliness is equally obscure. It may rely on Isaiah's encounter with Yahweh in the midst of smoke (Isa. 6:4). This idea may be behind the early Christian idea that connected the coming of the Spirit at Pentecost, not only with wind and fire but also with a sweet smell.[63] It is possible that the sustenance received in heaven is no less than the perfume of the Spirit of God.

Just as Perpetua had awakened from her first vision with the taste of something sweet in her mouth, Saturus seems to have awakened from his vision with a feeling directly related to the vision. He woke up "happy" or "rejoicing." He had apparently not only achieved his goal of providing the necessary oracle to Optatus but he had also seen into his own future: a successful martyrdom and a welcome in Paradise from his Lord. Thus, the vision of Saturus appears to have brought a word of comfort to Saturus and probably Perpetua in a time of significant stress, but it brought also a clear word of exhortation to the church at Carthage. The bishop had work to do. The church must quit its bickering. It remains now, to show how the redactor of these visions wove them together within the historical context, so as to determine the final role and function for which their publication was intended.

CHAPTER SEVEN

THE REDACTOR'S USE OF THE DIARIES

In the previous four chapters I have attempted to show how the martyrs Perpetua and Saturus interpreted the visions they received while awaiting execution and what factors may have influenced their interpretations. In some cases, notably in the visionary accounts left by Perpetua, the interpretation of the vision appeared in the diary left by her and has been incorporated into the text of *The Passion*. Thus, Perpetua, because of the ladder, concluded that the appropriate interpretation of the vision included the foreknowledge that she would be martyred for her faith. Her two visions of her deceased brother, Dinocrates, first raised and then alleviated her anxiety regarding his eternal state. Finally, the vision in which she saw herself in a life-or-death struggle with an Egyptian wrestler left her with the understanding that her contest was not so much with the wild animals she would soon face, but rather, it was with the devil who, if possible, would wrest from her the successful martyrdom she wished to undertake.[1]

Saturus's account was included with no contextual statements other than the redactor's assurance that Saturus had recorded his vision in his own hand. The account left by Saturus merely described in esoteric apocalyptic style the various features of the vision, including a single oracle, but the reader was left to provide the interpretation.

THE PURPOSE

The function of each of these visions, however, seems to be fairly straightforward. The visions appear to bring clarity, strength, comfort, and direction to an otherwise intolerable state of affairs. While Perpetua's visions tend to provide help in response to personal anxieties and questions, Saturus's vision ultimately has a place in the ecclesiastical life of the congregation at Carthage. It provides an oracle directed toward the bishop, Optatus (13.5–6), giving him the course of action he must follow to end a dispute in which his congregation is embroiled.

By way of contrast, the redactor saw much more in these accounts than their initial purposes. For the redactor they functioned with a larger purpose, a purpose unhindered by time or space. The redactor attempted to place these visionary accounts within a historical setting where they could be judged and, when judged, found to be genuine expressions of how God continues to meet the needs of God's people.

It is clear from the preface of *The Passion* that the redactor saw the martyrs of the Severan persecution as well as him- or herself standing within the stream of salvation history. Deeds and events such as those experienced by these young martyrs, with whom the redactor had apparently had some contact, had been written down since ancient times. The redactor's recollection of these deeds suggests that she or he was here referring to those books or letters that functioned as Scripture for the Christian community at Carthage at the beginning of the third century. In any case, the redactor understood that these deeds had been recorded previously for one of two purposes, perhaps for both. These deeds had been recorded, first, to act as proofs of God's favor or as evidences of God's grace. They provided an apologetic argument for the graciousness of God. Second, they had been recorded for the edification of those who would take the time to read them. Hence, they also had a pastoral focus in mind. The redactor's summary statement included the fact that they were written to honor God and to comfort the people of God.[2]

In a logical extrapolation from this precedent, the redactor sought to meet the spiritual needs of the day as well as those of future generations. The redactor was not concerned to write history merely for the sake of writing history, as Harris and Gifford have pointed out, for even the martyrdoms to which the redactor bore witness were "subservient to the visions."[3] Rather, the redactor was convinced that if the written records of the ways in which God had dealt with the people of God in the past, brought glory to God and comfort to the people of God, then to continue recording such dealings in written form would likely continue to produce similar results. Perpetua had laid down a challenge for someone to tell the whole story of her martyrdom. The redactor understood it to be a Spirit-impelled duty to meet her challenge (1.1; 10.15; 16.1). Furthermore, the redactor seems to have felt a need to respond to a contemporary argument related to the decline of the more spontaneous charismata in the church. To record these prophetic visions was to bear witness to the fact that the Holy Spirit was still present and active in the church, giving gifts to the people of God (1.3–6). To record these accounts for posterity was to document and thereby provide credibility to the claims of those who experienced prophecies and visions in the redactor's own day. Thus, the redactor saw his or her own contribution as having both an apologetic and a pastoral function in much the same way as the writers of an earlier age had.

Overall, the redactor of *The Passion* approached the task as a pastor. It is true to say, first of all, that the redactor understood the work to have an evangelistic thrust to it. She or he wished for it to provide to nonbelievers a witness to the fact that God's promises are sure. Thus, in its evangelistic thrust, it was also apologetic in nature (1.5).

Second, it had a focused pastoral function for members of the church. It provided an up-to-date witness to the fact that God's power or "supernatural grace" was present in the church at the beginning of the third century, just as it had been in an earlier age (1.5). Those who were weak in their faith and those who despaired could take heart in knowing that God was yet with them.

The redactor also desired to help Christian readers recognize their own place as part of the ongoing parade of personalities who had made up the church through the ages. Indeed, it was this notion of the communion of saints which led to the hope that, in recording the acts of these Severan martyrs, Christians of the redactor's day as well as those in years to come might have fellowship with them (1.6).

The redactor also spoke to those who, as Christians, had witnessed the martyrdom of Perpetua, Saturus, and their comrades. She or he hoped to rekindle in them the recollection of the glory of the Lord that surrounded their martyrological witness (1.6).

Ultimately, of course, the redactor was concerned that this editorial undertaking might serve as a catalyst to promote the glory of God. This would occur by the testimony it brought to the unbeliever regarding God's faithfulness, by the edification it brought to the church, and perhaps even through a fellowship with the Lord himself through a shared communion with the martyrs (1.1, 5, 6; 21.11).

THE RATIONALE

Whereas the redactor's purposes are primarily pastoral in their orientation, the arguments set forth in support of these purposes are largely theological. The theological arguments for producing The Passion are based, first, on a citation from Peter's Pentecost sermon recorded in Acts 2, and on an allusion to 1 Cor. 12.[4] The redactor's citation from Peter's sermon is a paraphrase based on Acts 2:17–18, which is itself a paraphrase of the earlier prophecy of Joel 2:28 (MT 3:1). That the redactor has worked with the text of Acts rather than that of Joel is clear from the opening words of the paraphrase, "In the last days." These words do not occur in Joel's prophecy, but clearly represent Peter's interpretation of Joel's וְהָיָה אַחֲדֵי־כֵן. The redactor is certain that she or he is living in the time that may be considered to be "the last days." It is because of this certainty that the redactor believes the miraculous events in the visions

FIGURE 3

Acts 2:17–18 (NRSV)	The Redactor's Paraphrase, *The Passion* 1.4
A. In the last days *it will be*, God declares, that *I will pour out* my Spirit upon all flesh, and *your* sons and *your* daughters shall prophesy,	A. In the last days, says the Lord, *I am pouring out* my Spirit upon all flesh, and *their* sons and daughters shall prophesy;
B. and *your* young men shall see visions, and *your* old men shall dream dreams;	C. and upon my menservants and my maidservants *of my Spirit I am pouring out;*
C. Even upon my slaves, both men and women, *in those days* I will pour out my Spirit; and *they shall prophesy.*	B. and young men shall see visions, and old men shall dream dreams.

and martyrdom of Perpetua and her friends are so significant. They represent the "extraordinary graces" that are to be present in the final period of time.

It is precisely at this point and in connection with this theological view of history that the redactor has introduced as evidence this paraphrase of Acts 2:17–18. To help in our discussion of the redactor's use of the passage, in Figure 3 it has been set beside the NRSV translation of the Greek text.

Several items have been changed in this paraphrase to highlight the redactor's point. First, the verb in "I will pour out" has been changed from the future tense in which it appears in the New Testament to the imperfect *effundam*. The emphasis has been switched from some future point in time to the present in which the Lord is said to be acting in just the way he had previously promised it. Second, and of equal significance, the redactor has chosen to invert a portion of the passage (part B) in such a way as to list the young men with their visions and old men with their dreams last. The change adds emphasis to this section of the paraphrase and provides a sound basis for the redactor's concern that the visions which Perpetua and Saturus experienced were in direct fulfillment of this prophetic word and thus indicative that the redactor's basic assumption of its being "the last days" is accurate. Finally, the redundant emphasis on the clause "and they shall prophesy" found in Peter's version is deleted from part C of the redactor's paraphrase. This is probably because the redactor assumes that prophecy continues to function within the church. After all, the redactor argues, "we hold in honor and acknowledge . . . prophecies . . ." (1.5a), and both prophecies and new or recent visions are granted in fulfillment of the promise in Acts 2.

This passage with its mention of "prophecies and new visions as equally promised" has led some to imply or even to argue that herein lies a clear indication of the Montanist leanings of the redactor.[5] But it is equally possible to argue that this passage merely bears witness to an effervescent form of Christianity detached from Montanism altogether.[6] Robinson's argument, for instance, can be turned against him by noting that the Greek translation was made sometime after the New Prophecy had clearly emerged in Carthage. As such, while striving to preserve the best aspects of the martyrology, the Greek translator merely eliminated those references that, when they originally appeared in Latin, had no meaning beyond a simple literal interpretation of Acts 2, whereas now they had become dangerously loaded by their similarities to the teachings the New Prophecy was espousing.

Weinrich has clearly demonstrated that the use of the paraphrase in Acts 2:17–18 sets the redactor at odds with the way in which the New Prophecy employed it. While adherents of the New Prophecy and the redactor believed themselves to be living in "the last days," the New Prophecy proponents held to an imminent parousia in ways that the redactor of *The Passion* did not. The redactor was writing for future generations. Weinrich's conclusion, with which I heartily concur, is that "the 'last days' began with Pentecost and that the events of the *Passion* are simply the most recent of those acts of the Spirit which bear the imprint of the 'last days.' The Spirit is working now in the Church in equal measure and in the selfsame manner as in the earliest days of the Church. That, and no more, is the contention of the redactor."[7] The redactor's view of history is one of continuity rather than of discontinuity. The redactor did not subscribe to a form of restorationism, but might well have argued that *The Passion* would have fit as another chapter at the end of the Book of Acts.

In addition to the emphasis on the promise of Acts 2, the redactor wished to acknowledge the whole of the Spirit's gifts to the church. These gifts were "other powers/capacities" of the Spirit. It was the role of the Spirit to distribute these "gifts" to everyone, just as it was the role of the Lord to apportion to each one individually. These gifts were intended to be the equipment of the church (1.5), and among these gifts were prophecy, visions, and martyrdom. Prophecies and visions were understood and acknowledged as coming in fulfillment of the promise found in Acts 2:17–18, based on the presupposition that the redactor lived during the period described as "the last days." Furthermore, these visions, or esteemed revelations, and these martyrdoms were also understood to be manifestations of divine grace made evident in the redactor's day through the lives and deaths of these Severan martyrs.[8]

CONFIRMATION THROUGH FULFILLMENT

With this as the foundation, it is easy to see why the redactor did not attempt to interpret the vision of Saturus. Perpetua's visions, all personal in nature, carried with them their respective interpretations. Saturus's vision did not; it was necessary only to show that he had received such a revelation in order for the redactor to believe that its purpose had been served. Besides, it is quite probable that the content of Saturus's vision had been conveyed first to Optatus and then on to the entire congregation. There was no need to interpret it, for that had been done in public already. Its fulfillment within the context of Saturus's martyrdom was all that was essential to make the redactor's point.

Whoever the redactor was, she or he was privy to an eyewitness account of the last hours and the executions of the martyrs whose visionary prophecies were chosen to be incorporated into *The Passion*. Furthermore, the redactor chose to use this eyewitness account, whether experienced by him- or herself or by others close to the martyrs, to verify the legitimacy of the visions she or he preserved, particularly the visions of Perpetua. The redactor recorded these events in some detail, and with the necessary allusions to Perpetua's visions to provide the visions with full credibility.

On the day of her execution, Perpetua and the other martyrs were brought to the amphitheater from their place of confinement. Their mood was said to be joyful as they went to the amphitheater. Perpetua was singled out and described by the redactor as going "with a shining countenance and calm step" (18.1). Upon reaching the amphitheater, the prisoners were commanded to don the robes of the pagan cults, the men dressed as the priests of Saturn, the women as the priestesses of Ceres. But Perpetua resisted so strongly that the military tribune agreed not to force the issue. Thus, the prisoners were brought along to the arena in their prison clothes.

Upon reaching the arena, the redactor informs us that Perpetua began to sing a psalm. The redactor's judgment of this act led to the pronouncement that she was "already treading on the head of the Egyptian."[9] In this obvious allusion to Perpetua's third vision, that of her wrestling match

with the Egyptian (10.10–11), the redactor established his or her judgment that Perpetua's prediction, spiritualized though it might be, was
nonetheless coming to pass. Thus, the redactor was convinced that one
form of testing which could be undertaken on the predictive aspects of
these visions was the test of fulfillment.

This was borne out in a second allusion to this same vision a bit later in
The Passion. Perpetua had stated in her third vision that she recognized the
reality of her martyrdom to encompass a fight, not merely with wild
beasts, but most directly with the devil. The redactor concurred in this
assessment, noting that a mad heifer had been prepared for her execution
by none other than the devil.[10]

As the scene was played out in the arena, however, Saturus was the first
to die. On this fact, the redactor remarked that each of the martyrs,
having been wounded by their respective adversaries, was put to death by
the sword. "The others took the sword in silence and without moving,
especially Saturus, who being the first to climb, was the first to die. For
once again he was waiting for Perpetua." This third allusion clearly refers
to Perpetua's initial vision, in which Saturus scaled the ladder before her
and then waited at the top to direct her in her movement past the dragon
and up the ladder.[11] Here again, the redactor presents a case for the
genuineness of one of Perpetua's visions. It had predicted, however subtly,
that Saturus would die before Perpetua. The redactor makes it clear for all
subsequent readers that this was, indeed, the case when the prisoners were
martyred.

With the record of the deaths of the Severan martyrs duly recorded, the
redactor broke out in a note of praise for these martyrs who had served
their Lord faithfully to the end. "Truly," she or he wrote, "are you [the
Severan martyrs] called and chosen for the glory of Christ Jesus our Lord"
(21.8). By so exulting in their triumph, the redactor reiterated his or her
foremost concern that the lives and deaths of these martyrs might bring
edification to the church and thereby issue in God's glory. These recent
manifestations of God's power would bear witness to "one and the same
Spirit who still operates, and to God the Father almighty, to his Son Jesus
Christ our Lord, to whom is splendor and immeasurable power for all the
ages" (21.8).

In summary, several statements may be made regarding the visions of
Perpetua and Saturus and their use by the redactor. First, Perpetua's
visions appear to have been primarily personal in nature, providing her
with strength and comfort in her last days. Second, whereas Saturus's
vision would have brought some measure of strength or consolation to the
martyrs, it also played a role in the congregation served by the bishop,
Optatus. It provided the congregation with help through the impartation

of a specific and timely oracle directed toward the bishop. The oracle commanded him to use his proper authority to settle a problem of disunity within the congregation. A third factor which appears in *The Passion* and specifically in the redactor's conclusions concerning the visions of Perpetua is that they were to be understood as prophetic gifts of the Holy Spirit, with purposes and results consistent with Scripture. Fourth, after being convinced of the divine origin of these visions and therefore of their genuineness, first, by the fact that Saturus died before Perpetua as she had predicted and, second, by the fact that these two martyrs had undergone a triumphal martyrdom as both of them had predicted (that is, by using the test of fulfillment), the redactor put them together in a historical framework that served three purposes. It provided an evangelistic apologetic to the unbeliever, showing that God's promises are trustworthy. It brought consolation and edification to the church by emphasizing the fact that God still empowers God's people, therefore making God the more relevant to the contemporary situation. And, it brought glory to God.

That Tertullian a few years later would use portions of Saturus's vision to argue a doctrinal point and that Augustine nearly two centuries later would preach at least four sermons based on this work, and engage in theological apologetics based on Perpetua's visions concerning the fate of Dinocrates, underscore the significance of the ongoing role these visions played in the life of the larger church in North Africa well into the fifth century.

PART TWO

PROPHETIC GIFTS IN THE WRITINGS OF TERTULLIAN

CHAPTER EIGHT

INTRODUCTION TO PROPHETIC GIFTS IN TERTULLIAN

The subject of "prophetic gifts" surfaces a number of times in Tertullian's writings. It appears in his recitation of or reference to specific oracles or sayings[1] and in his recalling of various visions.[2] It also occurs in some of Tertullian's arguments that support the continuing role of the Paraclete.[3] Nonetheless, it is significant to note that, prior to A.D. 207, he wrote very little on this subject.

PRE-MONTANIST CONCERNS

In the works that Tertullian wrote prior to his association with the so-called New Prophecy, he argued that charismata had been given by God to believers.[4] During this period, his concerns covered the subject of charismata more generally than they did in his later writings. In his tract *On Baptism*, for instance, he wrote a section addressed specifically to those who would shortly be baptized. Tertullian enjoined these catechumens to ask God for charismata. This is one of the earliest documents to suggest that it was common for the newly baptized to expect, to ask for, or to anticipate receiving charismata as part of their rite of initiation. The initiative of giving the gifts was understood clearly to lie in God's hands, but the newly baptized were expected to anticipate the bestowal of charismata for life in the church.[5]

By this instruction to the newly baptized, Tertullian was saying that the possession and use of these charismata was not optional. They played an important part in the Christian walk. They were not to be understood as something for a "spiritual elite," nor merely for mature believers, because Tertullian's specific audience was the newly baptized.

Tertullian viewed the possession and use of charismata as something that God willed for the church. In his tract *On Prayer*, he argued that the Lord (Jesus) accomplished the will of God in preaching, in working, and enduring. He then paralleled this with the idea that, as Christians, "we are now provoked, just as unto exemplars, to preach, to work, to endure even unto death."[6] While he did not clearly detail what the "works" were, they undoubtedly included such items as miracles, healings, and acts of mercy.[7] A gift of martyrdom may also have been understood as part of his comment on endurance unto death.

Tertullian saw more than just one or two charismata operating within the church of his day. He wrote of various ones that, he observed, had made their appearance in the church until the time of Marcion (circa A.D. 140) and Valentinus (A.D. 165). In his *Prescription against Heretics*, he argued eloquently against the Marcionite and Valentinian claims that they alone possessed the truth. If they alone possessed the truth, went his argument,

> during the interval [from Jesus to Marcion and Valentinus] the gospel was wrongly preached, men wrongly believed; so many thousands were wrongly baptized; so many works of faith were wrongly wrought; so many miraculous gifts; so many spiritual endowments were set in operation; so many priestly functions, so many ministries were wrongly executed; and to sum up the whole, so many martyrs wrongly received their crowns![8]

Tertullian went on to argue that this was clearly not the case. The works of faith, miraculous gifts, spiritual endowments, and ministries had been fully in line with the revealed Gospel. Although he used the past tense and, therefore, did not explicitly claim the presence of these things within his own day, his argument loses all its force if one does not understand him to mean that such things continued to exist throughout the church on a regular basis right up through the time of the Marcionites and Valentinus.

In his treatise *On Patience*, Tertullian argued for the continuation of faith, hope, and love, but he also argued for the continuation of tongues, knowledge, and prophecies.[9] These latter three items, however, were to be put away at the consummation.[10] It seems, then, that Tertullian argued that they legitimately continued in his own day, although in his writings that predate his interest and participation in the New Prophecy he did not describe or reflect on these phenomena in any depth.

With specific reference to prophecy, Tertullian mentioned certain false prophets who gave deceptive predictions of the future, just as he mentioned false apostles who preached a perverted gospel.[11] Little of what he thought about contemporary prophets or prophecy can be derived from this statement other than that he thought of prophecy primarily in a predictive sense of the word. It would take the works from his so-called Montanist period to provide a fuller explanation of prophecy as Tertullian understood it.

MONTANIST CONCERNS

As we turn from Tertullian's earliest works to those when he closely identified with Montanism, or the New Prophecy, we find that his concern with charismata of the Spirit became more specialized. Tertullian wrote about several of these, but his real concern was with prophetic gifts. Of the approximately sixty-five instances in which he wrote of charismata during this period, at least fifty had direct reference to the gift or charisma of prophecy.

General Concerns on Charismata

His most complete statement on the charismata comes in his work *Against Marcion*. Because of who his opponent was, Tertullian attempted to establish his doctrine of charismata firmly within the Old Testament. God the Creator, through Isaiah the prophet, promised that spiritual gifts would come to earth through Christ, the flower of Jesse.[12] Tertullian argued that the Spirit was taken from Judah until such time as this promise would be fulfilled in Christ.[13]

Tertullian went on to argue that Christ did indeed possess these gifts. In fact, in one place he argued that they culminated or ceased in Christ.[14] His intention at this point seems to have been to show that all prophecies and visions were, in essence, sealed in Christ's advent.[15] Thus, Tertullian argued that in Christ "the whole *substantia* of the Spirit would have to rest."[16] As a result, the entire operation of the Spirit rested in Christ.

Once his groundwork had been laid, Tertullian went on to argue that Scripture was correct to record that when Christ ascended to heaven at the end of his earthly ministry, "he led a host of captives, and he gave gifts to men."[17] These gifts were the charismata. Tertullian's analysis of Eph. 4:8 led him to believe that the latter half of this verse was fulfilled on the Day of Pentecost with the coming of the Spirit as prophesied in Joel 2:28–29 (see Acts 2:1–21, esp. 17–18).

Tertullian believed that the gifts found in the Pauline catalog (1 Cor. 12:8–10) and those found in Isaiah's prophecy (Isa. 11:1–3) were the same. His analysis of their correspondence is charted in Figure 4.[18]

Once Tertullian had established that the God of the Old Testament (the Creator) was the one who promised and delivered the promise regarding charismata and was convinced that the charismata were readily present among the Christian faithful, he challenged Marcion to demonstrate the presence of such charismata from among his own following. Thus, Tertullian used these arguments in particular to confirm the contin-

FIGURE 4

1 Cor. 12:8–10	Isa. 11:1–2
1. word of wisdom	1. spirit of wisdom
2. word of knowledge	2. (a) spirit of understanding
	(b) and counsel
3. faith	3. (a) spirit of religion
	(b) and the fear of the Lord
4. (a) gifts of healing	4. spirit of might
(b) working of miracles	
5. (a) prophecy	5. spirit of knowledge
(b) discerning of spirits	
(c) tongues	
(d) interpretation of tongues	

uance of (1) prophecy, (2) the interpretation of tongues, and (3) the gift of tongues. These signs were readily available in the churches with which he was familiar.[19]

The Gift of Prophecy

It has already been noted that, even prior to his identification with the New Prophecy, Tertullian believed that the gift of prophecy would continue to appear among Christians until the consummation. He based this conception on several passages of Scripture. His first and foremost argument was based on 1 Cor. 13:8–10.[20] But, like Peter on the day of Pentecost, Tertullian saw such a belief as consistent with the fulfillment of Joe's prophecy in Joel 2:28–29.[21] God's Spirit had been poured out on God's servants and handmaidens. The result was prophetic utterance.

While charismata received their fullest meaning in Christ,[22] they would nonetheless be present in the church from the time of the apostles onward. In fact, Tertullian argued, "apostles have the Holy Spirit properly, who have Him fully, in the operations of prophecy."[23] It was the Holy Spirit or Paraclete who was responsible for distributing this gift.[24]

Tertullian was equally aware of the presence of false prophecy in the church, and he charged that it was there because of the influences of false prophets and fallen spirits.[25] True prophecy came with an ecstatic experience, but it did not produce disorder when spoken.[26] And while it had several functions, Tertullian understood the Paraclete's (Holy Spirit's) role,[27] even in prophetic utterances, primarily as a teaching role.[28] He was quite explicit in what he saw as valid utterances from or by the Paraclete through individual Christians. They might be the words of the Spirit that came when a Christian was hard-pressed for an answer before the magistrates.[29] They might be words of prediction or of revelation of the secrets of one's heart.[30] They might be the explanation of previously hidden mysteries.[31] They might also be utterances of guidance in matters of discipline and ethics.[32] Yet, even with these possibilities for prophetic utterance, the true prophet would be trustworthy because his or her own conceptions or teachings would not enter into the utterances.[33]

Ecstasy and Prophecy: Background

Prophecy has often been described as an "ecstatic" experience, especially for some of the Old Testament prophets.[34] Although this position is held by many psychologists, commentators, and theologians, the term "ecstatic" is not always clearly defined. In some instances it is understood as a kind of raving mania.[35] Others hold to a more conservative understanding of ecstasy in which it may refer to a heightened sensitivity to God.[36] Still others argue that the term "ecstasy" is too ambiguous and too full of baggage to merit use in describing what happens in prophecy.[37] Yet this concept was related to the manifestation of prophetic gifts in Tertullian's thought. It would be helpful in our understanding of Tertullian to see how this concept was understood in earlier times.

The relationship between prophecy and ecstasy will become more apparent as we look at several important Greek terms. The first of these is ἔκστασις, a word used approximately thirty times in the Septuagint (LXX) to translate a variety of Hebrew terms.[38] The largest percentage of LXX usages involving ἔκστασις is in the phrase "fear of the Lord" (ἔκστασις κυρίου). In no case does it ever refer to a prophet or to the activity of prophesying. In the LXX, as well as secular literature, ἔκστασις normally has a meaning associated with physical or mental displacement and shock.[39]

Plutarch wrote of Solon that when he could no longer endure a certain disgrace, he pretended to be out of his head (ἐσκήψατο μὲν ἔκστασις τῶν λογισμῶν),[40] and through his family he leaked a report to the Athenians that he showed signs of madness. Examples of ἔκστασις that refer to mental displacement are also available in the writings of Hippocrates. On one occasion he wrote, "For madness to be followed by . . . raving (ἔκστασις), is a good sign."[41] He also used the term to denote physical rather than mental displacement.[42] But, even though the word ἔκστασις is used in the LXX and its meaning in both the LXX and secular literature refers to some type of ecstatic, mental displacement, it is never used to describe either the Old Testament prophets or their activities in the LXX.

The noun ἔκστασις also appears seven times in the New Testament. In four of these cases it is probably best translated as "astonishment" or "terror."[43] In the remaining three references, it refers to a "trance." Both Peter and Paul experienced such a trance (Peter in Luke's description in Acts 10:10 and his own description in Acts 11:5; Paul in Acts 22:17). In these instances, the apostles each received direction and guidance from God. The experience included both visionary and auditory components. Peter received a vision of clean and unclean animals, with the instructions that (1) he was not to judge as common what God had cleansed and (2) he should go with three men who sought him. In essence, it was a call for him to accept Gentiles into the church. Similarly, Paul received a vision that someone beckoned him to get out of Jerusalem. He was told, "Go, for I will send you far away to the Gentiles." Both of these instances, then, lend support to the term as a legitimate descriptor of a visionary activity within the New Testament.

A second word that is closely related to ἔκστασις is the verb form ἐξίστημι. It is used seventeen times in the New Testament.[44] In fifteen of these instances, the word is best translated as "amazed" or "astonished." In the remaining two, the word indicates existence apart from oneself (Mark 3:21, 2 Cor. 5:13). In only the 2 Corinthians passage can it be argued that there is a possible relationship to prophetic activity. Paul remarks simply, "For if we are beside ourselves (ἐξέστημεν), it is for God; if we are in our right mind (σωφρονοῦμεν), it is for you." His primary concern seems to be that everything he does is done for God *and* for the Corinthian people.[45] In any case, it *may* include prophetic activity, but only as a possible understanding. It is far more likely that this statement refers to charges by the Corinthians that Paul was thought to be out of his mind.[46]

A second term that may help clarify our thinking is the term μάντις. This term, as well as its related forms (μαντεία, μαντεῖον, and μαντεύομαι) is found approximately thirty times in the LXX. In most cases, this group of words takes on the meaning of "diviner" or the practice of "divining."[47] However, the term is never used in reference to the genuine prophet of God,[48] but, on the contrary, to one who prophesies by his or her own power or that of a demonic power.[49]

For the most part secular literature had the basic understanding that μάντις did not refer to a prophet, although, according to Plutarch, the μάντις was one who was inspired and possessed by Apollo.[50] But Plato moved the parallel between secular usage and LXX usage closer. He wrote that God gave human foolishness a gift of divination, since "no man achieves true and inspired divination when in his rational mind, but only [μαντικῆς] when the power of his intelligence is fettered in sleep or when it is distraught by disease or by reason of some divine inspiration."[51]

Continuing on, he reasoned, the one who had been or presently was in this state of frenzy was in no condition to judge and interpret his own messages. The role or function of the prophets (τῶν προφητῶν) came into play at this point.[52] Thus, Plato understood the μάντις to be an ecstatic possessed by the god Apollo, while the προφήτης was quite rational. Likewise, the προφήτης was on a plane superior to that of the μάντις, for it was up to the προφήτης to make intelligible to the people the ravings of the μάντις.

Plato's understanding of προφήτης was similar in some ways to that of the LXX, but for Plato the source of the prophet's message was the μάντις and the source of the diviner's ravings was his god. The LXX differs dramatically, however, precisely at this point. It claims that the μάντις is a false diviner, while the true προφήτης receives a message directly from God.[53]

We must conclude, then, that while the μάντις was one who may or may not experience frenzy or display a frenzied demeanor, the term was never used by the LXX translators to describe a genuine prophet of God or that prophet's activities. It did, however, apply to the prophet who practiced false divination, who spoke by his or her own authority and attributed his or her own words to God.

In the New Testament the noun μάντις does not occur. The verb form μαντεύομαι occurs once in Acts 16:16. In this case it is quite clear that the reference is to a young demoniac woman and her ability to prophesy or engage in soothsaying. Once again, then, this word is not used to describe the activity of a genuine prophet of God, but it is used here to describe demonically inspired speech.[54] The terms are used similarly in the *Shepherd of Hermas*.[55] The references in that early work are to soothsaying, an act attributed to those who provide false information according to the desires of those who seek them out.

A third term, ψευδοπροφήτης, is used in the LXX ten times, nine of which occur in Jeremiah.[56] Reiling has rightly pointed out that in these passages the LXX never uses ψευδοπροφήτης as a translation of the Hebrew נָבִיא שֶׁקֶר (false prophet), but only of נָבִיא (prophet).[57] One is left to the context of these passages, specifically the activities in which these נְבִיאִים are engaged, to determine that the translation ψευδοπροφήτης is applicable. The term ψευδοπροφήτης is used in connection with μάντις in Jer. 36 (29):8,[58] and with μαντεύομαι in Jer. 34 (27):9.[59]

It is obvious that on both of these occasions, Reiling's assertions concerning ψευδοπροφήτης may be borne out. In addition, while Jeremiah may have been using the terms נְבִיאִים and קֹסְמִים synonymously in 36 (29):8, it appears in Jer. 34 (27):9 that he was referring to two distinct groups of individuals. If these are two distinct groups in both passages, then the term μαντευομένων that translates קֹסְמֵיכֶם in 34 (27):9 sheds little additional light on the meaning of ψευδοπροφητῶν and ultimately on נְבִיאִים. Their function is merely similar, not identical. If, however, the terms are synonymous in both passages, then it may be said of the נְבִיאִים that their function was similar, if not equivalent, to that of the קֹסְמֵיכֶם, and thus they may have been involved in ecstatic behavior. Jeremiah uses the term μάντις and its cognates only three times. The first, in connection with the term προφήτης, is in 14:14, referring to the divinations that the prophets falsely gave; the second is ambiguous with respect to its equivalency with נְבִיאִים (36 [29]:8); and the third time refers to a group distinct from the נְבִיאִים. Therefore, it is difficult to come to a dogmatic position in Jeremiah regarding the ecstatic character of נְבִיאִים from its relationship either to μάντις or ψευδοπροφήτης.

In the New Testament the term ψευδοπροφήτης occurs only eleven times.[60] In most of these cases, the writers remark that these individuals will rise up from among those who appear to be within the church. In no instance is the term directly related either to μάντις or ἔκστασις.

Such early Christian writings as the *Didache* do not seem to be concerned with ecstatic or mantic behavior on the part of false prophets, but Hermas connects the concepts closely in *Mandate* 11.2.[61]

Ecstasy and Prophecy: Tertullian's Understanding

The concepts of prophecy and ecstasy are inextricably interwoven in Tertullian's mind. The Holy Spirit is the source of each. Ecstasy is understood to be the medium through which prophecy is made possible. In *On the Soul*, Tertullian calls ecstasy "the Holy Ghost's operative virtue of prophecy."[62] He describes the medium of such activity with various phrases such as being "in the Spirit,"[63] "in a rapture,"[64] or "in an ecstasy."[65] Yet, he seems to use these terms interchangeably.

Tertullian's idea of ecstasy was deeply influenced by discussions of the subject in the New Prophecy as well as with its opponents.[66] In some ways it centered around the ideas of dreams and their relationship to sleep. Sleep is, according to Tertullian, a natural state, not something of a supernatural character,[67] and as a result it may be described as "a reasonable work of God."[68] When people are infused with the spiritual quality that is ecstasy,[69] they lose a certain amount of sensation.[70] They bear an external resemblance to one who is mad, for they stand outside their senses.[71] Tertullian understood this to be absolutely essential, for in the ecstatic state the person is overcome by God's power.[72] It is at this very point, however, that questions of prophetic methodology were raised against those who followed the Paraclete by those whom Tertullian chose to label "*psychici.*"[73]

When Tertullian notes that a person loses a certain amount of sensation "in the Spirit" or "in ecstasy," he likens that state to one experienced by a person who dreams when asleep. Sleep comes upon one's body, while ecstasy comes upon one's soul. When both sleep and ecstasy come to a person, that person dreams. Ecstasy removes that person's soul from rest, whereas the body remains asleep.[74] Tertullian continues his argument by noting that while people dream they are detached from their senses. There is no *real* anxiety, or feeling, or suffering, or joy, or sorrow, or alarm that can be experienced in a dream. There is, in fact, *no reality* in a dream.[75]

Since dreams, or visions, or prophecies are produced by an external force (*ecstasi*), he argued, the soul is without mastery over these things. Yet the ecstatic condition brings with itself, memory.[76] It is at this point that Tertullian argues most strongly for possession of one's total mental capacity even in the ecstatic condition. In his own words he notes, "that . . . which memory supplies is a sound mind; and that which a sound mind [ecstatically] experiences while the memory remains unchecked, is a kind of madness."[77] Similarly, he observes, "It is one thing to shake, it is another thing to move; one thing to destroy, another thing to agitate."[78] Through the use of chiasmus, Tertullian argues that while at times an ecstatic condition may appear to indicate madness (to move, or to destroy), in reality it is still in the realm of sanity (to shake, or to agitate). One must, therefore, look closely at ecstatic behavior. This is especially important because an evil spirit may have a similar effect on a person, thereby producing initial confusion regarding the source of the experience. What appears to be genuine may ultimately prove to be false.

Within this discussion, Tertullian attempts to establish that those who are "in ecstasy" are in possession of their mental faculties.[79] However, he is willing to concede that, in the state of ecstasy, this possession of one's mental faculties is not exercised to its full potential. It is partial or diminished, but not to the extent of being destroyed. When someone receives visionary or auditory perceptions in an ecstasy, they are less aware of their actual surroundings, but they are not totally *unaware* of them.[80]

It is necessary to enter this special ecstatic condition, in essence a trance or trancelike state, before one is able to receive an auditory or visionary oracle from the Spirit of God.[81] Tertullian cites at least two illustrations from Scripture to describe what he means. The first of these involves an argument first used by Phrygian Montanists, an argument that refers to Adam's prophetic state in Gen. 2:21–23.[82] In that passage, God caused a deep sleep to come over Adam, then took one of his ribs and fashioned a woman. Upon awakening from his sleep, God presented the woman to Adam who said:

> This at last is bone of my bones
>   and flesh of my flesh;
> she shall be called Woman
>   because she was taken out of Man

The spontaneity or immediacy with which Adam "prophesied" what came to be called in Eph. 5:31–32 the great or profound mystery (τὸ μυστήριον; Tertullian, *sacramentum*) led Tertullian, like the Phrygian Montanists before him, to believe that Adam's prophecy was rooted in the ecstasy of sleep.[83] But while Adam experienced this state of ecstasy, a natural event in that it involved sleep, yet at the same time a supernatural process whereby the ecstasy worked upon his soul to keep it from sleep,[84] once he awakened from his temporary state of sleep and prophesied the "great mystery," he returned to the normal state of the *psychicos*.[85]

A second illustration of ecstatic revelation provided by Tertullian was that of Peter at the time of the Transfiguration of Jesus. Tertullian argued that at the time of Christ's transfiguration, Peter was in a state of *amentia*.[86] The reason Tertullian was so sure of this was that it was Peter who recognized Moses and Elijah, and it was Peter who did not know what he had said.[87] How else could Peter have known them, Tertullian quipped, except by being "in the Spirit"? Jewish law did not allow for pictures or statues of these men, so Peter had nothing with which to compare these figures. He did not *know* what he said. Peter's instant ability to recognize and identify these figures had to have been the result of a revelation in the Spirit.

Thus, Tertullian described what one could expect to experience in an ecstasy. Ecstasy brought with it images of soundness and wisdom as well as aberration or distortion.[88] Prophets spoke not from their own knowledge, but by what has been revealed to them by the Spirit.[89] It was only because their knowledge was "revealed" knowledge, received while the prophets were in an ecstasy, that prophets could (1) predict things to come and (2) expose the secrets of one's heart.[90] Likewise, ecstasy provided the medium by or through which psalms, visions, prayers, and the interpretation of tongues, if not the gift of tongues itself, were given.[91]

CHAPTER NINE

TERTULLIAN'S USE
OF RECORDED VISIONS AND ORACLES

Up to this point we have attempted to understand some of the factors at work in Tertullian's view of "prophetic gifts." From what we have learned to this point we may conclude that Tertullian saw a legitimate place for such phenomena in the church of his own day. These "prophetic gifts" like other charismata were understood to have their origin in the Spirit of God, and they came in conjunction with some form of ecstatic experience not unlike the dream state. Furthermore, Tertullian did not see these more recent "revelations" as competing with or undermining the more-or-less fixed canon of Scripture to which he was committed.

It is necessary now to see how Tertullian used such revelations in his own life and teaching. Fortunately, his writings contain references to the vision of Saturus and to six older "Montanist" oracles. Furthermore, he has given examples of two visions that were part of his own congregational life. The vision of Saturus will be treated first along with the older recorded oracles since they were all surely in circulation in some written form at the time Tertullian referred to them.

TERTULLIAN'S USE OF SATURUS'S VISION

"How is it that the most heroic martyr Perpetua on the day of her passion saw only her fellow-martyrs there, in the revelation which she received of Paradise, if it were not that the sword which guarded the entrance permitted none to go in thereat, except those who had died in Christ and not in Adam?"[1]

With this question Tertullian introduces us to the way in which he allowed recorded visions and oracles to function in his own life and writings.[2] But this question appears to be directly related not to a specific vision that Perpetua experienced, but rather to the vision experienced by Saturus, also recorded in *The Passion*.[3] It is true that Perpetua experienced at least three visions and that in the vision of her own passion she came to an immense garden in which there were many people wearing white garments. Such clothing was normally understood to be the dress of martyrs.[4] Yet, neither the garden nor the people were named, and white robes, while often descriptive of the clothes of martyrs, were never the sole possession of martyrs.[5]

It is in Saturus's vision that at least one of Tertullian's observations is readily apparent, and it is clear that the events Saturus describes take place after he and Perpetua have died. In this case, Saturus does not use the term "paradise." He merely acknowledges the fact that he and Perpetua "received his [the Lord's] promise," possibly a reference to eternal life or to a successful passion; and he notes that he and Perpetua are taken to a great open space, a garden complete with roses and other flowering plants and trees.[6] Within this "paradise" Saturus and Perpetua meet four martyrs, and recognize what is described by Saturus as "many of our brethren, martyrs among them."[7]

Tertullian was probably citing this reference from memory. This may be supported by two pieces of data. First, he errs in attributing the vision to Perpetua. It was actually Saturus who had the vision to which Tertullian makes reference, not Perpetua. Had he had the document in front of him, he would have known this to be the case. Yet, it could be argued that Perpetua's name carried more impact for his audience than that of Saturus. Since she had been mentioned in the vision as accompanying Saturus to this place of paradise the argument could be justified that she had, in essence, "seen" what Saturus described.

Second, the vision of Saturus does not fully support the point that Tertullian is making in his *On the Soul*. Even if we should allow that Perpetua as well as Saturus "saw" the martyrs in Paradise as Tertullian contends, the martyrs were not the only ones they saw. They also saw "many of our brethren" as well as "martyrs," and not just their "fellow-martyrs," as Tertullian has asserted. Still, one could argue that Tertullian was engaged in an act of selective memory while in the heat of debate, but this would hardly seem to be the case, for Tertullian could easily be exposed as a fraud by simple reference to *The Passion*.

Tertullian makes use of this vision in an argument concerning the abode of the righteous dead. The question is raised first in his *On the Soul*, 54.1. There he argued that the soul of a human being remains in the flesh until the precise moment of death.[8] "Where does it go once the person has died?" he asked. To this question he suggested several possible solutions. First among these arguments was that even though most philosophers held to the immortality of the soul, they argued for various ultimate destinations for the soul. The unwise were generally relegated to Hades, while the wise went to the ether, the air, or even to the moon. Tertullian argued that even Christ, following his death, descended into Hades so that "He might there make the patriarchs and prophets partakers of Himself."[9] Christians, Tertullian went on, should not be disturbed with the possibility that they would need to spend time in Hades as well. To do otherwise would be to become "servants above their Lord, and disciples above their Master." If Christ could do it, the church need have no higher expectation for itself.[10]

At this place in the argument, Tertullian attempted to address the suggestion that Hades might be the proper abode for the unrighteous dead, but Paradise would be the abode of the righteous dead in the intermediate state. To this assertion he responded with two questions. The first was based on Rev. 6:9. It was a rhetorical question to which he seems not to have wanted a reply, only agreement. "How is it, then," he asked, "that the region of Paradise, which as revealed to John in the Spirit lay under the altar, displays no other souls in it besides the souls of the martyrs?"[11]

From this question it is clear that Tertullian wanted to argue that the obvious reason John saw only martyrs in Paradise was because only martyrs were present there. But two points about this argument are interesting. First, this argument was based on a visionary experience of the apostle John in a work that Tertullian understood to be Scripture. Thus, Tertullian seems to have understood the process of inspiration at this point to have included a "prophetic activity," and his argument was based on the word of an apostle who, like Saturus, described what he saw "in the Spirit."[12] Second, while the text of Rev. 6 may be understood or interpreted as dealing with events occurring in "Paradise," the text does not say this. John was invited to enter an open door in heaven (Rev. 4:1), but it was heaven, not Paradise, that was mentioned, although one could argue they are one and the same.

If the most significant point to be made is that his initial argument for the abode of the righteous dead as Hades is based on Scripture, then the second most significant point lies in his use of Saturus's vision to substantiate this point further. Tertullian argued first on the basis of Scripture that Christ descended into Hades (Matt. 12:40; John 3:13; Eph. 4:9; 1 Pet. 3:19) and that all John saw in his vision of Paradise were martyrs. Then, he used the vision he ascribed to Perpetua as a secondary argument.[13] How is it, he argued, that Perpetua, like John, saw only her fellow martyrs there? But to this question he had also applied a condition.

The obvious answer to this question lay in the fact that, were it not for the sword which guarded the entrance to Paradise, Perpetua would not herself have been able to enter it. The sword kept out those who died only "in Adam," but allowed those to enter who were "in Christ." But even this answer was not sufficient, for Tertullian argued that it was the special case, the rare and special individual, who was allowed to enter directly into Paradise. Such treatment was granted only to the martyr. "The sole key to unlock Paradise is your own life's blood,"[14] he wrote.

Finally, there are two more points worthy of note here. First, he observed that the Paraclete had counseled Christians to lay down their lives for God "not in mild fevers and on your beds, but in martyrdoms."[15] To do so was merely to obey the words of Jesus and take up the cross and follow Him (Matt. 16:24; Luke 9:23–24). Yet, it is clear that his allusion to the Paraclete referred in part to another oracle to be treated below. Again, an oracular saying was being invoked to provide secondary substantiation to his argument.

Second, Tertullian noted that, prior to writing *On the Soul,* he had written a treatise *On Paradise* which is no longer extant. In that work, he claimed, he had "established the position that every soul is detained in safe keeping in Hades until the day of the Lord."[16]

Tertullian used Saturus's vision, then, to provide a secondary witness to a point he believed to be taught in Scripture, a point he had already argued at some length in a document that has since disappeared. He appealed to the witness of "Perpetua" because he believed it had been a genuine revelation of the Spirit given and received while "she" was in the Spirit. Since, in his understanding, Scripture taught that the righteous dead dwelt in Hades until the consummation and that the martyrs dwelt in Paradise, his citation of Saturus's vision can only be construed as providing secondary support. It is important to note, however, that a key hermeneutical principle to which Tertullian subscribed required consistency for all revelations of the Spirit. The new did not contradict the old; and thus, the vision of Saturus, revealed in the Spirit, would not contradict the vision of John who was in the Spirit on the Lord's Day.[17]

TERTULLIAN'S USE OF "NEW PROPHECY" ORACLES

The subjects of persecution and martyrdom were favorites among those Christians who were associated with the New Prophecy. It should not be surprising, then, to realize that the subject was addressed by various oracles of the New Prophecy from time to time. Their argument would not be only that the prophecy supported their belief but that their prophecy provided clarification to an existing Christian truth. We will consider six of these oracles. (Also, see appendix E.)

In one letter addressed to a Christian named Fabius, Tertullian quoted two such oracles. Each will be studied in turn.

[1.] It is good for you to be publicly exposed. For he who is not exposed among men is exposed in the Lord. Do not be disturbed; righteousness brings you before the public. Why are you disturbed when you are receiving praise? There is opportunity when you are observed by men. [18]

Tertullian incorporates this oracle into his treatise *On Flight in Persecution* without citing the *Sitz-im-Leben* in which the oracle first appeared. The original audience is unknown, but, based on the oracle itself, the audience was probably a group of Christians who were feeling the sting of public reproach. They may even have faced martyrdom. Frustrated and troubled by their situation, they complained to Montanus, to whom this oracle is attributed, and he, in turn, delivered the mind of the "Spirit," one which encouraged or consoled them in their most uncomfortable position. Thus, this word, which Aune has described as parenetic,[19] was designed to encourage these believers to suffer graciously rather than to avoid suffering. It may originally have come in the pattern shown in Figure 5, with Montanus or another Montanist prophet speaking.

The essence of this oracle is that public reproach, of which both suffering and martyrdom are examples, can be good for Christians since it may come to them as a consequence of their righteousness. They should be pleased to suffer, because in their suffering their righteousness is made evident: it takes on a sacramental meaning before those who see them. The message of this oracle appears to have some relationship to Jesus' teaching that "those who are persecuted for righteousness' sake," are blessed, "for theirs is the kingdom of heaven" (Matt. 5:10; cf. Luke 6:22–23). Persecution is an inevitable outgrowth of righteousness when righteousness is manifest in a perverse world. Yet, those who are persecuted receive their vindication: the kingdom of the heavens. God is their reward.

A second biblical passage that may be in focus here is Jesus' warning that "whoever denies me before others, I also will deny before my Father in heaven."[20] The idea is clear that between these two sayings of Jesus there is a strand of teaching that calls for total commitment. This commitment may ultimately lead to some form of persecution or even to martyrdom, which should be viewed as a legitimate, if not an anticipated, outcome of living a righteous and committed Christian life in a sinful world.

The oracle that Tertullian quotes, then, appears to be a more specific restatement of this strand of Jesus' teaching, but with a slightly different emphasis. Jesus spoke before the fact of persecution. The oracle itself

FIGURE 5

MESSENGER FORMULA (Conjectured)	(*The Spirit says*)
(A) ASSERTION Rationale	It is good for you to be publicly exposed. For he who is not exposed among men is exposed in the Lord.
(B) EXHORTATION Rationale	Do not be disturbed; Righteousness brings you before the public.
(B′) RHETORICAL QUESTION	Why are you disturbed when you are receiving praise?
(A′) ASSERTION	There is opportunity [*potestas*] when you are observed by men.

appears to have come after persecution had begun and after those who received the oracle had been confounded by the experience. Furthermore, the element of opportunity—or more literally, of power—is raised. Those who experience persecution for the sake of righteousness will also note a corresponding rise in power. As to what the object of that power might be, we may only speculate. It may be the power to rise above the effects of the suffering and appropriate the reward of the righteous. More likely, it has to do with the effectiveness of Christian testimony, which when publicly put to the test stands out before those who persecute the righteous.[21]

Tertullian penned his work *On Flight in Persecution* about A.D. 212,[22] and he incorporated this oracle in response to the question whether a Christian was permitted to flee when persecution comes. In the ninth chapter of this work, he argued that if one wanted to justify such a flight from persecution by using the examples of the apostles, particularly Paul or John, one could not find such a justification. The apostles did not command that Christians flee from city to city.[23] Paul pleaded with Christians to shine like children of light, not hide like children of darkness.[24] In a similar fashion, John had argued that "perfect love casts out fear" (1 John 4:18). Tertullian's comment on this verse was, "who will flee from persecution, but the one who fears? Who will fear, but the one who has not loved?"[25]

Tertullian did not allow the words of Jesus recorded in Matt. 10:23 to be raised against him in this argument. He understood Jesus' words to have been specific to their context. "The declarations of the Lord," he argued, "have reasons and laws of their own."[26] His command had no universal force or implication. The interpreter of Matt. 10:23 must conclude that the verse was specific to the times and circumstances in which the first-century apostles, not third-century Christians, found themselves.[27]

Tertullian went on to query of his reader, Fabius, "But if you consult the Spirit, what does he approve more than that word of the Spirit?" Nearly all of the Spirit's words, Tertullian claimed, "exhort to martyrdom, not to flight, as we are also reminded by his saying."[28]

Tertullian's treatment of this oracle, which, although it makes its appearance among the Montanist *testimonia*, is considered to be genuine, reveals several important insights. First, Tertullian claims that it was given by the Spirit. Since it was an oracle most probably offered some time in the last quarter of the second century, Tertullian's recognition of the Spirit as its source points to his belief that practical guidance for Christians could be obtained directly from the Spirit, guidance that apparently posed no threat to his understanding of a developing canon and/or the existing *regulae fidei*. Furthermore, his assertion that this oracle was from the Spirit indicates his own belief that it was a genuine prophetic exhortation.

Second, Tertullian was writing to someone whom he believed to be already aware of this same oracle. He addressed the saying as "that oracle," and his use of the demonstrative suggests specificity. He is not referring to just any oracle, but to a specific oracle: "that oracle." His words may carry the force that transforms his statement into a comment like "the famous oracle" or "the oracle with which we are both familiar." Hence, he expected a genuine response from Fabius when he asked the question, "If you consult the Spirit, what does He approve more than that word of the Spirit?" The anticipated reply would be "nothing more. The Spirit does not encourage flight, but rather, endurance in the face of persecution."

Third, since Fabius was apparently also aware of the oracle that Tertullian has cited, the oracle must have been (1) widely known in the church of North Africa in some form of oral tradition or (2) it had been written down and circulated among the members of the church. If it is a direct quotation of an oracle delivered by Montanus himself, it would have come from Asia Minor some forty or more years earlier. It probably belonged to a corpus of written prophetic material that circulated in North Africa during Tertullian's day.

Fourth, there is no known reference to Montanus as the one through whom this oracle had been delivered. Tertullian mentions it simply as a genuine utterance received from the Spirit, but he makes no mention of the one through whom the Spirit had spoken. That it may be easily accepted as an oracle of the New Prophecy seems fairly clear. Tertullian commented in his treatise *The Chaplet* that just as most Christians who served in Caesar's army "have refused the prophesies [sic] of the same Holy Spirit [they] intend to reject the martyrdoms too."[29] This work, like his *On Flight in Persecution,* is a work that dates from the period in which he was associated with the New Prophecy. The concerns are parallel; the messages comparable. It would seem odd that so many Christians would choose to ignore the "genuine" oracles of the Spirit, those which the orthodox church might accept. However, should these oracles come as the claim of the Spirit speaking through the questionable New Prophets at the close of the second century and the dawn of the third, they might easily be ignored.[30]

Finally, it may be argued that the prophecy or oracle was so widely known that it was considered to have general implications for nearly all Christians. Tertullian seems to suggest this was the case. This oracle bore repetition, he wrote, for "nearly all his [the Spirit's] words exhort to martyrdom not to flight." But Labriolle is helpful at this point by observing that Tertullian was no doubt exaggerating. "It is," after all, "an address of encouragement to a confessor who suffers for the faith."[31] Although this oracle was used to exhort many people to desire a death in martyrdom, it is probably inaccurate to assume that nearly all North African Christians could be incited to follow its paraenesis. Nevertheless, this oracle may have left many beleaguered and battered Christians facing heavy persecution and suffering, with their spirits upbuilt, their hearts encouraged, and their minds consoled. There was, after all, a purpose to all this chaos, for God had spoken.

[2.]
> Wish not to die in your beds
>   nor   in miscarriages
>   and   mild fevers,
>   but   in martyrdoms,
> that he who has suffered for you
>   may be glorified.[32]

This paraenetic oracle[33] is both simple and straightforward. It comes within the same context as the previous one. The person or persons originally addressed in this oracle were encouraged to view the death of martyrs with desire, because through a martyr's death they would bring glory to Christ who had suffered for them. Like the previous oracle, this one seems to have developed along the lines of a biblical passage. The most likely candidate is 1 Pet. 4:15–16, which exhorts the Christians of the dispersion in Asia Minor: "But let none of you suffer as a murderer, a thief, a criminal, or even as a mischief-maker. Yet if any of you suffers as a Christian, do not consider it a disgrace, but glorify God because you bear this name."[34] Froehlich, I believe, has rightly called this an exhortation to the *imitatio Christi* and more.[35] In this oracle, Montanus encourages the desire for martyrdom in the *imitatio Christi*. What is not the case is a clear statement by Montanus that his followers are to seek martyrdom.

Evidently the oracle describes or depicts a concern among adherents of the New Prophecy. Should they avoid martyrdom or should they embrace it when it lies before them? Labriolle suggests that not only does the Spirit convey support for martyrdom to those who may have heard this oracle but also the Spirit goes far beyond a passive support of martyrdom to exhort them actively to desire or embrace it as the best, if not the only, form of death that can have meaning.[36] Any other form of death pales into insignificance in comparison, and the underlying assumption that no other form of death appears to bring much, if any, glory to Christ is clear. Thus, this oracle appears on the surface, at least, to be quite severe. The actual words of the oracle belie this interpretation, however, as does the context in which we find them.

Tertullian has moved from a discussion on the general role of the suffering of righteous Christians evidenced in the previous oracle to a more specific form of suffering, namely, death by martyrdom. This oracle is connected to the previous one by the simple phrase "so also elsewhere." Thus, in his move from the general subject of suffering to the specific subject of martyrdom, Tertullian tries to lead his reader logically and progressively to the point where Fabius will accept his argument.

In addition to this line of logic, the oracle under consideration parallels the previous one at several points. Like the previous oracle, this one, by implication, is attributed to the Spirit. In this case, Tertullian included it among the "divine exhortations" of God.[37] While it, too, was most probably circulated in written form among certain Christians of North Africa, it may not be from the same source as the previous oracle, as is indicated by the phrase "so also elsewhere," although it may have appeared elsewhere within a volume containing a variety of New Prophecy teachings and prophecies. Finally, just as with the previous oracle, Tertullian sought to use this oracle of the Spirit to encourage Fabius, the confessor, to persevere in his confession even to martyrdom if that were necessary.

That this particular oracle held an important position in Tertullian's thought is evident not only by its inclusion in the present argument as substantiating what was previously taught by the apostles but also by his inclusion of it in paraphrased form in his *On the Soul* 55.5. There it takes part in his argument surrounding the differences that may be observed between a pagan and a Christian at the time of death. In fact, this oracle is related to the same overall argument he drew from Saturus's vision to support it.

The immediate context of Tertullian's paraphrase of this oracle reads in the following manner:

> Notice, therefore, the difference between the pagan and faithful man in death! If you should die in God, as the Paraclete instructs, not in mild fevers and on your beds, but in martyrdoms, if you take up your cross and follow the Lord as he himself commands (cf. Matt. 10:38; 16:34), your blood is the complete key of Paradise. [38]

From this passage several similarities as well as several differences are to be noted when this reference is compared with the oracle as it occurs in *On Flight in Persecution*. This reference is clearly a paraphrase, not a direct quotation. But there are enough similarities to convince us that we are dealing with the same oracle. Among them are his references to the terms "in bed" and "mild fevers," although the word order of the latter is reversed. In this case, death in bed or death resulting from fevers is apparently something to be avoided, whereas martyrdom is something to be embraced. The significant omission from the paraphrase includes death in abortion or childbirth. Similarly, in the paraphrase, there is a new emphasis on taking up one's cross, following the Lord, and coming through to full martyrdom by which one may enter Paradise. Thus, the cross to be borne is clearly the cross of martyrdom, and the reward to be obtained is Paradise. Tertullian, then, pushes Montanus's words further than their original intent, thereby encouraging martyrdom.

Finally, there is one other significant difference in the contexts of these two passages. In Tertullian's *On Flight in Persecution*, the inference is that this oracle has come from the Spirit. In the present passage from *On the Soul*, Tertullian has introduced the paraphrased oracle as a word of counsel from the Paraclete. While it is clear that Spirit and Paraclete in these passages are to be understood as equivalents—that is, the Holy Spirit is the Paraclete to whom Tertullian is making reference—it also seems that Tertullian's "New Prophecy" interests have surfaced here.

Tertullian's message is clear. He knows of at least two oracles that he believes exhort Christians to endure the difficulties and hardships or persecution. He intends to exhort Fabius, the confessor, to remain faithful, and he does so by citing the examples and teachings of the apostles Paul and John. To supplement his argument, he maintains that another famous oracle teaches the same thing. Indeed, wherever the Spirit speaks, one can expect consistency. Since Paul and John encourage endurance over flight, and the Spirit, by revelation, says the same thing, the message is to be viewed as normative. And as if one oracle is insufficient to support his point, Tertullian is prepared to cite a second one that supports it even more convincingly. The second oracle seems to be a favorite of his, for he alludes to it in another of his works as well, *On the Soul* (55.5):

[3.]

> The Church can pardon sin
> but I   will not do it
> lest they also commit other offenses.[39]

It is difficult to approach this "oracle" without thinking of Jesus' words to Peter: "And I tell you, you are Peter, and on this rock I will build my church, and the gates of Hades will not prevail against it. I will give you the keys of the kingdom of heaven, and whatever you bind on earth will be bound in heaven, and whatever you loose on earth will be loosed in heaven" (Matt. 16:18–19). It may be that the original setting in which this "oracle" was uttered involved the discussion and application or an appeal to this passage in support of pardons. What we do know for certain is that Tertullian acknowledged this oracle as originating from "the Paraclete Himself" in the persons of "the new prophets."[40] This is to be understood, then, as a genuine oracle of the New Prophecy. The names of the "new prophets" are not given, but the appearance of the oracle in this context would lead one to believe that this oracle dates from the earliest days of the New Prophecy in Asia Minor and may have been part of a circulating tradition among those in North Africa who embraced the New Prophecy.

The oracle is given in the first person singular with the assertion, "I will not do it." On the surface, at least, the reader may be confused about the identity of the speaker. The oracle is meant to convey the idea that, while the church is able to remit sins, the Paraclete, who speaks through the new prophet, is opposed to such action. The oracle consists of the theological claim that the church has the power or authority to remit sins, followed by further elaboration that reveals why this power will not be exercised. It may be lawful for the church to forgive, but there are factors that render it inexpeditious to do so.

In one way, this saying appears to be less a prophetic oracle than it is a teaching for which the inspiration of the Paraclete is claimed. This position may be supported by the fact that it would be doubtful the Holy Spirit would have inspired such a saying which seems to contradict or work against itself. Why would the church be given the power to pardon sins on the one hand, but be asked to withhold that pardon on the other? The answer appears to be that those who know sins will be punished rather than forgiven will be kept from sinning. In short, the oracle or teaching was employed to support a policy of deterrence.

Eusebius records an incident cited by Apollonius that demonstrates Tertullian's concerns. There was a man named Alexander who called himself a martyr. Apollonius claimed that, in fact, Alexander was a robber who ran with a woman prophet associated with the New Prophecy. While relating the story of Alexander and the prophet, Apollonius asked, "Which of these forgives the sins of the other? Does the prophet the robberies of the martyr, or the martyr the covetousness of the prophet?"[41] The forgiving of sins to which Apollonius refers would appear to be a frequent occurrence that Tertullian understood as encouraging the continuation of sinful acts. To claim the inspiration of the Spirit for an oracle or to teach that which questions the expediency of frequent or flimsy forgiveness was to invoke divine criticism of "cheap grace."

Tertullian's *On Modesty*, in which this saying appears, was apparently occasioned about A.D. 212 by the issuance of an edict by one described ironically as the "*Pontifex maximus*" (that is, "bishop of bishops").[42] The edict announced that the bishop remitted the sins of adulterers and fornicators for those who had duly satisfied the requirements of repentance. Tertullian disapproved of the edict.

The immediate context in which this saying lies is addressed to the bishop, and it calls into question the ability of anyone but God to forgive such sins.[43] To carry the argument one step further, Tertullian suggested that even if he conceded that the apostles (21.3) or the ancient prophets (21.5) had forgiven sins, this could be done only because they possessed the power of God to do so, as was evidenced by their ability to perform miracles. The apostles had raised the dead, healed the sick, and inflicted plagues on such people as Elymas the sorcerer and Ananias. Likewise, the prophets had granted pardon for murder and adultery, but they, like the apostles, had manifest "proofs of severity."[44]

At this point in his argument, Tertullian put a challenge to his opponent, "Apostolic sir," to exhibit as a sample of this power his own "prophetic evidences" so that Tertullian might be convinced of his power to forgive such sins.[45] If, however, he should lack such power as might be demonstrated by his inability to exhibit either prophetic or apostolic evidences on his behalf, then Tertullian would be forced to conclude that the bishop merely possessed not the power of God to forgive, but the discipline and the duty to minister that discipline.[46]

Tertullian anticipated the bishop's response: but "the Church has the power of forgiving sins,"[47] which would make possible a logical argument by which the bishops in some sense constituted the church. This point (that the church could forgive sins) Tertullian readily acknowledged; and noting that, he cited the oracle under consideration. Yet again, Tertullian raised a rhetorical question on behalf of the bishop: "What if a pseudo-prophetic spirit has made this declaration?"[48] This charge he just as readily discounted on the grounds that it would have been the role of a true subverter to encourage both clemency and loose living. Moreover, even if one were to grant that a "pseudo-prophetic spirit" wished to effect this line of thought, following the "Spirit of truth," then "it follows that the 'Spirit of truth' has indeed the power of indulgently granting pardon to fornicators, but will not to do it if it involves evil to the majority."[49] Following this argument, Tertullian moved on to provide his own understanding of Matt. 16:18–19.

From his use of this oracle, delivered by the new prophets, it is clear that Tertullian believed he quoted a genuine word from the Paraclete. But Tertullian was equally convinced that the bishop he addressed would not judge this oracle to be genuine. In a sense, he was engaged merely in a rhetorical argument, but he believed his case could be sustained by other means. Tertullian's use of the oracle was of a secondary nature. Its primary role was to act as a supporting argument to his main point that he believed could be demonstrated by the appropriate exegesis of Matt. 16:18–19. After all, Christ had conferred this power personally upon Peter, but it was not a power to bind or to loose the "capital sins of the faithful."[50] Rather, it had to do with which portions of the law would be abandoned by the church and which ones would be preserved. It was to "spiritual people" that this power had been granted, the apostles and prophets. The church did not consist merely in a number of bishops, but it was the church of the Spirit that involved spiritual people who would truly forgive sins.[51] It is evident that part of the struggle in which Tertullian was engaged was the interface between Spirit and structure, office and spontaneity. But Tertullian firmly believed "there were certain sins which they [the bishops] could not forgive,"[52] and if they chose to claim that they had such powers, their actions would be to the detriment of the church.

Finally, it is clear this oracle helped to maintain a belief held within the North African church that could be applied to the question of the *lapsi* if needed. The tendency among North African adherents to the New Prophecy was to take the more stringent approach to the question of sin, especially concerning the *lapsi,* and this oracle seems to have supported a more stringent line.

[4.]

> For purification produces harmony
> and they [the pure] see visions
> and when they turn their faces downward
> they also hear salutary voices
> as clear as they are secret.[53]

That this is an early Montanist oracle is clear from Tertullian's attribution of it to "the holy prophetess Prisca."[54] The *Sitz-im-Leben* in which it was originally given is unknown, but it is probable that we are here dealing with an oracle which had been preserved in written form for some forty years before it was included in Tertullian's work.

In his *On Exhortation to Chastity*, Tertullian addressed a Christian friend who had recently become a widower, advising him to remain single. His reason was that this man's continence would be a means by which he could gain holiness. By denying the flesh he could gain the Spirit.[55]

Tertullian held that any sexual contact was a carnal act. He cited Scripture as teaching Christians to be spiritual rather than carnal, holy rather than unholy, and as such, he concluded, it was better to remain free than it was to remarry. After all, one could while single concentrate more fully on spiritual things.

Tertullian's primary basis of support for this position was first and foremost his interpretation of several passages of Scripture. From what he described as the "prophetic voice" of the "Old Testament" he cited Lev. 11:44, "be holy, for I am holy," and he continued his retinue of proof texts by quoting from Ps. 18:25–26. He finished his argument from Scripture by citing Paul in Rom. 8:6, "To set the mind on the flesh is death, but to set the mind on the Spirit is eternal in Christ Jesus our Lord."[56]

In 1 Cor. 7:5, Paul had written that Christian couples might appropriately refuse one another sexual contact by mutual agreement and for a limited time so that they could devote themselves to prayer. Tertullian believed that Paul intended his readers to understand this as a positive means of growth in spirituality. Tertullian codified what Paul only conceded. Tertullian, then, argued the negative side of Paul's intention here. Paul wrote to a situation in which some Christians apparently chose to subdue *all* sexual desires, even within the bonds of marriage, to the extent that some partners were being tempted into immorality. But for Tertullian, the efficacy of prayer was obviously improved through abstinence. How much more so could it be improved through complete continence![57]

It is at this point that Tertullian introduced the oracle attributed to Prisca. The previous passages from the Old Testament were said to have been given by the "prophetic voice." This had been followed by a citation from the apostle. In short, the point had been established from what he had otherwise called "spiritual men," and he moved on to identify Prisca in the same light as the "holy prophetess." From Tertullian's perspective, then, Prisca continued to function in the same tradition as the prophets and apostles, the primary difference being that she prophesied later.[58]

Lawlor has pointed out, and rightfully so, that this oracle "does not enjoin the annulling of marriages already contracted."[59] It is thought, rather, to be a call to continence addressed primarily to the single Christian, whether never married or widowed. It is interesting to note, however, that the words for continence (*continentia* or *temperantia*) are totally missing from this oracle. Instead, the word *purificantia*, a rare word, is used. Thus, it is actually purity that is enjoined.[60] This understanding is further substantiated by the remarks by Tertullian as he introduced this oracle, that "the holy minister should know how to administer purity of life."[61] *Sanctimonia* and *sanctitas* are both synonyms with purity and are works wrought by the Spirit.[62]

The New Prophecy was said to have annulled marriages.[63] Likewise, it is thought to have employed an order of virgins.[64] Whether this oracle was originally addressed specifically to the question of annulment or the question of second marriages, however, is impossible to say. Yet, that is the interpretation and the usage we find in Tertullian. Purity can encompass continence, but it would not seem necessary to equate purity with continence.

If this should be the case, the oracle may have had a wider sphere of application than Tertullian chose to relate. It could be said that it called Christians to a total life-style commitment to the concept that Christians could actually be holy even as their heavenly Father is holy and that if they would submit to this expectation they could be the beneficiaries of God's grace and charismata.

Labriolle has indicated that Priscilla's prophecy is reminiscent of Joel 2:28.[65] Thus, those who have submitted to the ministry of the Spirit, a ministry of purity, are to become recipients of both visionary and auditory phenomena. Hence, the prophetic oracle of Priscilla could be interpreted as teaching that Christians are those who are eligible for "charismatic" gifts. These charismata may come in the form of visions (visions and visions yielding prophecies) or in auditory forms (word of wisdom, word of knowledge, prophecy, tongues, and interpretation of tongues). The reference to the bowed heads suggests a humble stance before God. As Christians submit to the work of the Spirit in moral improvement, growth in holiness or sanctification, and as they humble themselves before God, they can experience the fulfillment of Joel's prophecy.

There are two words Tertullian employs to describe these experiences.

They are, first of all, *salutares*. That is, they are found "to be truly profitable for their moral improvement."[66] Second, they are *occultas*: hidden, secret, or mysterious. It would seem, then, that these voices would not always be understood or that their words would have to undergo a process of interpretation. This would tend to support the idea that such gifts as prophecy, tongues, and the interpretation of tongues are in view here. Each of these gifts, prophecy and tongues, at times needs clarification or interpretation.

[5.]

> They are   flesh
> and they hate the flesh.[67]

As has been the case with the other oracles cited by Tertullian, very little of the original *Sitz-im-Leben* in which this oracle was given has been shared with us. Yet, just as in the cases of the previous oracles, at least two facts regarding the present oracle may be affirmed. First, Tertullian believed that this oracle was a genuine oracle or utterance whose source was the Paraclete. Second, like the one we have just analyzed, it has been attributed to the prophet Prisca.[68] If this is the case, once again, the oracle is at least four decades old and it comes from Asia Minor.

There is a strong possibility that this oracle originated in a context in which there were present within the church those who were teaching a docetic form of the faith. J. G. Davies has suggested that the New Prophecy as a whole arose in order to combat heresy and that this oracle in particular was aimed at a docetic group of heretics.[69] This suggestion is supported in the final chapter of Tertullian's *On the Resurrection of the Flesh* by the statement that God, by pouring out the Spirit upon all flesh (Joel 2:28), has "animated the struggling faith in the resurrection of the flesh."[70] Indeed, God has "dispersed all the former ambiguities . . . by the new prophecy which is overflowing from the Paraclete."[71]

Tertullian's assessment of this oracle was that it was a "splendid," "brilliant," or "shrewd" saying.[72] Clearly, then, he had a high regard for the wisdom it represented, particularly since he believed that it held relevance to the heresy against which he was writing. But this attitude may also reflect how Tertullian felt about many of the Phrygian oracles to which he had access, again pointing to the possibility that they had been preserved in some written form to his own day.

The treatise in which this oracle makes its appearance addressed the heresy which asserted that only the soul could experience immortality, whereas the body would disappear in corruption. Tertullian confronted this idea squarely by stating in his opening sentence that "The resurrection of the dead is the Christian trust."[73] By that statement, Tertullian meant the resurrection of the body.

Tertullian argued his position point by point. The body was created by God even before it became a living soul. God took great care in forming the flesh, for one day Christ, too, would become human flesh; and the flesh is nobler than its origin, dust, because of God's manipulation of it. Indeed, the flesh now enables the soul to act out its desires in the flesh.[74]

His argument then moved on from his interpretation of the Genesis accounts of creation to the unique significance of the flesh for Christianity. No soul ever finds salvation apart from the flesh, he maintained. Furthermore, it is the flesh that is baptized, anointed, signed, imposed, and martyred.[75] How can all this be true, he asked, and not experience resurrection? How can the flesh "so often brought near to God, not rise again?"[76]

Finally, Tertullian took his argument to Scripture. Although there were passages within Scripture that spoke disparagingly of the flesh, there were also passages that spoke highly of the flesh. As examples, Tertullian cited Isaiah's comment (Isa. 40:7) that "all flesh is grass" and contrasted it with Isaiah's other comment (Isa. 40:5) that "All flesh shall see the salvation of God." Similarly, he contrasted the LXX reading of Gen. 6:3 with Joel 2:28 (M.T. 3:1). He concluded that Paul spoke disparagingly of the *acts* of the flesh (Rom. 8:18; Gal. 5:17) but that Paul spoke highly of the flesh itself. After all, it carries the marks of the Lord Jesus (Gal. 6:17), is the temple of God (1 Cor. 3:16), and becomes a member of Christ (1 Cor. 6:15). And Paul exhorted his readers to glorify God in their bodies (1 Cor. 6:20).[77] Thus, he asked those who hold to the final corruption of the flesh,

> If, therefore, the humiliations of the flesh thrust off its resurrection, why shall not its high prerogatives rather avail to bring it about?—since it better suits the character of God to restore to salvation what for a while He rejected than to surrender to perdition what He once approved.[78]

Thus, Tertullian's arguments for the resurrection of the flesh were both biblical and theological. At this point he broke off the argument to speak out against the inconsistency of his opponents. In part, their inconsistency lay in how they chose to live their lives. Tertullian's concerns were not purely theological; they were as clearly directed to the subject of Christian praxis and discipline. He argued that his opponents actually catered to the flesh, while at the same time denying that it would be resurrected. They did so by despising discipline, and they held no belief in the reality of the punishment of the flesh.[79]

Here, then, was where the prophecy of Prisca came into play. It provided no new theological insight. It neither comforted nor encouraged. It merely provided a parallel between the opponents whom Tertullian faced at the moment and a group about whom Prisca had spoken nearly half a century earlier in Asia Minor: "They are flesh, and they hate the flesh." The inconsistency of what they taught and how they acted had been exposed.[80] Perhaps Tertullian even expected his opponents to change as a result of this revelation corroborated by the Paraclete.[81] For his opponents not to act would mean that this oracle should be understood as a "judgment" oracle.[82] Scripture had not convinced them. Perhaps this revelation would.

[6.]	For	God	brought	forth the Word . . .
	as	the root	brings	forth the tree,
	and	a fountain		a stream,
	and	the sun		a ray.[83]

Tertullian's *Against Praxeas* is important to our understanding of the New Prophecy for the picture it gives of the interaction between that sect and the bishop of Rome. Tertullian's contention was that for a time the bishop of Rome, most likely Eleutherus (A.D. 174–189), had been favorably disposed toward the prophetic gifts of Montanus, Prisca, and Maximilla to the extent that by formal letter he had admitted certain New Prophecy churches of Asia and Phrygia to communion.

Later, the bishop, now Victor (A.D. 189ff), was greatly influenced by Praxeas to withdraw the letter of admission to these churches. This was accomplished in a two-pronged approach. First, Praxeas set forth what Tertullian called "false accusations" against the prophets thereby undermining the legitimate expression of their charismata as well as their churches. He also insisted on the authority of Eleutherus's predecessors who had not granted such a letter of admission. The end result was that Praxeas successfully convinced Victor to withdraw support for the New Prophecy, while Praxeas, himself, gained a foothold for his own ideas concerning Patripassianism.[84]

Tertullian's summary of this action was that "Praxeas attended to two matters of the devil at Rome: he expelled prophecy and introduced heresy; he put the Paraclete to flight and crucified the Father."[85] Subsequently, those members of the New Prophecy, who followed the Paraclete, acknowledged the action of the Roman bishop and withdrew from communion with Rome.[86]

Tertullian's primary concern with Praxeas, however, was not his perspectives on the New Prophecy (he had an argument for that) so much as it was the introduction of Patripassianism. It had gained a foothold in

North Africa, a foothold that needed attention. Thus, Tertullian responded to Praxeas's assertion that the Father had been born and suffered in the person of Jesus Christ by noting that he, and others with him, believed only in one God who "has also a Son, His Word, who proceeded from Himself."[87] Tertullian affirmed through a type of *regula fidei*, creedal in form, that it was the Son who had been born, being both human and God, and that it was he who had suffered and died and been raised up by the Father.[88] The interesting thing to note, however, is that Tertullian claimed that while he had always held to this *regula fidei*, he was able the more to affirm it "since we have been better instructed by the Paraclete, who leads men indeed into all truth."[89] Furthermore, within this same *regula fidei*, he equated the Paraclete with the Holy Spirit.

We might ask, in what way did the Paraclete instruct those who heard him on such topics as the Trinity? It may well be that what we have in the saying or oracle under examination is exactly that, a statement on the Trinity, although, as Pelikan has clearly noted, it is a statement whose contribution toward a fully developed doctrine of the Trinity is extremely meagre.[90] Yet, the fact of the matter is that Tertullian acknowledged the source of this saying as "the Paraclete."[91] That various persons of the Trinity were mentioned in other oracles—indeed, that the whole Trinity was mentioned in a single oracle—lends credibility to Tertullian's statement suggesting that even in matters as intricate as Trinitarian doctrine the Paraclete was understood to be at work providing clarification.[92]

It is not completely clear that we have here a prophetic utterance from the Spirit-Paraclete. There is a possibility that this is no more than a teaching of Montanus, the Paraclete. Labriolle, for instance, has argued that in the first two chapters of *Against Praxeas*, Tertullian has used the term to refer to the one who inspired Montanus, Maximilla, and Prisca to prophesy. It is the Holy Spirit. Yet, in the passage under consideration, Labriolle concludes that without a doubt the Paraclete mentioned by Tertullian is "Paraclet-Montan." Furthermore, the term "oracle" may be a misnomer, even though the saying represents Montanus's own teaching on the subject.[93] It is not possible to establish beyond a doubt that this saying is a prophetic oracle. That it was understood by Tertullian to convey the mind of the Paraclete and therefore the Paraclete's teaching on the Trinity is, however, clear. Furthermore, Tertullian's reference in close proximity to this statement (i.e., in 9.3) clearly equates the Paraclete with the Holy Spirit. Thus, a case that identifies this saying as a prophetic oracle can be made, and, as such, this passage must be studied further.

The immediate context in which this saying appears is heavily influenced by Johannine thought. Tertullian has attempted to demonstrate that the Son has gone forth from the Father, yet they are one. The Son knows the Father completely, unlike the Aeon sent forth from the Valentinian deity. To support this contention, Tertullian has quoted from such passages as Matt. 11:27, which declares that only the Son knows the Father; John 1:18, which states that the Son unfolded "the Father's bosom"; John 8:26, which acknowledges that the Son knows and declares what the Father has made known to him; John 6:38, which affirms that the Son came to do the will of the Father; as well as John 1:1, 10:30, and 14:11, each of which affirms the deity of the Word and/or the unity of the Godhead.

Only after he has made his point from the biblical text does he introduce what the Paraclete has said. His argument is to be secondary and supportive of his understanding of the biblical text. It is to provide a more contemporary illustration of a truth he believes has already been established. The Paraclete declares a simple theological statement supported by three similes, each drawn from the realm of nature and each designed, according to Tertullian's argument, to demonstrate procession while maintaining a unity of substance. The root brings forth a tree, a river proceeds from a spring or fountain, and a ray of light makes its way from the sun. In like manner, God brought forth the Word.[94]

From the actual quotation of this saying, Tertullian moves on to interpret and apply it so as to make his theological point regarding the procession of the Son from the Father in the Trinitarian unity. Thus, he does not hesitate to identify the tree, or the river, or the ray with the Son, "because every original source is a parent and everything which issues from the origin is an offspring." Furthermore, both root and tree, like fountain and river, and ray and sun remain connected, "nor, indeed, is the Word separated from God."[95] Yet, even as they are not separated, the Word and God or the Son and the Father, like the various features in each of the Paraclete's analogies they are distinctly two things, but correlatively joined. Thus, "everything which proceeds from something else must needs be second to that from which it proceeds, without being on that account separated."[96]

Finally, Tertullian moves the analogy one step further in each of these similes to accommodate the presence of the Spirit. The tree that sprang from the root produces fruit, the fountain-produced river yields a stream, and the sun's ray an apex. Similarly, the Spirit is third, from Father and Son. Nothing of the three is alien from the other. Hence, "the Trinity, flowing down from the Father through intertwined and connected steps does not at all disturb the Monarchy whilst it at the same time guards the state of the economy."[97] His argument is complete. The saying, by extrapolation, has enabled him to describe his idea of the "economic" Trinity.

Yet, even the aspects of the saying that are so interpreted by Tertullian may have had their background in Scripture. The actual teaching that the Word proceeded from the Father certainly has its roots in the Johannine Prologue (John 1:1–18). Ernest Evans has pointed out the relationship between Heb. 1:3 and the simile of the sun and rays as well as the relationship between John 7:38–39a and the fountain-stream simile.[98] Pelikan has also suggested that it is possible the root-tree simile is built on the example of Isa. 11:1.[99]

We must conclude, then, that the usage of this saying has been consistent with the ways in which Tertullian has employed other oracles of the Paraclete obtained by prophetic utterance through the various prophets of the New Prophecy. Neither is this word at odds with Scripture. Its function appears to be that of providing contemporary, *ad hoc*, secondary support derived from a prophetic oracle and applying it to a particular theological position where help was needed. Finally, Tertullian once again affirms the *regula fidei* in which the Father, Son, and Holy Spirit are inseparable from one another, an affirmation that has been all the more easy to make, since, according to Tertullian, the Paraclete has so instructed the church.[100]

TERTULLIAN'S USE
OF CONTEMPORARY VISIONS

In the previous section our attention was focused on certain visions, oracles, and sayings that were cited in several of Tertullian's works. Most of these oracles had originated as "Paraclete sayings" in the early days of the New Prophecy in Asia Minor. Most of these oracles had been re-corded, then made their way into that facet of North African church life represented by Tertullian and his friends. Only the vision that Tertullian incorrectly ascribed to Perpetua had originated in North Africa, and it, too, had been recorded for posterity.

There were other visions of which Tertullian was equally conscious. These originated in the church at Carthage, and they functioned uniquely within that setting. In at least two instances, Tertullian took the time to record these visions and use them to support his written arguments. The first of these was a vision seen by a woman with whom Tertullian was personally acquainted. It was incorporated into his *On the Soul,* written about A.D. 212, a treatise in which he also had occasion to cite Saturus's vision (55.4) and the paraphrase of an early Montanist oracle (55.5) at which we have already looked. The second of these visions was recorded in his *On the Veiling of Virgins* (17.3). It, too, was seen by a female worshipper. In this chapter we shall analyze these two visions.

THE VISION OF THE SOUL

One of the most fascinating examples of prophetic phenomena to appear in the writings of Tertullian is found in his *On the Soul.* It is fascinating on two counts. First, the context in which the vision lies includes a description of the situation in which the vision was originally experienced, the *Sitz-im-Leben;* and second, it provides a clear example of the value of such phenomena for his theological argument.

Tertullian wrote *On the Soul* to combat heresy. He was frustrated by the ever-present reality of false teaching in the church. Heresies tried his strength, although they played a positive role, in his thinking, by provid-ing a vivid backdrop against which the truth would stand out.[1] Since the philosophers had been the source of such heresies as the denial of the immortality of the soul and since they had raised doubts concerning the soul's form, substance, and various faculties, as well as its origin and its ultimate destination (3.2), Tertullian felt that he was compelled to respond. Furthermore, he believed nothing should be accepted that did not agree with what he termed "the true system of prophecy which has arisen in this present age."[2]

He began the treatise with a brief discussion on the origin of the soul, noting that it was God who had breathed on the human form the breath of life, whereby it became a living soul. Hence, he concluded, the soul did not have its point of origin in matter (3.4; cf. Gen. 2:17). That question being settled, Tertullian moved on to a discussion of the condition or state of the soul. The soul, as he put it, was a "spiritual essence," a fact he willingly acknowledged had also been demonstrated by Stoic philosophy. Yet, the soul could also be described as a "corporeal substance" (5.2). After citing several other philosophers who held this same position, Tertullian concluded that "the soul is endued with a body" (5.6).

As he turned from the reasoning of philosophy, he did so to embrace the teachings of the church. His next move was to attempt a demonstration of the truth of the corporeal nature of the soul by citing two examples from Scripture. The first passage he chose was the Lukan account of Lazarus and the rich man immediately following their deaths (Luke 16:19–31, esp. vv. 23–24). Tertullian noted that the biblical text mentioned the rich man's request for Lazarus to dip his finger into water and bring it to the rich man. "Unless the soul possessed corporeality," he argued, "the image of a soul could not possibly contain a finger of a bodily substance, nor would the Scripture feign a statement about the limbs of a body, if these had no existence" (7.2). In short, his literal interpretation of the text of the Gospel led him to the conclusion that the biblical text taught the corporeality of the soul in Hades. Furthermore, he contended that logic would yield the conclusion he had reached from this text. "Whatever is incorporeal," he argued, "is incapable of being kept or guarded in any way; it is also exempt from either punishment or refreshment" (7:3–4).

Tertullian's second argument was based on Rev. 6:9–11. He had stated that the corporeal nature of the soul was invisible to the flesh, but quite visible to the spirit. John the apostle had provided proof of this when he wrote that "while he was in the Spirit of God, [he] beheld plainly the souls of the martyrs" (8.5).

From his arguments based on Scripture, Tertullian moved on to summarize his own position and then to point out that by arguing for the corporeality of the soul he wanted to note that the soul had both accidents and dimensions of form—that is, length, breadth, and height. "We inscribe on the soul the lineaments of corporeity," he went on, "not simply from the assurance which reasoning has taught us of its corporeal nature, but also from the firm conviction which divine grace impresses on us by revelation" (9.3).

It is at this point that he introduced as corroborating evidence of his position, the account of a certain woman and her vision. From his language, it seems probable that Tertullian was personally acquainted with the woman he described, for he noted that she was "among us," and the detail which he uses to describe the context in which the vision was seen, tends to confirm a firsthand knowledge.[3]

In any case, he claimed that he, and others with him, acknowledged spiritual gifts or charismata, in particular prophetic gifts, and that this woman had been favored with various gifts of revelation. While he did not name these gifts, it is not unthinkable that visions and prophecies, perhaps even tongues or the interpretation of tongues might have been among them. In this particular passage the unnamed woman was said to receive a vision in which some oracular utterance was given. Tertullian incorporates as evidence for his argument the description of the vision and its message. Furthermore, his close linkage between the point that "we" have merited the attainment of prophetic gifts and the sister who experienced gifts of revelation of which one such manifestation was visions, should be sufficient to demonstrate that her vision was a result of the prophetic gift.

From Tertullian's language it is clear that this woman was no novice in the use of prophetic gifts. Her ability was routinely engaged for the benefit of the local congregation, or at least for a portion of that congregation. It was done on the Lord's Day, and on this particular occasion it happened at the conclusion of the regular service. It is then that two groups within the church became most visible, for "the people" had been dismissed from the church and the woman reported her experience to another group designated by the pronoun "us." Such a division within the congregation strongly suggests that adherents to the New Prophecy were still a regular part of the worshipping community in Carthage. It is evident that no formal break had yet taken place, although Tertullian's choice of words indicate that there were deeply held ideological differences which separated these groups on occasion.[4]

One such occasion took place at the end of a particular service. This woman may well have been considered a visionary of the "New Prophecy" who received revelations from God within the context of the worshipping congregation. But belief in the legitimacy of such revelations *may* have been the crux of what separated those who were dismissed or who chose to leave from those who stayed to hear her out. Tertullian is clear, in spite of these differences, that her revelations were not indiscriminately accepted. Those who stayed could not be accused of gullibility or of injudiciously accepting any type of oracle prefixed by a "Thus saith the Lord." His statement is direct and to the point in this regard, for, according to Tertullian, all her visions were examined with the most scrupulous care in order that their truth could be tested and probed (9.4). Undoubtedly such analysis took seriously Tertullian's convictions that the Spirit's most recent revelations must be consistent with all previous revelations and that the genuine prophet said only what God wanted to be said, not inserting his or her own "conceits."[5]

It is also clear that Tertullian's examination went further. First, he looked to the person who was involved in the prophetic experience. He described her as a "sister" who dwelt among them, a sister who on numerous occasions had manifested various revelatory charismata, such charismata as were the possession and expectation of believers.[6] Second, he had had sufficient opportunity to observe her life-style and ministry. He noted that she had communicated with angels, and even more significantly, on occasion, he alleged, she had conversed with the Lord himself.

In spite of this woman's spiritual insights and her exposure to the intricacies of the revelatory gifts, Tertullian pronounced her as one who was not so captivated by the spiritual realm that she had lost her relevance to everyday life. He seems to have intended to head off any charge of fanaticism. The woman was concerned with the needs of those around her, and Tertullian bore witness to the fact that when she saw such needs she did her best to satisfy them. It is evident also that she exercised a significant level of wisdom and understanding of life's problems, for Tertullian pronounced her competent to provide counsel. In summary, then, this woman appears, by Tertullian's description, to have been a gifted, balanced, mature Christian woman who served her congregation well in a variety of ways.

Third, Tertullian accepted the method involved when this woman received her revelations. She was described as being "by ecstasy in the Spirit" when she was engaged in the reception of such revelations.[7] Yet, it is clear from the record of this incident that, whatever "by ecstasy in the Spirit" meant, it was not a disorderly phenomenon. She experienced such a vision even while others around her were more centrally involved in a community worship experience. Indeed, Tertullian remarked that she received such revelations sometimes during the singing of psalms, during the reading of Scripture, during the time of prayer, or even while the preacher expounded the Word. As a matter of regular practice, however, she held these revelations until the conclusion of the service, at which time she passed them on to those who chose to hear them. She caused no major disruption to the proceedings around her, but rather waited for the appropriate occasion.[8]

This woman's action appears to be consistent with Paul's observation that "the spirits of the prophets are subject to the prophets" (1 Cor. 14:32). She shared her revelations at an appropriate time, at the end of the regular service. She did not interrupt the normal liturgical order. Tertullian's understanding of Paul apparently did not allow for women speaking out in the formal worship service. He did not take a position prohibiting the *use* of a particular gift such as prophecy. He may, in fact, have encouraged it. But his concern had to do with *when* the charisma was to be expressed. Tertullian and the congregation at Carthage seem to have followed the lead of Paul in this regard, expanding Paul's concern for the orderly use of prophecy by anyone, regardless of gender. For Tertullian it was legitimate for a woman to prophesy, but the time for her to do so was at the end of the service.[9]

Tertullian was concerned also to note that a significant activity in which the community engaged when this woman shared her revelations involved what might be described under the rubric of "discernment of spirits" or, in this particular case, content analysis. As he put it, "her visions are also described very carefully that they may also be tested."[10]

With respect to content, Tertullian remarked that this woman had a number of items to convey, of which he has chosen to incorporate only one (see Figure 6).

At this point we are not privy to the ensuing discussion, if any, that determined whether this word should be accepted as genuine. We are put on notice, however, that this vision and what it purports to teach was judged a genuine revelation by Tertullian. He sums it up with the words, "This was her vision, and for her witness there was God; and the apostle [Paul in 1 Cor. 12:1–11; 13:8–10; etc.] most assuredly foretold that there were to be 'spiritual gifts' in the Church" (9.4).

It must be noted here that, even though I have painted a picture of Tertullian's objectivity in dealing with the testing of prophetic gifts as they appear in this particular account, others have not necessarily been of the same mind. H. J. Lawlor, for example, has argued that Tertullian did not objectively test this revelation at all, but rather that the discussion of the sermon supplied the material for the vision. "It is sufficient to observe," he wrote,

> that the preacher obviously, though he was unconscious that he had done so, produced the vision, while the vision in its turn was adduced to impart divine sanction to the preacher's doctrine. A new tenet was thus added to the official teaching of African Montanism, nominally, by a revelation, really by the personality of Tertullian.[11]

FIGURE 6

THE REVELATION	SUBSTANCE	QUALITY	
SHAPE	A soul was exhibited to me in a spirit appeared,	bodily form,	and but
TEXTURE	it was of a being	not of an empty vacuous quality quality could be grasped soft	and but rather that would suggest it and
COLOR	of the	bright color of the air	and and
SHAPE		resembling the human form in all respects[12]	

That such an assessment must be taken seriously should go without saying. Tertullian himself has noted that it is possible that this particular revelation had been given at the conclusion of a discussion or sermon on the soul. His use of the term *nescio,* however, shows his recollection at this point to be faulty. He was somewhat unsure of the original context, although he did not rule out any contextual discussion of or sermon on the soul. Furthermore, while it is possible for one to argue that psychological suggestion is a logical conclusion to draw from the proximity of a sermon/discussion on the nature of the soul and a revelation of the soul, such a conclusion may not necessarily be the best or the correct conclusion. It is possible, as Tertullian suggests, that here is a legitimate expression of a prophetic gift designed to confirm or explain a previously revealed truth of Scripture. In short, then, the preacher could have been understood as providing a message of exposition and the revelation provided a confirmatory word.[13]

The discussion of this incident thus far has demonstrated that there were a number of Christians in Carthage who attempted to reckon with manifestations of prophetic gifts in their midst. Unfortunately, there is not enough information available on those who were identified with the New Prophecy at Carthage to give more definitive examples of how they tested such revelations. But Tertullian's judgments are clear. It would be difficult to assume that he would have ever accepted the sayings of the New Prophecy without first being satisfied that what he read and heard was in fact true and had judged them to be so. With this in mind, we may now conclude our discussion on how Tertullian employed this particular revelation on the nature of the soul in *On the Soul.*

If the role that prophetic gifts played in the Carthaginian congregation was a significant one, as may be judged both by the frequency of such things as Tertullian has mentioned here and by the care with which such things were judged, then it is easy to understand how some of these came to be recorded. Tertullian's use of this particular vision clearly functioned for him in the same way that the earlier oracles had functioned. He had built his case for the corporeality of the soul first from borrowed philosophical speculation and then from Scripture. He moved on to employ the account of this vision in a supplementary fashion. Reason in the form of philosophical speculation, revelation in the form of Scripture, and experience in the form of this woman's vision all pointed to the same conclusion. The soul was not simply an ill-defined nothingness, a formless and airlike substance; it had form and shape. Perhaps it could even be described as corporeal.

Tertullian went on to provide a minimal exegesis to the vision of the soul. Since he assumed his point concerning the soul's corporeal nature to have been proven, he inferred that it must also have color, for every bodily substance has color. "Now what color would you attribute to the soul," he queried, "but an ethereal transparent one?" (9.5). The apparent answer was obvious to him.

From color, he moved to the subject of shape: "Likewise, as regards the figure of the human soul, you can well imagine that it is none other than the human form; indeed, none other than the shape of that body which each individual soul animates and moves about" (9.7). Thus, he employed the vision in a defense against the Platonic reasoning that left the soul without a figure (9.2). Finally, he wished to show that this premise was once again disclosed in the Scriptures. After all, the rich man had a tongue, Lazarus had a finger, Abraham had a bosom, and the martyrs under the altar could be recognized.[14] None of this, Tertullian argued, could take place without the corporeality of the soul.

Two final thoughts need to be raised in conjunction with Tertullian's arguments for the corporeal nature of the soul. The first of these is merely to note that the Stoics were not alone in their affirmation of this position. The idea seems to have had some basis in popular Greek and Roman parallels of the afterlife.[15] Similarly, this representation of the soul is not unlike that taught by Augustine's later antagonist, Vincentius Victor.[16]

THE VISION OF THE VEIL

It may have been as early as A.D. 207 when Tertullian penned his ascetical work *On the Veiling of Virgins*. He had addressed the subject prior to A.D. 200 in his work *On Prayer*, 20–22, and again in his treatise *On the Dress of Women*, 2.7.2–3. He may even have written an earlier Greek document on the subject.[17] In this work he again turned to the subject, thereby pointing to its importance as a topic for the church at Carthage.

As he began his discussion of the subject he informed his readers that it was truth, not custom, into which he would be inquiring.[18] It was progressive truth, but it was a truth that would be found to be consistent with the *regula fidei*.[19] Important to his argument was his conviction that it was the Holy Spirit's role to reveal the truth of God in an ongoing manner. This was essential to the welfare of the church, "since human mediocrity could not grasp everything at once, discipline could, little by little, be directed and regulated, and brought to perfection by that vicar of the Lord, the Holy Spirit."[20] It was the Spirit-Paraclete's role to accomplish three tasks. First, the Spirit was to provide direction to the discipline of the church. Second, the Spirit would reveal the Scriptures, a thought that appears to approximate the concept of illumination. And, third, the Paraclete would reform the understanding.[21]

As Tertullian developed his argument, he made the point that those who had received the Paraclete, "preferred truth to custom. Those who have heard him prophesying even to the present, veil virgins."[22] It is clear that Tertullian believed the Holy Spirit was actively directing discipline, illuminating Scripture, and reforming minds in his own day. Those who allowed the Spirit to do so, through the gift of prophecy, also taught the veiling of virgins. It may even be safe to suggest that some of these prophecies attributed to the Spirit consisted of what Aune might call "prescriptive oracles," oracles in which the speaker enjoined "a particular type of action or behavior,"[23] and that part of the behavior, so prescribed, was the veiling of virgins.

Tertullian's argument, then, rested on his interpretation of John 16:12–13a, in which Jesus had told his disciples, "I still have yet many things to say to you, but you cannot bear them now. When the Spirit of truth comes, he will guide you into all the truth." His interpretation was clear, and his argumentation easily followed. He began with Jesus' promise of a Paraclete who would come to guide the church into all truth. Tertullian believed the reason the Paraclete was sent by Jesus was that, in the brief amount of time which Jesus had on earth, he was not able to say all that he wanted to say. Had he done so, his followers would not have been able to bear it. Hence, a little bit at a time would be revealed, particularly in matters of discipline. Tertullian's conclusion was that the Spirit of truth continued to provide such guidance in his day by means of prophetic gifts.[24]

Tertullian's arguments were not based totally on either his understanding of John 16 or his expectations of prophetic gifts. Both custom and Scripture had spoken to the subject at hand. He cited Greek churches, even the majority of them, which still kept their virgins covered. There were also some North African churches that practiced this custom.[25] In spite of this custom, the matter had come to be one of individual choice, and also in spite of this custom, Tertullian argued that his concern was for truth.[26]

He was concerned to show that the veiling of virgins was consistent with Paul's teaching in 1 Cor. 11:2–16.[27] His primary concern in so doing was to combat the suggestion that while Paul had expected the veiling of women, he did not mean virgins. Tertullian argued that the term "virgin" was a subset of the generic term "woman." Thus, he concluded that he had adequately defended his opinion "in accordance with Scripture, in accordance with nature, and in accordance with discipline."[28]

As the argumentation of Tertullian moved forward, he turned his attention to married women. These, too, he admonished to wear the veil. He chided those who did what they believed was minimally acceptable and normal, those who obeyed the letter of the law but flaunted the spirit of the law. Tertullian contended that the limits of the head included the face and neck reaching down to the point where the robe began. The region of the veil needed to extend as far as the woman's hair extended when it was unbound.[29] In spite of this, there were those who thought themselves covered when they donned linen caps that came down to the ears[30] or when they placed small fringes, tufts of cloth, threads, or even their hands on their heads while worshipping.[31] Tertullian naturally disdained such casuistic activity in fulfillment of the Lord's wishes.

The fact of the matter is, argued Tertullian, "To us the Lord has, even by revelation, measured the space over which the veil is to extend."[32] This simple assertion made three important points. First, it claimed that the Lord was concerned with veils. The authority for Tertullian's teaching on the subject was not to be understood as one of his own making. Ultimate authority rested in the One these women sought to worship. It was the Lord who had made his wishes known and, therefore, by plain logic it would be the Lord whom they would offend by not conforming to his wishes. On this point, then, Tertullian argued in a way consistent with his understanding of the Paraclete saying in John 16:12–13a. The Lord,

Jesus, would declare those items essential for the church to know. They would be revealed through the Paraclete.

Second, Tertullian contended that particular words or teachings on the subject of veils had come by means of "revelations." It may be that he understood these revelations to have been shared first with adherents of the New Prophecy. This idea is supported by his use of the words "to us," which indicates who it was that received the revelations. It may have been a generic reference to all the Christians in North Africa, but that is unlikely, for earlier in this same work Tertullian had noted that those who received the Paraclete had set "truth before custom."[33] While nothing explicit is mentioned at that point, it is surely the case that there were those who had ignored or did not receive the prophesyings of the Paraclete. Tertullian would have been hinting at the presence of those who put their own customs ahead of revealed truth. They would undoubtedly have been those who chose not to veil their women or virgins or those who chose to meet the rule with a minimalist commitment and little or no conviction.

This second point, then, would also have been consistent with Tertullian's understanding of John 16:12–13a. The Lord would reveal his mind to the church. In Tertullian's way of thinking, this happened through ongoing revelations and/or prophecies mediated by the Paraclete. It is significant to note, however, that in this particular passage regarding the veiling of women, no Paraclete is mentioned. It is merely noted that revelations on the subject had been given.

Third, the content of these revelations originating from the Lord was said to have extended to such details as the size of the appropriate veil. Tertullian taught that the Paraclete had been sent to urge God's people on "toward perfection"[34] in their spiritual walk, this to be accomplished in part by the direction of discipline and the revelation of Scripture.[35] This particular concern expressed through the Lord's revelations, then, may be consistent with what Tertullian believed to be the type of revelation one might legitimately anticipate from the Paraclete. After all, if Scripture taught that women should be veiled, as Tertullian contended that it did, then it was a small step, but an appropriate one, for him to argue that the Lord, through the Paraclete, wanted to inform the church what size that veil should be. According to Tertullian, then, the church would first be told to veil its women, and when they could bear more, they would be told, by revelation, the proper dimensions of those veils.

Here, Tertullian provided an example of an occurrence that underscored the necessity of the veiling of women to which he had been referring. He introduced the account of a "certain sister of ours,"[36] a designation once again that may refer to a prophet of the New Prophecy, indeed, a designation similar to that which introduced the woman who had the vision of the soul.[37] It is even possible, although neither provable nor essential, that the two women were actually the same individual. Yet, whoever this woman was, Tertullian represented her as being addressed by an angel who also beat her neck "as if in applause."[38]

Very little of the original *Sitz-im-Leben* in which this event took place is presented by Tertullian. It is probable, although it is not stated, that this event took place during a worship time, whether in a community setting or in private devotions—more likely in a community setting. It is also probable that this event is to be understood as having come in a visionary form, for the woman is said to have been addressed by an angel. Although we are not told that she actually saw the angel, one might wonder how she knew it was an angel who had addressed her unless she also saw the angel.[39] It is also possible that the context of this vision, like that of the vision on the soul, was comparable in that it could have come in relation to the discussion of veiled heads and angels. Thus, this account may have had its origin in a discussion of 1 Cor. 11:10 in which Paul had urged women worshippers to veil their heads "because of the angels."[40]

Whatever the original occasion in which the "revelation" was given, Tertullian has recorded it as represented in the angel's words:

> Elegant neck
> and deservedly bare!
> It is well that you should be unveiled continuously from head to loins,
> lest indeed, your neck's freedom be not to your advantage.[41]

With these words, then, we have one more example in Tertullian's retinue of arguments all serving to extend the length of the veil. The words recorded appear to be the angel's words designed to show exactly how the angel is affected by the nakedness of the "sister's" neck. The angel's comment seems to have described the action of the woman as something that could ultimately prove to be his downfall, if not hers. After all, the reason for not wearing a suitable veil would be the elegance of her neck, the exposure of which might profit her in some way.

The obvious use to which Tertullian wished to put this "revelation," was to encourage women to take more seriously the discipline of veiling. Not to do so would yield a much deserved and severe chastisement.[42] That this angel's words were well said should be a lesson to all who refused to wear veils, for "of course, what you have said to one you have said to all."[43] Thus, Tertullian understood the revelation of the angel to have universal implications. It is probably not an overstatement to note that any revelation from the Lord on the subject would have been understood similarly. Indeed, the angel may have spoken on the Lord's behalf to admonish this woman and, thereby, all who would hear. The implication of the revelation that Tertullian claimed to be the message to the church was also understood by him to be a reaffirmation of his own interpretation of Paul's teaching in 1 Cor. 11:4–6.

CHAPTER ELEVEN

THE ROLE OF THE PARACLETE IN CONTINUING REVELATION

Thus far we have looked at certain general items related to the subject of prophetic gifts in Tertullian's writings, and we have explored his use of nine different oracles, visions, or sayings reputed to have been received through prophetic gifts of one type or another. We now turn our attention to one final subject in our study of the role and function of prophetic gifts for Tertullian: the role of the Paraclete in ongoing revelation.

This subject is not new in that even in his *On the Veiling of Virgins*, Tertullian laid some groundwork on this subject through (1) his appeal to John 16:12–13a, (2) his argument that the Paraclete was now acting as the vicar of Christ on earth, and (3) his contention that the Paraclete was present to speak to matters of discipline.[1] This chapter will be limited to two such issues, marriage and fasting. Similar studies could be conducted on other areas of personal holiness addressed by Tertullian that would yield similar results.

MARRIAGE

Tertullian approached the question of marriage, and particularly of second marriages, in much the same way he approached the question of the veiling of virgins. In his treatment of marriage, however, his hermeneutical presuppositions are more clearly explained and more easily understood. There are several of these that are either explicitly stated or else clearly implied in his work *On Monogamy*.

The first of these presuppositions is that he had a high regard for existing Scripture. This was true for the Old Testament, the Gospels—particularly John's gospel—and the writings of Paul. He believed that the Scriptures gave the law of God. One element of this law was the law of the sanctity of marriage. Tertullian argued that his teaching of continence was, in fact, honoring that law.[2]

The second presupposition was that the Spirit had been sent, the Paraclete had come, to act as the *restitutor* rather than the *institutor* of discipline.[3] Tertullian appealed to Jesus' words in John 16:12–13a that the Spirit would be sent to lead the church into all truth. Jesus had not been able to say many things because his disciples had been unable to bear them. Yet the Spirit's role would be to speak those things that were told to him.[4] As a result, Tertullian argued, Jesus let the church know that the Paraclete, the Spirit, "will inform fully of things [teachings] which can both be considered to be *new,* in that they have never been made known before, and sometimes *burdensome,* in that they had not been made known for that very reason"[5] (italics mine).

When the accusation is raised that this leaves the church open to the possibility that *any* new or burdensome teaching that someone may suggest may be attributed to the Spirit, Tertullian is ready with an eloquent response. No, these teachings must be judged! False teachings will be apparent because of the diversity of preaching that has its origin in the adulteration of the *regula fidei.*[6] What one believes affects or spills over into what one does. Hence, when a person has a faulty understanding of God and Christ, he or she will give faulty teaching with regard to discipline.[7] A false teacher or a false prophet will be uncovered according to what she or he believes regarding Christ.[8]

The Spirit is known to teach the truth in the area of discipline, for it comes in the proper context. The Spirit, whether through teacher or prophet, begins by bearing witness to and glorifying Christ.[9] Only after this is done, can the Spirit move into instruction on disciplinary matters. Thus, Tertullian suggested that any further teaching, new revelation, or disciplinary matters taught by the Spirit, even as taught in the New Prophecy, must come under the guidance and judgment of the apostolic writings of kerygmatic truth. Inconsistency was to be understood as a sign of falseness. Tertullian thus saw the continuation of the gift of prophecy as providing illumination and application on a secondary or supplementary level. Scripture, or the apostolic writings, was the norm.

This position is further borne out by two other factors. First, Tertullian argued that the Spirit introduced no *new* or *novel* teachings, but rather illuminated existing knowledge.[10] Second, Tertullian claimed that "What Scripture does not note, it denies."[11] This is not an argument posed by one who expects *new* or *novel* "revelation," but rather it is an argument offered by someone with a high view of the authority and completeness of Scripture as the norm. Scripture has spoken, and where it is silent, nothing can be added because the silence argues against additions.

Tertullian's teaching on second marriage seems to be a result of two things. The first of these is that the teaching of monogamy (Tertullian's term for a single marriage as opposed to digamy, which refers to second marriages; cf. *On Monogamy*, 12.3) is a teaching of the New Prophecy.[12] It is a teaching thought to have its origins in the Spirit, who conveys the mind of Jesus.[13]

Second, Tertullian's teaching is based on his perception of the role of the Spirit, a role defined partially by his primitive dispensationalism. He believed that hardness of heart had reigned until the time when Christ came and that infirmity of flesh had reigned until the coming of the Paraclete.[14] Yet, now was the time of the Spirit-Paraclete, and a new period had been inaugurated, a period when the Spirit enabled believers to endure temptations of the flesh.[15]

Tertullian saw distinct parallels between Jesus' teaching on divorce and the teaching of the Paraclete on remarriage. In both cases, marriage was allowable. In fact, Tertullian saw the teaching of the New Prophecy as a mean between two equally dangerous extremes. His comment was that "The heretics desist from marriages; the psychics heap them up. The former do not marry *even* once; the latter do not stop with one marriage."[16] So, the New Prophecy neither denied marriage totally nor condoned remarriage once a spouse had died. The New Prophecy did, however, regulate marriage.[17]

The parallel Tertullian saw between Moses and Paul as well as between Jesus and the Paraclete may be stated briefly. Tertullian contended that, in the beginning, God intended for human beings to have one spouse and not to allow for divorce.[18] Likewise, he argued, it was God's intent that there be single marriages from the beginning.[19] In the case of divorce due to the hardness of human hearts, however, God allowed Moses to declare that a bill of divorce could be acquired under certain circumstances. Moses' declaration was perceived by Jesus as a concession to human weakness and, therefore, less than ideal. His command was, "And I say to you: whoever divorces his wife except for unchastity, and marries another, commits adultery" (Matt. 19:9).

In the case of marriages, Tertullian argued that Paul had conceded the *possibility* of second marriage.[20] He obviously had in mind here 1 Cor. 7:8–9, in which Paul had written, "To the unmarried and the widows I say that it is well for them to remain unmarried as I am. But if they are not practicing self-control, they should marry. For it is better to marry than to be aflame with passion." It is clear here, too, that Paul's concession was based on the weakness of flesh.

In a move which Tertullian argued was parallel to that of Jesus, the Spirit, in the form of the New Prophecy, abrogated second marriages.[21] Tertullian went on to argue, if Jesus is accepted as coming from God rather than being demonic in origin, what is so different in the way we have accepted the teaching on marriage given by the Spirit?

This question points to the continuing problem raised by ongoing prophetic tradition in the form of a gift of prophecy. If this teaching came as a prophetic oracle, it demanded a judgment.[22] The judgment was to be made, at least partly, on the basis of content. The church judged it as false, claiming it to be "new" and "burdensome."[23] It did not coincide with the perception of the Catholic tradition, but rather it appeared to be a "new gospel."

Similarly, Tertullian also must have judged this teaching, for in other similar experiences he has already been shown to have demonstrated credibility in his willingness to judge prophetic teaching, and he appears to have had a high regard for the authority of Scripture. It was the norm by which the New Prophecy must be judged. The continuing gift of prophecy was secondary in its authority since it was secondary to Scripture. Thus, Tertullian, in this instance was forced to measure this teaching against the norm of Scripture.

His problem was twofold. First, if he judged it to be false, he took a stand against *at least this tenet* of the New Prophecy. He could judge it the way the Catholics did, but he chose to criticize their position by saying, "But the things which are of the Spirit are not pleasing to the psychics who do not receive the Spirit."[24] In other words, he charged them with having already made up their minds that the Paraclete of the New Prophecy was not to be identified with the Holy Spirit. Hence, their judgment was based on the presupposition that this teaching was not from God because it had come through the New Prophecy.

The second problem for Tertullian was highlighted by the fact that he was flying in the face of the judgment of the majority of the church. What had been proclaimed by the New Prophecy to be a further illumination of a teaching for the church was thought by the majority of the church to be a totally new revelation that stood over against the tradition and, therefore, it had been judged as falling outside the realm of legitimate prophetic utterance.

It seems, then, that Tertullian was governed by at least three presuppositions. The first was that the Holy Spirit was, indeed, speaking in and through the prophets of the New Prophecy. The presupposition of the church that denied this fact was wrong. Second, prophecy was defined by Tertullian largely as illumination and application of previously existing Scripture to specific situations with which the church was confronted. It was a means of guidance that the church should heed. Third, the position on marriage that the New Prophecy held was considered to be nothing more than further illumination by the Spirit of Paul's letter to Corinth. It came in the form of the gift of prophecy, with an application of this illumination to the contemporary situation in the form of newly revised standards of holiness. With these presuppositions, as well as Tertullian's personal interest in an ascetic life-style, Tertullian came to view this teaching on marriage as consistent with Scripture and, therefore, a command of the Holy Spirit that must be obeyed.

FASTING

Just as Tertullian devoted works to the disciplines of the veiling of virgins and of monogamous marriages, both teachings of the Paraclete supported by the New Prophecy, so he also devoted another work to the discipline of fasting. It was a discipline derived from early Montanism, for Tertullian traced it to Montanus, Priscilla, and Maximilla themselves.[25] It is probable that the discipline of fasting among members of the New Prophecy was instituted, at least in part, on the basis of one or more "prophetic oracles" on the subject.[26]

It seems that the larger church had some difficulty arriving at the decision that this teaching was based on false prophecy. Tertullian's comment that the teaching had to be judged as heretical if it were a humanly contrived teaching and as false prophecy if it were spiritually (other than from the Holy Spirit) derived leads one to understand that both opinions were maintained by parties within the church.[27] Some apparently thought that Montanus, Priscilla, and Maximilla were personally responsible for the injunction on fasting, while others seemingly attributed it to a form of demonic bondage being proclaimed through a false gift of prophecy. In either case, the claim was that what the New Prophecy taught was *novel* and, therefore, not to be accepted.

Tertullian listed the teachings the church regarded as new or novel. They included the keeping of fasts proclaimed by the New Prophecy as mandatory, the prolonging of stations, observing of xerophagies, and various dietary limitations.[28] The church as a whole believed that adherents to the New Prophecy were guilty of practices which Paul had condemned among the Galatians.[29] The New Prophecy was thought to bind the church with mandatory regulations at points where the church believed a level of personal freedom should reign.[30] Tertullian charged that the church had chosen to limit God in both the means and the extent to which God would work. He wrote, "But you [Psychics] again set up boundary-posts to God as with regard to grace, so with regard to discipline; as with regard to gifts so, too, with regard to solemnities: so that our observances are supposed to have ceased in like manner as His benefits."[31]

Thus, Tertullian began with this as his foundation and proceeded to argue by means of a few biblical examples to show that the teaching of the Paraclete was the same as the teaching of Scripture. His acceptance of the

Paraclete, his understanding of prophecy, and his use of Scripture was much the same as it was in his arguments on marriage.

Tertullian, then, took seriously the role of the Spirit-Paraclete in his own day. This meant, too, that he took the charisma of prophecy seriously, not merely as a forgotten vestige of some previous apostolic generation but as a genuine charisma with practical implications, for life in his own congregation. Prophetic gifts functioned authoritatively for him and especially for others connected with the New Prophecy that had rooted itself within the culture of North African Christianity. Various oracles were recorded throughout his writings, and in each case he sought to display them as subordinate to Scripture and in some cases the *regula fidei* to which the North African church subscribed. Additionally, these oracles were interpreted as supportive of a particular interpretation of that canon or that rule. Thus, the ongoing function of prophetic gifts in Tertullian's writings cannot be better stated than by applying to them the statement he applied to the Paraclete. They appear to have been given to the Christian community of third-century North Africa to lead them on to perfection by directing them in discipline, making plain the Scriptures and renewing their mind.[32]

PART THREE

PROPHETIC GIFTS IN THE WRITINGS OF CYPRIAN

CHAPTER TWELVE

INTRODUCTION TO PROPHETIC GIFTS IN CYPRIAN

As we approach the midpoint of the third century, it is obvious that Cyprian was aware of the presence of certain charismata of the Spirit which functioned in Carthage during his lifetime, but he has left us no comprehensive treatment of the subject. What we know of the charismata during his time must be gleaned from his often incidental comments both in his *Letters* or *Epistles* and in his *Treatises*. Among those items of which Cyprian speaks are visions, or what might be called visionary prophecies. While many historians have noted that Cyprian was a "visionary," only Adolf von Harnack has given more than a cursory treatment to this aspect of Cyprian's life and writings.[1]

Cyprian's term as bishop of Carthage (circa A.D. 248–258) was punctuated with visionary revelations from beginning to end. On numerous occasions, Cyprian referred to specific individuals,[2] to groups that included various unnamed individuals,[3] and even to himself[4] as having received visions. The range of the recipients addressed by Cyprian makes it clear that there were many who knew of these happenings, from the laity in Carthage to fellow bishops of the North African Synod and from confessors in the mines to the bishop who ruled in Rome.[5]

While it is clear that many Christians in Cyprian's day believed and trusted in the validity of divine revelation through visionary experiences, it is equally clear that not everyone was willing to accept visions as a legitimate method of discerning the Lord's leadership in a given situation. In fact, Florentius Puppianus led a group of insurgents from the congregation at Carthage and ridiculed Cyprian with the nickname "the dreamer"[6] because of Cyprian's repeated appeal to his own visions. What was Cyprian's understanding of these "prophetic gifts"? What was his perception of divine inspiration?

Cyprian wrote that visions were ecstatic experiences whereby messages were conveyed from God to human beings.[7] The Spirit was the source of these revelations since they took place when the subject was "filled with the Spirit";[8] the thoughts the prophetic figure had while "filled with the Spirit," however, were said to be given by the Lord. These visionary experiences often took place during the day,[9] although certain nocturnal dreams also fell within the same category.[10] At times they involved only visual stimulation, but more often than not, they also included an interpretive word, an *audible* voice, or a verbal application.[11]

Cyprian's understanding of the role of visions in the church was wide-ranging. He used no fewer than sixteen verbs to explain the purposes of visions.[12] While the recipient of such experiences was thought to occupy an honorable position for having received them, there were really only two purposes for which these revelations were given. God wished to show or to reveal God's will to the church. In a negative sense, they were used to warn or admonish.[13] In their more positive expressions, they were said to instruct.[14] The fact that a fixed canon of Scripture had not been completely settled by this time *may* have played a part in the understanding and value Cyprian placed on such experiences. Still, there is no evidence that the visions and prophecies to which Cyprian appealed posed a conflict either with the developing canon used at Carthage during his tenure as bishop or with the *regula fidei* to which the church was then committed. Cyprian's view of contemporary prophecy and/or visionary experiences, though, points toward certain judgments as being essential when dealing with such phenomena.

Cyprian clearly recognized that there were both true and false manifestations which might be called prophecy by some, but he seems to have had a clear perception of what one might call the authority of the *regula fidei* that was different from the authority of contemporary visions and prophecies or prophetic visions.

Cyprian's understanding of what constituted Scripture included the Old Testament and what he termed the "apostolic tradition" and the "evangelical authority,"[15] or the Gospels and the epistles written by the apostles.[16] These writings were revealed by the Holy Spirit,[17] and Cyprian argued that they were God's truth.[18] These inspired writings demanded obedience from those who came to understand them.[19] Those who knowingly or willfully disobeyed them were guilty of sin without the possibility of pardon. Thus, Cyprian held to a view of Scripture that saw it as a normative *canon* whereby the events of life could be assessed and behavior and thought brought under judgment.

Alongside this view of Scripture, Cyprian held to the understanding that Jesus' warnings of the coming of false prophets were something which continued to be relevant to events and practices in Cyprian's own day.[20] That is, he believed there would be those who would rise up in his time and profess to have the truth of God, but who would actually speak words of deception. It was important to Cyprian that they be identified and exposed.

Foremost among those whom Cyprian saw as false prophets were those persons who set *themselves* up as priests and bishops of the church. They were the ones who appointed themselves to the task of pastoring the church, but who had not been ordained or recognized by the presiding bishop. This was a problem that repeatedly troubled the congregation of Carthage in Cyprian's absence.

Felicissimus apparently led several presbyters who, in Cyprian's absence from Carthage, proclaimed themselves to be in control of the congregation and, as such, who claimed that they were able to grant full pardon to the lapsed. Of these men Cyprian wrote:

> There is the proclamation which God has spoken: "Heed not the talk of false prophets for the dreams in their own hearts deceive them. They speak, but not out of the mouth of the Lord. They say to those who reject the word of the Lord: peace shall be yours."
> So, too, they are now offering peace, whilst they have no peace themselves; they will not let the Church call back and lead back the fallen, whilst they have forsaken the Church themselves. [21]

Cyprian's judgment of these men was clear. The Old Testament had called for the death sentence for such dreamers. [22] The church should not accept their claims.

In essence, then, Cyprian's treatment of Felicissimus provides two methods of determining or discerning the differences between true and false prophecy. Both of them relate to the person who prophesies. First, he maintained, it is possible to receive genuine prophecy from those within the church, but not from those outside the church. In other words, since Felicissimus had left the church through the act of establishing his own priesthood, his words were to be judged as nothing more than self-fabricated visions. [23] According to Cyprian, Felicissimus had knowingly removed himself from the umbrella of responsible accountability within the Christian community and under Scripture. He had willfully chosen to disobey the Spirit-inspired truth of God, thereby bringing the wrath of God down upon himself. Scripture, then, provided the judgment that Felicissimus's promises were in fact examples of false prophecy. Christians could prophesy a genuine form of prophecy. Those outside the church could not. The genuine manifestation of this charisma was limited to the church. What posed as prophecy from those outside was actually false prophecy.

A second test involved assessing the fruit of the speaker. Cyprian argued that the false prophecies of Felicissimus produced division and scattering. Those who followed in this line were in danger of perishing outside the church and beneath the wrath of God. [24] Thus, one could in part, determine the presence of false prophecy by assessing the fruit it bore. According to Cyprian's assessment, the prophesying of Felicissimus was threatening the stability of the congregation in Carthage and, therefore, the fruit produced was to be viewed as not of the Spirit.[25]

The question of the church's treatment of the lapsed produced several occasions for Cyprian to speak to the question of contemporary prophecy. He argued that if the church adopted a hard line against the lapsed, the church was abandoning them to the influence of false prophets.[26] Apparently it was this pastoral concern that brought about a meeting of a large number of bishops to consider the subject of the lapsed. Cyprian described the meeting as follows:

> there gathered in Council a generous number of bishops who had been preserved safe and unharmed thanks to their own staunch faith and the protection of the Lord. Scriptural passages were produced, in a lengthy debate, on both sides of the issue and eventually we arrived at a balanced and moderate decision, striking a healthy mean.[27]

The concern of these bishops was to find a scriptural method of dealing with the lapsed, one which balanced grace and mercy against justice. They wished neither to deny all hope of realignment with the church nor to allow such a relaxing of standards that there would be no real need for repentance.

It is interesting to note, however, that when Cyprian wrote the official statement regarding the treatment of the lapsed, and thereby represented the bishops who took part in this conference, the synodal decree described the convention as having included visionary experiences as part of the evidence pointing toward the eventual decree. The decree of the bishops of the Synod of North Africa, addressed to Cornelius, bishop at Rome, read:

> And so, prompted by the Holy Spirit and counselled by the Lord through many explicit visions, we came to the decision, seeing that it is foretold and revealed that the Enemy is close upon us, to collect together the soldiers of Christ within the battlements, and after examining each case to grant reconciliation to the fallen, or, to put it another way, to supply with weapons all those who are soon to fight. And we believe that you too, being sensible of God's paternal compassion, will agree with our decision.[28]

It can be said, no doubt with a great deal of truth, that in writing the decree, Cyprian worded it in a way that represented his own mind on the subject. That is, the emphasis on the role of visions might not have been present in the decree had it been penned by another. Yet, there seems to be little doubt that visions played a significant role in the North African church during the first half of the third century even in synodical life. This may be true, in part, because of the influence of the New Prophecy under the able apologetic direction of Tertullian of Carthage, but Perpetua and Saturus had been martyred before the New Prophecy's role was clear in Carthage. Besides, the New Prophecy had already begun to decline in its influence and Tertullian had been dead perhaps as long as twenty-five years. In Asia Minor, the New Prophecy had been judged as heretical.[29] This may be the reason that, although Cyprian held Tertullian in high esteem personally,[30] he never mentioned him by name in any of his writings.

It should be said, however, that the decision of the North African council of bishops was not based entirely on visions. If Cyprian is to be believed, one must say that the decision was accomplished by a careful evaluation of various types of evidence. The question was debated in the light of Scripture.[31] The signs of impending persecution were also considered.[32] It was also thought that a number of visionary experiences both foretold of a coming period of persecution and that they may have hinted at a solution to the continuing problem of the lapsed. What is not clearly stated is whether Scripture or contemporary visions took precedence in the final decision. The form of argumentation would seem to indicate that Scripture held the final solution. Cyprian's view of its authority also points in that direction.

I would suggest, then, that the council met to discuss the issue and was guided largely by Scripture in its deliberations. The pros and cons were brought forth and debated. Various passages of Scripture were raised that were thought to bear on the issue. Among those passages discussed were the parable of the shepherd seeking the one lost sheep (see Luke 15:3–7) and Paul's examples of employing a variety of methods to save as many as possible.[33] On the other side of the debate was the concern to exercise proper discipline. Undoubtedly, such passages as Matt. 18:15–17 and 1 Cor. 5:1–13 might provide insight into such a discussion.

The pastoral problems were intense. If left without the possibility of repentance, the church would, in part, be responsible for contributing to the judgment of the lapsed. It would, in essence, be guilty of judging that which only God should rightfully judge.[34] A lack of repentance on the part of the lapsed, however, would surely weaken the church, and a lack of penitence over a protracted period of time might have a demoralizing effect on those who had remained faithful. Too strong a response would demoralize the lapsed, while too weak a response would not deter more Christians from joining their ranks in any future persecution.

It would seem, then, that before the council considered visions, it considered Scripture. Yet, the fact remains that it did consider what Cyprian described as "many explicit (literally *multas et manifestas*) visions."[35] But apparently these visions were considered to be of a confirmatory nature, only emphasizing the fact that some action was necessary. Similar councils met that recognized visions as confirmatory in nature.[36] This, coupled with the fact that Cyprian, as well as his colleagues, tended to judge such experiences according to some standard or norm, points toward the priority of Scripture as the canon for their debate.

Cyprian maintains that among the items revealed by these visions was a warning of an imminent period of renewed persecution. In essence, these visions foretold and, as such, would need to be weighed in light of current events. If this epistle was written about A.D. 252 as it appears to have been, then it came at the end of the Decian persecution and just five years prior to the extreme period of persecution under Valerian.

Cyprian took seriously the testing of prophetic oracles and the discerning between true and false visions. It seems credible, therefore, that his associates dealt with such things in a similar manner. To make a prediction by referring to a vision left the burden of proof on the person who had the vision. Cyprian, for one, believed that the test of fulfillment continued to be an important test for distinguishing between true and false prophecy.[37] It does not appear too problematic, then, to assume that the council tested all that was said in accordance with scriptural guidelines. If this was done, then Scripture was, indeed, the canon on which their action was based and the visions would be viewed as not in conflict, but in a secondary confirmatory relationship.

Although it is clear that Cyprian held scriptural authority in high esteem, it must also be noted that he valued personal inspiration. He claimed this inspiration for himself, recognizing that God often revealed things to him by way of vision.[38] Yet, his claims of inspiration were not for himself alone. Cyprian viewed these phenomena as broadly present among the clergy because God inspired the priesthood in such a way to enable it to govern properly.[39]

Thus, in Cyprian's thinking there was a sense of the *ad hoc* when dealing with contemporary manifestations of prophetic gifts. Visions were given to meet needs in specific circumstances. They were not necessarily meant to have a universal application. They were meant to communicate to an individual,[40] a congregation,[41] a small group of individuals,[42] or even a synod.[43] In essence, while they could provide divine guidance, they were not to have the same level of applicability and, hence, authority as did Scripture. They had to be assessed in light of or in relationship to Scripture.

Even in their *ad hoc* character, however, they had a modicum of authority. While it may be said to be a derived or secondary authority in that these visionary experiences were tested and judged according to Scripture and only when they had been found to be in accordance with that norm were they ruled acceptable, they were still to be considered seriously. Cyprian wrote that they were not given merely to be concealed.[44] They were to be received, tested, accepted, and shared. They were not to be hidden, but because they might be applicable to a larger group, they were to be passed along so that the message conveyed by God to them might also be obeyed. Obedience and conformity to God's will as conveyed through visions was very important.[45]

Cyprian argued that the knowledge gained through such experiences was only partial knowledge. It did not convey the entire picture.[46] His assertion was based on his understanding of 1 Cor. 14:29–30.[47] He argued from this passage that a vision or prophecy could be reversed or changed if God chose to supersede it by granting a new one:

> there are many matters on which revelation may come to particular individuals, bringing improvement, and . . . no man ought stubbornly to do battle in defence of an opinion he once acquired and has long held; rather he should eagerly embrace another viewpoint if it is an improvement and of greater benefit.[48]

One should not be surprised, then, that Cyprian calmly wrote that he was directed by God, by means of a vision, to leave Carthage and take a respite[49] and that he fully expected God to reverse that direction by another similar experience.[50] His obedience to such revelations could not be said to violate Scripture, nor to supersede it, nor even to possess its same level of inspiration. Scripture stood and provided a standard for testing all experiences, but one needed to remain open to the possibility that instruction by the Spirit might be given which superseded previous visionary revelations. Thus, these visions were truly *ad hoc*, but they were also authoritative in the situation.

What were these visionary revelations to which Cyprian referred? Into what categories did they fall? How were they understood and assessed by Cyprian's contemporaries? It is to such important questions that we now turn our attention. For purposes of clarity, Cyprian's accounts have been divided into four main categories: (1) visions that suggested clerical appointments, (2) visions that comforted confessors and martyrs, (3) visions that exhorted the congregation at Carthage, and (4) visions that brought personal guidance to Cyprian.

REVELATIONS INTRODUCING ECCLESIASTICAL APPOINTMENTS

In at least six epistles, Cyprian mentions the role and value of visions in the appointment of candidates to various ecclesiastical offices.[1] These epistles span a period of five years, and are addressed to a variety of people ranging from the laity and clergy in Carthage,[2] to a major ecclesiastical opponent,[3] to a personal friend,[4] and to Cornelius, the bishop of Rome.[5] One letter is apparently a synodical epistle and is addressed from Cyprian and thirty-one of his colleagues to some eighteen other clerics in North Africa.[6]

Because these epistles (1) cover such an extensive geographical area (from the unknown retreat where Cyprian lived during the Decian persecution to the Synod of North Africa, and even Rome itself); (2) are addressed to the full range of church membership (from laity to bishop); and (3) extend over a five-year period, it may be assumed that the practice of appealing to visions in making ecclesiastical appointments was fairly well known and widespread during the middle of the third century. In fact, Cyprian mentions that the number of bishops appointed by divine *dignatione*, a term Cyprian repeatedly uses for visions, was a superlative one.[7] In similar fashion, it is the one who is honored by God's *dignatione* who rules the church.[8] The way Cyprian states this is:

> One can now trace the source from which schisms and heresies have arisen and do arise: they occur when the bishop, who stands alone and who is the appointed leader in the Church, is held in contempt by the proud and arrogant, and when the man whom God had deigned to honor as worthy of office [alternatively—"the man who is honored by God's condescension," ANF 5:373] is deemed unworthy by men.[9]

Thus, it is possible that Cyprian understood many bishops to have been appointed through a divine visitation, or *dignatione*. In all probability this was a vision or a prophecy,[10] but clearly some form of a prophetic gift was involved.

To a certain degree, the priesthood was also filled in this manner. Cyprian described God's activity in a twofold fashion. First the Lord elects or chooses the candidates, and then appoints or constitutes them as priests in the church. The Lord's choice and appointment was made known by means of the *dignatione,* for Cyprian writes of the Lord: *"ut Dominus qui . . . dignatur."*[11] Furthermore, Cyprian together with thirty-one other bishops maintained that the bishops involved in the synod meeting of A.D. 255 administered the priesthood of the Lord by means of, or according to, the Lord's *dignationem.*[12] This administration included the ability to constitute priests following these visitations, to justify the priests thus appointed, and to repudiate attempts to stop these appointments by those who were unwilling to accept such actions.[13]

Two of Cyprian's epistles deal in detail with specific individuals who were appointed to clerical positions by means of these visitations. In a third one, Cyprian defends his own appointment against the aggression of Florentius Puppianus.

THE CASE OF CELERINUS

Cyprian addressed *Epistle* 39 to the presbyters, deacons, and laity (his brethren in the Lord) of the church in Carthage about A.D. 251 while he was in retreat during the Decian persecution. Its purpose appears to have been the recommendation of Celerinus to the clergy within the Carthaginian congregation.

Celerinus was a celebrated confessor of the third century who came from a family of martyrs.[14] He was described by Cornelius, bishop of Rome, in a letter to Fabius as "a man who by the grace of God most heroically endured all kinds of torture, and by the strength of his faith overcame the weakness of the flesh, and mightily conquered the adversary."[15] According to Cornelius, Celerinus had for a time defected to Novatus, the third-century schismatic who argued against the restoration of the *lapsi,* but who later returned to the main body of the church and was a member in good standing.

In Cyprian's treatment of Celerinus, he is called "our brother" and praised both for his courage and his character as a confessor.[16] His analysis of Celerinus was shared by many, for he wrote that he had various colleagues who, along with himself, wished to see Celerinus join "our clergy."[17] This decision was made, in part, because of an outstanding testimony presented by an unnamed person who had previously been responsible for persecuting Celerinus. This former persecutor had been filled with wonder at Celerinus's stability and at his Christian witness.[18]

Cyprian's description of the events surrounding the appointment of Celerinus make it clear that he did not wish to have the appointment questioned by the people to whom he was writing. He argued that it was not a human recommendation that placed Celerinus among the other clerics, but rather a divine visitation (*divina dignatione*). Any question the congregation might raise against the ordination of Celerinus would be construed as an act of rejecting God's will and not as an argument against Cyprian and his unnamed colleagues. They were merely passing on the revealed will of God by recommending Celerinus to the church.

Cyprian's account of the *divina dignatione* points to the idea that in an executive meeting of the church, Celerinus was recommended to be elevated to the ranks of the clergy. At first, Celerinus had refused this advancement, but during a recess of the meeting overnight, he became convinced that he should accept their request to advance him to the status of reader among the clergy.

Cyprian remarks that Celerinus changed his mind as a result of a vision or dream he had received during the night.[19] According to Cyprian, in this vision, Celerinus was constrained by the church. The church, through some visual phenomenon, apparently accompanied by an oracle addressed specifically to Celerinus, was said to have admonished and exhorted him not to refuse its persuasions (those of the bishops) to join the ranks of the clergy. In a sense, then, Cyprian argued that Celerinus was appointed by the Lord with the concurrence of the church.

Celerinus's interpretation of this vision included a straightforward line of reasoning. He believed that, without a doubt, the vision had been the result of a divine visitation. He perceived himself as one whom the Lord had honored with the dignity of heavenly glory.[20] Thus, he reasoned, it would be neither right nor proper for him not to be honored by the church when he had already been honored by the church's Lord.[21] The result of the invitation by the church to join the clergy and the vision in which he was admonished to accept the honor, together with Celerinus's understanding of these events, were sufficient for him to reverse his previous rejection of the ecclesiastical honor and to accept it as God's will. Hence, Cyprian noted, the Lord *and* the church had prevailed over Celerinus in the decision. Even Celerinus could not withstand the force of events.[22]

The function of the vision, as far as Cyprian was concerned, was confirmatory in nature. The bishops had known that Celerinus should be ranked among the clergy. Celerinus had hesitated, refusing a recommendation to join. Apparently he was not convinced that this was the direction in which God was calling him (whether because of humility or other factors). His judgment of the church's recommendation was negative, although he may have had some idea as to the direction his own relationship to God was pointing him. It was only by means of the vision that he came to a place in which he knew he should, indeed, submit himself to the will of the church and, in this case, to what he believed to be the will of his Lord. The bishops, in turn, judged the vision to be a legitimate confirmation of their own prior decision to include Celerinus among the clergy.

The equation just set out is an interesting one that has been addressed most clearly by Adolf von Harnack. It is the equation of the church (here identified with the episcopate) and the Lord on whose behalf the church through its episcopacy speaks. Cyprian's account of Celerinus's vision was that *the church* had admonished and exhorted Celerinus. Yet, Celerinus saw it as an honor of *the Lord,* and Cyprian made it clear to the people to whom he was writing that it was a *divina dignatione.* In short, the decision of the church to add Celerinus to the clergy was, according to Cyprian, ultimately God's decision.

Adolf von Harnack has argued that Cyprian had done nothing more than employ a literary form to motivate a malicious or antagonistic congregation to do as he says. Von Harnack paints the picture in the following manner: The Decian persecution was under way. Cyprian, with various other members of the clergy, had withdrawn to their undisclosed retreat. While he was gone, the congregation he had left in Carthage came under the power of others. In order to maintain his power in the Christian community of Carthage, he was forced to communicate with them. He had to remove the community from the power of these inter-lopers who had replaced him and, as a result, he was forced to resort to his most powerful weapon. Thus, Cyprian, a follower of *The Shepherd of Hermas,* appealed to visionary experiences or prophecies, thereby appeal-ing to divine authority to make his point.[23]

Standing at Cyprian's side was a tried and proven supporter whom he believed to be loyal to his position. The man was Celerinus. In order to place Celerinus in a position to act on his behalf within the congregation at Carthage, Cyprian resorted to a visionary claim. He was appointing Celerinus, but it was not he, it was God who provided the confirmation.[24] Thus, the people of Carthage had God to answer to if they did not accept his recommendation. Cyprian had cleverly removed himself from crit-icism by claiming the Lord's intervention.

Von Harnack's position is a plausible one, but its presuppositions need to be examined. This will be done following the analysis of a second specific example from Cyprian's *Epistles,* the appointment of Numidicus, and the analysis of a third passage written to Florentius Puppianus.

THE CASE OF NUMIDICUS

As in the case of Celerinus, Cyprian wrote a similar letter, *Epistle* 40, to the Christians in Carthage in support of the appointment of Numidicus.

Both *Epistles* 39 and 40 appear to have been written about the same time, and von Harnack dates the one written about Celerinus as the first, with that concerning Numidicus coming slightly later.[25]

Cyprian's letter regarding Numidicus is one in which he tries to communicate his concern for the welfare of the church in Carthage. They are Cyprian's "brethren," and they are "dearly beloved."[26] It is because he is concerned for their welfare that he has information he wants to share with them, information he believes will bring both joy and glory to the Carthaginian congregation. It is the joy of a new presbyterial appointment.

In this letter, Cyprian makes no specific mention of "colleagues" who share with him the desire to make an appointment to the presbytery of Carthage, nor does he mention that Numidicus received a divine visitation of any sort confirming such a recommendation. In addition, whereas Cyprian relates in *Epistle* 39 that Celerinus had a vision, a *divina dignatio* recorded in the third person, in *Epistle* 40 he records a first-person experience of a *dignatio divina*. Thus, he is writing to Carthage with a claim that Numidicus has been named to the presbytery of Carthage totally by divine revelation.

Cyprian's words regarding the incident are few. "You ought to know," he writes, "that we have been advised and instructed by the grace of God (*dignatione divina*), that the presbyter Numidicus, . . . should be enlisted in the ranks of our Carthaginian presbyters, and that he should take his seat with us amongst our clergy."[27]

In von Harnack's mind, Cyprian had made a logical leap that enabled him to maintain control of the church in Carthage. In Celerinus's case, the clergy voted to elevate Celerinus, and the Lord confirmed the vote through a vision. In Numidicus's case, the Lord spoke directly to Cyprian in a revelation, indicating that Numidicus should be a presbyter. It is, according to von Harnack, a climax (*Steigerung*) in Cyprian's method,[28] a risky political move with which he hopes the congregation will be satisfied.[29]

THE CASE OF FLORENTIUS PUPPIANUS

Two or three years after Cyprian wrote to the church at Carthage recommending both Celerinus and Numidicus, he was faced with another problem. It came in the person of Florentius Puppianus. Puppianus was apparently a socially significant layperson who rose up within the congregation at Carthage to confront the strongly vision-supported leadership of Cyprian. He accused Cyprian of being the cause of the dispersion of certain members of the Carthaginian congregation,[30] and he charged him with immorality because he had left his flock at a time when they needed him.[31] Cyprian responded to Puppianus's charges in written form, and again Puppianus wrote to Cyprian. It is this latter exchange that provides the occasion for the epistle now under discussion.

Throughout the epistle, Cyprian addresses himself to the questions Puppianus has raised. In each case he affirms that he has been duly appointed to the episcopate by the Lord. The overall argument, indeed, the summary argument, to which Cyprian resorts is based on his own revelation (*dignatio*) from the Lord. He describes it briefly for us:

> For I am mindful of the revelation which has already been made to me, or rather, to phrase it better, what the Lord God in His authority has enjoined upon an obedient and God-fearing servant. Among other things which He vouchsafed to reveal and disclose, He imparted this warning: "And so, whoever does not believe in Christ when He appoints a bishop shall begin to believe hereafter in Christ when he avenges that bishop."[32]

For the first time, Cyprian has recorded an actual oracle that deals with the appointment of priests and their vindication before the one who dares to question their authority. It is clear that he has in mind Puppianus when he refers to the person who does not believe, just as it is clear that he sees himself as the priest or bishop who has been duly appointed by Christ.

There are several items of interest that should be addressed regarding this incident. First, Cyprian has here referred to this experience as a *dignatio*, this time without the adjective *divina*. The context is clear, however, that the same thing as a *divina dignatio* is meant here, for it is, as Cyprian contends, a revelation from the Lord and God (*dominica et divina*). The two verbs he chooses to describe the action of this revelation are "to reveal and disclose."

Second, there are things to which Cyprian has been privy in previous revelations that he is not planning to write in his present statement. What he does plan to pass on is an oracle that addresses the root problem he faces: the problem of the genuineness of his ecclesiastical authority in the eyes of Puppianus. It is a judgment oracle that Cyprian unmistakably attributes to the authority of the Lord.

Third, the oracle is given as a simple statement of fact that seems to have its basis in the ideas expressed in Ps. 105:15: "Do not touch my anointed ones; do my prophets no harm." The ones who have been appointed by God to specific tasks must not be undercut. It is clearly a warning to those who would undertake such a task to allow those whom God has set in place to do God's work unhindered.[33]

Fourth, the oracle itself is given without its *Sitz-im-Leben*. It seems clearly to be a statement addressed to the problem Cyprian currently faces, but he states that it was given on some previous occasion. There is, however, no reference as to when or where that was. There is no historical context. Given Cyprian's long-standing feud with Florentius Puppianus, it could date from early in their dispute. But it is also possible that it is unrelated in any way to this specific ongoing argument. Cyprian may have simply viewed it as a useful parallel and, therefore, used it better to illustrate his point.

Fifth, this oracle was clearly meant to be understood as being added to things the Lord had "revealed and disclosed." Most certainly, we are led to believe that it was spoken by the Lord or, at least, by someone speaking on behalf of the Lord. The oracle itself is in the third person, and a case may be fairly easily built that Cyprian's description was not meant to convey the idea that Jesus himself was speaking, but rather that what is here recorded is a prophetic oracle given by the Spirit who spoke through Cyprian, its recipient. The oracle honored Christ, Christ's ability to make priests and Christ's readiness to protect them. Its purpose would be that to which Cyprian is now applying it: to bring order out of chaos and to show a clear connection between the Lord and those whom the Lord calls into service. The idea seems to parallel Jesus' own words regarding himself in John 14:21: "those who love me will be loved by my Father, and I will love them and reveal myself to them." It even more closely parallels his thoughts in Matt. 10:32–33: "Everyone therefore who acknowledges me before others, I also will acknowledge before my Father in heaven." It is especially interesting to note this latter parallel, since it falls within the immediate context of Matt. 10:19–20, a passage to which Cyprian refers on a number of occasions regarding the role of the Spirit in teaching what one should say in the hour of intense persecution.

Sixth, the context of this oracle makes it quite clear that Cyprian did not really expect Florentius Puppianus to be persuaded by his argumentation, even though it was said to be based on a revelation from God. He recognized the presence of skeptics, particularly among those whose minds were set to ignore the priests of God. For Cyprian, to apply this oracle to a specific situation was not to see the problem necessarily resolved. He anticipated its rejection even as he wrote, for Puppianus probably could be numbered among those persons to whom dreams seem ridiculous and visions foolish, since he clearly did not recognize Cyprian as the priest of God.[34]

To show the extent to which Cyprian believed the truth of what he himself said and the extent to which he realized he would not be believed by Puppianus, he related the Joseph narrative of Gen. 37:19–20. In essence, he likened himself to Joseph the dreamer who would not be believed even by his brothers, but whose dreams were true nonetheless. Joseph's brothers had ultimately come to bow at his feet. In a final thrust to make his point, Cyprian claimed to have a pure conscience before God. His ultimate hope would be a vindication of the truth of his position on the day of judgment.

Adolf von Harnack continues his analysis of Cyprian by looking at this passage. His argument begins with the idea that, in the extended absence of Cyprian from Carthage, the congregation, led by Puppianus, began to revolt against Cyprian's leadership. In his response to Puppianus, Cyprian once again appealed to a revelation, this time, however, to support his own position. The weakness of Cyprian's argument lies in the fact that he was apparently the recipient of the revelation used to justify his own position.[35] Hence, von Harnack writes that "episcopal power and enthusiasm have, in Cyprian, been tightly bound together."[36] The expectation was that no one could resist the combination of the authority of the ecclesiastical office and the power of the Spirit.

In dealing from his position of power, Cyprian could write to Puppianus that, whereas he was recognized by the Lord, Puppianus was outside the fold. If Puppianus would listen to Cyprian, and believe that Christ both appointed Cyprian and now ruled his church at Carthage through him, Cyprian would minister on his behalf. Cyprian informed Puppianus that he would consult his Lord to see whether he should receive entrance into the church, and he argued that the answer would come from the Lord.[37] In order to cover himself, in the event that Puppianus did not cede to his wishes, Cyprian shrewdly acknowledged beforehand that Puppianus probably would not accept his word.

Von Harnack's arguments, once again are clearly plausible. There are, however, several items that must be considered within his arguments, and these three incidents, the appointments of Celerinus and Numidicus as well as Cyprian's own defense, need to be analyzed together.

First, a number of persons were involved in the decision-making process that proposed the advancement of Celerinus to the level of reader. Cyprian's account of the visionary experience which Celerinus had suggests that the vision played a confirmatory role in the minds of Celerinus, of Cyprian, and of the other bishops with him. Cyprian did not act alone. Nor was Celerinus appointed solely by the *divina dignatio*; his appointment was merely ratified through it.

Second, in the case of Numidicus, the situation is slightly more obscure. There is no explicit mention of anyone other than Cyprian who was involved in the decision to thrust Numidicus into the ranks of the presbyters of Carthage. To say that Cyprian was the one who experienced the *dignatio divina*, however, is to say more than the text demands. He appeals to the first-person plural when talking of this experience. It is "we" who have been admonished and instructed by this visitation, and it is "with us" that Numidicus has been mandated to sit. Von Harnack's decision to interpret this as a case of circumlocution is one possible interpretation,[38] but the other might be that the same persons who were present for the appointment of Celerinus were present also in the deliberation on Numidicus.

There are two problems with this second interpretation, however. First, it is an argument from silence, for in the epistle regarding Celerinus, Cyprian specifically mentions those who were with him when the series of events took place.[39] In the epistle regarding Numidicus, no such statement is made. This problem may be minimized, however, if one assumes three things. First, the letter regarding Numidicus was written about the same time as the one concerning Celerinus, an assumption von Harnack himself admits. Second, the congregation at Carthage knew who was in retreat with Cyprian and how such appointments normally took place. It was not necessary to think that Cyprian was alone responsible for the appointment of Numidicus. Third, the "we" and "with us" were genuinely meant to be understood as plurals, not circumlocutions, and thus referred to this group, one member of which had experienced a visitation from God.

The second problem is that if "we" is accepted as a genuine plural, still to be dealt with is who received the vision or revelation. It was most probably not a group experience, but would have been an experience either of Cyprian or one of his colleagues. Again, the argument that the plural is genuine and not a case of circumlocution is harmed by the fact that the text is silent on the subject.

Third, in the case of Cyprian, the text does seem to read the way von Harnack has interpreted it. Cyprian is apparently the recipient of the oracle, although again the point is debatable. It can only be maintained if one equates the two clauses:

| what has already been manifested to me | = | what has been prescribed by the authority of our Lord and God to an obedient and fearing servant. |

This equation can be questioned by Cyprian's use of *immo,* which clearly separates these two clauses and regulates their relationship. If *immo* is translated as "yes, indeed," one may argue that Cyprian is speaking of himself. Yet, *immo* is often translated as meaning "on the contrary" or "nay, rather."[40] Thus, the clauses would relate as follows: "For I remember what has already been manifest to me, no rather [*immo*], what has been prescribed by the authority of our Lord and God to an obedient and fearing servant." While one can still argue that "me" and the "servant" are the same and that Cyprian employed *immo* to emphasize his own humility before God, it is as easily argued that the obedient and fearing servant is another person and that Cyprian remembered, midsentence, who it was.

None of this argumentation then, either pro or con, is definitive, and perhaps it is not even that important. Probably of more importance are what appear to be von Harnack's presuppositions concerning such supernatural manifestations as genuine visitations. His basic position seems to be that Cyprian saw himself in much the same way as Hermas did. In thinking through the realities of his own precarious situation, he chose to employ accounts of visions (whether genuine or not) to solidify his own political power base. Von Harnack's appraisal is that while Cyprian may claim to be a prophet, one needs also to look at the politics of the situation. In light of the possibility that Cyprian was merely using "prophecy" in a self-serving way, von Harnack rejected the genuine character of Cyprian's claims. Instead he chose a position similar to a "modern" secularist viewpoint.[41] It must be conceded that a significant political dimension did exist in Cyprian's relationship to the Christians at Carthage. However, it is not essential to assume that the politics dictated his "visions."

That they had political and practical uses, particularly in bad times, did not make their authenticity suspect. They were facts of psychic life recognized by the whole community. They could be used, as were other facts, to support or attack practices and institutions. To infer fictitiousness or conscious calculation would be to yield to too much skepticism.[42]

Clarke, too, criticizes von Harnack's skepticism: "We may well be inclined to react unsympathetically to Cyprian's exploitation of what appears to be unduly convenient heavenly illumination as knock-down argument in order to assert control over his turbulent clergy. But we ought at least to recall that this is written in a society where such inspiration was considered as a normal part of affairs."[43] In light of the criticisms raised by Sage and Clarke, it may be that von Harnack credits too much of Cyprian's motivation to design.[44]

CHAPTER FOURTEEN

VISIONS CONVEYING COMFORT TO CONFESSORS

A second major category of visions in Cyprian epistles is centered on the confessors. These were the persons who, like Perpetua and Saturus, had publicly confessed they were Christians and had been sentenced to hard labor in the North African prisons or mines and/or who had been sentenced to death, but had not yet been martyred. The accounts regarding visions and confessors are found in four epistles,[1] which once again involve a variety of destinations and recipients and cover a period of some eight years.

THE EXPERIENCES OF SERGIUS AND ROGATIANUS THE PRESBYTER

The earliest of these (*Epistle* 6) was addressed to Sergius, Rogatianus, and other confessors who were with them. It was written during Cyprian's first period of seclusion in mid A.D. 250.[2] In this epistle, Cyprian attempts to encourage these confessors to continue in their stand as Christians and not to turn back. He tries to help them see the glory of their calling as confessors about to become martyrs. Within this epistle, however, Cyprian notes the role of the Spirit and divine visitations four times, and he gives us a glimpse of the theological and practical significance of these experiences in the lives of the confessors.

The first such mention reads:

> I send my congratulations to you, as well as my exhortations that you persevere with steadfast courage in your glorious and holy confession. You have entered upon the pathway of the Lord's blessings (*et ingsressi viam dominicae dignitonis*). May you press forward along it with spiritual valor (*spiritale virtute*) so that you may gain your crown, having as your guard and guide the Lord who said: "And see, I am with you all days, even to the end of the world."[3]

Several items should be noted regarding this passage. The term *dignatio* appears once again, but this time in the phrase *dominicae dignationis*. Thus,

whatever it was to which Cyprian made reference, he saw it as an experience from the Lord. It may safely be assumed, then, that his *dominicae
dignationis* is equivalent to the term we have already assessed, *divina
dignatio.*

Second, whatever this *dignatio* was, Cyprian described it as a "way"
upon which these confessors could travel. It appears, then, that these
dominicae dignationis were entered at one point in time, and Cyprian's
encouragement centered on a continuing progression along the same way.

Third, Cyprian pointed out two reasons why the confessors should be
encouraged. They were able to continue to draw upon the resources of the
Spirit for strength (*spiritali virtute*), and they had been promised both
guidance and protection by the Lord. It was the same Lord who had
promised never to leave them.[4]

After his initial word of encouragement, Cyprian continued with an
exhortation. "There should now be found in your hearts and minds," he
writes,

> nothing but those divine precepts and heavenly ordinances, whereby the
> Holy Spirit has ever encouraged us to endure sufferings.[5]

Here, Cyprian once again makes reference to a strengthening role of
the Spirit. It is a role of animation toward endurance, a role that produces
an ability within confessors to endure their suffering. It is a role by which
the Spirit will bring before these confessors certain information: namely,
divine precepts and heavenly commands. The larger context of this
passage seems to indicate that Cyprian had in mind here the role of the
Spirit as set forth by Jesus in John 14:26[6] and that these precepts and
commands were nothing more than passages of Scripture or other writings
which, when brought to the remembrance of the confessors and applied
by the Spirit, would bring strength.[7]

A third statement in this epistle which addresses the subject of visions
and revelations among the confessors is a short one that casts a little more
light on the two just discussed. It reads simply, "God in His goodness
(*divina dignatio*) has allied with you in glorious confession young boys as
well."[8] This passage helps us understand most fully what the divine
condescension was as it related to the confessors.

According to Cyprian, God's goodness—literally, the divine condescension—was directly related to the confessors' act of confession. It
seems, then, that Jesus' words as recorded in Luke's gospel may help in
gaining an understanding of Cyprian's reference both to the *divina dignatio*
in this passage and his previous reference to spiritual strength. Jesus told
his disciples:

When they hand you over, do not worry about how you are to speak or what you are to say; for what you are to say will be given to you at that time; for it is not you who speak, but the Spirit of your Father speaking through you.[9]

In summary, Cyprian's reference to the *dignatio* was an attempt to remind the confessors of the Lord's promise never to leave those who serve him as well as his promise to send spiritual strength through the Holy Spirit in such times of need. Sergio and Rogatianus, like many others in North Africa at this time, had been brought before the Roman tribunal on charges that they were Christians. They had confessed to the charges as stated, and Cyprian's belief was that it was in the act of confession that the Lord, by means of the Holy Spirit, spoke through the confessors. It may have referred to a simple affirmative reply or to an extended dialogue with the Roman officials, but whatever it was, it was understood to be the Spirit, or the Lord through the Spirit, who spoke through these confessors. It was, no doubt, an expression of a word of wisdom or of the gift of prophecy at its best. In essence, the Spirit defended the confessors before their accusers in a spontaneous way. This act of confession placed them on the road of the Lord's blessing.

Once the confession had been made and the confessors imprisoned, the role the Spirit played was to strengthen and empower them so that they might not turn back from their confession. The Spirit brought to their remembrance the words of Jesus from the pages of Scripture, Jesus' own reminder that they should look to the future with hope and not remorse. It was the Spirit who enabled them to endure the suffering of privation and persecution and to experience the ultimate blessing of God (*divina dignatione*) in the transition from death unto life.[10]

THE EXPERIENCE OF MAPPALICUS

The confessor and martyr Mappalicus is mentioned in an open epistle "to the martyrs and confessors of Jesus Christ our Lord."[11] Cyprian's purpose in writing this letter was to encourage the manifold confessors and martyrs of North Africa to persevere in their confession. In this epistle, he reminds his readers that when they should be delivered before the authorities, they are literally the promise of Jesus that the Spirit of their Father will speak through them.[12] To help them understand more fully what is meant by this important passage, Cyprian cites the martyrdom of Mappalicus as a vivid example of what we have previously examined: the practical value of the divine blessing. Cyprian wrote:

The present battle [the Decian persecution] has given proof of this [saying]. A voice filled with the Holy Spirit broke forth from the martyr's lips when the most blessed Mappalicus, in the midst of his torments, cried out to the proconsul: "The contest you will see tomorrow." And the words he spoke giving witness to his fortitude and his faith, the Lord has fulfilled. A heavenly contest was shaped, and the servant of God did win his crown, striving in the contest which he had promised.[13]

From this fascinating account we note first that Cyprian believed sufficiently in the validity and truth of Jesus' promise and instruction to expect its complete fulfillment. That is, Cyprian understood and believed that the Spirit had a unique empowering role in the life of believers who were under pressure from persecution, and he believed that this role could be observed by those who watched. He viewed that role as a prophetic role. The Spirit spoke through the confessor in the form of either a word of wisdom or of prophecy. Cyprian did not state which of these it was or whether indeed it was some combination that was in effect at the time the believer was confronted by the magistrates. But there can be little doubt he understood the Spirit of prophecy to have been in effect at such moments.[14]

Second, he chose as an illustration of his belief the example of Mappalicus. We know nothing more about this martyr than what is contained in Cyprian's accounts.[15] It seems obvious, however, that Cyprian was acquainted with the case of this martyr from a firsthand source, and he used the example in a way which would lead one to believe that his readers knew of the case as well.

Third, from the way he described how Mappalicus responded to the proconsul in his confession, it is clear he wanted his readers to understand that Mappalicus acted as little more than a mouthpiece for the words and thoughts of the Spirit. He described this act in the following manner: "A voice filled with the Holy Spirit broke forth from the martyr's lips."[16] The words attributed to the "voice full of the Holy Spirit" were simple: "The contest you will see tomorrow." They were future tense and, therefore, predictive in their orientation, and they appear to have been directed to the tribunal. A summary of the situation could be constructed something like the following.

Mappalicus had been arrested and imprisoned on charges of being a Christian. His imprisonment must have covered some period of time, and perhaps the tribunal gave him one last chance to recant from his Christian confession. His choices were "Recant, or face death in the contest tomorrow."[17] Mappalicus did not recant, but continued steadfast in his confession. The word he returned to the tribunal was both a confession and a prediction: "The contest you will see tomorrow." Cyprian argued it was a voice full of the Holy Spirit that responded to the tribunal. The Spirit was the One who was really responsible for the confession, through words spoken by Mappalicus. The Spirit was the Power behind the confession. Yet, Mappalicus spoke these words with virtue and faith.[18] It was, therefore, a cooperative effort.

Cyprian added a footnote regarding the fulfillment of this predictive word. His analysis was that what Mappalicus had said when full of the Holy Spirit was fulfilled by the Lord.[19] Mappalicus went into the contest and was crowned a martyr. The contest, however, was more than man against man or man against beast, for in Cyprian's mind its reality lay in the fact that it was a spiritual or heavenly contest. It was a case of "spiritual" warfare, and it was the Spirit who enabled Mappalicus to move from confessor to martyr, from death into life.

In conclusion, then, Cyprian understood the role of the Spirit as one who enabled a servant of God to be thus crowned. Mappalicus, with an overwhelming faith in the trustworthiness of God, prophesied by means of the Spirit both a confession and a prediction. Cyprian understood it to be a concrete example of the fulfillment of Jesus' instructions in Matt. 10:19–20. Mappalicus did not recant his faith, but held to it even though martyrdom was the test applied to the prophetic oracle, "The contest you will see tomorrow." The prophecy was judged as genuine because it was fulfilled.[20] The Lord's promise was confirmed, and the confessors to whom Cyprian was writing would be encouraged.[21]

CYPRIAN'S INSTRUCTIONS TO CHRISTIANS IN THIBARIS

At the onset of the Gallian persecution (about A.D. 253), Cyprian addressed a letter to the Christians who lived in Thibaris, a city some seventy-five to eighty miles inland from Carthage. Apparently the Christians in this city had repeatedly requested that Cyprian visit them, but due to continued persecution he had been unable to do so. Rather, he chose to respond to their requests by letter, a letter by which he meant to encourage them in their Christian walk. This was not easily done, however, since they seem to have been in fairly immediate danger of being martyred because of their Christian convictions. His task, therefore, became one of exhorting them to the prize of martyrdom, which was already on the horizon.

As Cyprian began this letter he shared with the Thibarians the fact that he believed the Lord had dealt with him on numerous occasions about persecution. Once again he used the term *dignatio* to describe these events. Let us take a closer look at the passage:

> We have been receiving numerous urgent warnings by which the Lord in His goodness (*nam cum Domini instruentis dignatione*) seeks to instruct us. It is our duty, accordingly, to make known to you also the anxious warnings that are being communicated to us.[22]

In his introduction, Cyprian wanted to make it clear that what he was about to put on the page was a message he believed the Lord had given to him. It was a message he claimed the Lord had given through condescensions for two specific purposes: to instigate or stimulate them to action and to warn them. Thus, he began his message to the Thibarians:

> You have to realize, you have to be utterly convinced, you have to hold as certain that the day of affliction is now dawning overhead: The demise of the world and the time of Antichrist are nigh. Hence we must all take our stand, being at the ready to go into battle; we should have no thought other than for the glories of eternal life and the crown that is won by confessing the Lord. Neither should we regard what is coming as in any way comparable with what has already been; the battle that now looms over us is more serious and savage by far. For it, the soldiers of Christ must equip themselves with the weapons of unblemished faith and valorous strength, reflecting that the reason why they drink each day the cup of the blood of Christ is that they themselves may thus also be enabled to shed their blood for Christ's sake.[23]

Cyprian wrote with a singleness of purpose: to prepare the Thibarian Christians for any eventuality. He fully expected them to be persecuted, and he chose to prepare them by passing along to them the message in which he had been instructed. His understanding of why the message had been given to him also led him to incorporate these facts into his message. Thus, he stressed heavily that they "have to realize, . . . be utterly convinced" of and "hold as certain" the truth of his message.

Cyprian's message was given in apocalyptic terms. It was, indeed, a message of warning. In it he declared, "the day of affliction is now dawning overhead: the demise of the world and the time of Antichrist are nigh."[24] It was a message that pointed toward the end of the current fray while acknowledging its apparent power, and it presented a warning for those who shortly must face the onslaught of its power to prepare.[25] It was a picture that interpreted the times in the same way the apostle John had interpreted them to the recipients of his epistles. Only the identity of antichrist was different. For John, it included largely the docetic teachers of Asia Minor (see 1 John 4:1–3; 2 John 7), but for Cyprian, antichrist was embodied in those who were persecuting the Christians of North Africa, and the persecution was imminent. Its imminence demanded immediate preparation.

The preparation Cyprian suggested had to do with how these Christians would respond to the persecution. It did not stress the concerns for material things or personal relationships or even concerns of the persecution itself. It stressed preparation for the battle, for which they should look forward only to "the glories of eternal life and the crown that is won by confessing the Lord" (cf. Heb. 12:1–2).

It is difficult to assess whether the method of preparation Cyprian suggested was part of what he received in the *dignatione* or whether the message had been a simple statement that he freely applied to the contemporary situation. It would seem, however, that the latter might have more validity.

Cyprian, in essence, reiterated the message clearly within this passage. He stated, "the day of affliction is now dawning overhead: the demise of the world and the time of Antichrist are nigh." The implication of this warning was also clear: "we must all take our stand."[26] Thus, Cyprian claimed the Lord had instructed him by means of a *dignatione*, an instruction that equated the day of affliction, the end of the age, the time of antichrist, and Cyprian's own day. He believed that while past persecutions had been severe, they were yet building in a crescendo to a climax in which the embodiment of antichrist would become clear and that that time was fast approaching.

Cyprian's personal reactions to the message of instruction included two closely related ideas. The first was an immediate response that "we must all take our stand." The second clarified further this initial reaction: "The battle that now looms over us is more serious and savage by far [than has ever before been witnessed]. For it, the soldiers of Christ must equip themselves."[27] Through these related responses, Cyprian provided basic guidelines from which he believed the Thibarian Christians might profit.

Cyprian's guidelines were simple enough and may be summarized briefly. First, the Thibarian Christians were told to think of nothing other than the ultimate outcome of the imminent challenge. They were to keep their minds on the glory of eternal life and the crown they would receive for being consistent in the confession of their faith. They were to look beyond their suffering to eternal glory. Second, they needed to prepare for the ultimate confrontation with uncorrupted faith and robust courage. Cyprian maintained that their faith could be increased and their courage strengthened through daily participation in the Eucharist.

In summary, then, if Cyprian's reference to *dignatione* is a reference to the gift of prophecy, as it seems to be, it demonstrates a purpose for the gift the apostle Paul suggested might be present (see 1 Cor. 14:3). Cyprian had received a revelation from the Lord. It included nothing more than the statement in 1 John 2:18. Yet, he saw in it a message for his time and a clear application to the situation in which the Christians residing in Thibaris were soon to find themselves. Having received the message, he passed it on to the Thibarians, adding his own interpretation to the message, which he believed was directed toward their situation. He gave them some simple guidelines that he hoped would help them in the troubled days ahead. It was a word of prophecy that would be tested ultimately by the historical events in the intense persecution which, within a very short time, involved much of North Africa.

Elsewhere in this same epistle, Cyprian spoke briefly of the promise and instruction found in Matt. 10:19–20. As he continued to exhort and encourage the Thibarian Christians toward their future in martyrdom, he reminded them of the three young men of Israel who had been placed in the fiery furnace for refusing to worship the image that King Nebuchadnezzar had made. He visualized the Thibarians as being in a position similar to that occupied by the three young men, a position from which the young men believed God could deliver them. But they were not afraid to have their faith tested, nor were they afraid of the death that might overtake them. It was in their confession of this very fact (see Dan. 3:16–18) that they proved the truth of Jesus' words in Matt. 10:19–20.

In his elaboration on this passage, Cyprian showed clearly that he had a gift of prophecy in mind:

> He [Jesus] has said that what we may say and answer will be granted and presented to us at that hour through divine power, and that at that time it is not we who speak but the Spirit of God the Father. And as He neither departs nor is parted from those who confess Him, He is the one who not only speaks but also is crowned in us. [28]

It should probably be noted that the words used at the moment of confession are given to the speaker in a spontaneous manner. They would not be carefully prepared remarks but, rather, *ad hoc* statements made at the time of confrontation. Furthermore, the confessor appears to be not much more than a mouthpiece, for Cyprian wrote, "it is not we who speak, but the Holy Spirit of God." Thus, we could also say that it is the Spirit who inspires or conveys the message.

In summary, then, Cyprian had a concept of prophecy which (1) assumed a semipassive role for the confessor; that is, the Spirit spoke through the confessor's lips; (2) gave an active role to the Spirit, who was the real speaker in this situation; (3) claimed a message that was addressed *ad hoc*, but (4) which originated spontaneously from God. Thus, the confessor who spoke a prophetic word did so only as long as he or she spoke what had been supplied, and in so doing, it was God who really spoke. The martyrdom that came as a result could be pictured as a victory for God. The theme is clearly one of *Christus in martyre*.[29]

THE CASES OF LUCIUS, NEMESIANUS, AND COMPANIONS

A letter addressed to Cyprian from Lucius makes it clear that Cyprian knew what the gift of prophecy was. This same letter also informs us that Cyprian himself exercised this gift.[30] Lucius was one of Cyprian's fellow bishops who, during the early part of the Valerian persecution, was enslaved in the mines of North Africa. Awaiting his martyrdom alongside a number of other brethren,[31] Lucius and the others had received a letter from Cyprian, a letter meant to bring comfort during their oppression.[32] According to Lucius, it did bring the comfort Cyprian had intended for it to bring. He wrote to Cyprian that on reading the letter, it had "eased the burden of our chains, . . . brought us solace in our distress, and support in our urgent need."[33]

Not only did Cyprian's letter soothe these martyrs, but Lucius wrote that it brought strength to them as well. In his own words, we read, "we have been fired with fresh vigour and spirit to confront any further punishments that may await us."[34] Continuing on, Lucius informed Cyprian that

> by your words you have fully prepared us, steeling us with the determination to bear those very sufferings we now bear; but we remain confident of our reward in heaven, of our crown of martyrdom and of the kingdom of God, *following that prophecy which you, filled with the Holy Spirit, pledged to us in your letter.*[35] (Emphasis mine.)

It is immediately evident from Lucius's letter that he understood a portion of what Cyprian had penned to be prophetic in its origin and content, for he refers to it as *ad prophetiam*. This is further clarified by Lucius's recognition that Cyprian promised it while "filled with the Holy Spirit." What is not immediately clear is which portion of Cyprian's letter Lucius had in mind or whether it was the entire letter to which he referred.

Cyprian wrote of many things in his letter to Lucius and Nemesianus, but there are two or three in particular that may lead to a better understanding of what was meant by "prophecy" and "mysteries revealed." On two occasions, Cyprian mentioned a "divine favor" or "divine honor." The first of these is found in *Epistle* 76.1, which reads as follows:

Is it conceivable that I could restrain my tongue in silence and hold my peace at a time when I have learned of the many glorious exploits of dearest friends of mine? Through those deeds God has favored [literally, *divina dignatio*] and honored you: some of your number have already gone on ahead to receive from the Lord their crowns for their deserts, having brought their martyrdom to its accomplishment.[36]

What is meant here is not completely clear from the context, but it seems to suggest the *Christus in martyre* theme once again. The "glorious exploits" of the confessors are clearly to be identified with their ability to make their confession. As a result, or as part of the very act of confession, God has provided divine favor, thereby bringing honor to their number. Should this be a reference to the prophetic phenomenon, as it seems to be, the emphasis Cyprian makes is on the gracious bestowal of this charisma as a response to a faithful act of confession under pressure.

The second instance is found further along in the same epistle:

Clearly now [that everyone of you stands near to the promised reward of God] your word has become all the more effectual in supplication, for prayers made in the midst of persecution are answered all the more readily. Ask and pray, therefore, with all the greater fervour that through God's bounty [*dignatio divina*] we may, all of us, bring our confession to its completion.[37]

Cyprian's use of *dignatio divina* within this context, while translated by Clarke as "God's bounty," is perhaps more clearly identified as a type of beatific vision that one might attain in the transition from death unto life at the time of martyrdom. Yet, it suggests that this is a future event and still to be achieved. Perhaps an analysis of its basis, "For each of you now awaits in readiness God's promised reward," would lead us to a clearer understanding of what Lucius may have had in mind when he referred to Cyprian's prophecy.

In order to accomplish this, however, we must examine *Epistle* 76.5, where Cyprian encouraged the martyrs by reminding them of the two passages in the gospels already discussed: Matt. 10:19–20 and Luke 21:14–15.[38] His repeated use of these passages provides us with a clue to the fervency with which the North African church claimed these promises within their experiences of persecution. It is also very probable that the application of these promises to the situation of Lucius (which was understood) is the basis for the prophecy Lucius had received from Cyprian.

To undertake a detailed study of *Epistle* 76 provides little additional help in our quest for an explicit example of a prophetic gift. There is no clear "messenger formula," no "Thus saith the Lord." There is no claim of prophetic inspiration, and there appears to be no clearly stated prophetic oracle. Yet, there *is* a comforting stance within the letter that Cyprian made clear. He writes that the confessors have been promised the presence and power of the Spirit in the time of persecution, and he reminds them that "the sufferings of the present time are not worth comparing with the glory about to be revealed to us."[39] In short, Cyprian promised these martyrs that they would succeed in their martyrdom and, in their very act of dying for their faith, that they would have a guaranteed security from the judgment of God.

Lucius, it seems, seized on this truth. He recognized in it, since it came from Cyprian, the fullness of the Spirit. He recognized in it "the promise of our crown of martyrdom and of the kingdom of God."[40] He recognized the truth that had been applied in his situation, and he was comforted and sustained by it. He saw himself as now steeled and fully armed for the struggle. He also viewed himself confidently as one already made a conqueror in the battle that was to follow, a battle in which he would be martyred. Again, all of this seems to be consistent with what the Apostle Paul had in mind when he penned 1 Cor. 14:3. Those who prophesy, Paul wrote, "speak to other people for their upbuilding and encouragement and consolation." By his own words, Lucius recognized in Cyprian far more than mere Christian fellowship. He heard a prophetic oracle, written down for his own "upbuilding and encouragement and consolation," a sustaining word that was inspired by the Holy Spirit. It brought to him strength, confidence, and determination to live out his remaining days in faithfulness to his Christian confession.

CHAPTER FIFTEEN

VISIONS EXHORTING TO CHRISTIAN UNITY

Perhaps the most interesting and the most controversial of Cyprian's visions are those found in *Epistle* 11. There are at least four visions recorded in this letter, which is addressed to the presbyters and deacons of Carthage during Cyprian's first retirement.[1] Cyprian's letter was directed toward meeting a problem that had arisen in Carthage in the midst of the Decian persecution. The flock was scattered or scattering, and a division had arisen among the clergy as to the future of those who had lapsed. Cyprian argued that it was this division which had resulted in the problems the church now faced.[2]

Cyprian's concern was to bring unity to the congregation and to encourage the clergy to spend more time in prayer. He accused the church of having broken God's law and of departing from the path of God's judgments. As a result, these Christians were feeling God's rod of chastisement and, according to Cyprian, their response should be to ask for forgiveness. With this as his background, he began to illustrate his concern by citing a series of visions.

"ASK AND YOU SHALL HAVE"

The first vision Cyprian mentions is given with a few words of introduction. Cyprian wrote that he had chosen to describe the vision in his letter to the Carthaginians because it had been revealed by the Lord and it contained an important oracle. His introductory statement reads:

> You ought to know what has particularly induced, indeed, driven me to write this letter to you. The Lord thought fit to manifest and reveal a vision. In it, these words were spoken: "Ask and you shall have."[3]

It is important to note several things regarding this introductory statement. We are not told who the recipient of the vision was, only that there was a vision. The introduction is written in a passive third person. It would not seem to be overly speculative to suggest, as many do, that Cyprian was the vision's recipient since he is the one driven to write as a result, but since later in this same epistle (11.5.1) he is explicit about his own role in receiving another vision, the question must remain open.

It was clearly a *vision* that Cyprian described, for he himself used the Latin term *visione*. The Lord is described as the source of the vision, and in true visionary fashion, the purpose for this manifestation was to reveal something. As a vision, it was not merely a silent picture, nor does it seem to have been a fully narrated one. There was, however, as part of the total visionary experience, what one might describe as a "prescriptive" oracle.

An unnamed individual gave or spoke the oracle. Although we are not told this, whoever spoke the oracle was probably a character in the vision itself. It may have been the Lord from whom the vision was said to come. It may have been someone else. The words of this short "prescriptive" oracle were similar to Jesus' words recorded in Matt. 7:7: "Ask, and it will be given you; search, and you will find; knock, and the door will be opened for you."[4] The difference between Jesus' words and the oracle in this vision lies in the emphasis on the "having" that Cyprian describes and "giving" that, according to Matthew, Jesus had originally emphasized. The situation confronting the clergy at Carthage seems to have demanded the emphasis on having, so it is that Cyprian applies it to the Carthaginian situation.[5]

In order to make this oracle more understandable in the Carthaginian context, Cyprian elaborated on it. The context is not totally clear, and the extent or limits of the vision in the text is debatable.[6] What follows, however, appears to be part of the whole visionary experience.[7] A crowd of people is described, and they are told to pray for certain persons who were pointed out to them. The identity of the crowd is not clear, but Cyprian's intention suggests that it symbolized the Christians at Carthage.

When the crowd was told to intercede for the individuals pointed out to them, they did as they were instructed. It soon became evident, though, that they were praying at cross-purposes. They had raised dissonant or discordant voices. Because of the resulting conflict, Cyprian described the person who had commanded "Ask and you shall have" as greatly displeased. How Cyprian became aware of his displeasure is not clear, although were he the "seer," he would be recording something he had seen himself, a firsthand experience.

Adolf von Harnack describes the *Sitz-im-Leben* as one in which the community of believers had gathered together, filled with grief and apprehension concerning their imprisoned brother [Cyprian]. Then a voice broke in and directed them to offer a prayer of intercession on his behalf as well as one for those who were with him. Not everyone was willing to participate in praying for their brother. A few did, but there was disharmony present, and God was displeased and unable to act.[8]

Here the vision seems to break off and the interpretation or application begins. Cyprian interpreted the vision as a picture of the actual situation within the Carthaginian congregation. While it is possible that the vision itself included an application, this does not appear to be the case. In the interpretation of the vision there is the repeated use of a first-person plural. That is, while the oracle itself is directed as a command, "Ask, and you shall have," to a group designated by the second-person plural, the interpretation and proof-texting that follows includes the speaker or writer among those who have been instructed by the Lord. To assume that it is God who speaks in the vision and that God is also instructed by the Lord makes no sense. (See appendix J for an outline of this vision.)

Apparently, the congregation was in great internal conflict. So great was the trouble that their prayer was not even heard. With this as his background, Cyprian appealed to a number of biblical references so that he could remind his parishioners of the importance of Christian unity.[9] He urged upon them the value of uniting in one accord in order to bring about an end to their persecution and in order to obtain the release of those who were currently experiencing peril to their salvation and faith due to imprisonment.[10]

The application of the vision to the situation revolving around Cyprian's own retreat from the church at Carthage is summarized in an indictment against those involved in dissension. In fact, suggests Cyprian, "these evils would not have befallen our community had they all been of one mind together."[11]

These seem clearly to be the words of Cyprian. They were meant to provide the existential situation, or *Sitz-im-Leben,* to explain *why* the vision was given. In this case, the Christian community was confused and disoriented by the current political events. Persecution had come. Some of their number were imprisoned or, as in Cyprian's case, they were in a secret place of retirement. Now the congregation was disunited in their attempts to reach a solution on how to act. In order to help them, Cyprian contended, the Lord had given a vision in order to reveal how their plight might come to a satisfactory conclusion. To whom God revealed the vision is unimportant in the long run. What is important is that the vision was allegedly given for the purpose of directing a confused and persecuted church.

By the one test still available to us today—its consistency with Scripture—the vision seems to have constituted a genuine manifestation of a prophetic gift.[12] That it was attributed to the Lord by Cyprian, that it was addressed *ad hoc,* that its purpose seems to have been for the ultimate edification of the local body, and that it was based on a biblical passage all tend to indicate that it could be considered to be an example of a genuine vision/prophecy dating from the middle of the third century. This vision/prophecy, however, is connected both logically and grammatically to a second one on the same general theme to which we now turn our attention.

THE VISION OF THREE MEN

Within the context of Cyprian's *Epistle* 11, a second vision relating to the first one and addressing the same situation is connected grammatically by the clause, "Now this was also revealed."[13] No reference is made to the situation in which this vision was revealed, only that it was given at a time prior to the persecution in which the Carthaginian Christians now found themselves. Once again, no indication is given as to the identity of the person who received the vision. Its relationship to the first vision, although introduced by Cyprian's use of "*nam*," is abundantly clear from the content of the vision/prophecy itself.

Cyprian may be the one who received both of these visions. This is the position von Harnack has adopted,[14] and it is a credible position because the detail of the vision is lucid. It appears to be a firsthand rather than a secondhand report. One is able to see the faces and feel the emotions of those who are described, and all of this detail lends itself to an indication of a genuine firsthand experience. The attribution of these visions to Cyprian himself gains added credibility when it is coupled to the fact that he claims to have experienced a third and a fourth vision within the immediate context of this epistle.

It is probably best to allow Cyprian to speak for himself and describe the various elements of the vision. It is immediately obvious that the elements of this vision are once again familiar (see Figure 7).[15]

There are personalities present in this vision who are not unknown, and the context of the vision makes it clear that its three characters beg for identification. This vision uses one key figure who appears in a variety of visions within the setting of the early church. It is the figure of a young man,[16] and in the present context, it is undoubtedly meant to be understood as Jesus.

He is the one who sits at the right hand of his father and grieves because his commandments are not observed. In the interpretation of the previous vision, the congregation is disunited because it has not taken seriously the command of the Lord "that you love one another."[17]

Once the identification of Jesus has been completed, the identity of the father quickly falls into place. It remains only to identify the third party who stands with the net. His identity is further qualified by the remark that he had received the power of destroying. Such imagery seems to point

FIGURE 7

The Vision	. . . the father of a household was seated, with a young man sitting on his right. This young man looked worried and somewhat aggrieved as well as distressed as he sat mournfully holding his chin in his hand. But there was another person standing on the left side; he was carrying a net and he kept threatening to cast it and ensnare the crowd of bystanders.
Transition to Interpretation	And when the person who saw the vision wondered what this meant, he was told that
The Interpretation Given within the Visionary Experience	the young man who was sitting like that on the right was grieving and sorrowful at the neglect of his precepts, whereas the one on the left was jubilant at being given the opportunity of obtaining from the father of the household leave to rage and destroy.

toward Satan as the third party,[18] and the vision makes clear that all of his power is a derived power. He is operating not from his own strength, but is being allowed by God to cause disruption in the life of the church because the church has chosen not to obey the commandments of Jesus. They are being confirmed in the consequences of their disobedience.

Thus, the interpretation of the vision is important in the overall understanding of the vision. It conveys the idea that it is through disobedience that trouble has come to the Christians at Carthage. This disobedience has grieved Jesus and pleased Satan. The inevitable conclusion is that the church is involved in sin, and it is essential in Cyprian's application of the vision to recognize its implications for his own retreat from Carthage.

The transition within the vision from the picture to the interpretation involves the seer with the revealer. The seer marvels at the vision, wonders at its meaning. An unnamed voice begins to unfold the mystery of the revelation, and it is this unfolding that brings clarification. Once again we have a vision complete with speaking parts. Cyprian's use of the passive (*dictum est ei*) and the past tense throughout the interpretation suggests that the content of the vision recorded in this epistle is not a true oracle. It is simply a summary of events.

The application of the vision/prophecy is clearly parallel to that of the first vision, "Ask and you shall have" (see first section of this chapter). And Cyprian applies it forcefully:

so long as we hold in scorn the precepts of the Lord, so long as we do not observe the saving ordinances of the law which He has given, the enemy gains power to do harm and with a cast of his net holds us enmeshed, too ill-armed and off-guard to repel him.[19]

There is little doubt that Cyprian has in mind his ecclesiastical opponents in the divided congregation when he refers to "those who are too ill-armed and off-guard to repel." By their selfish actions they have been guilty of not keeping the commandments, such as to love one another. Cyprian, therefore, uses the vision to address what he perceives to be the problem of sin and weakness in his congregation. Their unwillingness to obey Christ has led to their current state of affairs.

The understanding of this vision as a sample of a "prophetic gift" is, once again, something to be considered. Several simple tests may be applied in our evaluation of the material. The first of which involves Cyprian's own presentation. That it is a prophetic gift from the Lord in the form of a vision can be seen by Cyprian's use of "Now this was also revealed," which ties it to the first vision, which was clearly denoted by the words, "The Lord thought fit to manifest and reveal a vision."[20] It was, in Cyprian's mind at least, a revelation and, thereby, may be treated as in some way prophetic.

To this revelation, Cyprian applies an ancient test, the test of fulfillment. Although the vision and interpretation were recorded in the past tense, Cyprian remarks explicitly that a great deal of time has elapsed since the vision was seen. His judgment of the contemporary situation within the congregation is that the description of the division was forewarned. It was predicted, and thus, it has provided its own test for fulfillment. "This revelation was made long ago," noted Cyprian, "before the present storm arose. And we see now fulfilled what was then revealed."[21] Division had occurred within the congregation, division that Cyprian viewed as sinful and avoidable. Thus, he used the vision to support his claim that the Carthaginian Christians were participants in their own destinies and living testimonies to the veracity of the vision.

A third test is to see whether this vision is consistent with Scripture. There appears to be no obvious problem except for the question of whether Satan could ever legitimately be understood as a member of the same family as Jesus. Cyprian does not designate who the members of the family are, but the scene is suggestive of a father and two sons. If, however, the literary form is understood to be a parable, the difficulty is overcome without further elaboration since the logical connections of real life do not need to be pressed. In this case, there is no reason to suggest that the vision is inconsistent with Scripture.

Tests regarding the original *Sitz-im-Leben*, the seer, who remains name-less, and any reference to ecstasy are not recorded. They are beyond recovery. So, the final test must be the test of purpose. Once again, here, it passes. The purpose served by transmitting this prophetic manifestation is a parenetic or prescriptive one. The Christians are again alerted to the problem of disunity. The vision calls them to account for their sin. It assesses blame in its interpretation and application to the situation at Carthage, but it also allows Cyprian freedom to encourage the congrega-tion to return both to the commandments of Christ and to his salutary laws. In short, it, too, seems to be a genuine example of a third-century prophetic gift.

"WATCH AND PRAY"

At this point in *Epistle* 11, Cyprian begins to relate what can best be described as his own personal experiences with these prophetic gifts. He changes from the third person (it was said, and it was shown) to the first person (I was told). Cyprian clearly continues on the path he had already set in the epistle. He has thus far established that (1) the congregation has failed to obey Jesus' commands, (2) Jesus has been grieved, (3) Satan has been allowed to bring further disruption to the Christian community, and (4) the Christian community is in disarray with divisions and persecutions as a result. Cyprian's obvious intention is to bring order out of chaos and a sense of unity among the believers at Carthage. He chose to do so by relaying to them another vision; this time, one he has seen himself:

> We must be urgent in prayer and raise our mournful cries (*Oremus . . . et . . . ingemescamus*) with incessant supplication. For I must tell you, my very dear brothers, that not so long ago in a vision this reproach was also made to us.[22]

This introduction is of interest for several reasons. First, its tone is once again prescriptive. Cyprian's exhortation is to pray (*oremus*) and to groan (*ingemescamus*) with continual petitions. It is not completely clear to what the term "to groan" (*ingemescamus*) actually refers, but two possibili-ties quickly present themselves. It may be merely that he is referring to a groan of anguish or a lament. But it may also be that he has in mind the type of prayer mentioned in Rom. 8:26–27:

> Likewise the Spirit helps us in our weakness; for we do not know how to pray as we ought, but the Spirit himself intercedes with sighs too deep for words. And God, who searches the heart, knows what is the mind of the Spirit, because the Spirit intercedes for the saints according to the will of God.[23]

The depth of anguish is such that the congregation is incapable of praying adequately without the aid of the Spirit.

Second, Cyprian does not exempt himself from the exhortation. He always involves himself with those who should pray and groan, and he claims already to have sat beneath the judgment of the vision. Yet, the reproach may be aimed at his own unwillingness or failure in the past to exhort the congregation to vigilance. Since, like his congregation, he has been less than vigilant, he feels the rebuke personally. It is at this point, then, that he believes he must share his vision with his flock.

The vision is summarized briefly with the words, "We are slumbering in our supplications, I was told; we are not watchful in prayer." Thus, two things may be noted about this vision. First, there is no graphic picture or illustration set forth for interpretation like those present in the first two visions. There is merely a statement dealing with a relaxed attitude toward prayer that points to spiritual laxity in the Carthaginian Christian community. Second, the oracle seems to have its basis in Jesus' exhortation, "Stay awake and pray that you may not come into the time of trial, the spirit indeed is willing, but the flesh is weak" (Matt. 26:41; see also 1 Thess. 5:17 and 1 Peter 4:7). At the least, it appears to be an exhortation based on a biblical principle, which is once again applied to a specific situation.

Cyprian seems to take responsibility for interpreting the vision himself. It is not attributed to a voice within the vision; rather, it is simply a logical deduction based on his understanding that the members of the congregation are sheep over whom Bishop Cyprian is the shepherd. His reaction is to interpret the present discord as a sign of God's rebuke. Thus, he has carried his argument one step further. The persecution and division that has resulted from the casting of the net by Satan—a power given to him by the Father—is merely a tool by which God is attempting to bring the congregation to a point of conformity with the commands of his Son, Jesus.[24]

Cyprian's point is that God is currently rebuking the congregation for their sin. They deserve the rebuke, for they have forgotten their Lord's command to love one another. However, they should take note of the fact that the rebuke is actually a sign of God's love and that its purpose is to correct, so ultimately the congregation will be preserved.

Cyprian goes on to make a major parenetic appeal based on God's revelation:

> if He goes to such pains for us and for our transgressions [as He has through the revelation about] watching and praying, it follows that we ought all the more to be urgent in prayer and supplication, firstly making our plea to the Lord Himself, and then, through Him, making our amends to God the Father.[25]

His application of the word conveyed through a vision is again a fulfillment of one purpose in the gift of prophecy: namely, exhortation.

With all these factors in mind, it seems that we have another example
of a genuine prophetic gift. Cyprian's claim is that it came in the form of a
vision. His deduction is that it was a timely message of exhortation from
God: it spoke to the situation at Carthage; it followed the guideline of
purpose set down by Paul in 1 Cor. 14:3; its basis was biblical; its result was
a call to a closer walk with God through prayer.

"THERE IS . . . A SHORT DELAY"

The fourth vision contained in this epistle is an equally interesting one.
It is said to have come to one described as "the least of His servants."[26] He
is also said to be undeserving of the Lord's favor (*dignatione*), but despite
his unworthiness, God has condescended toward him.[27] Cyprian's use of
"for us" *may* indicate that he has someone other than himself in mind in
this description,[28] but that is rather unlikely given the context in which
he is writing.

Exactly how the condescension took place in this instance we are not
told. The Lord may have spoken, as von Harnack suggests, through an
angel who delivered the message.[29] The message consists of the most
extensive oracle, a "parenetic oracle of assurance,"[30] that is recorded in
Cyprian's writings:

> Tell him . . . not to be anxious, for there is going to be peace, but there
> is, meantime, a short delay, for some are left still to be tested.[31]

The message falls into two parts. It recognizes a continuation of the
persecution for a short time, but it promises that the period of persecution
is to be followed by a period of peace.

Cyprian wrote this in the midst of the Decian persecution and could not
have known the importance his statement would come to hold. No doubt
those who refused to believe the prediction would argue that Cyprian's
word was of such an indeterminate length that it would be meaningless in
their circumstance. Yet, it has been pointed out that within a very short
period, Decius was unexpectedly killed in battle, and there came a respite
from the persecution.[32]

Like those oracles already studied, this one holds several items of
importance for our discussion. First, the source from which the oracle
originated seems to be God, for God is the one who ultimately has chosen
to favor "the least of His servants." The oracle was given to an intermedi-
ary to carry to its recipient. That the Lord commanded the messenger to
"tell him" may point toward Cyprian as the recipient of the message and

divine favor. That the messenger was described as *minimum famulum suum*, however, tends to indicate that the messenger was not Jesus but, rather, an angelic messenger. It may even be that such a messenger appeared as a shining young man. However, the text offers no further hints.

Second, the oracle is predictive in nature. It predicts a time of peace and exhorts the recipient to be comforted by this knowledge. In a day of persecution, no doubt, such a prediction would have brought a sense of peace and security to the one who knew it to be a promise from the Lord. Yet, all were not promised safety, for in the interim between the time of the prophetic word and the time of its predicted fulfillment, there would continue to be a short period of turmoil. The reason the messenger gave for a delay to the end of persecution is that there were some who still needed to be tested.

What follows is Cyprian's application of this oracle to the situation in Carthage. He interpreted the vision as an admonition, a means whereby those who would receive its message might be both warned or admonished as well as instructed and guided.[33]

Cyprian understood it to contain a warning against laxity and an instruction toward a rigorous life-style:

> we are admonished to be abstemious in diet and sober in drink. I have no doubt that this is to prevent hearts now uplifted with heavenly strength from being emasculated by worldly allurements or souls from being less watchful in prayer and petition by being weighed down with lavish feasting.[34]

Yet, food and drink were only a small portion of Cyprian's exhortation regarding the Christian life-style at Carthage. They were both symptomatic of and contributing to an ill. As Cyprian understood it, the ill was actually a laxity in prayer and supplication. Indeed, Cyprian's purpose for recording this divine intervention was consistent with the previous three prophetic acts. It was to stir the clergy remaining at Carthage, who would, in turn, stimulate the laity at Carthage to pray in unity for an end to the persecution, for strength and protection in the persecution, and for the restoration of Cyprian to his rightful place as shepherd of the flock at Carthage.

What remains, then, is to test this oracle in the same way the previous three have been assessed. Cyprian claimed that the oracle was pronounced in a vision. While the test of form is not possible since there is no vivid description of the method involved, one can judge it on at least three criteria provided by Cyprian's narrative. First, he says that it was given by God to a servant of God, one who was unworthy, but who, nonetheless, was a servant. Thus, its source is said to be God and its medium a visionary or prophetic gift as exercised by a Christian. Second, the content when analyzed shows that the oracle is consistent with the concerns of Scripture. It includes exhortation as well as comfort. It satisfies the guidelines of 1 Cor. 14:3. Third, it also apparently survived the test of fulfillment. It involved a predictive word that there would be a short time of persecution followed by a period of peace. If Cyprian recorded this oracle soon after its delivery (A.D. 250), then it was a matter of a few short months until it was fulfilled, for Decius met his untimely death in the year 251 and the time of persecution ended. In short, then, this visionary experience with accompanying oracle is likely to be a genuine example of a prophetic gift in the tradition of Paul, expressed midway through the third century at Carthage.

Revelations Providing Personal Direction

It is possible that nearly all visions or revelations addressed to this point could be lumped together under the present heading. This heading, however, has been selected to describe Cyprian's own experiences of personal guidance at critical times in his life. There are two incidents in particular which point to the fact that Cyprian took visions or "divine favor" very seriously when they applied to his own welfare.

A PROTECTIVE WORD

Early in Cyprian's term as bishop of Carthage, he went into hiding in response to the immediate dangers of persecution.[1] The selective nature of the persecutions that at particular times pursued church leaders urged him in this action. But his action led to questions regarding his ability to lead a congregation in the midst of persecution when he, himself, had run from that persecution into a place of hiding.[2] In essence, it touched off an attack on his credibility as bishop, the shepherd of the sheep.[3] How could he help others face the crisis in which they found themselves if he was afraid to pay the ultimate price? The sheep could not be expected to outperform the shepherd.

In order to answer the charges leveled against him and to clear up a libelous account of his behavior, Cyprian defended himself by addressing a letter to the Roman presbyters and deacons:

> Right at the very first onset of the troubles, when the populace clam-oured for me violently and repeatedly, I followed the directives and in-structions and withdrew for the time being. I was thinking not so much of my own safety as the general peace of our brethren; I was concerned that if I brazenly continued to show myself in Carthage I might aggravate even further the disturbance that had begun.[4]

This statement is not the whole story behind the flight of Cyprian in the face of the persecution that had been leveled at him. He indicates in another epistle that he moved from Carthage to the retirement estate at the clear direction of the Lord. It was, he wrote, "the Lord who bade me withdraw."[5] Exactly how the Lord made known this wish for Cyprian to retire is not completely clear, but it seems to be the case that Cyprian was directed to retreat by means of a vision. Evidence on behalf of this position comes from several sources.

The first passage in which Cyprian speaks of the Lord's immanent direction is a passage in which he also mentions visions and ecstasies. The immediate context provides an interesting commentary on his action, for he writes:

> For in addition to visions of the night, during the day also innocent young boys, who are here with us, are being filled with the Holy Spirit, and in ecstasy they see with their eyes and they hear and they speak words of warning and instruction which the Lord in His goodness gives (*dignatur*) to us. And you shall hear all of these things when the Lord *who bade me withdraw* has brought me back to you.[6] (Emphasis mine.)

It may be noticed almost immediately that Cyprian does not say in precise terms that the Lord directed him by means of a vision. However, there are several strong hints in this passage that indicate he meant that he had been directed by a vision to go into hiding.

It is clear that Cyprian is writing to the clergy in Carthage from his place of hiding. Among those who were with him were some young boys, who allegedly heard from the Lord regularly when they were filled with the Holy Spirit. Cyprian remarks that the Lord provided them with visions at any hour of the day or night. The process of seeing the visions was one involving some form of ecstasy. Of what that ecstatic state consisted, we are given no further information.

Along with the visual stimulation that occurred, there was sometimes an accompanying audio stimulation. That is, at times the visionary experience included a voice which provided both warning and instruction. It may well be just such a warning (*monere*) or instruction (*instruere*) that caused him to say the Lord had requested him to withdraw or retire.[7]

The use of *monere* is probably significant here, as could be the use of *instruere*. Cyprian's decision to retire from easy accessibility in Carthage to some hidden estate may easily be explained by his having received an instruction by reading Scripture or, more forcefully, by means of one of these two phenomena: a vision or a prophetic word. Since Cyprian had argued that the Lord in grace grants visionary manifestations to warn or to instruct, it is hardly unthinkable that Cyprian may have received such a warning or instruction—in essence, a prescriptive oracle from the Lord in just this manner—which prompted his decision to retire. His decision might be nothing more than his own interpretation of why the Lord asked him to withdraw. He had withdrawn so the rest of the congregation might have an easier time during the persecution with their bishop out of sight. Without visible leadership, the authorities might prove to be more lenient in seeking out the remaining practicing Christians.

Cyprian may even have kept some type of account or log of the words of instruction and warning conveyed in these visionary experiences, for he promised the clergy at Carthage that, when once again he stood in their midst, he would tell them everything. Although he did not specifically say he would tell them everything he had heard as a result of these visions, the context suggests this meaning in order to be fully intelligible.

Cyprian clearly showed himself to be totally open to the expectation that God would, sometime in the future, reverse this temporary warning or instruction and bring Cyprian back to occupy his rightful place as bishop of Carthage. He did not say precisely how he expected this to take place, but the inference to be drawn is that the Lord who bids him to retire, the Lord who speaks and shows through visions in an ecstasy so as to warn and instruct, the Lord who condescends, would one day, following the present time of persecution, return Cyprian to his rightful place in the church at Carthage in much the same way the Lord had directed him to retire.

The cumulative effect of these factors suggests, then, that Cyprian had been directed into hiding by a vision or prophecy from the Lord. Cyprian was merely waiting in retirement until such time as the Lord would indicate his will to be something other than what Cyprian, up until the time of writing this epistle, understood it to be. More than likely, he anticipated a personal visionary experience or one conveyed to him from among the boys who stood beside him in his retirement.

A second passage points even more strongly in this direction.[8] By the time Cyprian wrote this epistle, probably the earliest of his retirement, he had begun to feel the pangs of his isolation. He wrote to the clergy in Carthage informing them that he would return to Carthage when one of two things had taken place. He would return to Carthage (1) if the presbyters and deacons there wrote to him telling him that "affairs have been settled" and that he ought to come.[9] More important for our present understanding is the statement with which he concluded: he would return to them before they should write (2) if the Lord should condescend and tell him to leave his place of retirement or provide him with a sign to that effect.[10]

Cyprian's use of *dignatus* clearly places his thought here in the visionary/prophetic realm. It is by far the most frequent term he employed when referring to visionary experiences. Thus, this passage makes clearer what was intimated in the previous one. Cyprian was open to be shown (*osten-*

dere), to be warned (*monere*), or to be instructed (*instruere*) by means of visions.

A third passage makes it patently clear that, indeed, Cyprian was led into retirement by means of a vision. It is a passage, however, which Cyprian did not write, but which was written after his death by one of his devotees, a man named Pontius. Pontius wrote about Cyprian and his magnanimous spirit. It was by the Spirit's direction that Cyprian had been led into retirement,[11] recalled Pontius. Thus, the Spirit made it possible for Cyprian to live long enough to show forth his true generosity.

It must be understood that in writing of this incident, Pontius was performing a posthumous apologetic task on behalf of Cyprian. "Do you wish to be assured that the cause of his withdrawal was not fear?" Pontius asked.[12] In order to reassure his reader that such had *not* been the case, Pontius continued:

> fortunately, it occurred then, and truly by the Spirit's direction that the man [Cyprian] who was needed for so many and so excellent purposes was withheld from the consummation of martyrdom.[13]

Pontius went on to argue that if Cyprian had been driven merely by a mortal fear of death or fear for his own well-being, he could just as easily have avoided martyrdom by hiding once again. But Cyprian was directed by the Lord himself, and he went forth to martyrdom when he was instructed to do so. In Pontius's words:

> this suffering [martyrdom] he assuredly would have evaded as usual, if he had evaded it before. It was indeed that fear—and rightly so—that fear which would dread to offend the Lord—that fear which prefers to obey God's commands rather than to be crowned in disobedience. *For a mind dedicated in all things to God, and thus enslaved to the divine admonitions, believed that even in suffering itself it would sin, unless it had obeyed the Lord, who then bade him seek the place of concealment.*[14]

Thus, it appears Cyprian believed that God sent visions, revelations, or prophecies to individuals in the church of North Africa during the middle of the third century. Others, like himself, had received personal guidance through visions,[15] and he, like them, took seriously the dreams and visions in which he believed the *vox Dei* spoke to him regarding his personal welfare.

A PREDICTIVE WORD

If it can be said that Cyprian received direction through a vision to seek a place of hiding during the early years of his ministry as the bishop of

Carthage, that vision was ultimately reversed toward the end of his ministry. He had been in hiding during the time of the Decian persecution. North Africa had for a few short years enjoyed a relative relaxation of the persecution occasioned by the sudden death of Decius. However, with the accession to the throne of Valerian in A.D. 253, the spectre of persecution rose once again. It did not strike North Africa until the summer of 257.

During that summer, Valerian, at the suggestion of Egyptian Magi and the recommendation of his chief financial officer, Macrianus, sent forth an edict which "insisted that the Christian leaders should perform some act of acknowledgement to the traditional Roman ceremonies."[16] While we do not have an extant copy of the edict, its content is fairly assured on the basis of a conversation recorded in Eusebius's *Ecclesiastical History* between Dionysius and Aemilianus, the deputy prefect of Egypt at the time.[17] It was as a result of violating this edict that Dionysius, as well as Cyprian, was ordered into exile. Cyprian was fortunate in that his place of banishment was a pleasant seacoast town named Curubis.[18]

On the day of his arrival at Curubis, Cyprian experienced a vision that he shared with Pontius. This apparently took place on 14 September A.D. 257.[19] The vision is recorded by the hand of Pontius in his *Life and Passion of Cyprian, Bishop and Martyr*. The vision is presented here to help up in our evaluation of it:

> there appeared to me . . . ere yet I was sunk in the repose of slumber, a young man of unusual stature, who, as it were, led me to the praetorium, where I seemed to myself to be led before the tribunal of the proconsul, then sitting. When he looked at me, he began at once to note down a sentence on his tablet, which I knew not, for he had asked nothing of me with the accustomed interrogation. But the youth, who was standing at his back, very anxiously read what had been noted down. And because he could not then declare it in words, he showed me by an intelligible sign what was contained in the writing of that tablet. For, with hand expanded and flattened like a blade, he imitated the stroke of the accustomed punishment, and expressed what he wished to be understood as clearly as by speech,—I understood the future sentence of my passion. I began to ask and to beg immediately that a delay of at least one day should be accorded me, until I should have arranged my property in some reasonable order. And when I had urgently repeated my entreaty, he began again to note down, I know not what, on his tablet. But I perceived from the calmness of his countenance that the judge's mind was moved by my petition, as being a just one. Moreover, that youth, who already had disclosed to me the intelligence of my passion by gesture rather than by words, hastened to signify repeatedly by secret signal that the delay

was granted which had been asked for until the morrow, twisting his fingers one behind the other. And I, although I rejoiced with a very glad heart with joy at the delay accorded, yet trembled so with fear of the uncertainty of the interpretation, that the remains of fear still set my exulting heart beating with excessive agitation.[20]

On reading the account of Cyprian's vision, which has been preserved for us by Pontius, we are struck by several important facts, not the least of which is its genuine flavor. There are at least three factors that are strongly suggestive of its genuineness. First, Pontius says he is recording the vision as told to him by Cyprian. He begins the account by writing, "'there appeared to me' said he." Thus his claim is that he is recording not his own account of the event, but one given to him by Cyprian.[21]

A second factor that points to the genuineness of the account is the detail involved in the vision. References are to the unusual stature of the young man, his anxiety as he read the sentence, and the secret signal that consisted of a young man "twisting his fingers one behind the other." All of these seemingly insignificant details point to a genuine account.[22]

The third factor which directs us to accept this vision as legitimate is the fact that, even in his description, Cyprian did not attempt to cover the details of his own fears. His references to his trembling with fear, the fear of uncertainty, and his relating how he was so filled with terror at the thought that his heart beat "with excessive agitation" paint a graphic picture one would expect only from the actual participant.[23]

Incidental to the subject of genuineness is that in recording the vision of Cyprian, Pontius moved from his typical third-person narrative style to a definite first-person involvement. Each of these facts lead us to the same conclusion: the vision is probably a genuine account based on the actual words of Cyprian.

Pontius also notes that Cyprian apparently experienced the vision while he slept. It came in the form of a dream that only later was related to Pontius and perhaps others who were with him during Cyprian's final period of exile. There are no fewer than five words employed by Cyprian and Pontius to describe this event.[24] The fact that the vision was predictive in nature and judged by Pontius to have been fulfilled, coupled with the concept that it was a revelation (*revelatione*), seems to indicate that the word "prophecy" (*praedictio*) could also have been employed to describe it.

The vision includes several other features that may be delineated. First, it was equipped in typical visionary fashion with both visual and symbolic phenomena. Cyprian saw himself as though he were watching another person.[25] He also saw two other figures. The first was one whom he understood to be the tribunal of the proconsul. The second was a figure of a young man.

Cyprian described the young man as being of unusual stature. His role within the vision was to act as the messenger who would convey the message of Cyprian's upcoming passion. He communicated not by words but, rather, by signs. His meaning, however, was clearly understood. His appearance in this vision parallels the appearance of young larger-than-life messengers in other early Christian visions.[26]

The message was predictive in its orientation. It conveyed the fact that Cyprian would be martyred by the sword, and it provided for a specific time lapse after which the execution would take place. In essence, it was a prophecy that foretold an event which was to come, and, thereby, it provided guidance to its recipient.

The fact that the messenger used no words, but resorted to symbolic gestures instead is particularly interesting in this account.[27] It was disconcerting to Cyprian, for it left him in a position where he was not completely certain as to their meaning. In short, these gestures meant that their meaning had to be interpreted.

If Cyprian was alarmed by the use of gestures rather than words in the communication he received, Pontius was not. He understood the meaning more clearly than perhaps did Cyprian, for in writing on Cyprian's life and passion, he had the benefit of hindsight. Yet, his assessment of the vision, and most particularly the message meant to be conveyed by it, was that it was a predictive word that was ultimately fulfilled.[28] This judgment was based in large part on one symbol found within the vision. It is the symbol of the delay "until the morrow."

According to his own account, Cyprian was fearful because of the "uncertainty of the interpretation."[29] Yet Pontius, looking back on the event remarked of Cyprian:

> He asks for delay till the morrow, when the sentence of his passion was under deliberation, begging that he might arrange his affairs on the day which he had thus obtained. This one day signified a year, which he was about to pass in the world after his vision. For, to speak more plainly, after the year was expired, he was crowned, on that day on which, at the commencement of the year, the fact had been announced to him.[30]

Pontius's explanation is not without difficulty, as even Pontius was willing to indicate. He was, however, committed to the truth of this interpretation of the symbolism. He argued that the time span was revealed only by symbol "because the utterance of speech was reserved for the manifestation of the time itself."[31] Its duration was at first not totally clear since, as Pontius pointed out, even Scripture does not normally equate "one day" with "one year."[32] But, Pontius insisted that Scripture made use of symbolism which provided a precedent for symbolism in this vision.[33]

Only after the passion of Cyprian took place was the true interpretation available and understood, for, as Pontius admitted, "no one knew why this had been shown to him [Cyprian], until afterwards, when, on the very day on which he had seen it he was crowned. Nevertheless, in the meantime, his impending suffering was certainly known by all, but the exact day of his passion was not spoken of by any of the same, just as if they were ignorant of it."[34]

It remains to note that while Valerian's initial decree carried no death-penalty clause, in August of A.D. 258, a second edict was issued in which summary execution was mandated for all bishops, presbyters, and deacons of the church.[35] It was this second edict that brought Cyprian's passion to its culmination. The date, 14 September A.D. 258, was one year to the day from the time Cyprian had received his vision. Thus, current events worked together to provide a fulfillment to an otherwise vague vision. Pontius immediately understood the meaning of the vision to have been fulfilled.

Cyprian's response to the vision and his recognition that he would have some indeterminate length of time to set his house in order provided him occasion to help the needy, especially among the confessors.[36] He looked forward to the day of his martyrdom, anticipating the promise of Matt. 10:19–20 to be appropriated for himself and encouraging other confessors to expect its fulfillment in their passions as well.[37]

PART FOUR

Conclusions

CHAPTER SEVENTEEN

CONCLUSIONS

At the outset of this study, our attention was drawn to the agenda proposed in 1981 by John Panagopoulos regarding future studies on the gift of prophecy. This agenda included (1) the examination of both form and function as well as the development process the phenomenon had undergone; (2) the disclosure of relevant historical and theological factors that contributed to this development; (3) the investigation of distinctive and common elements that might relate to its form, content, or purpose; and (4) the attempt to build a historical outline of prophecy to Montanism. Since the "New Prophecy" appeared in Asia Minor most probably about A.D. 172[1] and then moved to North Africa at the beginning of the third century, it is clear that the fourth point could not be covered in this study. Yet, portions of the first three points could be applied to each of the documents or writers to yield a variety of conclusions.

DEVELOPMENTS IN FORM AND FUNCTION

The present study makes clear that the vision was the primary form which prophetic gifts took in North Africa. Perpetua, Saturus, Cyprian, and others of his acquaintance all experienced what they believed to be genuine revelations from God in the form of visions. Tertullian, while making no personal claims of prophetic activity, was nonetheless a believer in such things and he recorded two visions experienced by women worshippers at Carthage.

Not all visions that have been preserved in this literature included oracles or oracular sayings given by the various characters or actors in the visions, but many of them did. These oracles appear to have followed time-tested forms that may be found in much of the canonical (cf. Acts 10:3–6, 9–20; 16:9–10; 27:23–25) and other early Christian literature (cf. Ignatius, *To the Philadelphians*, 7; *Shepherd of Hermas*) written prior to the period covered in this study. Most of the oracles found in the literature were of two types. They were either "prescriptive" or "parenetic oracles," or they were "oracles of assurance." In this sense, they appear to fit the basic form and/or purpose set forth in 1 Cor. 14:3; that is, they provided to the church words or pictures for upbuilding, encouragement/exhortation, and consolation.

Those prophetic manifestations recorded merely as oracles, rather than oracles embedded in visionary material, were limited largely to Tertullian's writings and were most reflective of the New Prophecy in Asia Minor. However, that Tertullian chose to incorporate them into his own works without regard to their original *Sitz-im-Leben* has prevented us from knowing whether they, too, had been received in a visionary format. Cyprian, alone, preserves one or more oracles without a visionary context, but these are limited to what might be termed "confessional oracles," oracles thought to be reflective of the Spirit's role mentioned in Matt. 10:19–20, which enabled confessors to stand before the magistrates unafraid.

The form that virtually all the visionary or oracular accounts take also includes an interpretation. The notable exceptions to this are the vision of Saturus, which is simply recorded by him and then incorporated into *The Passion* to meet the redactor's purposes, as well as the oracles recorded by Tertullian, which had their origin in the New Prophecy of Asia Minor. Perpetua interpreted her visions in light of her training, and largely by implication. Tertullian taught or engaged in apologetics with those he recorded. Cyprian interpreted and applied his for purposes of edification and exhortation. At times, he also used his interpretations to establish the authority of the oracle or exhortation to be conveyed.

The imagery found in many of the visions received by third-century Carthaginian Christians is comparable to much that is shared by other Jewish and early Christian visions, especially those with an apocalyptic flavor. Thus, flights into paradise; the presence of angels; the figure of the Lord sometimes appearing as a shepherd, sometimes aged though youthful, and at other times having immense stature, or appearing with shining countenance were common throughout. Because of this clear relationship between such imagery and the visions received in Carthage, I would suggest that the early Christian training at Carthage included the reading of Jewish and Christian apocalyptic literature.

The visions analyzed in this study seem to meet several functional expectations. They appear largely to have functioned personally for Perpetua. Her visions tended to provide answers to personal concerns, bringing meaning to events that transpired around her. Cyprian spoke of visions that had directed him as well as others around him to undertake certain activities. Even Tertullian's account of the angel's words to the worshipping woman seem to indicate that the word was specifically addressed to her personally.

The prophetic manifestations analyzed also showed that they often had a corporate function, or a function in the lives of individuals whose actions had corporate implications. Thus, the vision of Saturus was apparently directed toward instructing the bishop, whose response would affect the Carthaginian congregation. The visions Cyprian received on Christian unity would be used to move the congregation to a new level of corporate acceptance of one another and of their bishop.

Throughout this study, the nature of the oracles and visions was clearly *ad hoc*. They spoke to needs that were pressing or immediate for a limited number of people at a particular time in a particular place. Only Tertullian tended to view them as having an expanded function, a function that included the communication of his own perceptions of the will of God for the whole church. Yet, he never used these visions or oracles to establish doctrine *per se*; he merely introduced them as corroborating testimony to what he believed to be the legitimate teaching of Scripture. In this sense, then, Tertullian's use of prophetic manifestations differed from the rest, and Perpetua's use more closely approximated that which was present at Carthage a half century later, when Cyprian was bishop.

The function to which Tertullian put the record of certain oracles and visions was clearly apologetic or didactic in nature, a function not dissimilar to that which the redactor of *The Passion* put Perpetua's and Saturus's visions. Both the redactor of *The Passion* and Tertullian understood the visions and oracles as coming in fulfillment of Joel's prophecy in 2:28 and reiterated in Acts 2. The redactor of *The Passion*, therefore, recorded the visions to convince his readers of the ongoing work of God in the midst of God's people. Tertullian, however, linked Joel 2:28 to John 16:12–15 to provide a classic perspective reflecting the interests of the New Prophecy. The function of the Paraclete was a continuing one which provided hard teachings that the church had not been able to bear previously.

The development of the form that prophetic gifts underwent was not particularly significant. The complexity of the visions and the symbolism used throughout the period was relatively consistent. There may have been a slight decrease in the apocalyptic elements present from Perpetua to Cyprian, but that decrease was not significant. There may have been a slight increase in eschatological interests as time went on, but that does not appear to be overly significant either. Probably the most significant development to occur in the period studied is related to the function the New Prophecy played in the Carthaginian church. The more closely the oracles were tied to the New Prophecy, the more likely they were to reflect doctrinal concerns; and the less closely they were attached to the New Prophecy, the more likely they were to address or reflect personal concerns.

SIGNIFICANT FACTORS AFFECTING PROPHETIC DEVELOPMENT

The most significant historical and theological factors that appear to have affected prophetic development for the church at Carthage in the third century are an intense, yet intermittent, persecution and the arrival of the New Prophecy. While *The Passion of Perpetua and Felicitas* showed some similarities to certain teachings of the New Prophecy, especially in the section penned by the redactor, it was shown that the document in its various parts as well as the whole was probably best assigned a pre- or, at most, a proto-Montanist position. Its language was found to be more consistent with the contemporary teachings of Christianity as a whole than to those teachings unique to the New Prophecy.

Tertullian, however, appears to have identified somewhat more closely with the New Prophecy, even though it was still effectively an *ecclesiola in ecclesia* about A.D. 207. Prior to that time his references to prophetic gifts were few and relatively general in nature. Those writings of his produced after A.D. 207 tended generally to speak highly of certain of the new prophets or to give a unique emphasis to the continuing role of the Paraclete. It is in these later writings, too, that Tertullian recorded the visions and oracles which were so intrinsically related to the teaching of the New Prophecy.

Cyprian appears to have represented a highly pneumatic form of Christianity in the sense that he recorded numerous condescensions, visions, and oracles. That he represents a type of post–New Prophecy form of spirituality, however, would seem to be indicated by several independent pieces of evidence. First, certain members of the New Prophecy had repeatedly been condemned in a variety of local councils even during the second century.[2] Second, Tertullian lamented that Praxeas had been successful in having the New Prophecy condemned in Rome by engineering the revocation of certain letters of fellowship which the bishop of Rome had previously issued.[3] Third, while Jerome records the fact that Cyprian was well versed in the writings of Tertullian to the point of treating him as his "master," he also notes that Cyprian rejected Tertullian's acceptance of the New Prophecy.[4] His choice not to appeal to the name of Tertullian in any of his writings may indicate that as bishop of Carthage, while he had a great personal regard for Tertullian's work, he wished to distance himself from what he perceived to be Tertullian's primary weakness.[5]

Persecution, however, was a theme that was constantly in the thoughts of the Carthaginian congregation throughout the period studied. Even before the martyrdom of Perpetua and her colleagues, and perhaps as early as A.D. 297, Tertullian had penned an exhortation *To the Martyrs*. But the third century brought even more intense and pointed persecution to the church. It was in these later persecutions that Perpetua, Saturus, and Cyprian all lost their lives. Weinrich has established the direct relationship of the Spirit to the confessor in such times of persecution,[6] while Lampe has gone even further to demonstrate that the confessor was a "Spirit-possessed and prophet-like person."[7] Both of these theses have been upheld in our study of prophetic gifts in third-century Carthage.

Yet, the role of the Spirit and of prophetic gifts in this period also moved independently of persecution. The Spirit and prophetic gifts in addition to persecution were clearly related to one another in the cases of Perpetua and Saturus as well as in the personal examples that Cyprian recorded. However, Tertullian's citations as well as his use of prophetic oracles, with two exceptions, appear not to be directly related to persecution or martyrdom. Similarly, the experiences of Celerinus, Numidicus, and Florentius seem to cover subjects independent of the theme of persecution, although one might conceivably argue that they were related to persecution since they provided for Christian leadership within the context of a persecuted church. In any event, while it is clear that the Spirit was working in and through confessors and martyrs of Carthage, the experience of prophetic gifts extended beyond that limitation to other clergy and lay manifestations, with purposes unrelated to persecution and martyrdom.

A final factor about which this study had very little to say is that of psychology. The presence of certain psychological factors was noted throughout, and it is clear from this study that further work in psycho-history and/or psychoanalysis would be helpful. At best, though, this study seems to indicate that there may be a relationship between the individual's psyche and the vision or oracle received. Exactly what that relationship is and how far it extends is not clear, but to ignore that such a relationship apparently does exist is not to take prophetic gifts seriously.

DISTINCTIVE AND COMMON ELEMENTS

In one sense, the question of certain distinctive and common elements of prophetic gifts has already been answered in the section on developments in form and function. One cannot trace developments without noting distinctive and common elements over a period of time. Still, there are a few comments which can be made that relate to matters of role and function.

It has already been noted that some of the visions and oracles studied were given to individuals to meet individual needs. Others came to meet needs of the larger Christian community. The role that prophetic gifts for the third-century Carthaginian congregation appears to have been at least constant, if not widening. Prophetic gifts played a role in the lives of new converts as well as those established in leadership positions. They played a role in the lives of laity as well as clergy, catechumen, and theologians. They were, in Cyprian's day, not limited to the bishop, but available to many, from young boys, to confessors, to clerical prospects, to worshipping women, to the bishop himself. Thus, Ash's thesis that the monarchial episcopate was well along in the process of capturing the prophetic gift is not completely borne out. That Cyprian made good use of prophetic gifts is not to be doubted, but he gave equal assent to the reality of those gifts expressed by others. One must, therefore, argue that the evidence for its widespread presence goes quite beyond the "traces" of the charisma which Ash suggests existed by Cyprian's day.[8] If one may argue that the monarchial episcopate did manifest such a gift, as well it did, one must argue equally strongly that such a gift was being "captured" by the confessors and martyrs as the later martyrological literature continues to bear out. Thus, the role played by prophetic gifts for the church in North Africa from Perpetua to Cyprian is remarkably parallel.

So, too, is the subject of testing to establish the validity or genuineness of such gifts. The redactor of *The Passion* was concerned with testing Perpetua's revelations by the test of fulfillment. Tertullian was greatly concerned to demonstrate that prophetic manifestations in his day were assessed in relation to Scripture and the *regula fidei*. And Cyprian was concerned with the test of fulfillment. Of most significance is the fact that testing played an important role throughout. That this testing took place with such consistency and regularity would tend to speak against Benjamin B. Warfield's old thesis that the genuinely miraculous disappeared from the church before the middle of the second century.[9] The third-century Carthaginian Christian would have had difficulty agreeing with his conclusion.

Consistency is also apparent in the way many of the oracles and visions were put to use. In no case were they ever understood as replacing what canons or *regulae fidei* existed. The redactor of *The Passion* saw them merely as contemporary witnesses to the presence of God's hand among God's people. Perpetua understood them in terms of specific guidance, in much the same way as if she had received good advice or assurance from another more mature Christian. Tertullian argued for the supremacy of Scripture and the role of the Spirit in illumination. His use of oracles was understood as clarifying the truth he believed already to be present in Scripture. Cyprian also seems to have understood the primacy of Scripture and the *regula fidei*. The very fact that each was concerned to test the truth of the various revelations by Scripture or scriptural norms would tend to confirm this. The primary difference would be in the results of the test. Cyprian seems to have disagreed with the results of the tests and the oracles as well as the use of the oracles that Tertullian recorded. But to argue this way without further evidence is futile.

All in all, this study has shown that the role of prophetic gifts in the church at Carthage between A.D. 202 and 258 was a wide and significant one. Prophetic gifts touched the lives of many people, and they set the agenda for the church in that area for years to come. The function of prophetic gifts was equally significant, and it was equally diverse. Indeed, one should probably speak of functions rather than any single function for prophetic gifts among the Christians of Carthage. Perhaps there are lessons to be learned from the example these persecuted brothers and sisters have left as their legacy to the church at the end of the twentieth century.

The Vision of the Ladder*
4.1–10

Circumstances producing the need for guidance	4. ¹Then my brother said to me: "Dear sister, you are greatly privileged; surely you might ask for a vision to discover whether you are to be condemned or freed." ²Faithfully I promised that I would, for I knew that I could speak with the Lord, whose great blessings I had come to experience. And so I said: "I shall tell you tomorrow."
Method employed	Then I made my request and this was the vision I had.
The vision	³I saw a ladder of tremendous height made of bronze, reaching all the way to the heavens, but it was so narrow that only one person could climb up at a time. To the sides of the ladder were attached all sorts of metal weapons: there were swords, spears, hooks, daggers, and spikes; so that if anyone tried to climb up carelessly or without paying attention, he would be mangled and his flesh would adhere to the weapons. ⁴At the foot of the ladder lay a dragon of enormous size, and it would attack those who tried to climb up and try to terrify them from doing so. ⁵And Saturus was the first to go up, he who was later to give himself up of his own accord. He had been the builder of our strength, although he was not present when we were arrested. ⁶And he arrived at the top of the staircase and he looked back and said to me: "Perpetua, I am waiting for you. But take care; do not let the dragon bite you." "He will not harm me," I said, "in the name of Christ Jesus." ⁷Slowly, as though he were afraid of me, the dragon stuck his head out from underneath the ladder. Then, using it as my first step, I trod on his head and went up. ⁸Then I saw an immense garden, and in it a grey-haired man sat in shepherd's garb; tall he was, and milking sheep. And standing around him were many thousands of people clad in white garments.
Oracle of salvation	⁹He raised his head, looked at me, and said: "I am glad you have come, my child." He called me over to him and gave me, as it were, a mouthful of the milk he was drawing; and I took it into my cupped hands and consumed it. And all those who stood around said, "Amen!"

Interpretation	[10]At the sound of this word I came to, with the taste of something sweet still in my mouth. I at once told this to my brother, and we realized that we would have to suffer
Effect of the message conveyed by the vision	and that from now on we would no longer have any hope in this life.

*Translation of vision in *The Passion* from Herbert Musurillo, *The Acts of the Christian Martyrs*, OECT (Oxford: Clarendon Press, 1972).

Perpetua's Dinocrates Visions*
7.1–10; 8:1–4

Circumstances surrounding the first Dinocrates vision	7. ¹Some days later when we were all at prayer, suddenly while praying I spoke out and uttered the name Dinocrates. I was surprised; for the name had never entered my mind until that moment. And I was pained when I recalled what had happened to him. ²At once I realized that I was privileged to pray for him. I began to pray for him and to sigh deeply for him before the Lord. ³That very night I had the following vision.
Vision 1A	⁴I saw Dinocrates coming out of a dark hole, where there were many others with him, very hot and thirsty, pale and dirty. On his face was the wound he had when he died.
Perpetua's Comment	⁵Now Dinocrates had been my brother according to the flesh; but he had died horribly of cancer of the face when he was seven years old, and his death was a source of loathing to everyone. ⁶Thus it was for him that I made my prayer.
Vision 1B	There was a great abyss between us: neither could approach the other. ⁷Where Dinocrates stood there was a pool full of water; and its rim was higher than the child's height, so that Dinocrates had to stretch himself up to drink. ⁸I was sorry that, though the pool had water in it, Dinocrates could not drink because of the height of the rim.
Perpetua's intermediate conclusion	⁹Then I woke up, realizing that my brother was suffering.
Circumstances surrounding the second Dinocrates vision	But I was confident that I could help him in his trouble; and I prayed for him every day until we were transferred to the military prison. For we were supposed to fight with the beasts at the military games to be held on the occasion of the emperor Geta's birthday. ¹⁰And I prayed for my brother day and night with tears and sighs that this favour might be granted me. 8. ¹On the day we were kept in chains, I had this vision shown to me.

Vision 2	I saw the same spot that I had seen before, but there was Dinocrates all clean, well dressed, and refreshed. I saw a scar where the wound had been, [2]and the pool that I had seen before now had its rim lowered to the level of the child's waist. And Dinocrates kept drinking water from it, [3]and there above the rim was a golden bowl, full of water. And Dinocrates drew close and began to drink from it, and yet the bowl remained full. [4]And when he had drunk enough of the water, he began to play as children do.
Perpetua's final conclusion	Then I awoke, and I realized that he had been delivered from his suffering.

*Translation of visions in *The Passion* from Herbert Musurillo, *The Acts of the Christian Martyrs,* OECT (Oxford: Clarendon Press, 1972).

Perpetua's Vision of the Egyptian*
10:1–4

Introduction	10. ¹The day before we were to fight with the beasts I saw the following vision.
Scene #1 The invitation to the amphitheatre	Pomponius the deacon came to the prison gates and he began to knock violently. ²I went out and opened the gate for him. He was dressed in an unbelted white tunic, wearing elaborate sandals. ³And he said to me: "Perpetua, come; we are waiting for you." Then he took my hand and we began to walk through rough and broken country. ⁴At last we came to the amphitheatre out of breath, and he led me into the centre of the arena.
The promise	Then he told me: "Do not be afraid. I am here, struggling with you." Then he left.
Scene #2a Enter the Egyptian	⁵I looked at the enormous crowd who watched in astonishment. I was surprised that no beasts were let loose on me; for I knew that I was condemned to die by the beasts. ⁶Then out came an Egyptian against me, of vicious appearance, together with his seconds, to fight with me. There also came up to me some handsome young men to be my seconds and assistants. ⁷My clothes were stripped off, and suddenly I was a man. My seconds began to rub me down with oil (as they are wont to do before a contest). Then I saw the Egyptian on the other side rolling in the dust.
Scene #2b The man of wondrous height The challenge	⁸Next there came forth a man of marvellous stature, such that he rose above the top of the amphitheatre. He was clad in a beltless purple tunic with two stripes (one on either side) running down the middle of his chest. He wore sandals that were wondrously made of gold and silver, and he carried a wand like an athletic trainer and a green branch on which there were golden apples. ⁹And he asked for silence and said: "If this Egyptian defeats her he will slay her with the sword. But if she defeats him, she will receive this branch." ¹⁰Then he withdrew.

Scene # 3 The fight	We drew close to one another and began to let our fists fly. My opponent tried to get hold of my feet, but I kept striking him in the face with the heels of my feet. [11]Then I was raised up into the air and I began to pummel him without as it were touching the ground. Then when I noticed there was a lull, I put my two
Oracle of Salvation	hands together linking the fingers of one hand with those of the other and thus I got hold of his head. He fell flat on his face and I stepped on his head. [12]The crowd began to shout and my assistants started to sing psalms. Then I walked up to the trainer and took the branch. He kissed me and said to me: "Peace be with you, my daughter!" I began to walk in triumph towards the Gate of Life.
Interpretation	[14]Then I awoke. I realized that it was not with wild animals that I would fight but with the Devil, but I knew that I would win the victory.

*Translation of vision in *The Passion* from Herbert Musurillo, *The Acts of the Christian Martyrs,* OECT (Oxford: Clarendon Press, 1972).

Saturus's Vision*
11.1–13.8

Redactor's Introduction	11.¹But the blessed Saturus has also made known his own vision and he has written it out with his own hand.
Scene 1 The ascent to the garden	²We had died, he said, and had put off the flesh, and we began to be carried towards the east by four angels who did not touch us with their hands. ³But we moved along not on our backs facing upwards but as though we were climbing up a gentle hill. ⁴And when we were free of the world, we first saw an intense light. And I said to Perpetua (for she was at my side): "This is what the Lord promised us. We have received his promise." ⁵While we were being carried by these four angels, a great open space appeared, which seemed to be a garden, with rose bushes and all manner of flowers. ⁶The trees were as tall as cypresses, and their leaves were constantly falling. ⁷In the garden there were four other angels more splendid than the others. When they saw us they paid us homage and said to the other angels in admiration: "Why, they are here! They are here!" Then the four angels that were carrying us grew fearful and set us down. ⁸Then he walked across to an open area by way of a broad road, ⁹and there we met Jucundus, Saturninus, and Artaxius, who were burnt alive in the same persecution, together with Quintus who had actually died as a martyr in prison. We asked them where they had been. ¹⁰And the other angels said to us: "First come and enter and greet the Lord."
Scene 2 Within the city whose walls seem to be constructed of light	12.¹Then we came to a place whose walls seemed to be constructed of light. And in front of the gate stood four angels, who entered in and put on white robes. ²We also entered and we heard the sound of voices in unison chanting endlessly: "Holy, holy, holy!" ³In the same place we seemed to see an aged man with white hair and a youthful face, though we did not see his feet. ⁴On his right and left were four elders, and behind them stood other aged men. ⁵Surprised, we entered and stood before a throne: four angels lifted us up and we kissed the aged man and he touched our faces with his hand. ⁶And the elders said to us: "Let us rise." And we rose and gave the kiss of peace. Then the elders said to us: "Go and play." ⁷To Perpetua I said: "Your wish is granted." She said to me: "Thanks be to God that I am happier here now than I was in the flesh."

Scene 3 The concern for unity	13. [1]Then we went out and before the gate we saw the bishop Optatus on the right and Aspasius the presbyter and teacher on the left, each of them far apart and in sorrow. [2]They threw themselves at our feet and said: "Make peace between us. For you have gone away and left us thus." [3]And we said to them: "Are you not our bishop, and are you not our presbyter? How can you fall at our feet?" We were very moved and embraced them. [4]Perpetua then began to speak with them in Greek, and we drew them apart into the garden under a rose arbour. [5]While we were talking with them, the angels said to them: "Allow them to rest. Settle whatever quarrels you have among yourselves." [6]And they were put to confusion.
Parenesis	Then they said to Optatus: "You must scold your flock. They approach you as though they had come from the games, quarrelling about the different teams." [7]And it seemed as though they wanted to close the gates. [8]And there we began to recognize many of our brethren, martyrs among them. All of us were sustained by a delicious odour that seemed to satisfy us.
The vision's effect	And then I woke up happy.

*Translation of vision in *The Passion* from Herbert Musurillo, *The Acts of the Christian Martyrs*, OECT (Oxford: Clarendon Press, 1972).

Prophetic Oracles Recorded in Tertullian's Works*

1.	MESSENGER FORMULA (Conjectured)	(*The Spirit says*)
	(A) ASSERTION Rationale	It is good for you to be publicly exposed. For he who is not exposed among men is exposed in the Lord.
	(B) EXHORTATION Rationale	Do not be disturbed; Righteousness brings you before the public
	(B') RHETORICAL QUESTION	Why are you disturbed when you are receiving praise?
	(A') ASSERTION	There is opportunity [*potestas*] when you are observed by men.

Tertullian, *On Flight in Persecution* 9.4

2.	Parenesis	Wish not to die in your beds
		      nor in miscarriages
		      and mild fevers,
		      but in martyrdoms,
		that he who has suffered for you
		      may be glorified.

Tertullian, *On Flight in Persecution* 9.4

3.	Parenesis	The Church can pardon sin but I will not do it lest they also commit other offenses.

Tertullian, *On Modesty* 21.7

4.	Parenesis	For purification produces harmony
		and they [the pure] see visions
		and when they turn their
		faces downward
		      they also hear salutary
		      voices
		      as clear as they are secret.

Tertullian, *On Exhortation to Chastity* 10.5

5.	Parenesis		They are and they hate the	flesh flesh.

Tertullian, *On the Resurrection of the Flesh* 11.2

6.	Parenesis	For God brought forth the Word . . . as the root brings forth the tree, and a fountain a stream, and the sun a ray.

Tertullian, *Against Prakeas* 8.5

*Translations of citations from Tertullian are from Ronald E. Heine, *The Montanist Oracles and Testimonia*, PMS, 14 (Macon, Ga.: Mercer University Press, 1989).

Appendix F

Visionary Woman[*]

THE REVELATION	SUBSTANCE	QUALITY	
SHAPE	A soul was exhibited to me in a spirit appeared,	bodily form,	and but
TEXTURE	it was of a being	not of an empty vacuous quality quality could be grasped soft	and but rather that would suggest it and
COLOR	of the	bright color of the air	and and
SHAPE		resembling the human form in all respects.	

Tertullian, *Treatise on the Soul* 9:4

Anonymous Woman

Angelic teaching	Elegant neck and deservedly bare! It is well that you should be unveiled continuously from head to loins, lest indeed, your neck's freedom be not to your advantage.

Tertullian, *On the Veiling of Virgins* 17:4

[*]Translation of citations from Tertullian from Ronald E. Heine, *The Montanist Oracles and Testimonia*, PMS, 14 (Macon, Ga.: Mercer University Press, 1989).

APPENDIX G

Prophetic Oracles Recorded in Cyprian's Correspondence[*]

MAPPALICUS

1.	Promise	"The contest you will see tomorrow."

Cyprian, *Epistle* 10.4

SPEAKER UNKNOWN

2.	Parenesis	"Ask and you shall have."

Cyprian, *Epistle* 11.3

3.	Announcement of judgment	"And so, whoever does not believe in Christ, when He appoints a bishop shall begin to believe hereafter in Christ when He avenges that bishop."

Cyprian, *Epistle* 66.10

CYPRIAN

4.	Announcement of salvation	"Tell him, . . . not to be anxious, For there is going to be peace but there is, meantime, a short delay, For some are left still to be tested."

Cyprian, *Epistle* 11.6

The following oracle is conjectured, based on the content and form in which it appears in Cyprian's *Epistle* 58.1.

5.	Apocalyptic saying	" . . .the day of affliction is now dawning overhead. the demise of the world and the time of Antichrist are nigh."

Cyprian, *Epistle* 58.1

[*]Translations of Cyprian texts from G. W. Clarke, *The Letters of St. Cyprian*, 4 vols. ACW, 43, 44, 46, 47 (New York: Newman Press, 1984, 1986, 1989).

Appendix H*

CELERINUS	NUMIDICUS
1. Cyprian addresses the whole congregation.	1. Cyprian addresses the whole congregation.
2. Cyprian and others recommend Celerinus to the clergy.	
3. Celerinus at first refuses.	
4. Celerinus receives *divina dignatio* called a nocturnal vision (*visione per noctem*).	2. Someone (*nos*) receives *dignatio divina* called that which is revealed (*quod ostenditur*).
5. The recipient of the *divina dignatio* is (a) admonished (*admonitu*) (b) encouraged (*horatu*).	3. The recipient of the *dignatio divina* is (a) advised (*admonitos*) (b) instructed (*instructos*).
6. Celerinus agrees with Cyprian and others to a place among the clergy as a reader.	
7. Celerinus is recommended to the Carthaginians as a reader.	4. Numidicus is recommended to the Carthaginians as a presbyter.
8. Attributes for office are listed.	5. Attributes for office are listed.
9. Appeal is made for his acceptance. "There is no place more proper for him to be stationed than on the pulpit. . . ."	6. Appeal is made for his acceptance. "In the meantime, let us carry out what is revealed to us. . . ."

Notice the parallel forms in the way these two incidents are recorded from *Epistles* 39 and 40, respectively.

*Translation is from G. W. Clarke, *The Letters of St. Cyprian*, vol. 2, ACW, 44 (New York: Newman Press, 1984).

Comparison Chart of Vision Forms in Cyprian, *Epistle* 11*

	EPISTLE 11.3	EPISTLE 11.4	EPISTLE 11.5	EPISTLE 11.6
INTRO-DUCTORY STATEMENT	You ought to know what has particularly induced, indeed, driven me. . . . The Lord thought fit to manifest and reveal a vision.	Now this was also revealed:	We must be urgent in prayer and raise our mournful cries with incessant supplication. For I must tell you, my very dear brothers, that not so long ago in a vision this reproach was also made to us.	Finally, even the least of His servants, set as he is in the midst of very many trans-gressions and undeserving of His favour, He favoured nevertheless in His goodness towards us with these instructions:
VISION AND/OR ORACLE	In it, these words were spoken: "Ask and you shall have." And then the congregation standing by was enjoined to ask on behalf of certain people pointed out to them, but in putting their request their voices were discordant, their wills conflicting; and He who had said "Ask and you shall have" was exceedingly displeased	the Father of a household was seated, with a young man sitting on his right. This young man looked worried and somewhat aggrieved as well as distressed, as he sat mournfully holding his chin in his hand. But there was another person standing on the left side; he was carrying a net and he kept threatening to cast it and ensnare the crowd of bystanders.	We were slumbering in our supplications, I was told; we are not watchful in prayer.	Tell him, he said, not to be anxious, for there is going to be peace, but there is, meantime, a short delay, for some are left still to be tested.

	EPISTLE 11.3	EPISTLE 11.4	EPISTLE 11.5	EPISTLE 11.6
INTERPRE-TATION OF VISION	at the fact that the people were divided and at variance, and that amongst the brethren there was no one, uniform agreement and harmonious concord. And this, despite the fact that it is written; *God who makes men dwell united together in a house,* and even though we read in the Acts of the Apostles; *The multitude of those who believed were of one heart and mind.* Likewise the Lord has commanded with His own lips: *This is My commandment, that you love one another* and again: *But I say to you that if two of you are in agreement on earth in seeking any matter, it shall be granted to you by My Father who is in heaven.*	And when the person who saw this vision wondered what this meant, he was told that the young man who was sitting like that on the right was grieving and sorrowful at the neglect of his precepts, whereas the one on the left was jubilant at being given the opportunity of obtaining from the father of the household leave to rage and destroy.	It is undoubtedly true that God loves the man whom He chastens. When He chastens, He chastens in order to improve him, and He improves him in order to save him.	

	EPISTLE 11.3	EPISTLE 11.4	EPISTLE 11.5	EPISTLE 11.6
APPLICA-TION OF VISION	Now, if two, united together, have such power, what could be accomplished if all should be united together? Had there been agreement amongst all the brethren, in conformity with the peace which the Lord has given us, we would long ago have gained from our merciful God what we are seeking, neither would we now have been tossed for so long on these waves which jeopardize our faith and our salvation. In fact, these evils would not have befallen our community had they all been of one mind together.	This revelation was made long ago before the present devastating storm arose. And we see now fulfilled what was then revealed: so long as we hold in scorn the precepts of the Lord, so long as we do not observe the saving ordinances of the law which He has given, the enemy gains power to do harm and with a cast of his net holds us enmeshed, too ill-armed and off-guard to repel him.	We must, therefore, cast off and burst the bonds of sleep and pray with urgency and watchful-ness. . . .	And further, through God's favor, we are admonished to be abstemious in diet and sober in drink. I have no doubt that this is to prevent hearts now uplifted with heavenly strength from being emasculated by worldly allurements or souls from being less watchful in prayer and petition by being weighed down with lavish feasting.

*Translation from G. W. Clarke, *The Letters of St. Cyprian*, vol. 1, ACW, 43 (New York: Newman Press, 1984), 77–79.

Structure of the First Vision Occurring in *Epistle* 11.3*

INTRODUCTION	You ought to know . . .
	The Lord thought fit
	    to manifest (*ostendere*) and
	    reveal (*revelare*)
	      a vision.

PRESCRIPTIVE ORACLE	"Ask and you shall have. . . ."

DESCRIPTION OF THE VISION
(This follows the oracular utterance. It is a narrative of events that transpired in the vision.)
	And then [following the giving of the oracle]
	    the congregation standing by was enjoined
	      to ask on behalf of certain people pointed out to
	them,
	but in putting their request
	    their voices were discordant,
	    their wills conflicting;
	and He who had said
	    "ask and you shall have"
	was exceedingly displeased
	    at the fact that the people
	        were divided
	        and at variance,
	and that amongst the brethren
	    there was no one, uniform
	                    agreement
	          and harmonious
	            concord.

SCRIPTURAL CITATIONS (These are summoned by Cyprian to authenticate the validity of the VISION.)	Ps. 68.6 John 15.12 Acts 4.32 Matt. 18.19

APPLICATION OF VISION (*Ad hoc*)	Now,
	    if two, united together, have such power,
	    what could be accomplished if all should
	      be united together?
	
	    Had there been agreement amongst all the brethren,
	      in conformity with the peace which the
	      Lord has given us,
	    we would long ago have gained from our merciful
	      God what we are seeking,
	neither,
	    would we now have been tossed for so long on
	      these waves which jeopardize
	      our faith and our salvation.

SUMMARY OF APPLICATION	In fact, these evils would not have befallen our community had they all been of one mind together.

*Translation from G. W. Clarke, *The Letters of St. Cyprian*, vol. 1, ACW, 43 (New York: Newman Press, 1984), 77.

Comparative List of Cyprian's *Epistles*

The following list of Cyprian's *Epistles* compares the numerations found in Alexander Roberts and James Donaldson, eds., *The Ante-Nicene Fathers* (Grand Rapids: Wm. B. Eerdmans, 1971), vol. 5, with those found in Guilelmus Hartel's edition of Cyprian's writings found in the Vienna series of Latin fathers, Corpus Scriptorum Ecclesiasticorum (1868–71). Hartel's list is shared by the Oxford edition of Cyprian's writings as well as the edition of Cyprian's letters in the Ancient Christian Writers series and by G. W. Clarke, *The Letters of St. Cyprian*, 4 vols., ACW, 43, 44, 46, 47 (New York: Newman Press, 1984, 1986, 1989). This study follows the Hartel/Clarke numbering system.

ANF	Hartel	*ANF*	Hartel	*ANF*	Hartel
1	NA	11	17	21	22
2	8	12	18	22	27
3	9	13	19	23	29
4	5	14	20	24	28
5	14	15	37	25	31
6	13	16	23	26	33
7	11	17	26	27	34
8	10	18	24	28	35
9	16	19	25	29	36
10	15	20	21	30	30
31	32	41	45	51	55
32	38	42	47	52	56
33	39	43	46	53	57
34	40	44	48	54	59
35	7	45	49	55	58
36	12	46	51	56	60
37	41	47	50	57	61
38	42	48	52	58	64
39	43	49	53	59	62
40	44	50	54	60	2
61	4	71	72	81	80
62	63	72	73	82	81
63	65	73	74		
64	3	74	75		
65	1	75	69		
66	68	76	76		
67	67	77	77		
68	66	78	78		
69	70	79	79		
70	71	80	6		

REFERENCES

List of Abbreviations

AC	*Antike und Christentum*
ACW	Ancient Christian Writers
ANF	*Ante-Nicene Fathers* (Roberts and Donaldson)
BEHE	Bibliothèque de l'enseignement de l'histoire ecclesiastique
BFLS	*Bulletin de la Faculte des lettres de Strasbourg*
BJRL	*Bulletin of the John Rylands University Library of Manchester*
BUSPR	Boston University Studies in Philosophy and Religion
BWANT	Beitrage zur Wissenschaft vom Alten und Neuen Testament
Byz	*Byzantion*
BZNW	Beiheft zur Zeitschrift für die neutestamentliche Wissenschaft und die Kunde der alteren Kirche
CC	Calvin's Commentaries
CH	*Church History*
CJT	*Canadian Journal of Theology*
Col	*Colloquium: The Australian and New Zealand Theological Review*
CSEL	Corpus Scriptorum Ecclesiasticorum Latinorum
DS	*Daughters of Sarah*
ETH	Études de Théologie Historique
Hel	*Helmantica*
HNTC	Harper's New Testament Commentaries
HTR	*Harvard Theological Review*
ICC	International Critical Commentary
Int	*Interpretation*
JAAR	*Journal of the American Academy of Religion*
JAC	*Jahrbuch für Antike und Christentum*
JBL	*Journal of Biblical Literature*
JETS	*Journal of the Evangelical Theological Society*
JRS	*Journal of Roman Studies*
JSNT	*Journal for the Study of the New Testament*
JTS	*Journal of Theological Studies*
LCL	Loeb Classical Library
LCP	Latinitas Christianorum Primaeva
LRB	*La Revue Bénédictine*
LW	Luther's Works
MTL	Marshall's Theological Library
MTS	Münchener Theologische Studien
NCB	New Century Bible
NFTL	New Foundations Theological Library
NICNT	New International Commentary on the New Testament
NIGTC	New International Greek Testament Commentary
NovTSup	Novum Testamentum Supplement
NPNF	*Nicene & Post-Nicene Fathers* (Schaff and Wace)
NT	*Novum Testamentum*
NTS	*New Testament Studies*
OCA	Orientalia Christiana Analecta
OECT	Oxford Early Christian Texts

OTL	Old Testament Library
PG	*Patrilogia Graecae* (Migne)
PJSPS	*Pneuma: The Journal of the Society for Pentecostal Studies*
PMS	Patristic Monograph Series
QD	Quaestiones Disputatae
RAM	*Revue d'ascétique et de mystique*
REA	*Revue des Études Augustiniennes*
REL	*Revue des Études Latines*
RHE	*Revue d'Histoire ecclesiastique*
RMP	*Rheinisches Museum für Philologie*
RQCAK	*Rhomische Quartalschrift für christliche Altertumskunde und Kirchengeschichte*
RSHLL	Aeta Reg. Societatis Humaniorum Litteratum Lundensis
SBL	Society of Biblical Literature
SBT	*Studia Biblica et Theologica*
SBT	Studies in Biblical Theology
SC	*The Second Century*
SC	Sources Chrétiennes
SGLG	Studia Graeca et Latina Gothoburgensia
SNT	Studien zum Neuen Testament
SNTS	Society for New Testament Studies, Monograph Series
SP	*Studia Patristica*
SR	*Studies in Religion/Sciences Religieuses*
T	*Theology*
TDNT	*Theological Dictionary of the New Testament*
TH	Théologie Historique
TNTC	Tyndale New Testament Commentaries
TR	*Theological Renewal*
TS	*Theological Studies*
TTS	Theology Today Series
T&U	Texte und Untersuchungen
TZ	*Theologische Zeitschrift*
VC	*Vigiliae Christianae*
ZNTW	*Zeitschrift für die neuetestamentliche Wissenschaft*

CHAPTER ONE

1. *The Passion of Perpetua and Felicitas*, 1.1–5. On the use of this passage by the Montanists, see P. C. Atkinson, "The Montanist Interpretation of Joel 2:28, 29 (LXX 3:1, 2)," T&U, 126, *Studia Evangelica* 7 (1982): 11–15, although the use of Scripture by the Montanists is more generally assessed in F. E. Vokes, "The Use of Scripture in the Montanist Controversy," T&U, 103, *Studia Evangelica* 5 (1968): 317–20, and in Dennis E. Groh, "Utterance and Exegesis: Biblical Interpretation in the Montanist Crisis," in *The Living Text: Essays in Honor of Ernest W. Saunders*, ed. Dennis E. Groh and Robert Jewett (Lanham, Md.: University Press of America, 1985), 73–95.

2. Tertullian, *On Patience* 12.10.

3. But see the study by Gerald Lewis Bray, *Holiness and the Will of God: Perspectives on the Theology of Tertullian*, NFTL (Atlanta: John Knox Press, 1979), 56, in which he argues that Tertullian may have defended the Montanists, but he did not himself "propogate their beliefs."

4. Suggestions on his actual date of death vary with the latest date, circa A.D. 240, suggested by W. H. C. Frend, *The Early Church* (London: Hodder and Stoughton, 1965), 92.

5. Eugenio Corsini, "Proposte per una Lettura della 'Passio Perpetua'," in *Forma Futuri: Studi in Onore del Cardinale Michele Pellegrino* (Torino: Bottega d'Erasmo, 1975), 481–541; F. J. Dölger, "Antike Parallelen zum leidenden Dinocrates in der Passio Perpetuae," AC 2 (1930): 1–40; idem., "Der Kampf mit dem Ägypter in der Perpetua-Vision: Das Martyrium als Kampf mit dem Teufel," AC 3 (1932): 177–88; Peter Dronke, *Women Writers of the Middle Ages* (Cambridge: Cambridge University Press, 1986), 1–17; Marie-Louise von Franz, "Die Passio Perpetuae," in *Aion: Untersuchungen zur Symbolgeschichte*, ed. C. G. Jung, Psychologische Abhandlungen, 7 (Zurich: Racher Verlag, 1951), 389–496; Michel Meslin, "Vases sacrés et boissons d'éternite dans les visions des martyrs africains," in *Epektasis: Mélanges patristiques offerts au Cardinal Jean Daniélou*, ed. Jacques Fontaine and Charles Kannengieser (Paris: Beauchesne, 1972), 139–52; Patricia Cox Miller, "'A Dubious Twilight': Reflections on Dreams in Patristic Literature," CH 55 (June 1986): 153–64; R. Petraglio, "Des influences de l'apocalypse dans la 'Passio Perpetuae' 11–13," in *L'apocalypse de Jean: Traditions exégétiques et iconographiques IIIᵉ–XIIᵉ siècles*, ed. R. Petraglio et al. (Geneva: Librairie Droz, 1979), 15–29; Johannes Quasten, "A Coptic Counterpart to a Vision in the Acts of Perpetua and Felicitas," Byz 15 (1940/41): 1–9; David M. Scholer, "'And I Was a Man': The Power and Problem of Perpetua," DS 15 (September–October 1989): 10–14; A. de Waal, "Der leidende Dinocrates in der Vision der heil. Perpetua," RQCAK 17 (1903): 339–47.

6. Kurt Aland, "Bemerkungen zum Montanismus und zur frühchristlichen Eschatologie," in *Kirchen geschichtliche Entwürfe: Alte Kirche, Reformation und Lutherum, Pietismus und Erweckungsbewegung*, ed. Kurt Aland (Gütersloh: Gerd

Mohn Verlagshaus, 1960), 105–48; A. A. R. Bastiaensen, "Tertullian's Reference to the *Passio Perpetuae* in *De Anima* 55, 4," *SP* 17(2) (1982): 790–95; Wolfgang Bender, "Der Montanismus in Tertullians Lehre über den Heiligen Geist," in *Die Lehre über den Heiligen Geist bei Tertullian,* ed. Joseph Pascher und Klaus Morsdorf, MTS, II Systematische Abteilung, 19 (Munich: Max Hueber Verlag, 1961), 150–69; Karlfried Froehlich, "Montanism and Gnosis," in *The Heritage of the Early Christian Church,* ed. David Neiman and Margaret Schatkins, OCA, 195 (Rome: Pont. Institutum Studiorum Orientalium, 1973), 91–111; D. Powell, "Tertullianists and Cataphrygians," *VC* 29 (1975): 33–54; George Schöllgen, " 'Tempus in Collecto est': Tertullian, der Frühe Montanismus und die Naherwartung ihrer Zeit," *JAC* 27/28 (1984/1985): 74–96; R. Gregor Smith, "Tertullian and Montanism," *T* 46 (1943): 127–36.

7. A. d'Ales, "Le mysticisme de Saint Cyprien," *RAM* 2 (1921): 256–67; Adolf von Harnack, "Cyprian als Enthusiast," *ZNTW* 3 (1902): 177–91; Cecil M. Robeck, Jr., "Visions and Prophecy in the Writings of Cyprian," *Paraclete* 16(3) (Summer 1982): 21–25.

8. It is the case that two other documents, *The Martyrdom of Montanus and Lucius* as well as *The Martyrdom of Mary and James,* both come from North Africa and date from the end of the Valerian persecution in which Cyprian died. These two Acts, however, have been excluded from this study for two reasons. First, they hold very great similarities in both form and content to *The Passion of Perpetua and Felicitas,* thereby raising some question as to their overall reliability as historical documents. Second, they record events about A.D. 259, and only later were they put into final form. The most recent edition in which they may be found is Herbert Musurillo, *The Acts of the Christian Martyrs* (Oxford: Clarendon Press, 1972). On their reliability see J. Rendel Harris and Seth K. Gifford, *The Acts of the Martyrdom of Perpetua and Felicitas* (London: C. J. Clay and Sons, 1890), 26–27; contra J. W. Trigg, "Martyrs and Churchmen in Third-Century North Africa," *SP* 15 (1984): 242–46.

9. Von Franz, "Die Passio Perpetuae," 389–496.

10. Mary R. Lefkowitz, "The Motivations of St. Perpetua's Martyrdom," *JAAR* 44(3) (1976): 417–21.

11. Dronke, *Women Writers of the Middle Ages,* 1–17; cf. Elizabeth Alvilda Petroff, *Medieval Women's Visionary Literature* (New York: Oxford University Press, 1986), 45–46.

12. Von Harnack, "Cyprian als Enthusiast," 177–91.

13. In light of Paul's discussions of prophecy in 1 Cor. 12:1–11 and Rom. 12:6–8, in which the terms $\chi\acute{\alpha}\rho\iota\sigma\mu\alpha$ or its plural form $\chi\alpha\rho\acute{\iota}\sigma\mu\alpha\tau\alpha$ are the subjects and of which prophecy ($\pi\rho o\phi\eta\tau\epsilon\acute{\iota}\alpha$) is but one of several manifestations, it seems appropriate to use the term "gift" ($\chi\acute{\alpha}\rho\iota\sigma\mu\alpha$) "of prophecy" ($\tau\hat{\eta}\varsigma$ $\pi\rho o\phi\eta\tau\epsilon\acute{\iota}\alpha\varsigma$) without doing violence to Paul's meaning.

14. John Calvin on Rom. 12:6 in Ross MacKenzie, trans., *The Epistles of Paul the Apostle to the Romans and to the Thessalonians,* CC (Grand Rapids: Wm. B. Eerdmans, 1960), 269, wrote: "In the Christian Church, therefore, prophecy at the present day is simply the right understanding of Scripture and the

particular gift of expounding it, since all the ancient prophecies and all the oracles of God have been concluded in Christ and His Gospel"; Martin Luther, *Lectures on the Minor Prophets*, ed. Hilton C. Oswald, LW, 18 (St. Louis: Concordia Publishing House, 1973), 108, in his comment on Joel 2:28 wrote that "when Paul or the other apostles are manifestly interpreting Scripture, this interpretation is prophecy," and in his *Lectures on the Minor Prophets, III*, ed. Hilton C. Oswald, LW, 20 (St. Louis: Concordia Publishing House, 1975), 156, on Zechariah (1527), in the Preface he wrote, "With all Christian faithfulness I therefore ask and admonish everyone, teachers as well as students, first, not to despise those who can expound the Scriptures and ably interpret and teach the difficult books. For St. Paul tells us (1 Thess. 5:19f.) not to despise prophesying or quench the spirit." But see Oscar Cullmann, *Early Christian Worship*, trans. A. Stewart Todd and James B. Torrance, SBT, 1st ser., 10 (London: SCM Press, 1969), 20–21, and R. B. Y. Scott, "Is Prophecy Preaching?" *CJT* 1 (1955): 11–18. Both contend that prophecy is something other than preaching.

15. See on this phenomenon the thought-provoking article by W. Sibley Townes, "On Calling People 'Prophets' in 1970," *Int* 24 (1970): 492–509.

16. So argue Pentecostals Donald Gee, *Concerning Spiritual Gifts* (Springfield, Mo.: Gospel Publishing House, 1980), 57, and Harold Horton, *The Gifts of the Spirit* (Nottingham: Assemblies of God Publishing House, 1971), 167–68, and charismatics Arnold Bittlinger, *Gifts and Graces: A Commentary on I Corinthians 12–14*, trans. Herbert Klassen (Grand Rapids: William B. Eerdmans, 1976), 45, and Bruce Yocum, *Prophecy: Exercising the Prophetic Gifts of the Spirit in the Church Today* (Ann Arbor, Mich.: Word of Life, 1976), 32–45. This interpretation has never been the sole possession of Pentecostals or charismatics. See, for instance, J. R. Pridie, *The Spiritual Gifts* (London: Robert Scott, 1921), 97, and Karl Rahner, *Visions and Prophecies*, QD, 10 (New York: Herder and Herder, 1963), 106.

17. These definitions are found in David Hill, *New Testament Prophecy*, MTL (London: Marshall, Morgan & Scott, 1979) and NFTL (Atlanta: John Knox Press, 1979), 5–7.

18. Hill, *New Testament Prophecy*, 8–9.

19. David E. Aune, *Prophecy in Early Christianity and the Ancient Mediterranean World* (Grand Rapids: William B. Eerdmans, 1983), 10.

20. Aune's definition is found in M. Eugene Boring, "The Apocalypse as Early Christian Prophecy: A Discussion of the Issues Raised by the Book of Revelation for the Study of Early Christian Prophecy," in *Society of Biblical Literature 1974 Seminar Papers*, ed. George MacRae (Cambridge, Mass.: Society of Biblical Literature, 1974), 58, n. 5, sec. 2.

21. Boring, "The Apocalypse as Early Christian Prophecy," 58, n. 5, sec. 3.

22. Hill, *New Testament Prophecy*, 8–9, has provided the basis for this statement. The emphasis has merely been shifted from the person to the phenomenon.

23. 1 Sam. 9:9: "Formerly in Israel, when a man went to inquire of God, he said, 'Come let us go to the seer (עַד הָרֹאֶה)'; for he who is now called a prophet (לַנָּבִיא) was formerly called a seer (הָרֹאֶה)."

24. Cf. 1 Sam. 3:1; Isa. 1:1–2; 6:1–13; 29:10–12; Jer. 23:16, 23–32; Lam. 2:9; Ezek. 1:1, 4–28; 8:3–4, 40:4; Dan. 7:1–28; 8:1–27; Joel 2:28; Amos 7:1–2, 4, 7–8, 12–13; 8:1–2; 9:1; Obad. 1:1; Nah. 1:1; Hab. 1:1; 2:2; Zech. 5:1. For a short overview of prophecy see Cecil M. Robeck, Jr., "Prophecy, Gift of," in *Dictionary of Pentecostal and Charismatic Movements,* ed. Stanley M. Burgess and Gary B. McGee (Grand Rapids: Regency Reference Library/Zondervan Publishing House, 1988), 728–40.

25. Matt. 1:20, 2:12–13, 19, 22, 17:1–13; Acts 2:17–18; 9:10–17; 10:1–20; 11:1–18; 16:9–10; 18:9–10; but esp. Rev. 1:12–20; 4:1ff, where the prophet is particularly connected with visions.

26. James L. Ash, "The Decline of Prophecy in the Early Church," *TS* 37 (1976): 252.

27. Paul Monceaux, *Histoire littéraire de l'afrique Chrètienne depuis les origines jusqu'a l'invasion Arabe,* 7 vols. in 3 (Paris: Ernest Leroux, 1901–1905).

28. Dom H. Leclercq, *L'afrique Chrètienne,* BEHE, 2 vols. (Paris: Librairie Victor Lecoffre, 1904).

29. Aune, *Prophecy in Early Christianity and the Ancient Mediterranean World;* M. Eugene Boring, *Sayings of the Risen Christ: Christian Prophecy in the Synoptic Tradition,* SNTS, 46 (Cambridge: Cambridge University Press, 1982); T. M. Crone, *Early Christian Prophecy: A Study of Its Origin and Function* (Baltimore: St. Mary's University Press, 1973); Gerhard Dautzenberg, *Urchristliche Prophetie,* BWANT, 4 (Stuttgart: W. Kohlhammer, 1975); E. Earle Ellis, *Prophecy and Hermeneutic in Early Christianity* (Grand Rapids: William B. Eerdmans, 1980); Wayne A. Grudem, *The Gift of Prophecy in I Corinthians* (Washington, D.C.: University Press of America, 1982); idem., *The Gift of Prophecy in the New Testament and Today* (Westchester, Ill.: Crossway Books, 1988); Ronald E. Heine, *The Montanist Oracles and Testimonia,* PMS, 14 (Macon, Ga.: Mercer University Press, 1989); Hill, *New Testament Prophecy;* Ulrich B. Müller, *Prophetie und Predigt im Neuen Testament,* SNT, 10 (Gütersloh: Verlagshaus [Gerd Mohn], 1975); Ἰωάννου Παναγοπούλου, Ἡ Ἐκκλησία τῶν Προφητῶν. Τὸ Προφητικὸν Χάρισμα ἐν τῇ Ἐκκλησίᾳ τῶν δύο Πρώτων Αἴωνων (Ἀθηναι: ΙΣΤΟΡΙΚΕΣ ΕΚΔΟΣΕΙΣ ΣΤ, ΒΑΣΙΛΟΠΟΥΛΟΣ, 1979); J. Panagopoulos, ed., *Prophetic Vocation in the New Testament and Today,* NovTSup, 45 (Leiden: E. J. Brill, 1977); J. Reiling, *Hermas and Christian Prophecy: A Study of the Eleventh Mandate,* NovTSup, 37 (Leiden: E. J. Brill, 1973). I should also mention the study by E. Cothenet, "Prophétisme dans le Nouveau Testament," in *Supplément au dictionaire de la Bible* (Paris: Letouzey & Ané, 1971, 1972), fasc. 46–47, cols. 1222–1337.

30. Ash, "Decline of Prophecy," 227–52; D. E. Aune, "*Herm. Man.* 11.2: Christian False Prophets Who Say What People Wish to Hear," *JBL* 97(1) (1978): 103–4; idem., "The Odes of Solomon and Early Christian Prophecy," *NTS* 28 (1981/82): 435–60; Dronke, *Women Writers of the Middle Ages,* 1–35, esp. 1–23; W. H. C. Frend, "Montanism: A Movement of Prophecy and Regional Identity in the Early Church," *BJRL* 70(3) (1988): 25–34; Froehlich, "Montanism and Gnosis," 91–111; Heinrich Kraft, "Vom Ende Urchristlichen

Prophetie," in *Prophetic Vocation*, ed. J. Panagopoulos, NTS, 45 (Leiden: E. J. Brill, 1977), 162–85; Miller, "'Dubious Twilight'," 153–64; Cecil M. Robeck, Jr., "The Prophet in the *Didache*," *Paraclete* 18(1) (Winter 1984): 16–19; idem., "Prophecy in the *Shepherd of Hermas*," *Paraclete* 18(2) (Spring 1984): 12–17; idem., "Origen, Celsus, and Prophetic Utterance," *Paraclete* 11(1) (Winter 1976): 19–23; idem., "Hippolytus on the Gift of Prophecy," *Paraclete* 17(3) (Summer 1983): 22–27; idem., "Montanism: A Problematic Spirit Movement," *Paraclete* 15(3) (Summer 1981): 24–29; idem., "Tertullian and Prophetic Gifts," *Paraclete* 18(3) (Summer 1984): 16–21; idem., "Visions and Prophecy in the Writings of Cyprian," 21–25; idem., "Irenaeus and 'Prophetic Gifts'," in *Essays on Apostolic Themes*, ed. Paul Elbert (Peabody, Mass.: Hendrickson Publishers, 1985), 104–14; idem., "Canon, *Regulae Fidei*, and Continuing Revelation in the Early Church," in *Church, Word, & Spirit: Historical and Theological Essays in Honor of Geoffrey W. Bromiley*, ed. James E. Bradley and Richard A. Muller (Grand Rapids: William B. Eerdmans, 1987), 65–91; John E. Stam, "Charismatic Theology in the *Apostolic Tradition* of Hippolytus," in *Current Issues in Biblical and Patristic Interpretation*, ed. Gerald F. Hawthorne (Grand Rapids: William B. Eerdmans, 1975), 267–76; David F. Wright, "Why Were the Montanists Condemned?" *Themelios* 2(1) (September 1976): 15–22; idem., "Montanism: A Movement of Spiritual Renewal?" *TR* 22 (November 1982): 19–29.

31. d'Ales, "mysticisme de Saint Cyprian," 256–67; F. J. Dölger, "ΘΕΟΥ ΦΩΝΕ: Die 'Gottes-Stimme' bei Ignatius von Antiochien, Kelsos und Origenes," *AC* 5 (1936): 218–23; von Harnack, "Cyprian als Enthusiast," 177–91; Heinz Kraft, "Die altkirchliche Prophetie und die Entstehung des Montanismus," *TZ* 11 (1955): 249–71; H. J. Lawlor, "The Heresy of the Phrygians," *JTS* 9 (1908): 481–97; J. W. Wilson, "The Career of the Prophet Hermas," *HTR* 20 (1927): 21–61.

32. Howard Clark Kee, Review of *New Testament Prophecy* by David Hill, *JAAR* 49 (1981): 677.

33. John Panagopoulos, Review of *New Testament Prophecy* by David Hill, *JSNT* 10 (1981): 65.

34. Ibid.

35. Matt. 7:15–23; 10:19–20; 24:11, 24–25; Acts 2:17–18; 11:27–30; 13:1–4; 15:22–35; 16:16–18; 19:1–7; 20:17–23; 21:1–14; Rom. 12:1–8; 1 Cor. 11:1–16; 12:1–14:40; Eph. 2:19–3:6; 4:11–15; 1 Thess. 4:13–18; 5:19–20; 2 Thess. 2:1–5, 15; 3:6–13; 5:19–22; 1 John 4:1–3; 2 Pet. 2:1–3; Rev. 1:1–4, 19; 4:1–20:15; 22:6–10, 18–19; *Didache* 10.7–11.2; 13.1; 15:1–2; *Martyrdom of St. Polycarp*, 5; Ignatius, *To the Philadelphians*, 7; *Epistle of Barnabas*, 16; *Shepherd of Hermas, Mandate* 11; Justin Martyr, *Dialogue with Trypho*, 82, 87–88; Irenaeus, *Against Heresies*, 5.6.1; *Epideixis*, 99.

36. Irenaeus, *Against Heresies*, 1.13.1–7; 1.14.1; 2.31.3; 3.2.1; Hippolytus, *Refutation of All Heresies*, 6.37; 7.26.

37. Eusebius, *Ecclesiastical History*, 5.14.1–5.19.4; Epiphanius, *Panarion*, 48.2, 10–13; Didymus, *On the Trinity*, 3.41.1.

38. For an overview of how the claims of orthodox, Gnostic, and Montanist

were assessed see Robeck, "Canon, *Regulae Fidei* and Continuing Revelation," 65–91.

39. Adolf von Harnack, *History of Dogma*, trans. Neil Buchanan (New York: Dover Publications, 1961), 2:53.

40. Hill, *New Testament Prophecy*, 191; cf. Aune, *Prophecy in Early Christianity*, 338, who notes that:

> Throughout the entire second century the phenomenon of prophecy was primarily tied to dissenting voices and movements within various phases of Christianity. This does not mean that prophets became an endangered species primarily because of their increasing association with heretical movements, but it does suggest that the earlier role of the prophets as articulators of the norms, values, and decisions of the invisible head of the church was taken over by the visible figures of the teacher, preacher, theologian, and church leader.

41. See also Ernst Käsemann, "An Apology for Primitive Christian Eschatology" in *Essays on New Testament Themes*, trans. W. J. Montague (Philadelphia: Fortress Press, 1982), 188: "A ministry conferred by ordination is bound to be the natural opponent both of Gnosis and of primitive Christian prophecy."

42. Hans von Campenhausen, *Ecclesiastical Authority and Spiritual Power in the Church of the First Three Centuries*, trans. J. A. Baker (Stanford: Stanford University Press, 1969), 178.

43. Ash, "Decline of Ecstatic Prophecy," 252.

CHAPTER TWO

1. Louis Duchesne, *Early History of the Christian Church* (London: John Murray, 1909), 1:262–63.

2. W. H. C. Frend, "Open Questions Concerning the Christians and the Roman Empire in the Age of the Severi," *JTS*, n.s., 25 (1974): 340.

3. Ibid., 340–43.

4. W. H. Shewring, *The Passion of S. S. Perpetua and Felicity MM. Together with the Sermons of S. Augustine on these Saints* (London: Sheed and Ward, 1931), xiii.

5. Tertullian, *To Scapula*, 4.2: "*Quid enim amplius tibi mandatur quam nocentes confessos damnare, negantes autem ad tormenta revocare?*" The Latin text is from Tertullian, *Tertullian Opera: Corpus Christianorum Series Latina*, vol. 2, *Opera Montanistica* (Turnholti, Belgium: Typographi Brepols; Rome: Editores Pontificii, 1954), 1130. Hereafter denoted *Tertullian Opera*.

6. Tertullian, *To Scapula*, 4.2: "*Videtis ergo quomodo ipsi vos contra mandata faciatis, ut confessos negare cogatis*" (ibid.).

7. William Tabbernee, "Early Montanism and Voluntary Martyrdom," *Col* 17(2) (May 1985): 42, suggests that Saturus may have been their Montanist instructor. I am inclined to disagree with this designation, although he may have represented a form of proto-Montanism at Carthage. Even if Saturus were a teacher of the New Prophecy, his action of voluntary surrender to the authorities,

as Tabbernee has shown, is certainly no proof that Montanists supported voluntary martyrdom against the position held by non-Montanist Christians.

8. J. Rendel Harris and Seth K. Gifford, *The Acts of the Martyrdom of Perpetua and Felicitas* (London: C. J. Clay and Sons, 1890), and J. Armitage Robinson, ed., "The Passion of S. Perpetua," in *Texts and Studies* 1(2) (Cambridge: The University Press, 1891; reprinted in Nendeln/Liechenstein: Kraus Reprint, 1967), both include the longer and shorter Latin texts as well as the Greek text; Shewring, *Passion of SS. Perpetua and Felicity*, contains only the longer Latin text; Cornelis I. M. I. van Beek, *Passio Sanctarum Perpetuae et Felicitatis*, FP, 43 (Bonn: Petri Hanstein, 1938), offers both the longer Latin and Greek texts; and, most recently, Herbert Musurillo, *The Acts of the Christian Martyrs*, OECT (Oxford: The Clarendon Press, 1972), 106–30, gives the longer Latin text. The longer Latin text and translation provided by Musurillo will be followed throughout.

9. R. E. Wallis, "The Martyrdom of Perpetua and Felicitas," in *Ante-Nicene Fathers*, ed. Alexander Roberts and James Donaldson (Grand Rapids: Wm. B. Eerdmans, 1973), 3:699–706 (hereafter denoted *ANF*); R. Waterville Muncey, *The Passion of S. Perpetua* (London: J. M. Dent & Sons, 1927); Shewring, *Passion of SS. Perpetua and Felicity*, 22–24; Musurillo, *Acts of the Christian Martyrs*, 107–31; and Rosemary Rader, "The Martyrdom of Perpetua," in *A Lost Tradition: Women Writers of the Early Church*, ed. Patricia Wilson-Kastner et al. (Washington, D.C.: University Press of America, 1981), 1–32.

10. Ronald E. Heine, *The Montanist Oracles and Testimonia*, PMS, 14 (Macon, Ga.: Mercer University Press, 1989), 60–61, translates only 1.1–5 in the section titled "Testimonia Concerning Montanism in North Africa."

11. W. H. Shewring, "Prose Rhythm in the *Passion S. Perpetua*," *JTS* 30 (1929): 57.

12. Åke Fridh, *Le problème de la Passion des Saintes Perpétue et Félicité*, SGLG, 26 (Göteborg: Acta Universitatis Gothoburgensis, 1968), 11, 45.

13. T. A. Johnston, "The Passion of SS. Perpetua and Felicitas," *Month* 153 (1929): 120.

14. For a brief survey of the history of these manuscripts see Julio Campos, "El autor de la 'Passio SS. Perpetuae et Felicitatis'," *Hel* 10 (1959): 358–61.

15. Robinson, "Passion of S. Perpetua," 2–7; the argument being restated in Shewring, *Passion of SS. Perpetua and Felicity*, xviii–xxi, and further elaborated by Campos, "Autor de la 'Passio'," 326–67.

16. Harris and Gifford, *Martyrdom of Perpetua and Felicitas*, 13–18.

17. Fridh, *Problème de la Passion*, 82–83.

18. Gustav Bardy, *La question des langues dans l'Église ancienne*, ETH, I (Paris: Beauchesne et Ses Fils, 1958), 63. Translation mine.

19. *The Passion of Perpetua and Felicitas*, 1.6.

20. Timothy D. Barnes, "Pre-Decian *Acta Martyrum*," *JTS*, n.s., 19(2) (October 1968): 523–25.

21. All subsequent references in the text to *The Passion of Perpetua and Felicitas* will be cited in parentheses.

236 / NOTES TO PAGES 13–14

22. William C. Weinrich, *Spirit and Martyrdom: A Study of the Work of the Holy Spirit in Contexts of Persecution and Martyrdom in the New Testament and Early Christian Literature* (Washington, D.C.: University Press of America, 1981), 243 n. 2.

23. Tertullian, *On the Soul*, 55.4.

24. Frend, "Open Questions," 340.

25. Eusebius, *Ecclesiastical History*, 6.1; 6.3.13–6.4.3.

26. See Muncey, *Passion of S. Perpetua*, 2–4, as well as the *Depositio Martyrum* of the *Philocalian Calendar* (A.D. 354) in Ethel Ross Barker, *Rome of the Pilgrims and Martyrs* (London: Methuen, 1913), 338.

27. *Passion of Perpetua and Felicitas*, 2.1: "'Εν πόλει Θου(βου)ρβιτανῶν τῇ μικροτέρᾳ συνελήφθησαν νεανίσκοι κατηχούμενοι . . ." This Greek reading is provided by van Beek, *Passio Sanctarum Perpetuae et Felicitatis*, 11. Robinson, "Passion of S. Perpetua," 63, reads Θουρβιτάνων.

28. Robinson, "Passion of S. Perpetua," 22–26.

29. Gustav Bardy, *La Vie spirituelle d'après les pères des trois premiers siècles* (Tournai, Belgium: Desclée et Cie, 1968), 1:218, states that the martyrs were originally from (*originaire de*) Thurburbo Minus. While this is possible, it is yet unproven.

30. L. R. Holme, *The Extinction of the Christian Churches in North Africa* (New York: Burt Franklin, 1969), 12.

31. Eusebius, *Ecclesiastical History*, 4:27; 5.17.4.

32. It would seem that Tertullian, *Against Praxeas*, 1.5–6, wrote of Victor as the bishop of Rome who was talked into condemning the movement by the heretic Praxeas.

33. Eusebius, *Ecclesiastical History*, 5.3.4–5.4.3, makes mention of Eleutherus's receipt of several works published by church leaders in Gaul prior to the time Irenaeus became bishop of Lyons (circa A.D. 178). See W. H. C. Frend, *The Early Church* (London: Hodder and Stoughton, 1965), 81, and Cecil M. Robeck, Jr., "Irenaeus and 'Prophetic Gifts'," in *Essays on Apostolic Themes*, ed. Paul Elbert (Peabody, Mass.: Hendrickson Publishers, 1985), 106–9.

34. The editor of *The Passion of Perpetua and Felicitas*, 1.3–5, remarks that these phenomena are present and valid as fulfillments of the prophecy of Joel 2:28–29, which Peter quoted in Acts 2:17–21. Cf. A. d'Ales, "L'auteur de la passio Perpetuae," *RHE* 8 (1907): 12; P. C. Atkinson, "The Montanist Interpretation of Joel 2:28, 29 (LXX 3.1, 2)," *T&U*, 126, *Studia Evangelica* 7 (1982): 11–15.

35. See, for instance, Tertullian, *Against Praxeas*, 8.5; *On Flight in Persecution*, 9.4; *On Modesty*, 21.7; *On Exhortation to Chastity*, 10.5.

36. Holme, *Extinction of the Christian Churches*, 13.

37. Tertullian, *On the Soul*, 9.3–4.

38. John de Soyres, *Montanism and the Primitive Church* (Cambridge: Deighton, Bell and Co., 1878; Lexington, Ky.: The American Theological Library Association, 1965), 44–45. See also Harris and Gifford, *Acts of the Martyrdom*, 2, 5.

39. Soyres, *Montanism and the Primitive Church*, 140.

40. Bardy, *Vie spirituelle*, 1:216. Alvyn Pettersen, "Perpetua—Prisoner of Conscience," *VC* 41 (1987): 146, argues that it "seems to reflect a proto-Montanist theology."

41. Timothy David Barnes, *Tertullian: A Historical and Literary Study* (Oxford: Clarendon Press, 1971), 77.

42. Ibid.

43. Ibid., 78; *The Passion of Perpetua and Felicitas*, 7.1; 8.2.

44. Barnes, *Tertullian*, 78; *The Passion of Perpetua and Felicitas*, 13.1.

45. Barnes, *Tertullian*, 78; *The Passion of Perpetua and Felicitas*, 4.3, in which Saturus voluntarily surrendered to the authorities, and 21.4, in which Perpetua helped her young and inexperienced executioner with the sword. But see Tabbernee, "Early Montanism and Voluntary Martyrdom," 33–44, who convincingly demonstrates that this same activity was common among the orthodox as well.

46. Pierre de Labriolle, *La crise Montaniste* (Paris: Ernest Leroux, 1913), 341–42.

47. Weinrich, *Spirit and Martyrdom*, 227; cf. F. E. Vokes, "Penitential Discipline in Montanism," *SP* 14 (1976): 63.

48. Weinrich, *Spirit and Martyrdom*, 227; *The Passion of Perpetua and Felicitas*, 13.3.

49. Weinrich, *Spirit and Martyrdom*, 228. See also Tabbernee, "Early Montanism and Voluntary Martyrdom," 42.

50. Weinrich, *Spirit and Martyrdom*, 228. One could also cite *The Martyrdom of St. Polycarp*, 13, as providing an example of non-Montanist assistance to the persecutors.

51. Weinrich, *Spirit and Martyrdom*, 228.

52. A brief synopsis of this meeting is outlined in R. Braune, "Seance du 26 Mars 1955," *REL* 33 (1955): 80–81, which later appeared in the *BFLS* 34 (1956): 230–31; cf. Weinrich, *Spirit and Martyrdom*, 224.

53. The attitude of Montanism is to be found in one of its oracles quoted by Tertullian, *On Flight in Persecution*, 9.4: "Wish not to die in your beds, nor in miscarriages and mild fevers, but in martyrdoms, that he who has suffered for you may be glorified." This translation appears in Heine, *Montanist Oracles*, 73, and differs from the translation on p. 7 of the same work.

54. Weinrich, *Spirit and Martyrdom*, 229; *The Passion of Perpetua and Felicitas*, 15.1–7; 18.3.

55. Fridh, *Problème de la Passion*, 11.

56. Campos, "Autor de la 'Passio'," 381. Translation mine. A similar position is adopted by Barnes, "Pre-Decian *Acta Martyrum*," 522.

57. David M. Scholer, "'And I Was A Man': The Power and Problem of Perpetua," *DS* 15 (September–October 1989): 11.

58. Among these proponents are Labriolle, *Crise Montaniste*, 345; Robinson, "Passion of S. Perpetua," 47–58; Johannes Quasten, *Patrology* (Utrecht-Antwerp: Spectrum Publishers, 1975), 1:181; F. J. Dölger, "Der Kampf mit dem

Ägypter in der Perpetua-Vision: Das Martyrium als Kampf mit dem Teufel," *AC* 3 (1932): 188.

59. A. d'Ales, "L'auteur de la passio Perpetuae," 5–18.

60. Jerome, *Lives of Illustrious Men,* 53.

61. Tertullian, *On the Soul,* 55.4; *Tertullian Opera,* 2:862. The date is derived from Quasten, *Patrology,* 2:289.

62. d'Ales, "L'auteur de la passio Perpetuae," 8.

63. Most scholars argue for this date, although Harris and Gifford, *Martyrdom of Perpetua and Felicitas,* 28–31, suggest that Tertullian addressed *To the Martyrs* specifically to Perpetua and her companions at Carthage.

64. Robinson, "Passion of S. Perpetua," 47–58.

65. d'Ales, "L'auteur de la passio Perpetuae," 13, explains this as resulting from the fact that Tertullian's acknowledgments of Perpetua's passion as a "sacred trust" led him to act merely as a narrator so that Perpetua might receive the honor due her; *The Passion of Perpetua and Felicitas,* 16.1.

66. Cf. Tertullian, *On the Soul,* 55.4, and *The Passion of Perpetua and Felicitas,* 11.1, 9; d'Ales, "L'auteur de la passio Perpetuae," 13–14, argues that this may be explained on the basis of the fact that Tertullian wrote *On the Soul* some years later, and while the error is present, it is merely a defect of Tertullian's memory that, nevertheless, conveys the same general sense. But see A. A. R. Bastiaensen, "Tertullian's Reference to the *Passio Perpetuae* in *De Anima* 55.4," *SP* 17(2) (1982): 791, in which he claims that no such error took place.

67. See note 52 above.

68. It would seem to me that Augustine's words in *On the Soul and Its Origin,* 1.12, "Concerning Dinocrates, however, the brother of St. Perpetua, there is no record in canonical Scripture" must take on this meaning in order to be understandable. See also Quasten, *Patrology,* 1:181.

69. For these sermons, see Shewring, *Passion of SS. Perpetua and Felicity,* xxi, 45–49. Cf. Muncey, *Passion of S. Perpetua,* 8.

70. J. W. Trigg, "Martyrs and Churchmen in Third-Century North Africa," *SP* 15 (1984): 242–46, describes these visions as "prophetic."

CHAPTER THREE

1. Mary R. Lefkowitz, "The Motivations for St. Perpetua's Martyrdom," *JAAR* 44(3) (1976): 420, views Perpetua's relationship to her father as one of "'unconscious incest,' a close emotional pairing of father and daughter which results from a desperate attempt to keep a disintegrating family together." An older attempt to understand the psychology behind Perpetua's visions is that made by Marie-Louise von Franz, "Die Passio Perpetuae," in *Aion: Untersuchungen zur Symbolgeschicte,* ed. C. G. Jung, Psychologische Abhandlungen, 7 (Zurich: Racher Verlag, 1951), 389–496. While there were surely psychological factors at work in the events surrounding the martyrdom of Perpetua, such things are beyond the scope of this study and, in the absence of any possibility of personal analysis, are largely speculative.

2. *The Passion of Perpetua and Felicitas*, 3.5: "*mihi Spiritus dictavit non aliud petendum ab aqua nisi sufferentiam carnis.*"

3. Tertullian, *On Baptism*, 20.5; "*petite de domino peculia gratiae distributiones charismatum subiacere*" (*Tertullian Opera*, 1:295). On this text see the helpful discussion by Kilian McDonnell, "Communion Ecclesiology and Baptism in the Spirit: Tertullian and the Early Church," *TS* 49 (1988): 679–84.

4. While one might argue from silence that the Spirit revealed this through a prophetic utterance, her explicit use of *mihi*, which clearly individualizes this revelation, would seem to indicate that the recognition arose internally rather than coming externally from another in such a prophetic utterance.

5. *The Passion of Perpetua and Felicitas*, 4.1. Subsequent references in the text to this source are in parentheses.

6. Ibid.: "*iam in magna dignatione es, tanta ut postules visionem.*"

7. Ibid., 4.2: "*Et ego quae me sciebam fabulari cum Domino, cuius beneficia tanta experta eram.*"

8. One is readily reminded of the sister in the congregation at Carthage about whom Tertullian wrote, "she converses with angels, and sometimes even with the Lord (*conversatur cum angelis, aliquando etiam cum domino*)," *On the Soul*, 9.4; *Tertulliani Opera*, 2:792. This anonymous sister experienced these things while she was "in the Spirit by ecstasy (*per ecstasin in spiritu patitur*)." That Perpetua should not be identified with this anonymous sister, however, is apparent from the facts that (1) no catechumen would have been ascribed the level of trust that was given this sister whose utterances were understood to be tried and proven and that (2) whereas Perpetua was martyred in March 202/203, Tertullian wrote between A.D. 210 and 213 as though this woman was a contemporary of his (*Est hodie soror apud nos*).

9. *The Passion of Perpetua and Felicitas*, 4.2: "*Et postulavi, et ostensum est mihi hoc.*" For a translation of the vision, see appendix A. All appendices for *The Passion* are based on the translation provided by Musurillo.

10. Ibid., 4.10: "*intelleximus passionem esse futuram.*" Elizabeth Alvilda Petroff, *Medieval Women's Visionary Literature* (New York: Oxford University Press, 1986), 45, notes that "Close examination of her [Perpetua's] writing reveals a very conscious structuring of the relationships between vision and reality, between human confrontation and divine resolution." This is the first of such passages in which this structuring occurs.

11. This works two ways. On the one hand, visions and dreams played an important role in ancient life and, apparently, especially in North African life. As Patricia Cox Miller "'A Dubious Twilight': Reflections on Dreams in Patristic Literature," *CH* 55 (June 1986): 157, points out, "Perpetua betrays her oneness with her culture, which understood dream-speech as a kind of divine logic." On the other hand, she notes (p. 159) Perpetua shapes later tradition with her interpretations and descriptions, using her dreams/visions to some extent as "a mode of scriptural exegesis as well as a vehicle for theological reflection."

12. On the history of Phoenician Carthage see Alfred J. Church, *Carthage of the Empire of Africa* (Freeport, N.Y.: Books for Libraries Press, 1971).

13. Ibid., 296–301.

14. L. R. Holme, *The Extinction of the Christian Churches in North Africa* (New York: Burt Franklin, 1969), 18; J. Rendel Harris and Seth K. Gifford, *The Acts of the Martyrdom of Perpetua and Felicitas* (London: C. J. Clay and Sons, 1890), 1.

15. *The Passion of Perpetua and Felicitas*, 2.1: "*honeste nata, liberaliter instituta, matronaliter nupta.*" Timothy David Barnes, *Tertullian* (Oxford: Clarendon Press, 1971), 70, notes interestingly that "Three Vibii were proconsuls of Africa in the first century, and no proconsul of that name happens to be attested after the reign of Vespasian. If Perpetua's family had gained Roman citizenship from one of the three known Vibii, its standing in Carthage was no humble one." On her husband, we know nothing further of certainty, but Peter Dronke, *Women Writers of the Middle Ages* (Cambridge: Cambridge University Press, 1986), 282–83, n. 3, has done an excellent job of sorting through the existing options.

16. *The Passion of Perpetua and Felicitas*, 13.4: "*et coepit Perpetua graece cum illis loqui.*" Cf. William H. C. Frend, "Blandina and Perpetua: Two Early Christian Heroines," in *Les martyrs de Lyon (177)* (Paris: Éditions du Centre Nationale de la Recherche Scientifique, 1978), 575:169–70.

17. Dronke, *Women Writers of the Middle Ages*, 7, argues that "the most important *literary* stimulus to the images in her dreams may well be Virgil rather than the Bible." I am inclined to disagree with Dronke's emphasis, although his suggestion that secular ideas played a formative role in Perpetua's imagery is well taken.

18. See note 35 below.

19. Frend, "Blandina and Perpetua," 575:172.

20. J. Armitage Robinson, ed., "The Passion of S. Perpetua," in *Texts and Studies*, 1(2) (Cambridge: The University Press, 1891; Nendeln/Liechtenstein: Kraus Reprint, 1967), 26–43.

21. See Herbert Musurillo, *The Acts of the Christian Martyrs* (Oxford: The Clarendon Press, 1972), 86–89, for the text of *The Acts of Scillitan Martyrs*, an event dated at 17 July 180.

22. E. A. Andrews, ed., *Harpers' Latin Dictionary: A New Latin Dictionary*, rev. Charlton T. Lewis and Charles Short (New York: American Book, 1907), 612.

23. Gen. 3:1–5; Job 26:13; Isa. 27:1; Amos 9:3.

24. Job 7:12; Ps. 74:13; Isa. 27:1; 51:9; Jer. 51:34; Ezek. 29:3; 32:2. Ezekiel's prophecies against Egypt clearly identify Pharaoh (the state?) as a water-dwelling dragon (probably the crocodile—symbol of Egypt to the prophets) who will be destroyed by God.

25. Job 41:1; Pss. 74:14; 104:26; Isa. 27:1.

26. Job 9:13; 26:12; Pss. 87:4; 89:10; Isa. 30:7; 51:9. In the Psalms passages, Rahab may be identified as Egypt. Rahab, however, is traditionally the primeval chaos-producing sea-god that Yahweh overcomes in order to create the world in which we live. The implications derived from the Isaiah passages may expand this perspective from the nation of Egypt to a world system or world empire. Thus, Rahab could refer to evil as it is embodied within the world system. On this, see

Otto Kaiser, *Isaiah 13–39: A Commentary*, trans. R. A. Wilson, OTL (Philadelphia: Westminster Press, 1974), 223.

27. Job 40:15–24.

28. *Bel and the Dragon* for example is the story of a dragon god said to have been worshipped by the Babylonians during the time of Daniel. The cult of the dragon was overthrown by means of Daniel's clever detective work that revealed the mysterious disappearance of food offered to the dragon as a hoax perpetrated by its priests.

29. 2 Esd. 6:49–52; *1 Enoch* 60.7–9; *Testament of Asher* 7:3; *2 Bar.* 29.3–4; *4 Ezra* (or *Esdras*) 6.49–52; *Apocalypse of Abraham* 21.4; and *Psalms of Solomon* 2.29. In the *Psalms of Solomon* it seems that the Roman general Pompey is to be identified with the dragon.

30. Rev. 12:3–13:4, 11; 16:13.

31. For a brief and helpful overview of the dragon/serpent symbol in apocalyptic writing see D. S. Russell, *The Method and Message of Jewish Apocalyptic*, OTL (Philadelphia: Westminster Press, 1964), 123–24, 276–77. Also of help in understanding this figure is Edmond Jacob, *Theology of the Old Testament*, trans. Arthur W. Heathcote and Phillip J. Allcock (New York: Harper & Row, 1958), 281, n. 3.

32. Prior to the death of Perpetua (A.D. 202/203), Theophilus of Antioch, *To Autolycus*, 2.28 (circa A.D. 180), described Satan, deceiver of Eve, as "demon and dragon on account of his revolting from God (Δαίμων δὲ καὶ δράκων καλεῖται, διὰ τὸ ἀποδεδρακέναι αὐτὸν ἀπὸ τοῦ θεοῦ)" (translation mine). The Greek text is from J. P. Migne, ed., *Patriologiae Graecae* (Turnholti, Belgium: Typographi Brepols, 1978), vol. 6, col. 1098. Hereafter denoted PG. Prior to A.D. 200, Clement of Alexandria, *Exhortation to the Heathen*, 1.86, wrote of the evil one as tyrant and dragon (τύραννος καὶ δράκων), PG, 8:64; Irenaeus, *Against Heresies*, 3.23.3–7, identified Satan with the serpent of Gen. 3:1–5, 13–15; Ps. 91:13; and Rev. 20:5. Tertullian used similar language in his work *On Baptism*, 1:2 (circa A.D. 198–200), describing the heretic Quintilla as a serpent (*vipera*) (*Tertullian Opera*, 1:277), and in his *To the Martyrs*, 1 (circa A.D. 197), he wrote that Satan is the "outcharmed or smoked-out snake (*coluber*)" over which the martyrs are encouraged to triumph (*Tertullian Opera*, 1:3). In writing *To His Wife*, 1.6.3 (circa A.D. 200–206), Tertullian described the Roman vestal virgins as those who keep company with the dragon (*dracone*) himself, referring to Satan (*Tertulliani Opera*, 1.380).

33. Cyprian, *Epistle* 22.1.

34. Ibid., 39.2: "*et quamuis ligati nervo pedes essent, galeatus serpens et obtritus et victus est.*" The Latin text is from Guilelmus Hartel, *S. Thrasci Caecili Cypriani Opera Omnia*, CSEL (Vienna: C. Geroldi Filium Bibliopolam Academiae, 1871), 3.2, 528.

35. Bruce M. Metzger, *The Text of the New Testament: Its Transmission, Corruption, and Restoration* (New York: Oxford University Press, 1968), 72, and sec. *k*, p. 73. The Vulgate begun by Jerome in A.D. 382 used the term *draco* in such passages as Ps. 73(74):13–14; 90(91):13; 103(104):26; Isa. 51:9; Jer. 51:34;

Ezek. 29:3; 32:2; Dan. 14:22, 25–27 (Bel and the Dragon); Rev. 12:3, 4, 7, 9, 13, 16–17; 13:2, 4, 11; 16:13; 20:2. Although it is obvious that Perpetua did not use the Vulgate, the fact that some of Scripture had been translated into Latin in North Africa prior to her conversion (existing quite probably in an interlinear Greek/Old Latin fashion) coupled with the fact that the Vulgate was based in part on various Old Latin manuscripts make the parallel of the North African Christian understanding of Satan a real possibility in Perpetua's day. The Vulgate would seem to have preserved some of this earlier thinking.

36. Josephus, Antiquities, 8.2.5; this latter may be what Jesus alluded to in Luke 11:19: "And if I cast out demons by Beelzebub, by whom [by what authority, or in whose name] do your sons cast them out?"

37. Matt. 7:22. This passage seems to indicate that of primary importance is a previously existing relationship between the one invoking the name of Jesus and the Lord himself. Contrast this with the actions of the sons of Sceva in Acts 19:13–16.

38. Justin Martyr, Apology, 2.6; Irenaeus, Against Heresies, 2.32.4–5; Origen, Against Celsus, 3.24; 7.4; and Tertullian, Scorpiace, 1.3.

39. Mark 16:17, which occurs in the longer ending of the Gospel, is probably best dated sometime prior to A.D. 180, and it provides an interesting parallel. In words attributed to Jesus we are told that specific signs would accompany those who believe. Among the list of signs was included the statement that "in my name they shall cast out demons (ἐν τῷ ὀνοματί μου δαιμόνια ἐκβαλοῦσιν)." Here, it is once again clear that this authority over the demonic rested with those who believed (τοῖς πιστεύσασιν).

40. F. J. Dölger, "Der Kampf mit dem Ägypter in der Perpetua-Vision," AC 3 (1932): 184–85.

41. The text reads, "I saw a great beast like a whale/sea-monster (βλέπω θηρίον μεῖστον ὡσεὶ κατός τι)," Shepherd of Hermas, Vision 4.1.6; translation mine. Greek text for the Shepherd of Hermas is from Robert Joly, Le Pasteur, SC, 53 (Paris: Éditions du Cerf, 1958), 134.

42. Shepherd of Hermas, Vision 4.1.5–6.

43. Ibid., 4.1.7.

44. The Passion of Perpetua and Felicitas, 4.4; Shepherd of Hermas, Vision 4.1.7.

45. In The Passion of Perpetua and Felicitas, 4.6, Perpetua was encouraged by Saturus's words, "I am waiting for you. But take care; do not let the dragon bite you." Hermas, in the Shepherd of Hermas, Vision 4.1.7, was encouraged when he remembered the words, "Doubt not, Hermas! (Μὴ διψυχήσεις Ἑρμᾶ)" (Joly, Pasteur, 134).

46. Shepherd of Hermas, Vision 4.1.8a.

47. Ibid., 4.2.4a: "ὅτι τὴν μέριμνάν σου ἐπὶ τὸν θεόν ἐπέριψας καὶ τὴν καρδίαν σου ἤνοιξας πρὸς τὸν κύριον, πιστεύσας, ὅτι δι᾽ οὐδένος δύνη σωθῆναι εἰ μὲ διὰ τοῦ μεγάλου καὶ ἐνδόξου ὀνοματος" (Joly, Pasteur, 136).

48. Shepherd of Hermas, Vision 4.2.4a compared with The Passion of Perpetua and Felicitas, 4.6.

49. *Shepherd of Hermas,* Vision 4.2.5: "τὸ θηρίον τοῦτο τύπος· ἐστὶν θλίψεως τῆς μελλούσης τῆς μεγάλης" (Joly, *Pasteur,* 136).

50. Of course this passage appears in Peter's Pentecost sermon as a reference to the risen Jesus in Acts 2:34–35. Cf. also Matt. 22:44; Mark 12:36; Luke 20:42–43; Heb. 1:13; 10:12–13. The idea of submission to the name of Jesus on bended knee is also present in Phil. 2:9–11.

51. Dölger, "Kampf mit dem Ägypter," 183–85.

52. See Frend, "Blandina and Perpetua," 575:172, and Alvyn Pettersen, "Perpetua—Prisoner of Conscience," VC 41 (1987): 147. Gen. 28:12–15: "And he [Jacob] dreamed that there was a ladder set up on the earth, and the top of it reached to heaven; and behold the angels of God were ascending and descending on it! And behold, the Lord stood above it (וְהִנֵּה יְהוָה נִצָּב עָלָיו) and said: . . ." A potential, although later, parallel exists in the *Acts of Montanus and Lucius,* which dates from Carthage about A.D. 259. In 7.6, a presbyter named Victor, who was imprisoned with Montanus and Lucius and who himself was soon to die as a martyr, received a vision in which he asked the Lord for a sign of where heaven was. He wanted to share that knowledge with his fellow prisoners. His request was answered with the words "Give them the sign of Jacob (*Dic illis signum Iacobi*)." Presumably this referred to Jacob's ladder. See Musurillo, *Acts of the Christian Martyrs,* 219.

53. Johannes Quasten, "A Coptic Counterpart to a Vision in the Acts of Perpetua and Felicitas," *Byz* 15 (1940/41): 2–4.

54. *The Ascension of Isaiah,* 7:9, 13, 18, 24, 28, 32; 8:1; 9:1, 6–7. Philo, *De somniis* 1:22 (Secs. 133–35) (F. H. Colson, *Philo,* trans. G. H. Whitaker, LCL [Cambridge, Mass.: Harvard University Press, 1949], 5:369).

55. In *The Passion of Perpetua and Felicitas,* 21.8, the redactor sees the ladder as the transition from death to life or, more pointedly, as the act of dying. He/she wrote of Saturus, "*multo magis Saturus, qui et prior ascenderat, prior reddidit spiritum.*"

56. 1QS 3:13–4:26, esp. typified the way of light and the way of darkness.

57. *The Testament of Asher,* 3:1–2.

58. 4 *Ezra* 7:6–8 (R. H. Charles, *The Apocrypha and Pseudepigrapha of the Old Testament in English* [Oxford: Clarendon Press, 1913], 2:580). I find this to be a much more satisfactory parallel than Dronke, *Women Writers of the Middle Ages,* 8, who suggests Virgil's *Aeneid,* 2:469ff.

59. Matt. 7:14: "For the gate is narrow (τί στενὴ ἡ πύλη) and the way is hard (καὶ τεθλιμμένη ἡ ὁδός) that leads to life, and those who find it are few."

60. *Didache,* 1:1; "There are two Ways, one of Life and one of Death; but there is a great difference between the ways" (Phillip Schaff, *Teaching of the Twelve Apostles* [New York: Funk & Wagnalls, 1885], 162–63).

61. *Epistle of Barnabas,* 18–20.

62. Jean Daniélou, *The Origins of Latin Christianity: A History of Early Christian Doctrine before the Council of Nicaea* (Philadelphia: Westminster Press, 1977), 3:60.

63. Such an interpretation might also have parallels in Heb. 12:1–2: "There-

fore, since we are surrounded by so great a cloud of witnesses, let us lay aside every weight, and sin which clings so closely, and let us run with perseverance the race that is set before us, looking to Jesus the pioneer and perfecter of our faith, who for the sake of the joy that was set before him endured the cross, disregarding its shame, and has taken his seat at the right hand of the throne of God"; cf. Heb. 11:33–40.

64. Rev. 1:13b–16. Cf. C. H. Dodd, "The Appearances of the Risen Christ: An Essay in Form-Criticism of the Gospels," in *Studies in the Gospels: Essays in Memory of R. H. Lightfoot*, ed. D. E. Nineham (Oxford: Basil Blackwell, 1955), 21.

65. Dodd, "Appearances of the Risen Christ," 9.

66. Ibid., 10. Among the "concise" pericopes he includes Matt. 28:8–10, 16–20, and John 20:19–21.

67. Dodd, "Appearances of the Risen Christ," 10. Among the "circumstantial" pericopes Dodd cites Luke 24:13–35 and John 21:1–14.

68. Johannes Lindblom, *Gesichte und Offenbarungen: Vorstellungen von göttlichen Weisungen und übernatürlichen Erscheinungen im ältesten Christentum*, RSHLL (Lund: Gleerup, 1968), esp. 40, 53–54.

69. Elaine H. Pagels, "Visions, Appearances, and Apostolic Authority: Gnostic and Orthodox Traditions," in *Gnosis: Festschrift für Hans Jonas*, ed. Barbara Aland (Göttingen: Vandenhoeck & Ruprecht, 1978), 418.

70. Ibid.

71. H. P. Owen, "Stephen's Vision in Acts VII. 55–6," *NTS* 1 (1955): 226.

72. See Samuel Terrien's fascinating treatment of the "Glory of Yahweh" and the blinding light throughout Israel's history in his *The Elusive Presence: Toward a New Biblical Theology* (New York: Harper & Row, 1978).

73. Cyprian, *On Mortality* 19: *"paene morienti iuvenis honore et maiestate venerabilis, statu celsus et clarus aspectu et quem adsistentem sibi vix possit humanus aspectus oculis carnalibus intueri."* The Latin text is from Hartel, S. *Thrasci Caecili Cypriani*, 3.1:309. Contrast this with the description of the young man who from within the vision interprets Hermas's vision in the *Shepherd of Hermas, Vision* 3.10–13.

74. *1 Enoch* 89:59–67. It should be noted that God is here called "Lord of the sheep." Cf. *1 Enoch* 89:75.

75. Ignatius, *To the Philadelphians* 2.

76. Robert M. Grant, *The Apostolic Fathers: An Introduction* (New York: Thomas Nelson & Sons, 1964), 85; Joly, *Pasteur*, 14–15, dates it no later than A.D. 140; J. Reiling, *Hermas and Christian Prophecy*, NovTSup, 37 (Leiden: E. J. Brill, 1973), 23.

77. *Shepherd of Hermas, Vision* 5.1: *"σχήματι ποιμενικῷ, περικείμενος δέρμα αἴγειον λευκὸν καὶ πήραν ἔχων ἐπὶ τῶν ὤμων καὶ ῥάβδον εἰς τὴν χεῖρα"* (Joly, *Pasteur*, 140); translation mine.

78. *Shepherd of Hermas, Mandate* 12.6.1: *"Ἐγὼ δὲ ὑμῖν λέγω, ὁ ἄγγελος τῆς μετανοίας"* (Joly, *Pasteur*, 208); translation mine. Cf. *Mandate* 4.2.2 and *Similitude* 9.1.1.

79. *Shepherd of Hermas, Similitudes* 6.2.1 and 6.3.2; translation mine.

80. Edgar Hennecke, *New Testament Apocrypha*, ed. Wilhelm Schnee-melcher, trans. R. McL. Wilson (Philadelphia: Westminster Press, 1965), 2:634.

81. David E. Aune, *Prophecy in Early Christianity and the Ancient Mediterranean World* (Grand Rapids: William B. Eerdmans, 1983), 320.

82. Rom. 8:16; Eph. 5:1; Phil. 2:15; John 1:12; 1 John 3.1.

83. Mary addresses Jesus this way in Luke 2:48, and the term is used in one of Jesus' parables (Matt. 21:28) of a father's address to a son.

84. Jesus, for instance, uses the term in Matt. 9:2 and in Mark 2:5 when he addresses the paralytic.

85. Epiphanius, *Panarion* 49.2: "ταῦτά ἐστιν ἃ κατειλήφαμεν. Ἀρτο-τυρίτας δὲ αὐτοὺς καλοῦσιν ἀπὸ τοῦ ἐν τοῖς αὐτῶν μυστηρίοις ἐπιτιθέν-τας ἄρτον καὶ τυρὸν καὶ οὕτως ποιεῖν τὰ αὐτῶν μυστήρια" (Migne PG 41:881). Harris and Gifford, *Martyrdom of Perpetua and Felicitas*, 44–45, note, accepted this statement as fact.

86. Julio Campos, "El autor de la 'Passio SS. Perpetua et Felicitatis'," *Hel* 10 (1959): 376. However, John de Soyres, *Montanism and the Primitive Church* (Lexington, Ky.: The American Theological Library Association, 1965), 140, argued that whether one accepted this incident as indicative of Montanist use of cheese or as an example of such a practice in Montanism, the vision itself, obviously received in a state of ecstasy, was reason enough to link Perpetua to Montanism.

87. Pierre de Labriolle, *La crise Montaniste* (Paris: Ernest Leroux, 1913), 344; E. R. Dodds, *Pagan and Christian in an Age of Anxiety* (Cambridge: University Press, 1965), 51; A. d'Ales, "L'Auteur de la Passio Perpetuae," *RHE* 8 (1907): 17.

88. Musurillo, *Acts of the Christian Martyrs*, 111, 113.

89. Dodds, *Pagan and Christian*, 51.

90. Michel Meslin, "Vases sacrés et boissons d'éternité dans les visions des martyrs africains," in *Epektasis: Mélanges patristiques offerts au Cardinal Jean Dan-iélou*, ed. Jacques Fontaine and Charles Kannengieser (Paris: Beauchesne, 1972), 150, esp. n. 68.

91. Exod. 3:8, 17; 13:5; 33:3; Lev. 20:24; Num. 13:27; 14:8; 16:13–14; Deut. 6:3; 11:9; 26:9, 15; 27:3; 31:20; Josh. 5:6; Jer. 11:5; 32:22; and Ezek. 20:6, 15.

92. 1 Cor. 3:2; Heb. 5:12–13; 1 Pet. 2:2–3.

93. Meslin, "Vases sacrés et boissons d'éternité," 151; translation mine.

94. Tertullian, *The Chaplet*, 3.3. Pettersen, "Perpetua—Prisoner of Con-science," 148, cites this passage in Tertullian as well, but he sees in Perpetua a drawing together of baptismal and Eucharistic motifs.

95. Meslin, "Vases sacrés et boissons d'éternité," 150.

96. Tertullian, *On Modesty* 7.1; 10.12.

97. See Christopher Rowland, *The Open Heaven: A Study of Apocalyptic in Judaism and Early Christianity* (New York: Crossroad, 1982), 398; Daniélou, *Origins of Latin Christianity* 3:60; Meslin, "Vases sacrés et boissons d'éternité," 150.

98. 2 Cor. 12:2–4. On this *Himmelsreise*, see Russell P. Spittler, "The Limits of Ecstasy: An Exegesis of 2 Corinthians 12:1–10," in *Current Issues in Biblical and Patristic Interpretation*, ed. Gerald F. Hawthorne (Grand Rapids: William B. Eerdmans, 1975), 259–66, esp. 262, n. 19.

99. Gen. 2:8–10, 15–16; 3:1–3, 8, 10, 23–24; Isa. 51:3; Ezek. 28:13; 31:8–9; Joel 2:3.

100. Theophilus of Antioch, *To Autolycus* 2:26; Irenaeus, *Against Heresies* 5.5.1; 5.36.1; Origen, *Principles* 2.11.6.

101. Tertullian, *On the Resurrection of the Flesh* 43.4; *On the Soul* 55.4.

102. On this understanding of "Amen" one may cite 1 Kings 1:36, 1 Cor. 14:16, and probably Rev. 1:7; 22:20. See, on this, Klaus Berger, *Die Amen-Worte Jesu*, BZNW, 39 (Berlin: Walter de Gruyter, 1970), 161; also Heinrich Schlier, "Ἀμήν," in *Theological Dictionary of the New Testament*, ed. Gerhard Kittel, trans. and ed. Geoffrey W. Bromiley (Grand Rapids: Wm. B. Eerdmans, 1964), 1:335–38.

103. *The Passion of Perpetua and Felicitas*, 4.10; Miller, "'A Dubious Twilight'," 158, notes, "In the moment of her awakening, Perpetua's 'real' life has become a kind of prelude to the realization of her dream. The dream then becomes both frame and substance of her subsequent actions, a living parable of the relation between life and death."

104. *The Passion of Perpetua and Felicitas*, 5.6. Pettersen, "Perpetua—Prisoner of Conscience," 141, notes that Perpetua's willingness to suffer is central to her spirituality. She does not live in a predetermined historical context, but she allows herself the freedom to accept the circumstances that, in turn, reveal her genuine faith toward God.

105. The symbolism of Perpetua's confession may be interpreted more fully than merely as a confession of faith. It functions also as a "political act," a confrontation with existing life and culture in Carthage, including the breaking of traditional patterns of the day. See Lefkowitz, "Motivations for St. Perpetua's Martyrdom," 418, 421. Margaret R. Miles, "Patriarchy as Political Theology: The Establishment of North African Christianity," in *Civil Religion and Political Theology*, ed. Leroy S. Rouner (Notre Dame, Ind: University of Notre Dame Press, 1986), 172, goes so far as to suggest that North African "Women may have been attracted to the Christian movement by the opportunities for discovering and using their energy and talent without the restrictions of secular society."

CHAPTER FOUR

1. *The Passion of Perpetua and Felicitas*, 6.6. Subsequent references in the text to this source are in parentheses.

2. A. de Waal, "Der leidende Dinocrates in der Vision der heil. Perpetua," *RQCAK* 17 (1903): 340.

3. This is apparent from the redactor's perspective in *The Passion of Perpetua and Felicitas*, 1.5–6; 18.7; 21.8, 11; Tertullian, *On the Soul*, 55.4; and Augustine, *On the Soul and Its Origin*, 1:10; and his *Sermons*, 280–82.

4. Ernst Rupprecht, "Bemerkungen zur Passio SS. Perpetuae et Felicitatis," *RMP* 90(3) (1941): 185.

5. Frederick C. Klawiter, "The Role of Martyrdom and Persecution in Developing the Priestly Authority of Women in Early Christianity: A Case Study of Montanism," *CH* 49 (1980): 257; Michal Meslin, "Vases sacrés et boissons d'éternité dans les visions des martyrs africains," in *Ipektasis: Mélanges patristiques offerts au Cardinal Jean Daniélou*, ed. Jacques Fontaine and Charles Kannengieser (Paris: Beauchesne, 1972), 145; Waal, "Der leidende Dinocrates," 339; William C. Weinrich, *Spirit and Martyrdom* (Washington, D.C.: University Press of America, 1981), 227. See the later problems that developed at Carthage when confessors granted the *libelli faeis* to friends, etc.

6. In Rom. 8:26, Paul wrote: "Ὡσαύτως δὲ καὶ τὸ πνεῦμα συναντιλαμβάνεται τῇ ἀσθενείᾳ ἡμῶν· τὸ γὰρ τί προσευξώμεθα καθὸ δεῖ οὐκ οἴδαμεν, ἀλλὰ αὐτὸ τὸ πνεῦμα ὑπερεντυγχάνει στεναγμοῖς ἀλαλήτοις." The terms προσευχώμεθα and στεναγμοῖς have been rendered in the Latin Vulgate by *oremus* and *gemitibus*, respectively. Thus, Perpetua's prayer (*orationem*) corresponds to the Vulgate *oremus*, and her reference to deep groans (*ingemescere*) corresponds to the Vulgate *gemitibus*.

7. Augustine, *On the Soul and Its Origin*, 3.1.1.

8. Ibid., 3.9. Victor's thoughts on the subject of infant baptism are spelled out in ibid., 2.9–12.

9. Ibid., 2.10.

10. Ibid., 2.12.

11. Ibid., 2.11.

12. Ibid., 3.9.

13. Ibid., 1.10.

14. Ibid., 3.9.

15. This argument is used a number of times in precisely the same manner in Augustine's discussion of Dinocrates. See ibid., 1.10, 2.10, 3.9.

16. J. Armitage Robinson, eds., "The Passion of S. Perpetua," in *Texts and Studies*, 1(2) (Cambridge: University Press, 1891; Nendeln/Liechtenstein: Kraus Reprint, 1967), 29, n. 1.

17. Augustine, *On the Soul and Its Origin*, 1.10; 3.9.

18. Num. 16:30; Job 10:21–22, 17:13–16, 26:5; Ps. 88:10; Prov. 2:18; Isa. 14:9, 26:14, 19.

19. R. H. Charles, *The Book of Enoch* (Oxford: Clarendon Press, 1893), 168. For Homer's perceptions of Hades, see in text p. 49. Jeremias has noted also that "the OT שאול idea is in essential agreement with the conception of the future world found in popular Babylonian belief" (Joachim Jeremias, "Ἀδης," in *Theological Dictionary of the New Testament*, ed. Gerhard Kittel, trans. and ed. Geoffrey W. Bromiley (Grand Rapids: William B. Eerdmans, 1964), 1:147.

20. Dan. 12:2; Isa. 26:19; and possibly Ezek. 37:14–16.

21. Charles, *Book of Enoch*, 168, 169.

22. D. S. Russell, *Between the Testaments* (Philadelphia: Fortress Press, 1965), 151; Pss. 9:17; 16:10, 31:17; 49:14–15; 55:15.

23. Luke 16:22–23. The question, of course, is whether Abraham's bosom is to be considered a place within Hades or separate from it, although the former seems to be the case.

24. Charles, *Book of Enoch*, 169. Cf. Rev. 20:13–14; *1 Enoch* 63:10, 99:11, 103:7; *Psalms of Solomon* 14:4–6, 15:11. While Russell, *Between the Testaments*, 153–54, seems to view Sheol, Hell, and Gehenna as separate entities, the expectation in Revelation that Sheol is cast into hell would appear to make Charles's statement essentially, although not technically, correct.

25. It is noteworthy that Dinocrates seems to be totally oblivious to Perpetua, not even knowing she is looking in on him. There is, therefore, no direct communication between the dead and the living in this vision. Cf. Job 7:9. Luke 16:27–31, while not stating this idea, surely contributes to it with Abraham's denial of the rich man's second request.

26. *1 Enoch* 22:8–13; 2 Bar. 85:11–15; 2 Esd. 7:103–105.

27. F. J. Dölger, "Antike Parallelen zum leidenden Dinocrates in der Passio Perpetuae," *AC* 2 (1930): 37.

28. Homer, *Odyssey*, 6.10–12; 9.523–25; 10.560; 11.37–47, 155–57, 210–12; Hesiod, *Theogony*, 767–74, 850–52.

29. Homer, *Odyssey*, 11.36–41; A. T. Murray, trans., *Homer: The Odyssey*, LCL (London: William Heinemann, 1930), 389.

30. Homer, *Odyssey*, 11.155; similarly, Hesiod, *Works and Days*, 151–55.

31. Hesiod, *Theogony*, 721–25, 736–38, 807–10.

32. Ibid., 739. Diogenes Laertius, *Lives* 4.5.27, describes the underworld as the "abyss (ἄβυσσον) of Pluto."

33. Homer, *Hymns to Hermes*, 254–59; Hugh G. Evelyn-White, trans., *Hesiod, The Homeric Hymns and Homerica*, LCL (Cambridge: Harvard University Press, 1936), 383.

34. Plato, *Republic*, 10.615C.

35. Hesiod, *Theogony*, 767–74.

36. Cited in note 33 above.

37. Peter Dronke, *Women Writers of the Middle Ages* (Cambridge: Cambridge University Press, 1986), 11, suggests that this particular work lies behind Perpetua's description of Dinocrates.

38. Virgil, *Aeneid*, 6.236 ff., esp. 305–30.

39. Ibid., 6.426–29; H. Rushton Fairclough, trans., *Virgil: Eclogues, Georgics, Aeneid I–VI*, LCL (Cambridge: Harvard University Press, 1953), 1:535, 537; Plutarch, *De genio Socratis* 22.

40. Virgil, *Aeneid*, 6.494–99; Fairclough translation.

41. Ibid., 6.577–81; Fairclough translation.

42. Ibid., 6.660–64; Fairclough translation.

43. Ibid., 6.714–15; Fairclough translation.

44. Ibid., 6.711–23; Fairclough translation.

45. Ibid., 6.431–33 (judgment), 6.660–64 (reward); Fairclough translation.

46. Franz Cumont, *After Life in Roman Paganism* (New York: Dover Publications, 1959), 137.

47. Virgil, *Aeneid*, 6.494–99. Tertullian, *On the Soul*, 56.7, takes a position quite similar to this when he writes, "We . . . maintain that every soul, whatever be its age on quitting the body, remains unchanged in the same, until the time shall come when the promised perfection shall be realized in a state duly tempered to the measure of the peerless angels."

48. Virgil, *Aeneid*, 6.

49. Christian Maurer, "Apocalypse of Peter," in *New Testament Apocrypha*, ed. Edgar Hennecke, ed. Wilhelm Schneemelcher and trans. R. McL. Wilson (Philadelphia: Westminster Press, 1965), 2:664. Maurer notes that it probably originated in Egypt, perhaps as early as A.D. 100, but more probably about A.D. 135.

50. (Ethiopic) *Apocalypse of Peter* 8, English translation from Maurer, "Apocalypse of Peter," 2:674–75.

51. Clement of Alexandria, *Extracts from Prophetic Scripture*, 48, considered the *Apocalypse* to be the work of the apostle Peter, while Methodius, *Symposium on the Ten Virgins*, 2.6, judged it to be "Scripture inspired by God"; see respectively, J. B. Migne, ed., *PG* 9:720 and *PG* 18:57.

52. Robert Ombres, *The Theology of Purgatory*, TTS, 24 (Butler, Wis.: Clergy Book Service, 1978), 27; cf. Waal, "Der leidende Dinocrates," 339, but with restrictions, 347. But see Timothy David Barnes, *Tertullian: A Historical and Literary Study* (Oxford: Clarendon Press, 1971), 78.

53. Dölger, "Antike Parallelen zum leidenden Dinocrates," 37; Meslin, "Vases sacrés et boissons d'éternité," 146.

54. Ps. 75:8; Isa. 51:17, 22; Jer. 25:15–17, 28; 49:12; Ezek. 23:31–34; Hab. 2:15–17; Rev. 14:9–10; 16:19; 18:6.

55. Meslin, "Vases sacrés et boissons d'éternité," 146, esp. n. 48.

56. See above, note 43.

57. Augustine, *On the Soul and Its Origin* 4.18. Cf. Meslin, "Vases sacrés et boissons d'éternité," 146.

58. Marie-Louise von Franz, "Die Passio Perpetuae," 445, 454. But Perpetua had been baptized prior to these visions, *The Passion of Perpetua and Felicitas*, 3.5.

59. Marie-Louise von Franz, "Die Passio Perpetuae," in *Aion: Untersuchungen zur Symbolgeschichte*, ed. C. G. Jung, Psychologische Abhandlungen, vol. 7 (Zurich: Racher Verlag, 1951), 451. I am inclined with Dronke, *Women Writers of the Middle Ages*, 12, to disallow any suggestion that this fountain serves as an image of the baptismal font. As Dronke puts it, "He wants to drink, not to be immersed."

60. von Franz, "Die Passio Perpetuae," 452: "*und das Wasser des Bassins ist hier andeutungsweise ein Art von Taufwasser, als einem Symbol Christi oder des Heiligen Geistes.*" Translation mine.

61. Ibid., 453.

62. Eugenio Corsini, "Proposte per una Lettura della 'Passio Perpetuae'," in *Forma Futuri: Studi in Onore del Cardinale Michele Pellegrino* (Torino: Bottega d'Frasma, 1975), 502: "*un simbolo di una malattia morale, cioe di una colpa.*"

63. Ibid.: "*La coppa d'oro sull'orlo della piscina ristabilisce il nesso neotestamen-*

tario tra il primo battesimo e quell'altro, della passione, che Gesù ripetutamente richiama nella metafora di 'bere il calice'." Translation mine. Cf. Luke 12:50; Mark 10:35–40, esp. 39; Matt. 20:20–23.

64. Corsini, "Proposte per una Lettura della 'Passio Perpetuae'," 503.

65. Ibid., 504: "*Perpetua sembra risolverlo alla luce di una concezione mistico-sacramentale del battesimo.*" Translation mine.

66. Ibid.

CHAPTER FIVE

1. *The Passion of Perpetua and Felicitas*, 10.1, 15. Subsequent references in the text to this source are in parentheses.

2. See chapter 2, esp. note 52.

3. (*nobis ministrabant.*) Translation mine.

4. Mary R. Lefkowitz, "The Motivations for St. Perpetua's Martyrdom," *JAAR* 44(3) (1976): 419.

5. J. Armitage Robinson, ed., "The Passion of S. Perpetua," in *Texts and Studies*, 1(2) (Cambridge: University Press, 1891; Nendeln/Liechtenstein: Kraus Reprint, 1967), 30.

6. R. Waterville Muncey, *The Passion of S. Perpetua* (London: J. M. Dent & Sons, 1927), 40, n. 1.

7. *Shepherd of Hermas*, Vision, 4.2.1.

8. Heb. 12:1–2; cf. chapter 3, note 3.

9. At the very least, this statement may signal that Perpetua understood Pomponius to be one who truly was willing to bear her burdens with her (Gal. 6:2). Furthermore, it may signal the fact that Perpetua had a concept of the church as the Body of Christ in which when one suffers, all suffer (1 Cor. 12:26).

10. David E. Aune, *Prophecy in Early Christianity and the Ancient Mediterranean World* (Grand Rapids: William B. Eerdmans, 1983), 32, and also his treatment of the parallel passage in the *Shepherd of Hermas*, Mandate 12.5–7 on p. 305.

11. Robinson, "Passion of S. Perpetua," 30.

12. *Shepherd of Hermas*, Mandate 12.4.6.

13. Ibid.: "$\mu\grave{\eta}\ \phi\circ\beta\acute{\eta}\theta\eta\tau\epsilon\ \tau\grave{\circ}\nu\ \delta\iota\acute{\alpha}\beta\circ\lambda\circ\nu$" (Robert Joly, *Le Pasteur*, SC 53 [Paris: Éditions du Cerf, 1958], 204).

14. *Shepherd of Hermas*, Mandate 12.4.6–7a: "$\acute{\circ}\tau\iota\ \grave{\epsilon}\nu\ \alpha\grave{\upsilon}\tau\hat{\wp}\ \delta\acute{\upsilon}\nu\alpha\mu\iota\varsigma\ \circ\grave{\upsilon}\kappa\ \acute{\epsilon}\sigma\tau\iota\nu\ \kappa\alpha\theta'\ \acute{\upsilon}\mu\hat{\omega}\nu'\ \grave{\epsilon}\gamma\grave{\omega}\ \gamma\grave{\alpha}\rho\ \acute{\epsilon}\sigma\circ\mu\alpha\iota\ \mu\epsilon\theta'\ \acute{\upsilon}\mu\hat{\omega}\nu$" (Joly, *Pasteur*, 204, 206).

15. *Shepherd of Hermas*, Mandate 12.5.2: "$\Delta\acute{\upsilon}\nu\alpha\tau\alpha\iota\ \acute{\circ}\ \delta\iota\acute{\alpha}\beta\circ\lambda\circ\varsigma\ \grave{\alpha}\nu\tau\iota\pi\alpha\lambda\alpha\hat{\iota}\sigma\alpha\iota,\ \kappa\alpha\tau\alpha\pi\alpha\lambda\alpha\hat{\iota}\sigma\alpha\iota\ \delta\grave{\epsilon}\ \circ\grave{\upsilon}\ \delta\acute{\upsilon}\nu\alpha\tau\alpha\iota$" (Joly, *Pasteur*, 206). Cf. Eph. 6:12. Such a word has a strong parallel in James 4:7–8a.

16. Cf. Gen. 15:1; 21:17; 26.24; Isa. 41:10, 14; 43:1, 5: Jer. 30:10; 46:27–28; Luke 1:13, 30; 2:10; Acts 18:9, 27:24.

17. *Epistle of Barnabas* 4.10; 20.1. See on this Robert A. Kraft, *The Apostolic Fathers* (New York: Thomas Nelson & Sons, 1965), 3:19, 156. The offensiveness of such imagery that portrays evil as black, thereby implying that goodness is white, is problematic in the twentieth century. The contemporary context of

oppression and the historical context of slavery make that so. In Perpetua's day, and in the time when much of this imagery was developed in the Old Testament, Egypt was often the oppressor. The use of color is but one way of describing good and evil by pointing to opposites. Still, it is important in our times to be socially sensitive in the use of such pictures.

18. Cornelis van Beek, *Passio Sanctorum Perpetuae et Felicitatis*, Florilegium Patristicum, 43 (Bonn: Petri Hanstein, 1938), 34, n. 9.

19. Judg. 6:9; 10:11; Heb. 8:9; Jude 5.

20. Rev. 11:8: "and their dead bodies will lie in the street of the great city that is prophetically [spiritually] called Sodom and Egypt, where also their Lord was crucified."

21. Ezek. 29:1–3; 32:1–2. See chapter 3, note 24.

22. Naphtali Lewis, *Life in Egypt under Roman Rule* (Oxford: Clarendon Press, 1983), 90. According to Donald A. Mackenzie, *Egyptian Myth and Legend* (Portland, Maine: Longwood Press, 1976), 235–38, 368, Set was sometimes considered to be the crocodile deity, alternatively the devil.

23. Lewis, *Life in Egypt*, 26. Alvyn Pettersen, "Perpetua—Prisoner of Conscience," *VC* 41 (1987): 148, sees in this rubdown an allusion to baptism (cf. Tertullian, *On Baptism* 7), thus making the fight that follows the "ἀγών of the Christian life."

24. *Shepherd of Hermas*, Vision 4.1.5–6.

25. "*et expoliata sum et facta sum masculus.*" Cf. the discussion of this passage in Augustine's *On the Soul and Its Origin* 4.26.

26. For an introduction and translation of this text see H. Anderson, "4 Maccabees," in *The Old Testament Pseudepigrapha*, ed. James H. Charlesworth (Garden City: Doubleday & Company, 1985), 2:531–64. All quotations are from this translation.

27. It is interesting to note that the Montanist Prisc[ill]a once claimed that Christ came to her in a vision, in the form of a woman (Epiphanius, *Panarion*, 49.1). Many Gnostics seem also to have attributed the feminine element to the Godhead (Hippolytus, *Refutation of All Heresies*, 5.6; Irenaeus, *Against Heresies*, 1.11.1; 1.14.1).

28. Douglas M. Parrott, ed. "The Gospel of Mary," BG 7:8, in *The Nag Hammadi Library*, ed. James Robinson (San Francisco: Harper & Row, 1981), 472.

29. Thomas O. Lambdin, trans., "The Gospel of Thomas," in *The Nag Hammadi Library*, ed. James Robinson (San Francisco: Harper & Row, 1981), 121, "Jesus said to them, 'When you make the two one, and when you make the inside like the outside and the outside like the inside, and the above like the below, and when you make the male and the female one and the same, so that the male not be male nor the female female; . . . Then will you enter [the Kingdom].' " On this saying, see the notes in Robert M. Grant and David Noel Freedman, *The Secret Sayings of Jesus* (Garden City: Doubleday & Company, 1960), 143–44.

30. Lambdin, "Gospel of Thomas," 130. Cf. the thesis presented in Dennis

Ronald MacDonald, *The Legend and the Apostle: The Battle for Paul in Story and Canon* (Philadelphia: Westminster Press, 1983), in which he argues for such competing strains, male- and female-dominated texts, even in the Pauline writings.

31. Elaine Pagels, *The Gnostic Gospels* (New York: Vintage Books/Random House, 1981), 81.

32. Ibid., 58.

33. William H. C. Frend, "Blandina and Perpetua: Two Early Christian Heroines," in *Les Martyrs de Lyon (177)* (Paris: Éditions de Centre National de la Recherche Scientifique, 1978), 575:173.

34. Ron Cameron, ed., *The Other Gospels: Non-Canonical Gospel Texts* (Philadelphia: Westminster Press, 1982), 28.

35. Frend, "Blandina and Perpetua," 575:175. So too, Frederick C. Klawiter, "The Role of Martyrdom and Persecution . . .," *CH* 49 (1980):257–58.

36. Lefkowitz, "Motivations for St. Perpetua's Martyrdom," 421.

37. David M. Scholer, " 'And I Was A Man': The Power and Problem of Perpetua," *DS* 15 (September–October 1989): 14. Scholer assesses the 4 *Maccabees* passages and Logion 114 of the *Gospel of Thomas*, as well as passages in *Joseph and Asenath* (15.1–2) and *The Acts of Paul and Thecla* (25 and 40).

38. One obvious impact that Perpetua had was the "seminal role" her passion played on North African hagiography for years to come. Cf. Jaakko Aronen, "Indebtedness to Passio Perpetuae in Pontius' Vita Cyprian," *VC* 38 (1984): 74. Needless to say her impact went far beyond hagiography.

39. See chapter 3, pp. 30–35.

40. "Gospel of Peter," 10.39, in Edgar Hennecke, ed., *New Testament Apocrypha*, ed. Wilhelm Schneemelcher, trans. R. McL. Wilson (Philadelphia: Westminster Press, 1963), 1:186. Cf. *Shepherd of Hermas*, *Similitude* 9.6.1.

41. J. Rendel Harris and Seth K. Gifford, *The Acts of the Martyrdom of Perpetua and Felicitas* (London: C. J. Clay and Sons, 1890), 31, clearly identify the figure as Christ. They note too, the parallel in Tertullian's *To the Martyrs*, 3:3–4, in which Jesus leads the martyrs to the arena. God acts as the superintendent and the Holy Spirit is considered to be the trainer. The prize is an eternal crown. Whether or not Perpetua had read this work is not possible to know. But, the parallels to her own vision are striking.

42. W. H. Shewring, "En Marge de la *Passio des Saintes Perpétue et Félicité*," *LRB* 43(1) (January 1931): 17. Translation mine. Shewring bases his conclusions on conversations with Professor A. E. Houseman. He understands the passage to have evolved into its present form, reading originally *distinctus tunicum habens et purpuram inter duos clavos per medium pectus, habeus et gallieulas.* He argues that this is consistent with the remainder of Perpetua's linguistic style.

43. Jean Daniélou, *The Origins of Latin Christianity* (Philadelphia: Westminster Press, 1977), 3:60–61. Lev. 23:40 reads: "And you shall take on the first day the fruit of goodly trees, branches of palm trees, and boughs of leafy trees, and willows of the brook; and you shall rejoice before the Lord your God seven days."

44. Song of Sol. 2:3, 5; 7:8; 8:5.

45. Deut. 32:10; Ps. 17:8; Prov. 7:2; Lam. 2:18; Zech. 2:8.

46. This utterance appears to take the form of a "parenetic salvation-judgment oracle" in Aune's scheme of oracular systematization. Cf. Aune, *Prophecy in Early Christianity*, 326.

47. See 1 Cor. 9:25; 2 Tim. 2:5; 4:7–8; James 1:12; 1 Pet. 5:4; Rev. 2:10.

48. *Shepherd of Hermas, Similitude* 8.2.

49. Paul Monceaux, *Histoire littéraire de l'afrique Chrétienne* . . . (Paris: Ernest Leroux, 1901–1905), 1:88.

50. See chapter 3, pp. 23–26; cf. F. J. Dölger, "Der Kampf mit dem Ägypter in der Perpetua-Vision," *AC* 3 (1932): 183–85.

51. "I will put enmity between you and the woman, and between your offspring and hers; he will strike your head, and you will strike his heel." Cf. Muncey, *Passion of S. Perpetua*, 41, n. 1; Pettersen, "Perpetua—Prisoner of Conscience," 140.

52. Christopher Rowland, *The Open Heaven* (New York: Crossroad, 1982), 397.

CHAPTER SIX

1. *The Passion of Perpetua and Felicitas*, 11.1. Subsequent references in the text to this source are in parentheses.

2. William Tabbernee, "Early Montanism and Voluntary Martyrdom," *Col* 17(2) (May 1985): 42, argues that "Perpetua's description of Saturus (4.5) reveals that he was their instructor in the (Montanist?) faith. Hence it is more than likely that Saturus gave himself up voluntarily in order to prevent the possible apostasy of his *catechumens*."

3. *The Passion of Perpetua and Felicitas*, 13.8. The Greek text employs the term ἐξυπνίσθη from the verb ἐξυπνίζω, which generally refers to an arousal from sleep.

4. R. Petraglio, "Des influences de l'Apocalypse dans la 'Passio Perpetuae' 11–13," in *L'Apocalypse de Jean*, ed. R. Petraglio et al., vol. 13 of *Études et documents publíes par la Section d'Histoire de La Faculté des Lettres de l'Université de Genéve* (Geneva: Librairie Droz, 1979), 18, states that their "souls" have left their bodies.

5. The Greek and Latin texts should probably be emended here to read αὐτῶν and *eorum* instead of ἡμῶν and *nos* for the statement to be clear. See Petraglio, "Des influences de l'Apocalypse dans la 'Passio Perpetuae' 11–13," 18–19; Ernst Rupprecht, "Bemerkungen zur Passio S.S. Perpetuae et Felicitatis," *RMP*, n.s., 90(3) (1941): 187, *contra* Cornelis van Beek, *Passio Sanctarum Perpetuae et Felicitatis*, Florilegium Patristicum, 43 (Bonn: Petri Hanstein, 1938), 39, and J. Armitage Robinson, ed., "The Passion of S. Perpetua," *Texts and Studies*, 1(2) (Cambridge: University Press, 1891; Nendeln/Liechtenstein: Kraus Reprint, 1967), 79; Herbert Musurillo's English translation at this point is based on the emendation rather than the Latin *nos* in his *The Acts of the Christian Martyrs*, OECT (Oxford: Clarendon Press, 1972), 118–19.

6. Exod. 23:20; Num. 22:22; 1 Sam. 29:9; 2 Sam. 14:17; 19:28; 1 Kings 19:7; 2 Kings 1:3, 15; 19:35, etc.

7. *1 Enoch*, 20.1–8, lists Uriel as being over the world and Tartarus; Raphael is over the spirits of men; Raguel takes vengeance on the world of luminaries; Michael presides over the best part of humanity as well as chaos; Saraqael is set over the spirits who sin in the spirit; Gabriel rules paradise, the serpents, and cherubim; and Remiel is over those who rise.

8. *Testament of Abraham*, 20.12: "The angels escorted . . . [Abraham's] precious soul and ascended into heaven." The work is thought to be dated in its final form about A.D. 100 according to E. P. Sanders, "Testament of Abraham," in *The Old Testament Pseudepigrapha*, ed. James H. Charlesworth (Garden City, N.Y.: Doubleday & Company, 1983), 1:875. Cf. the *Testament of Job*, 52.1–12 and the later *Apocalypse of Paul*, 14; reference to this teaching may also occur in *The Shepherd of Hermas*, Vision 2.2.7, where Hermas writes, "Stand steadfast, therefore, ye who work righteousness, and doubt not, that your passage may be with the holy angels" (ἵνα γένηται ὑμῶν ἡ πάραδος μετα τῶν ἀγγελῶν τῶν ἀγίων) (Robert Joly, *Le Pasteur*, SC 53 [Paris: Éditions du Cerf, 1958], 92). See also the *Apocalypse of Peter*, 13: "The angels will bring my elect and righteous which are perfect in all righteousness, and shall bear them in their hands [*contra* Saturus's contention] and clothe them with the garments of eternal life" (Edgar Hennecke, ed., *New Testament Apocrypha*, ed. Wilhelm Schneemelcher, trans. R. McL. Wilson [Philadelphia: The Westminster Press, 1965], 2:679).

9. Tertullian, *On the Soul* 53.6 (*Tertulliana Opera*, 2:860–61); ANF, 3:230.

10. Petraglio, "Influences de l'Apocalyse dans la 'Passio Perpetuae' 11–13," 19.

11. *1 Enoch*, 108.12–15.

12. C. H. Dodd, *The Interpretation of the Fourth Gospel* (Cambridge: University Press, 1968), 201. Cf. "The Paraphrase of Shem," 7:7–13, in James Robinson, ed., *The Nag Hammadi Library* (San Francisco: Harper & Row, 1981), 309.

13. "And the city [the New Jerusalem] has no need of sun or moon to shine upon it, for the glory of God is its light, and its lamp is the Lamb." Cf. Rev. 22:5.

14. Jean Daniélou, *The Origins of Latin Christianity* (Philadelphia: Westminster Press, 1977), 3:61.

15. *1 Enoch*, 32.2–6. Christopher Rowland, *The Open Heaven* (New York: Crossroad, 1982), 400, refers to this place as "Paradise." Cf. *Testament of Job* 40.3 and 52.10.

16. On the direction, see *2 Enoch* 42.3 and Gen. 2:8; on the heavenly nature of paradise, see D. S. Russell, *The Method and Message of Jewish Apocalyptic*, OTL (Philadelphia: Westminster Press, 1964), 283, and 2 Cor. 12:2–4.

17. J. Armitage Robinson, ed., "The Passion of S. Perpetua," *Texts and Studies*, 1(2) (Cambridge: University Press, 1891; Nendeln/Liechtenstein: Kraus Reprint, 1967), 32.

18. *Shepherd of Hermas*, Vision 1.4.1–3 (Joly, *Pasteur*, 86).

19. *The Shepherd of Hermas*, Vision 3.4.1 (ibid., 108).

20. Robinson, "Passion of S. Perpetua," 32.

21. See William H. C. Frend, "Blandina and Perpetua," in *Les Martyrs de Lyon (177)* (Paris: Éditions du Centre National de la Recherche Scientifique, 1978), 575:172.

22. Gen. 2:8–10; Isa. 51:3; Ezek. 31:8–9; *Testament of Levi*, 18.10–11; *1 Enoch*, 32.3; 60.8; 61.12; *Apocalypse of Peter*, 16 (Ethiopic), 15–20 (Akhmim).

23. *The Passion of Perpetua and Felicitas* 11.6b, "*quarum folia cadebant sine cessatione (ἀκαταπαύστως δὲ κατεφέρετο τὰ δένδρα τὰ φάλλα αὐτῶν)*" (Musurillo, *Acts of the Christian Martyrs*, 120); Robinson, "Passion of S. Perpetua," 81.

24. See also Rev. 22:2, 14, 19.

25. Petraglio, "Influences de l'Apocalypse dans la 'Passio Perpetuae' 11–13," 19–20.

26. Robinson, "Passion of S. Perpetua," 38.

27. R. Waterville Muncey, *The Passion of S. Perpetua* (London: J. M. Dent & Sons, 1927), 44–45; see also W. H. Shewring, *The Passion of SS. Perpetua and Felicity MM* (London: Sheed and Ward, 1931), 13, n. 1, and 33; Daniélou, *Origins of Latin Christianity*, 3:61.

28. 1 Chron. 16:33; Ps. 96:12; Isa. 35:1–2; 44:23; 55:12.

29. *Testament of Abraham*, 3.3 (Sanders, "Testament of Abraham," 1:883).

30. Robinson, "Passion of S. Perpetua," 39.

31. See, for instance, Saint John of Damascus's work *Barlaam and Iosaph* in G. R. Woodward and H. Mattingly, trans., St. John Damascene, *Barlaam and Iosaph*, LCL (Cambridge, Mass.: Harvard University Press, 1953), 468–69, "*τὰ τε φύλλα τῶν δένδρων λιγυρὸν ὑπήχει*," "The leaves of the trees rustled gently," or as Robinson translates it in his "Passion of S. Perpetua," 38, "made a tuneful sound."

32. Jean Daniélou, *The Angels and Their Mission*, trans. David Heimann (Westminster, Md.: Christian Classics, 1976), 98.

33. Rowland, *Open Heaven*, 401.

34. The Latin texts A and C read simply, *qui introeuntes vestierunt stolas candidas*. The Greek text and the Latin text B appear to make an attempt at clarification consistent with Rev. 4:4; 7:9, etc. Their readings are *ἐνέδυσαν ἡμᾶς λευκὰς στολάς* and *introeuntes et nos vestiti stolas candidas*, thereby clearly placing the robes on the martyrs. The sense is helped by accepting the Greek and Latin B readings, but the Latin A and C reading is obviously original due to its vagueness. Daniélou, *Origins of Latin Christianity*, 3:61, and Petraglio, "Influences de l'Apocalypse dans la 'Passio Perpetuae' 11–13," have followed the Greek reading and understand the martyrs as being dressed in white robes; *contra* Robinson, "Passion of S. Perpetua," 14.

35. The significance of this observation is not understood, but it stands in stark contrast to the visionary experience of Perpetua in 10.8.

36. See above chapter 3, pp. 30–33; see also Frend, "Blandina and Perpetua," 575:172.

37. Rowland, *Open Heaven*, 401; Justin Martyr, *Dialogue with Trypho*, 75–80.

38. *Shepherd of Hermas, Vision* 3.10.4; 3.12.1; similar imagery also occurs in 4.2.1 (Joly, *Pasteur*, 126, 130).

39. Petraglio, "Influences de l'Apocalypse dans la 'Passio Perpetuae' 11–13," 22–23. Cf. Rev. 7:1.

40. Robinson, "Passion of S. Perpetua," 27.

41. J. Rendel Harris and Seth K. Gifford, *The Acts of the Martyrdom of Perpetua and Felicitas* (London: C. J. Clay and Sons, 1890), 10–11. Cf. Tertullian, *On Prayer* 18.3: "What prayer is complete if divorced from the 'holy kiss'?" This work dates from A.D. 198–200. See also Johannes Quasten, *Patrology* (Utrecht-Antwerp: Spectrum Publishers, 1975), 2:296; cf. Eusebius, *Ecclesiastical History*, 5.16.

42. *Shepherd of Hermas, Similitude* 9.11.4–5, employs the Greek verb παί-ζειν. Cf. Muncey, *Passion of S. Perpetua*, 47, n. 4.

43. Timothy David Barnes, *Tertullian* (Oxford: Clarendon Press, 1971), 75, n. 1.

44. Petraglio, "Influences de l'Apocalypse dans la 'Passio Perpetuae', 11–13," 27–28.

45. John de Soyres, *Montanism and the Primitive Church* (Cambridge: Deighton, Bell and Co., 1878. Reprint, Lexington, Ky.: The American Theological Library Association, 1965), 141.

46. Barnes, *Tertullian*, 78.

47. Eusebius, *Ecclesiastical History*, 5.16.16–17, notes the lack of submission to the bishops, for instance, and there were charges that the Montanists set up their own bishops.

48. William C. Weinrich, *Spirit and Martyrdom* (Washington, D.C.: University Press of America, 1981), 227.

49. Ibid.

50. Frederick C. Klawiter, "The Role of Martyrdom and Persecution in Developing the Priestly Authority of Women in Early Christianity," *CH* 49 (1980): 259.

51. Ibid.

52. Ibid.

53. Petraglio, "Influences de l'Apocalypse dans la 'Passio Perpetuae' 11–13," 28.

54. Tertullian, *To the Martyrs*, 1.6: "Some, not able to find this peace [the cessation of strife within the church] have been used to seek it from the imprisoned martyrs. And so you ought to have it dwelling with you, and to cherish it, and to guard it, that you may be able perhaps to bestow it upon others." Dates range from A.D. 197 to A.D. 202.

55. Rowland, *Open Heaven*, 399.

56. Petraglio, "Influences de l'Apocalypse dans la 'Passio Perpetuae' 11–13," 29. Translation mine.

57. See chapter 15. Cf. Cyprian, *Epistle* 11; 1 Cor. 1:10–17.

58. *The Passion of Perpetua and Felicitas*, 13.8. It is undoubtedly to this

passage and 11.9 that Tertullian referred in *On the Soul*, 55.4, where he mistakenly attributed it to Perpetua.

59. *1 Enoch*, 29.2: "And there I saw aromatic trees exhaling the fragrance of frankincense and myrrh"; cf. 31.3.

60. Ibid., 32.3–5.

61. *The Apocalypse of Peter* (Ethiopic) 16; (Akhmim 15–16) (Hennecke, *New Testament Apocrypha* 2:681–82).

62. Frend, "Blandina and Perpetua," 575:172.

63. See on this, Henry J. Cadbury, "The Odor of the Spirit at Pentecost," *JBL* 47 (1928), 237–56, who has traced this idea in the Syrian tradition of Ephrem.

CHAPTER SEVEN

1. *The Passion of Perpetua and Felicitas* 4.10; 7.8; 8.4; 10.14. Subsequent references in the text to this source are in parentheses.

2. *The Passion of Perpetua and Felicitas*, 1.1; further mention of these ancient accounts may be found in 21.11. Alvyn Pettersen, "Perpetua—Prisoner of Conscience," *VC* 41 (1987): 139–40, views *The Passion* as dependent on the notion of *imitatio Christi*, which presents to the reader "the acts of inner self-disclosure which the true follower of Christ in North Africa was expected to adopt in the pursuit of virtue and perfection."

3. J. Rendel Harris and Seth K. Gifford, *The Acts of the Martyrdom of Perpetua and Felicitas* (London: C. J. Clay and Sons, 1890), 6.

4. The allusion appears to be to 1 Cor. 12:4–11, 27. There may be an allusion to Rom. 12:3 here, as Herbert Musurillo, *The Acts of the Christian Martyrs*, OECT (Oxford: Clarendon Press, 1972), 107, n. 2, suggests, but that seems to be less likely due to the numerous factors that are shared between the redactor's argument and 1 Cor. 12 (e.g., the good of the church; the Spirit distributes gifts to all; the Lord apportions to each).

5. So appears the translation, "not only new prophecies but new visions as well, according to the promise," in Musurillo, *Acts of the Christian Martyrs*, 107. J. Armitage Robinson, "The Passion of S. Perpetua," *Texts and Studies*, 1(2) (Cambridge: University Press, 1891; Nendeln/Liechtenstein: Kraus Reprint, 1967), 6, compares the Latin and Greek texts here and concludes that "the . . . desire of the Greek translator to minimize the Montanist allusions to the work of the Holy Spirit" is evident from the fact that he does not translate the words *pariter repromissas*.

6. Pierre de Labriolle, *La crise Montaniste* (Paris: Ernest Leroux, 1913), 353. R. Waterville Muncey, *The Passion of S. Perpetua* (London: J. M. Dent & Sons, 1927), 13–15, is hesitant at this point, but seems to come down ultimately on this side; Rosemary Rader, "The Martyrdom of Perpetua: A Protest Account of Third-Century Christianity," in *A Lost Tradition: Women Writers of the Early Church*, ed. Patricia Wilson-Kastner et al. (Washington, D.C.: University Press of America, 1981), 2, notes it as having pro-Montanist tendencies because of its

apocalyptic imagery, "belief in prophecy," and "direct divine inspiration"—but she refrains from identifying it as a Montanist document; William C. Weinrich, *Spirit and Martyrdom* (Washington, D.C.: University Press of America, 1981), 232–36, esp. 235, states categorically, "There is, therefore, no reason to assume that the redactor of the *Passio* was a Montanist or that he tended toward Montanism."

7. Weinrich, *Spirit and Martyrdom*, 235; *The Passion of Perpetua and Felicitas*, 1.2.

8. *The Passion of Perpetua and Felicitas*, 1.5; cf. 1 Pet. 4:10–11; 1 Cor. 12:4–11; Rom. 12:3–8. It is possible that 1 Cor. 13:3 makes reference to the act of martyrdom as a charisma, an understanding commonly held by members of the early church. Note too the use of the words "esteemed revelations" to describe the martyrs' visionary experiences. These words are used repeatedly by Cyprian half a century later. See chapter 13.

9. *The Passion of Perpetua and Felicitas*, 18.7; cf. Gen. 3:15.

10. Compare *The Passion of Perpetua and Felicitas*, 10.14, in which Perpetua's remark is made, with the redactor's remark in 20.1.

11. *The Passion of Perpetua and Felicitas*, 21.8. Compare this with Perpetua's vision recorded in 4.5 in which *ascendit autem Saturus prior.*

CHAPTER EIGHT

1. Tertullian, *On Flight in Persecution*, 9.4 (2x); *Against Praxeas*, 8.5; *On Modesty*, 21.7; *On Exhortation to Chastity*, 10.5; *On the Resurrection of the Flesh*, 11.2. The most recent collection of these oracles may be found in Ronald E. Heine, *The Montanist Oracles and Testimonia*, PMS, 14 (Macon, Ga.: Mercer University Press, 1989), 4–7.

2. Tertullian, *Treatise on the Soul*, 9.4; 55.4; *On the Veiling of Virgins*, 17.3. The visions are counted among the *testimonia* in Heine, *Montanist Oracles and Testimonia*, 62–93.

3. Tertullian, *On Monogamy*, 2.1–4.5; *On Fasting*, 1.3–5; 10.5–6; 11.1–15.7; 16.8; etc. (Heine, *Montanist Oracles and Testimonia*, 77–78, 83–84, etc.).

4. I have chosen to treat as works that Tertullian wrote prior to his association with Montanism those works which make no mention of the New Prophecy or the Paraclete and which are generally accepted as "pre-Montanist." These works include *On Repentance*, *On Prayer*, *On Baptism*, *To His Wife I*, *To His Wife II*, *To Martyrdom*, *On Patience*, *Prescription against Heretics*, *Apology*, and *The Soul's Testimony.*

5. Tertullian, *On Baptism*, 20.5: "*cum de illo sanctissimo lavacro novi natalis ascenditis et primas manus apud matrem cum fratribus aperitis, petite de patre, petite de domino peculia gratiae distributiones charismatum subiacere*" (*Tertullian Opera*, 1:295). The English translations of Tertullian are those found in Alexander Roberts and James Donaldson, eds. *The Ante-Nicene Fathers*, vols. 3 and 4 (Grand Rapids: William B. Eerdmans, 1973, 1972). Hereafter denoted *ANF*. For an important discussion of this passage see Kilian McDonnell, "Communion Eccle-

siology and Baptism in the Spirit: Tertullian and the Early Church," *TS* 49 (1988): 679–90.

6. Tertullian, *On Prayer*, 4.3: "*nos velut ad exemplaria provocamur, ut et praedicemus et operemur et sustineanmus ad mortem usque*" (*Tertullian Opera*, 1:259–60).

7. There is no *explicit* textual warrant for this, but the idea of these works being 'miracles' is shared by Ernest Evans, ed. and trans., *Tertullian's Tract on the Prayer* (London: SPCK, 1953), 9.

8. Tertullian, *Prescription against Heretics*, 29 (*Tertullian Opera*, 1:209); ANF, 3:256.

9. Tertullian, *On Patience*, 12.10 (*Tertullian Opera*, 1:313).

10. Ibid.: "*evacuabuntur consummabuntur.*"

11. Tertullian, *Prescription against Heretics*, 4.4; ANF, 3:245.

12. Isa. 11:3; Tertullian, *Against Marcion*, 5.8.4. Cf. *On Monogamy*, 1.

13. Tertullian, *Against Marcion*, 5.8.5. Cf. Isa. 3:1–3. This seems to point to the idea that the gifts of the Spirit were found previously in Judah among

> the mighty man and the prophet
> the diviner and the elder
> the captain of fifty
>   and man of rank
> the counselor and the skillful magician
>   and the expert in charms.

14. Tertullian, *An Answer to the Jews*, 8:14: "*omnis plenitudo spiritalium retro charismatum in Christo cessavit*" (*Tertullian Opera*, 2:1362).

15. Tertullian, *An Answer to the Jews*, 8.14.

16. Tertullian, *Against Marcion*, 5.8.4 (*ANF*, 3:445). Tertullian showed a strong Christological interest in gifts of the Spirit. They were, after all, sealed in Christ by promise and given by Christ in the Spirit. Cf. here also *Against Marcion*, 5.17.4–5, and *Against Praxeas*, 28.12.

17. Eph. 4:8; Ps. 68:18. Tertullian used at this point a translation of this passage that spelled it out as gifts given to sons of men (*filiis hominum*). On this, see T. P. O'Malley, *Tertullian and the Bible*, LCP (Utrecht: Dekker and VandeVegt N. V. Nijmegen, 1967), 56–57.

18. Tertullian, *Against Marcion*, 5.8.9. Tertullian's analysis was, "See how the apostle agrees with the prophet both in making the distribution of one Spirit, and in interpreting His special graces" (*ANF*, 3:446). He seems to have thought nothing of the fact that there was no perfect one-to-one correspondence in these two lists.

19. Tertullian, *Against Marcion*, 5.8.12: "*si haec omnia facilius a me proferuntur*" (*Tertullian Opera*, 1:688). While Tertullian readily acknowledged the presence of such gifts in the church during his day, it should be noted that it was in the apostles that "the operations of prophecy, and the efficacy of (healing) virtues, and the evidences of tongues" were most fully found. In subsequent Christians, their appearance was only partial (*On Exhortation to Chastity*, 4.6; ANF, 4:53).

20. Tertullian, *On Patience*, 12.10. Cf. *Against Marcion*, 5.15.6.

21. Tertullian, *On the Soul*, 47.2; *On the Resurrection of the Flesh*, 63.7 and 9. The latter reference is the more explicit on this matter. Tertullian apparently saw no problem in having male and female prophets within the church. On the use of this passage, which supports an anticessationist perspective, see P. C. Atkinson, "The Montanist Interpretation of Joel 2:28, 29 (LXX 3:1, 2)," T&U, 126, *Studia Evangelica* 7 (1982): 11–15, esp. 13. Atkinson notes that Tertullian appeals to this passage in traditional ways, not exploiting it in ways the redactor of *The Passion of Perpetua and Felicitas* did.

22. Tertullian, *An Answer to the Jews*, 8.14.

23. Tertullian, *On Exhortation to Chastity*, 4.6 (ANF, 4:53); "*Proprie enim apostoli spiritum sanctum habent, qui plene habent in operibus prophetiae*" (*Tertullian Opera*, 2:1022).

24. Tertullian, *The Chaplet*, 1.4; *On the Soul*, 9.3 and 4; *Against Marcion*, 5.8.4–12.

25. Tertullian, *On the Soul*, 2.3.

26. Tertullian, *Against Marcion*, 4.4.5. Tertullian argued this from 1 Cor. 14:32.

27. Tertullian was usually explicit in his use of the term "Paraclete." In a few cases, whether he meant the Holy Spirit or Montanus is difficult to discern. Cf. *On the Soul*, 58.8; *Against Praxeas*, 1.7; 13.5. He spoke of the Holy Spirit explicitly as the Paraclete in *Against Praxeas*, 2.1; 9.3; *On the Veiling of Virgins*, 1.4–5; *On Modesty*, 31.7. Likewise, he called Montanus the Paraclete on several occasions; cf. *On Monogamy*, 14.3–4; *On Modesty*, 1.20; 12.1; *On Fasting*, 1.3; 12.4. It seems, however, that in Tertullian's mind Montanus and the Paraclete were *not* one and the same, even when he referred to them in a manner in which it could be inferred that they were the same. His remarks indicate quite clearly that Montanus received a gift of prophecy from the Spirit (*Against Praxeas*, 1.5). Likewise, other prophets received such gifts from the Spirit (Prisca and Maximilla in *Against Praxeas*, 1.5), and still others were said to have this gift as a result of the Paraclete (*On Modesty*, 21.7). His use of the term when describing Montanus, then, seems to have been his way of equating the words of Montanus with the teachings of the Spirit, not their persons.

28. Tertullian, *On the Veiling of Virgins*, 1.5; *The Chaplet*, 4.6. Cf. John 14:26.

29. Tertullian's example here is drawn from Num. 22–24, in which Balaam could speak only the words that God gave him to speak (*Against Marcion*, 4.28.7–8). Cf. also Luke 12:11–12.

30. Tertullian, *On the Flesh of Christ*, 2.3; *Against Marcion*, 5.8.23; 5.15.5. Cf. also 1 Cor. 14:24–25.

31. Tertullian, *Against Marcion*, 5.15.5; cf. Eph. 3:1–5. It should be noted at this point that, for Tertullian, prophecy as it was present in the New Prophecy was important in the application and explanation of *existing* Scripture, not in the creation of *new* Scripture. As F. E. Vokes, "The Use of Scripture in the Montanist Controversy," T&U, 103, *Studia Evangelica* 5 (1968): 320, has noted, "the New

Testament canon had emerged in broad outline by 193 A.D. and . . . it was treated with great circumspection." Tertullian had a strong commitment to this idea despite his commitment to the continuing revelatory role of the Spirit-Paraclete. Cf. Vokes, 319. The Holy Spirit, by means of prophecy, illumined Scripture and explained mysteries (*On the Resurrection of the Flesh*, 63); cf. chapter 1, note 14, to see the similarities and differences between Tertullian here and the subject as understood by the Reformers.

32. Tertullian, *The Chaplet*, 3.6–7. On this point particularly, see *On Flight in Persecution*, 9.4, where he argues that those who sought guidance from the Spirit were exhorted to martyrdom.

33. Tertullian, *Against Marcion*, 1.21.5: "*et definitio superior instructa est, non esse credendum deum, quem homo de suis sensibus composuerit, nisi plane prophetes, id est non de suis sensibus*" (*Tertullian Opera*, 1:463). This last suggestion points to a clear appreciation for a prophetic consciousness that enabled the prophet to distinguish his or her words from God's words.

34. This particular understanding is evident in studies on the prophets beginning with Gustav Hölscher, *Die Profeten: Untersuchungen zur Religionsgeschichte Israels* (Leipzig: J. C. Hinrichs'sche Buchhandlung, 1914), and is continued in such current works as Johannes Lindblom, *Prophecy in Ancient Israel* (Philadelphia: Fortress Press, 1973).

35. This is best illustrated by Theodore H. Robinson, *Prophecy and the Prophets in Ancient Israel* (London: Gerald Duckworth & Co., 1967), 50. He writes that the prophet might be mingling with the crowds, when "suddenly something would happen to him. His eye would become fixed, strange convulsions would seize upon his limbs, the form of his speech would change. Men would recognize that the Spirit had fallen upon him. The fit would pass, and he would tell to those who stood around the things which he had seen and heard. There might have been symbolic action, and this he would explain with a clear memory of all that had befallen him, and of all that he had done under the stress of the ecstasy."

36. H. H. Rowley, "The Nature of Old Testament Prophecy in the Light of Recent Study," chapter in *The Servant of the Lord* (Oxford: Basil Blackwell, 1965), 97–134. This chapter first appeared in *HTR* 38 (1945): 1–38. Cf. also Cyril G. Williams, "Ecstaticism in Hebrew Prophecy and Christian Glossolalia, *SR* 3 (1974): 331, where he argues that "When we say that prophets are susceptible to ecstatic states, we mean that they experience hyperaroused conditions with varying degrees of dissociation, ranging from trancelike states to those in which the consciousness is heightened to a pitch of unusual sensitivity and perceptivity."

37. See Robert L. Alden, "Ecstasy and the Prophets," *JETS* 9 (1966): 149–56, and Leon J. Wood, "Ecstasy and Israel's Early Prophets," *JETS* 9 (1966): 125–37. This latter article has been reworked in Leon J. Wood, *The Holy Spirit in the Old Testament* (Grand Rapids: Zondervan Publishing, 1976), 90–125.

38. Among the Hebrew words translated by ἔκστασις are (1) הֲרָדָה meaning "terror, fear" (Gen. 27:33; Ezek. 26:16); (2) פַּחַד meaning "fear, terror"

(2 Chron. 14:14 [13]); (3) שֵׁעַד meaning "horror" (Ezek. 27:35); and (4) תִּמָּהוֹן meaning "astonishment, consternation" (Deut. 28:28).

39. See G. Abbott-Smith, *A Manual Greek Lexicon of the New Testament* (Edinburgh: T. & T. Clark, 1964), 141; and H. A. A. Kennedy, *Sources of New Testament Greek* (Edinburgh: T. & T. Clark, 1895), 121–22. Later secular writings, of course, merely provide parallels.

40. Plutarch, *Solon*, 7.1, in Bernadotte Perrin, trans., *Plutarch: Solon*, LCL (Cambridge, Mass.: Harvard University Press, 1948), 1:421.

41. Hippocrates, *Aphorisms* 7.5, in W. H. S. Jones, trans., *Hippocrates: Aphorisms*, LCL (Cambridge: Harvard University Press, 1953), 4:195. Jones states (note 2) that "By ἔκστατις is meant an increase of the maniacal symptoms, helping to bring the disease to a crisis."

42. Hippocrates, ΠΕΡΙ ᾿ΑΡΘΡΟΝ 56, in E. T. Withington, trans., *Hippocrates: ΠΕΡΙ ᾿ΑΡΘΡΟΝ*, LCL (Cambridge: Harvard University Press, 1948), 3:331. In referring to persons who had prominent haunches, Hippocrates noted that it was διὰ τὴν ἔκστασιν τῶν ἄρθρων. Aristotle, *de Anima*, I, 3, p. 406ᵇ 13, uses it in much the same way. Cf. James L. Ash, "The Decline of Ecstatic Prophecy in the Early Church," TS 37 (1976): 229.

43. Mark 5:42, 16:8; Luke 5:26; Acts 3:10; William F. Arndt and F. Wilbur Gingrich, *A Greek-English Lexicon of the New Testament and Other Early Christian Literature*, ed. Walter Bauer (Chicago: The University of Chicago Press, 1957), 244.

44. Matt. 12:23; Mark 2:12, 3:21, 5:42, 6:51; Luke 2:47, 8:56, 24:22; Acts 2:7, 12, 8:9, 11, 13, 9:21, 10:45, 12:16; and 2 Cor. 5:13.

45. C. K. Barrett, *A Commentary on the Second Epistle to the Corinthians*, HNTC (New York: Harper and Row, 1973), 166. R. V. G. Tasker, *The Second Epistle of Paul to the Corinthians*, TNTC (Grand Rapids: Wm. B. Eerdmans, 1958), 84.

46. Albrecht Oepke, "ἔξίστημι," in *Theological Dictionary of the New Testament*, ed. Gerhard Kittel, trans. and ed. Geoffrey W. Bromiley (Grand Rapids: Wm. B. Eerdmans, 1964), 2:460; Jean Héring, *The Second Epistle of Saint Paul to the Corinthians*, trans. A. W. Heathcote and P. J. Allcock (London: Epworth Press, 1967), 41; Alfred Plummer, *Second Epistle of St. Paul to the Corinthians*, International Critical Commentary (Edinburgh: T. & T. Clark, 1970), 173–74.

47. Abbott-Smith, *Manual Greek Lexicon*, 278.

48. See J. Reiling, "The Use of Ψευδοπροφήτης in the Septuagint, Philo, and Josephus," NT 13 (1971): 155–56.

49. This is particularly evident in the passages of Jer. 14:14 and Ezek. 13:7, 8, which refer to those prophets of Israel who spoke even though they had received no revelation from God. Typical of this usage is Ezek. 13:7: "Have you not seen a delusive vision (ὅρασιν ψευδῆ), and uttered a lying divination (μαντείας ματαίας) whenever you have said, 'Says the Lord,' although I have not spoken?"

50. Plutarch, *Moralia* 758 E, in W. C. Helmbold, trans., *Plutarch: Moralia*,

LCL (Cambridge: Harvard University Press, 1961), 9:728. He writes, "There are several kinds of enthusiasm: the prophetic (τὸ μαντικὸν) comes from the inspiration (ἐπιπνοίας) and possession (κατοχῆς) of Apollo." See also *Moralia* 436 E.

51. Plato, *Timaeus* 71 E, in R. G. Bury, trans., *Plato: Timaeus*, LCL (Cambridge: Harvard University Press, 1952), 7:187: οὐδεὶς γὰρ ἔννους ἐφάπτεται μαντικῆς ἐνθέου καὶ ἀληθους, ἀλλ᾽ ἢ καθ᾽ ὕπνον τὴν φρονήσεως πεδηθεὶς δύναμιν ἢ διὰ νόσον ἢ διά τινα ἐνθουσιασμὸν παραλλάξας.

52. Plato, *Timaeus*, 72 A and B: ὅθεν δὴ καὶ τὸ τῶν προφητῶν γένος ἐπὶ ταῖς ἐνθέοις μαντείαις κριτὰς ἐπικαθιστάναι, νόμος· οὓς μάντεις αὐτοὺς ὀναμαζουσί τινες, τὸ πᾶν ἠγουηκότες ὅτι τῆς δι᾽ αἰνιγμῶν οὗτοι φήμης καὶ φαντάσεως ὑποκριταί, καὶ οὔ τι μάντεις, προφῆται δὲ μαντευομένων δικαιότατα ὁ νομαζοιντ᾽ ἄν (ibid., 186, 188).

53. Jer. 36 (MT 29):8–9; Mic. 3:7; Zech. 10:2.

54. It makes no difference that her prophecy, as recorded in Acts 16:17 is correct in content: "these men are slaves of the Most High God, who proclaim to you the way of salvation." Her source is a spirit of divination (πνεῦμα πύθωνα), and thus it must be judged as wrong.

55. Hermas, *Mandate* 11:2 (μάντιν); 11:4 (μαντεύονται).

56. Jer. 6:13; 33 (MT 26):7, 8, 11, 16; 34 (MT 27):9; 35 (MT 28):1; and 36 (MT 29):1 and 8.

57. Reiling, "Use of Ψευδοπροφήτης in the Septuagint, Philo, and Josephus," 147.

58. "For thus says the Lord of hosts, the God of Israel: 'Do not let your prophets (נְבִיאֵיכֶם, LLX οἱ ψευδοπροφῆται) and your diviners (וְקֹסְמֵיכֶם, LXX οἱ μάντεις ὑμῶν) deceive you . . . for it is a lie which they are prophesying to you in my name.'"

59. "So do not listen to your prophets (אֶל־נְבִיאֵיכֶם, LXX τῶν ψευδοπροφητῶν), your diviners (וְאֶל־קֹסְמֵיכֶם, LXX τῶν μαντευομένων ὑμῶν) . . . for it is a lie which they are prophesying to you."

60. Matt. 7:15, 24:11, 24; Mark 13:22; Luke 6:26; Acts 13:6; 2 Pet. 2:1; 1; John 4:1; Rev. 16:13, 19:20, 20:10.

61. "These doubters then go to him ['à false prophet (ψευδοπροφήτης), ruining the minds of the servants of God,' 11:1] as a soothsayer [μάντις] and inquire of him what will happen to them; and he, the false prophet (ψευδοπροφήτης), not having the power of a Divine Spirit in him, answers them according to their inquiries and according to their wicked desires, and fills their souls with expectations, according to their own wishes" (ANF, 2:27).

62. Tertullian, *On the Soul* 11.4: "*sanctu spiritus vis operatrix prophetiae*" (*Tertullian Opera*, 2:797); ANF, 3:191. Cf. *On the Soul*, 21.2, and, visionary dreams, *On the Soul*, 47.3.

63. Tertullian, *On the Soul*, 9.4; *Against Marcion*, 4.22.4–5; cf. *Against Marcion*, 5.8.12. The use of the terms *in spiritu* and *in extasi* in the *Passion of Perpetua and Felicitas*, 20.8, to describe a trancelike state of Perpetua when confronted with the beasts has led some to argue that Tertullian is the redactor of

that work. This is possible, of course, although prophetic activity is not connected with this state explicitly. What appears to be the case may be the experience described in the *Passion of Perpetua and Felicitas*, 15.6, where Felicitas describes her own suffering as that of another who is inside her.

64. Tertullian, *Against Marcion*, 4.22.4; 5.8.12; *On the Soul*, 21.2 and 45.3.

65. Tertullian, *Against Marcion*, 5.8.12. On the terms *amentia* and *ecstasis* as used in Tertullian, see O'Malley, *Tertullian and the Bible*, 33.

66. I say that it may be partially known because his seven volumes on ecstasy mentioned by Jerome in *Lives of Illustrious Men* are no longer extant.

67. Tertullian, *On the Soul*, 43:1.

68. Ibid., 43:7: "*rational aligood opus dei esse*" (*Tertullian Opera*, 2:846); cf. Patricia Cox Miller, "'A Dubious Twilight': Reflections on Dreams in Patristic Literature," *CH* 55 (1986): 157.

69. Tertullian, *On the Soul*, 21.2; *Tertullian Opera*, 2:813.

70. Tertullian, *Against Marcion*, 4.22.5: "*In spiritu enim homo constitutus, . . . necesse est excidat sensu*" (*Tertullian Opera*, 1:601).

71. Tertullian, *On the Soul*, 45.3: "*excessum sensus et amentiae instar*" (*Tertullian Opera*, 2:849).

72. Tertullian, *Against Marcion*, 4.22.5: "*obumbratus scilicet virtute divina*" (*Tertullian Opera*, 1:601). This is a point where those outside the New Prophecy seem to have attacked it. They appear to have argued that fasting as practiced in the New Prophecy was used to bring some sort of hallucinatory state on those fasting in which they would receive their "visions" or "prophecies." Tertullian argued that ecstasy was an external force brought on by God, and one did not "psych" oneself into receiving either visions or prophecies (*On the Soul*, 48.3). Cf. Hans von Campenhausen, *Ecclesiastical Authority and Spiritual Power*, trans. J. A. Baker (Stanford: Stanford University Press, 1969), 190.

73. Tertullian, *Against Marcion*, 4.22.5; *Tertullian Opera*, 1:601. Cf. William Tabbernee, "Dissenting Spiritualities in History," *The Way: A Review of Contemporary Spirituality* 28 (April 1988): 141.

74. Tertullian, *On the Soul*, 45.3: "*Somnus enim [Adam] corpori provenit in quietem, ecstasis animae accessit adversus quietem, et inde iam forma somnum ecstasi miscens et natura de forma*" (*Tertullian Opera*, 2:849).

75. Tertullian, *On the Soul*, 45.4. Thus, Tertullian goes on to argue that the lack of reality in dreams assures that "*non magis enim ob stupri visionem damnabimur quam ob martyrii coronabimur*" (*Tertullian Opera*, 2:850).

76. Tertullian, *On the Soul*, 45.5: "*Hoc [memoria] erit proprietas amentiae huius*" (*Tertullian Opera*, 2:850).

77. Tertullian, *On the Soul*, 45.6: "*Igitur quod memoria suppetit, sanitas mentis est; quod sanitas mentis salva memoria stupet, amentiae genus est*" (*Tertullian Opera*, 2:850).

78. Tertullian, *On the Soul*, 45.5 (*ANF*, 3:224). Cf. also *On the Soul*, 11.4.

79. Tertullian, *On the Soul*, 45.6: "*ideo et prudentes, si quando, sumus*" (*Tertullian Opera*, 2:850).

80. Tertullian, *On the Soul*, 45.6: "*Sapere enim nostrum licet obumbretur, non tamen extinguitur, nisi quod et ipsum potest videri vacare tunc, ecstasin autem hoc quoque operari de suo proprio, ut sic nobis sapientiae imagines inferat, quemadmodum et erroris*" (*Tertullian Opera*, 2:850). This sounds like a description of a person with a "one-track mind." The primary focus is on one thing, but there is not total obliviousness to various other things. See too, Wolfgang Bender, "Der Montanismus in Tertullians Lehre über den Heiligen Geist," in *Die Lehre über den Heiligen Geist bei Tertullian*, ed. Joseph Pascher and Klaus Morsdorf, MTS, II Systematische Abteilung, vol. 19 (Munich: Max Hueber Verlag, 1961), 161, who in analysis of Tertullian's concept of ecstasy writes, "*Der Mensch ist ganzlich passiv (passus), auch im Verlauf der Ekstase. Die wirkende Kraft (vis operatrix) in ihm ist der Heilige Geist.*" Pierre de Labriolle, *History and Literature of Christianity from Tertullian to Boethius*, trans. Herbert Wilson (London: Kegan Paul/N.Y.: Alfred A. Knopf, 1924), 92, says:

> In the eyes of Tertullian *ecstasis* was a state produced in a normal manner during sleep. The soul lost in that state its sense of its surroundings; its faculties of sense were suspended; the power of conscious reflection became stupefied; images, which it ceased to direct of its free will, assailed it. However, it preserved the memory of what it had thought it had seen and heard. God permitted this mode of special activity sometimes to take on a religious character and signification. Whether in sleep *or even apart from sleep*, the state of ecstasy, *amentia*, was the modification through which of necessity the human reason passes at the moment when it enters into direct relation with God. Visions and prophecies therefore postulated it of necessity.

81. Tertullian, *On the Soul*, 48.3.

82. Ibid., 11.4: "*accidentiam spiritus passus est: cecidit enim ecstasis super illum, sancti spiritus vis operatrix prophetiae*" (*Tertullian Opera*, 2:797). See too, *On the Soul*, 21.2; *On Fasting*, 3.2. It is difficult to know whether this argument is first used by Tertullian or whether it was used earlier by the New Prophecy. Tertullian obviously wrote his "Montanist" works sometime shortly after A.D. 207. Epiphanius, one of the two major sources for our knowledge of early Montanism, wrote his *Panarion* sometime between A.D. 367 and 400. In *Panarion*, 48.4–6, as found in Pierre de Labriolle, *Les sources de L'histoire du Montanisme* (Fribourg, Paris: Libraire de l'Université; Ernest Leroux, 1913), no. 88, 121–24), Epiphanius makes the statement that the New Prophecy attempted to make a case from Gen. 2:21 for its activity of ecstatic prophecy: Εἰ δὲ θελήσουσι παραπλώκειν τῇ ἀληθείᾳ τὸ ψεῦδος, καὶ ἀγνοεῖν τὸν νοῦν τὸν τῆς ἀκριβείας ἐπιμελόμενον, ἑαυτοῖς δὲ ἐρισωρεύειν λόγους, δι᾿ ὧν παραποιητεύονται τὴν ἑαυτῶν πλάνην ὁμοίαν τινὰ ἀροτελέσαι, παραστήσουσιν ἀπὸ τοῦ τὴν ἁγίαν γραπὴν εἰρηκέναι, Ἐπέβαλεν ὁ θεὸς ἔκστασιν ἐπὶ τὸν Ἀδάμ, καὶ ὕπνωσε. Two things point to the fact that this argument probably had its roots in Phrygian Montanism. First, Epiphanius, although writing 150 or more years later than Tertullian, does not quote Tertullian in connection with the New Prophecy. Second, in this context, Epiphanius's argument seems more to be

aimed at the prophetic words and style of Montanus himself. Cf. Karlfried Froehlich, "Montanism and Gnosis," in *The Heritage of the Early Christian Church*, ed. David Neiman and Margaret Schatkins, OCA, 195 (Rome: Pont. Institutum Studiorum Orientalium, 1973), 101–2.

83. Tertullian, *On the Soul*, 11.4; 21.2; 45.3. Dennis E. Groh, "Utterance and Exegesis: Biblical Interpretation in the Montanist Crisis," in *The Living Text: Essays in Honor of Ernest W. Saunders*, ed. Dennis E. Groh and Robert Jewett (Lanham, Md.: University Press of America, 1985), 85–86, rightfully follows Aune's lead by labeling this as an example of "charismatic exegesis." Cf. David E. Aune, *Prophecy in Early Christianity and the Ancient Mediterranean World* (Grand Rapids: William B. Eerdmans, 1983), 339–40. Groh then convincingly links Tertullian's argument to the one preserved in Epiphanius, *Panarion*, 48.

84. Tertullian, *On the Soul* 45.3: "*Sic et in primordio somnus cum ecstasi dedicatus: et misit deus ecstasin in Adam et dormiit. Somnus enim corpori provenit in quietem, ecstasis animae accessit adversus quietem, et inde iam forma somnum ecstasi miscens et natura de forma*" (*Tertulliani Opera*, 2:849). The two types of ecstasy, one natural, the other more spectacular, that emerge from Tertullian's thought shed light on why the Montanists were criticized at certain points. Although their content was heavily criticized in Tertullian's day, the style of the ecstatic state— literally, a παρέκστασις as represented by Epiphanius—was very much a part of the discussion in earlier days. On this, see William Tabernee, "Opposition to Montanism from Church and State," unpub. thesis, University of Melbourne, 1978, 97–102; William H. C. Frend, "Montanism: A Movement of Prophecy and Regional Identity in the Early Church," *BJRL* 70(3) (Autumn 1988): 28; and W. M. Calder, "Philadelphia and Montanism," *BJRL* 7(3) (August 1923): 329.

85. Tertullian, *On Fasting*, 3.2: "*Verum et ipse tunc in psychicum reversus post ecstasin spiritalem*" (*Tertullian Opera*, 2:1259). See also Bender, "Der Montanism in Tertullians Lehre über den Heiligen Geist," 162: "*Der Geist fordert Anerkennung; der Mensch—ohnehin von Sinnen, wenn der Geist uber ihn kommt—spielt keine grosse Rolle.*"

86. Tertullian, *Against Marcion*, 4.22.5. Even here, however, Tertullian clearly argues that neither Peter, James, nor John lost their reason or mind in such an experience (Tertullian, *Against Praxeas* 15.8). N. Bonwetsch, "Montanus, Montanism," in *The New Schaff-Herzog Encyclopedia of Religious Knowledge*, ed. Samuel McCauley Jackson (New York: Funk & Wagnalls, 1910), 7:486, writes, "For the ecstasy of the prophets the Montanists appealed to Gen. ii.7sqq.; Ps. cxvi.11; and Acts x.10, as well as to the prophecies recorded in Acts xv.32, xxi.11; and 1 Cor. xii.28, and to John the daughters (*sic*) of Philip, Ammia, and Quadratus, while they based the right of prophetesses on Miriam and Deborah." Calder, "Philadelphia and Montanism," 329, calls this *amentia* "trance."

87. It appears that Tertullian had in mind here the incident as recorded in Luke 9:33: "Just as they were leaving him, Peter said to Jesus, 'Master, it is good for us to be here; let us make three dwellings, one for you and one for Moses and one for Elijah'—not knowing what he said."

88. Tertullian, *On the Soul*, 45.6. Groh, "Utterance and Exegesis," 86–87,

demonstrates clearly the natural and supernatural aspects of ecstasy in Tertullian's thought.

89. Tertullian, *Against Marcion*, 5.8.12; *Tertullian Opera*, 1:688.

90. Tertullian, *Against Marcion*, 5.8.12. Cf. here, *On the Soul*, 9.4, where Tertullian records the account of a visionary woman who does this very thing: "*Est hodie soror apud nos revelationum charismata sortita, quas in ecclesia inter dominica sollemnia per ecstasin in spiritu patitur; conversatur cum angelis, aliquando etiam cum domino, et videt et audit sacramenta et quorundum corda dinoscit*" (*Tertullian Opera*, 2:792). Cf. also 1 Cor. 14:24–25.

91. Tertullian, *Against Marcion*, 5.8.12. Tertullian would like literally to let Marcion "*psalmum, aliquam visionem, aliquam orationem, dumtaxat spiritalem, in ecstasi, id est in amentia, si qua linguae interpretatio accessit*" (*Tertullian Opera*, 1:688).

CHAPTER NINE

1. Tertullian, *On the Soul*, 55.4; ANF, 3:231; *Tertullian Opera*, 2:862.

2. *The Passion of Perpetua and Felicitas*, 11–13, esp. 13:8. The practice of recording oracles and visions for later reference is still with us in certain sectors of Pentecostalism and the more recent charismatic renewal. For a discussion of some of the problems related to this practice, see Cecil M. Robeck, Jr., "Written Prophecies: A Question of Authority," *PJSPS* 2(2) (Fall 1980): 26–45.

3. A. A. R. Bastiaensen, "Tertullian's Reference to the *Passio Perpetua* in *De Anima* 55, 4," *SP* 17(2) (1982): 790–95, following the lead of J. H. Waszink, *Quinti Septimi Florentis Tertulliani De Anima* (Amsterdam: J. M. Meulenhoff, 1947), 561–62, argues that Tertullian actually had Perpetua's vision in mind rather than Saturus's vision. I remain unconvinced by their arguments.

4. *The Passion of Perpetua and Felicitas*, 4.8; cf. Rev. 6:9–11.

5. See, for instance, Rev. 4:4, where the twenty-four elders wear white robes; it is the dress of the 144,000 who come through the great period of tribulation in Rev. 7:9, 13–14; it is the attire of seven angels in Rev. 15:6 and the armies of heaven in 19:14. It may also be the attire of the Bride of Christ in 19:8, where the linen attire is said to be "fine linen, bright and pure," although it is not called white.

6. *The Passion of Perpetua and Felicitas*, 11.4–5.

7. "*multos fratres cognoscere sed et martyras*," *The Passion of Perpetua and Felicitas*, 13.8; see also 11.8.

8. Tertullian, *On the Soul*, 53.6.

9. Ibid., 55.2.

10. Ibid.; cf. Matt. 10:24.

11. Tertullian, *On the Soul*, 55.4.

12. In Rev. 1:10, John the apostle reveals that he received his vision when he was "in the spirit" on the Lord's day.

13. Bastiaensen, "Tertullian's Reference to the *Passio Perpetuae* in *De Anima* 55, 4," suggests that "Tertullian, here, in an unobtrusive way, puts the novel

spiritual revelation of the Paraclete on a par with the canonical revelation of the Scriptures." It may be conceded that Tertullian argues both from "the canonical revelation" and from "spiritual revelation" (=prophecy/vision), but that does not necessarily place them on a par. Two points, in fact, suggest that this is not the case. First, Tertullian always moves *from* Scripture *to* prophecy as though Scripture is the norm. Second, he often uses Scripture to "test" the validity of the prophecy.

14. Tertullian, *On the Soul*, 55.5.

15. Ibid.; cf. *On Flight in Persecution*, 9.4.

16. Tertullian, *On the Soul* 55.5; cf. 7.1–4.

17. Admittedly, this carries his argument found in his *On the Soul*, 21, that "The statements of holy Scripture will never be discordant with truth" one step further to the point that "two revelations by the same Holy Spirit will never be discordant with truth," but the logic seems to fit the present case admirably. Furthermore, Tertullian taught that the role of the Paraclete—and I understand him to mean by that the Holy Spirit—is to clarify already existing revealed truth: that is, Scripture (*On the Veiling of Virgins*, 1.5). See also J. H. Waszink, "Tertullian's Principles and Methods of Exegesis," in *Early Christian Literature and the Classical Intellectual Tradition: In Honorem Robert M. Grant*, ed. William R. Schoedel and Robert L. Wilkens, TH, 53 (Paris: Éditions Beauchesne, 1979), 28–29.

18. Tertullian, *On Flight in Persecution*, 9.4; Ronald E. Heine, *The Montanist Oracles and Testimonia*, PMS, 14 (Macon, Ga.: Mercer University Press, 1989), 73. "*Publicaris . . . bonum tibi est; qui enim non publicatur in hominibus, publicatur in Domino. Ne confundaris; justitia te producit in medium. Quid confunderis laudem ferens? Potestas fit, cum conspiceris ab hominibus*" (*Tertullian Opera*, 2:1147). For this and other oracles recorded in Tertullian's writings see appendix E. Cf. Robert M. Grant, *Second Century Christianity: A Collection of Fragments*, Translations of Christian Literature, series 6 (London: SPCK, 1957), 96.

19. David E. Aune, *Prophecy in Early Christianity and the Ancient Mediterranean World* (Grand Rapids: William B. Eerdmans, 1983), 315–16.

20. Matt. 10:33; Mark's version of this saying in 8:38 reads, "Those who are ashamed of me and my words in this adulterous and sinful generation, of them the Son of Man will also be ashamed when he comes in the glory of his Father with the holy angels." Cf. also Luke 12:9.

21. As William Tabbernee, "Early Montanism and Voluntary Martyrdom," *Col* 17(2) (May 1985): 37, notes, "The one event of martyrdom is viewed here from a double perspective: whilst the martyr is being put to shame at a human level, a supranatural event of a far greater significance is taking place. The martyr is declaring his or her faith *before Christ* and, consequently, is being invested with spiritual *potestas.*"

22. Johannes Quasten, *Patrology* (Utrecht-Antwerp: Spectrum Publishers, 1975), 2:310.

23. Tertullian, *On Flight in Persecution*, 3.1.

24. Ibid., 9.2; cf. 1 Thess. 5:5.

25. Tertullian, *On Flight in Persecution*, 9.4.

26. Ibid., 13.2. Cf. R. P. C. Hanson, "Notes on Tertullian's Interpretation of Scripture," *JTS*, n.s., 12 (1961): 276.

27. Tertullian, *On Flight in Persecution*, 6.1.

28. Ibid., 9.4; Heine, *Montanist Oracles and Testimonia*, 73; ANF 4:121: "*Spiritum vero si consulas, quid magis sermone illo Spiritus probat? Namque omnes paene ad martyrium exhorta[n]tur, non ad fugam, ut et illius commemoremur*" (*Tertullian Opera*, 2:1147).

29. Tertullian, *The Chaplet*, 1.4; Heine, *Montanist Oracles and Testimonia*, 73; ANF 3:93.

30. We are reminded of Celsus's account as recorded in Origen's work *Against Celsus*, 7.9, in which Celsus remarked that certain prophets went in and prophesied even "among armies."

31. Pierre de Labriolle, *La crise Montaniste* (Paris: Ernest Leroux, 1913), 52. Translation mine.

32. Tertullian, *On Flight in Persecution*, 9.4: "*Nolite in lectulis nec in aborsibus et febribus mollibus optare exire, sed in martyriis, uti glorificetur qui est passus pro vobis*" (*Tertullian Opera*, 2:1147).

33. Aune, *Prophecy in Early Christianity*, 315–16.

34. A. F. Walls, "The Montanist 'Catholic Epistle' and Its New Testament Prototype," *Studia Evangelica* 3(2) (1964): 441, n. 1, also suggests a Petrine influence here. Tabbernee, "Early Montanism and Voluntary Martyrdom," 36, rightly notes that this oracle attests to the fact that Montanus encouraged early Montanists to *desire* martyrdom, but it does not explicitly indicate that they were to *seek* death in martyrdom.

35. Karlfried Froehlich, "Montanism and Gnosis," in *The Heritage of the Early Christian Church*, ed. David Neiman and Margaret Schatkins, OCA, 195 (Rome: Pont. Institutum Studiorum Orientalium, 1973), 103.

36. Labriolle, *Crise Montaniste*, 53.

37. Tertullian, *On Flight in Persecution*, 10:1; *Tertullian Opera*, 2:1147.

38. Tertullian, *On the Soul*, 55.5; Heine, *Montanist Oracles and Testimonia*, 71; "*si pro deo occumbas, ut paracletus monet, non in mollibus febribus et in lectulis, sed in martyriis*" (*Tertullian Opera*, 2:863).

39. Tertullian, *On Modesty*, 21.7; Heine, *Montanist Oracles and Testimonia*, 93; "*Potest ecclesia donare delictum, sed non faciam, ne et alia delinquant*" (*Tertullian Opera*, 2:1326).

40. Tertullian, *On Modesty*, 21.7; *Tertullian Opera*, 2:1326.

41. Eusebius, *Ecclesiastical History*, 5.18.7; NPNF, 1:236.

42. Tertullian, *On Modesty*, 1.6; *Tertullian Opera*, 2:1281–82.

43. Tertullian, *On Modesty*, 21.2.

44. Ibid., 21.3–5.

45. Ibid., 21.5.

46. Ibid., 21.5–6.

47. Ibid., 21.7, "*potestatem ecclesia delicta donandi*" (*Tertullian Opera*, 2:1326).

48. Tertullian, *On Modesty*, 21.8.

49. Ibid.

50. Ibid., 21.10, 14.

51. Ibid., 21.17; cf. W. H. C. Frend, "The *Memoriae Apostolorum* in Roman North Africa," *JRS* 30 (1940): 36–37, reprinted in W. H. C. Frend, *Town and Country in the Early Christian Centuries* (London: Variorum Reprints, 1980) 18:36–37.

52. R. P. C. Hanson, *Tradition in the Early Church* (London: SCM Press, 1962), 160–61.

53. Tertullian, *On Exhortation to Chastity*, 10.5; Heine, *Montanist Oracles and Testimonia*, 67; "*Purificantia enim cum cor dat, ait, et visiones vident et ponentes faciem deorsum etiam voces audiunt salutares, tam manifestas quam et occultas*" (*Tertullian Opera*, 2:1030). It should be noted that there are at least three textual problems present in this oracle. (1) Labriolle, *Crise Montaniste*, 77, discusses briefly the fact that *On Exhortation to Chastity*, 10, is missing from various early manuscripts. This chapter, and particularly this oracle, however, has been judged genuine by Labriolle and Kurt Aland, "Bemerkungen zum Montanismus und zur frühchristlichen Eschatologie," in *Kirchen geschichtliche Entwürfe: Alte Kirche, Reformation und Luthertum, Pietismus und Erweckungsbewegung*, ed. Kurt Aland (Gütersloh: Verlagshaus Gerd Mohn, 1960), 145. (2) The words *cum cor dat* should probably read *concordat*, as attested in manuscript *Agobardinus*. Labriolle and Heine agree. (3) Labriolle has chosen the reading "*voces audiunt manifestas, tam salutares quam et occultas.*" This reading is also based on the manuscript *Agobardinus*. It has been further accepted by Quasten, *Patrology* 2:304–5, and Grant, *Second Century Christianity*, 96. Aland, however, has chosen to follow the text as outlined in *Tertullian Opera*.

54. Tertullian, *On Exhortation to Chastity*, 10.5; *Tertullian Opera*, 2:1030.

55. Tertullian, *On Exhortation to Chastity*, 10.1: "*Per continentiam enim negotiaberis magnam substantiam sanctitatis, parsimonia carnis spiritum adquires*" (*Tertullian Opera*, 2:1029).

56. Tertullian, *On Exhortation to Chastity*, 10.5. This reading is apparently a Tertullianic paraphrase, for both Greek and Latin texts read "life eternal and peace."

57. 1 Cor. 7:5; Tertullian, *On Exhortation to Chastity*, 10.2. On this passage see Gordon D. Fee, *The First Epistle to the Corinthians*, NICNT (Grand Rapids: William B. Eerdmans, 1987), 280–83.

58. Tertullian, *On Exhortation to Chastity*, 10.4–5. Cf. J. G. Davies, "Tertullian, 'De Resurrectione Carnis LXIII': A Note on the Origins of Montanism," *JTS* 6 (1955): 92, who points out that even the primitive Montanists were "concerned to maintain their link with the past, resting their teaching on the Old Testament and the apostolic writings."

59. H. J. Lawlor, "The Heresy of the Phrygians," *JTS* 9 (1908): 494; cf. Eusebius, *Ecclesiastical History*, 5.18.2, who quotes Apollonius as charging that the New Prophecy did teach the annulment of marriage. Cf. Epiphanius, *Panarion*, 48.9.

60. H. K. La Rondelle, *Perfection and Perfectionism: A Dogmatic-Ethical Study of Biblical Perfectionism and Phenomenal Perfectionism* (Berrien Springs, Mich.: Andrews University Press, 1971), 282, n. 176, writes that according to this passage, "Prisca is quoted as having said that chastity, sexual continence and purity are prerequisites for the spiritual communion and the reception of revelations."

61. Tertullian, *On Exhortation to Chastity,* 10.5.

62. D. P. Simpson, ed., *Cassell's New Compact Latin-English, English-Latin Dictionary* (New York: Funk & Wagnalls, 1963), 337; cf. Labriolle, *Crise Montaniste,* 80.

63. Eusebius, *Ecclesiastical History,* 5.18.2.

64. Epiphanius, *Panarion,* 49.2.

65. Labriolle, *Crise Montaniste,* 84; Davies, "Tertullian, 'De Resurrectione Carnis LXIII'," 92–3; cf. Acts 2:17.

66. Labriolle, *Crise Montaniste,* 84.

67. Tertullian, *On the Resurrection of the Flesh,* 11.2; Heine, *Montanist Oracles and Testimonia,* 75; "*Carnes sunt, et carnem oderunt*" (*Tertullian Opera,* 2:933).

68. Tertullian, *On the Resurrection of the Flesh,* 11.2.

69. Davies, "Tertullian, 'De Resurrectione Carnis LXIII'," 93.

70. Tertullian, *On the Resurrection of the Flesh,* 63.7; Heine, *Montanist Oracles and Testimonia,* 75.

71. Tertullian, *On the Resurrection of the Flesh,* 63.9; Heine, *Montanist Oracles and Testimonia,* 75.

72. Tertullian, *On the Resurrection of the Flesh,* 11.2.

73. Ibid., 1.1.

74. Ibid., 5.3, 8–9; 6.3, 7; 7.1, 7, 11–13.

75. Ibid., 8.1–6.

76. Ibid., 9.1.

77. Ibid., 10.2–4.

78. Ibid., 10.5.

79. Ibid., 11.1.

80. Ibid., 11.2.

81. Cf. 1 Cor. 14:24–25.

82. Aune, *Prophecy in Early Christianity,* 323.

83. Tertullian, *Against Praxeas,* 8.5; Heine, *Montanist Oracles and Testimonia,* 91; "*Protulit enim Deus sermonem quemadmodum etiam Paracletus docet, sicut radix fruticem et fons fluvium et sol radium*" (*Tertullian Opera,* 2:1167). It should be noted that Aland, "Bemerkungen zum Montanismus," 147, lists this oracle among those he calls the "remnants of the contents of oracles." Aune does not treat this "remnant."

84. Ronald E. Heine, "The Role of the Gospel of John in the Montanist Controversy," *SC* 6(1) (Spring 1987–88): 1–19, esp. 15, has made some useful regional observations on the New Prophecy and its opponents. While the opponents in Asia Minor rejected the New Prophecy on grounds that its prophets were

"false prophets," in Rome, the New Prophecy was rejected on grounds that the charisma of prophecy ceased to function following the deaths of the apostles. If this is the case, then it would appear that Praxeas might be identified as a cessationist.

85. Tertullian, *Against Praxeas*, 1.5; Heine, *Montanist Oracles and Testimonia*, 89.

86. Tertullian, *Against Praxeas*, 1.7. On the Roman acceptance, study, and rejection of the New Prophecy, see Cecil M. Robeck, Jr., "Irenaeus and 'Prophetic Gifts,'" in *Essays on Apostolic Themes: Studies in Honor of Howard M. Ervin*, ed. Paul Elbert (Peabody, Mass.: Hendrickson Publishers, 1985), 106–9.

87. Tertullian, *Against Praxeas*, 2.1.

88. Ibid., 2:1–2. On the subject of the *regulae fidei* in Tertullian's works see the helpful and informative study by L. Wm. Countryman, "Tertullian and the Regula Fidei," *SC* 2(4) (Winter 1984): 208–27.

89. Tertullian, *Against Praxeas*, 2.1: "*Nos vero et semper et nunc magis, ut instructiores per Paracletum, deductorem scilicet omnis veritatis . . . credimus*" (*Tertullian Opera*, 2:1160); cf. *Against Praxeas*, 13.5, for a similar claim. This contains an obvious allusion to John 16:13.

90. Jaroslav Pelikan, "Montanism And Its Trinitarian Significance," *CH* 25 (1956): 107.

91. Tertullian, *Against Praxeas*, 8.5.

92. Didymus, *On the Trinity*, 3.41; Epiphanius, *Panarion*, 48.11.1; 48.11.9; Eusebius, *Ecclesiastical History*, 5.16.17.

93. Labriolle, *Crise Montaniste*, 56: "*Il ne cite pas les propres paroles de Montan, il résume son enseignment.*"

94. Tertullian, *Against Praxeas*, 8.5.

95. Ibid.; *ANF*, 3:603.

96. Tertullian, *Against Praxeas*, 8.5; *ANF*, 3:603.

97. Tertullian, *Against Praxeas*, 8.7; *ANF*, 3:603.

98. Ernest Evans, *Tertullian's Treatise Against Praxeas* (London: SPCK, 1948), 242; Heb. 1:3a reads, "He reflects the glory of God and bears the very stamp of His nature"; John 7:38–39a reads, "He who believes in me, as the scripture has said 'Out of his heart shall flow rivers of living water.' Now this he said about the Spirit."

99. Pelikan, "Montanism and Its Trinitarian Significance," 106.

100. Tertullian, *Against Praxeas*, 9.1; cf. 2.1.

CHAPTER TEN

1. Tertullian, *On the Soul*, 3.2. Subsequent references to this source in the text are in parentheses.

2. Ibid., 2.3; *ANF*, 3.182; "*certos nihil recipiendum quod non conspiret germanae et ipso iam aevo pronatae propheticae paraturae*" (*Tertullian Opera*, 2:783–84).

3. Tertullian, *On the Soul*, 9.3–4; *Tertullian Opera*, 2:792.

4. The idea that what we have here is in fact an *ecclesiola in ecclesia* has been

convincingly argued by D. Powell, "Tertullianists and Cataphrygians," VC 29 (1975): 33–54. There is no conclusive evidence to suggest that there was a separate Montanist congregation at this time. See also William Tabbernee, "Opposition to Montanism from Church and State," unpub. thesis, University of Melbourne, 1978, 77.

5. Tertullian, On the Soul, 21; Against Marcion, 1.21.5.

6. Tertullian, On Baptism, 20.5.

7. Tertullian, On the Soul, 9.4; on the role of ecstasy in prophecy as understood by Tertullian, see chapter 8, "Ecstasy and Prophecy: Tertullian's Understanding."

8. Tabbernee, "Opposition to Montanism," 143, notes that this woman's self-control is indicative of a "sharp contrast" between her type of ecstasy and that type of ecstasy experienced by "the original Phrygian [Montanist] prophets." Cf. Eusebius, Ecclesiastical History, 5.16.7: "And he [Montanus] became beside himself, and being suddenly in a sort of frenzy and ecstasy (παρέκστασει), he raved and began to babble and utter strange things" (NPNF, 1.231).

9. 1 Cor. 11:5; 14:32–34; Tertullian, On the Veiling of Virgins, 9.2; Against Marcion, 5.8.11.

10. Tertullian, On the Soul, 9.4; Ronald E. Heine, The Montanist Oracles and Testimonia, PMS, 14 (Macon, Ga.: Mercer University Press, 1989), 71. See appendix F as well.

11. H. J. Lawlor, "The Heresy of the Phrygians," JTS 9 (1908): 487.

12. For this vision and that of another contemporary see appendix F; Tertullian, On the Soul, 9.4: " 'inter cretera,' inquit, 'ostensa est mihi anima corporaliter, et spiritus videbatur, sed non inanis et vacuae qualitatis, immo quae etiam teneri repromitteret, tenera et lucida et aerii coloris, et forma per omnia humana. Hoc visio' " (Tertullian Opera, 2:792–93); Heine, Montanist Oracles and Testimonia, 71.

13. There may be an example of this in Isa. 8:1–2; 30:8.

14. Tertullian, On the Soul, 9.8; Luke 16:23–24; Rev. 6:9–11.

15. Homer, Hymns to Hermes, 254–59; Virgil, Aeneid, 6.494–99.

16. Augustine, On the Soul and Its Origin, 1.5; 2.7–9; 4.17–28.

17. Tertullian, On the Veiling of Virgins, 1.1; cf. Johannes Quasten, Patrology (Utrecht-Antwerp: Spectrum Publishers, 1975), 2:306.

18. Tertullian, On the Veiling of Virgins, 1.1–2.

19. Ibid., 1.4.

20. Ibid.; Heine, Montanist Oracles and Testimonia, 63.

21. Tertullian, On the Veiling of Virgins, 1.5.

22. Ibid., 1.7; Heine, Montanist Oracles and Testimonia, 65.

23. David E. Aune, Prophecy in Early Christianity and the Ancient Mediterranean World (Grand Rapids: William B. Eerdmans, 1983), 321.

24. On the argument, see Ronald E. Heine, "The Role of the Gospel of John in the Montanist Controversy," SC 6(1) (Spring 1987–88): 16, who suggests that use of this passage began as an anticessationist argument in Rome, to which Tertullian later makes appeal. This suggests, as Heine points out, that the origin of the New Prophecy in North Africa appears to be Roman rather than Asian.

This fact may explain many of the differences between Asian and North African expressions of the New Prophecy.

25. Tertullian, *On the Veiling of Virgins*, 2.1.

26. Ibid., 3.1.

27. Ibid., 4.1–5; 7.1–4. In 1 Cor. 11, Paul commended the Corinthians because they "remember me in everything and maintain the traditions" even as he conveyed these traditions to them (verse 2). He argued, thereby, for the Corinthians to keep the tradition that is present in the other churches of God, a tradition Paul recognized as legitimate, namely, the veiling of the heads of women (verse 16). Paul employed several arguments to support his position: (1) as Christ is the head of every man, the husband is the head of his wife (verse 3); (2) man is the image and glory of God, woman is the glory of man (verses 4–7); (3) nonveiled hair on women in worship is offensive to angels (verse 10); (4) nature teaches that for man to wear long hair is degrading, for women it is a source of pride (verses 14–15); and (5) last of all, he argued as if his previous arguments had not totally convinced his readers that he recognizes only noncontentious, veiled females and so do all the churches with which he had had contact (verse 16).

28. Tertullian, *On the Veiling of Virgins*, 16.1; *Tertullian Opera*, 2:1225.

29. Tertullian, *On the Veiling of Virgins*, 17.2.

30. Ibid., 17.1.

31. Ibid., 17.4.

32. Ibid., 17.3: "*Nobis Dominus etiam revelationibus velaminis spatia metatus est*" (*Tertullian Opera*, 2:1226).

33. Tertullian, *On the Veiling of Virgins*, 1.7.

34. Ibid., 1.4.

35. Ibid., 1.4, 5.

36. Ibid., 17.3; *Tertullian Opera*, 2:1226.

37. Tertullian, *On the Soul*, 9.4: "*Est hodie soror apud nos revelationum charismata sortita*" (*Tertullian Opera*, 2:792).

38. Tertullian, *On the Veiling of Virgins*, 17.3: "*Nam cuidam sorori nostrae angelus in somnis cervices, quasi applauderet*" (*Tertullian Opera*, 2:1226).

39. I suppose it is possible that Tertullian's understanding of prophetic inspiration is at this point similar to that which was introduced in Hermas, *Mandate* 11.9: namely, ὁ ἄγγελος τοῦ πνεύματος τοῦ προφητικοῦ. J. Reiling, *Hermas and Christian Prophecy*, NovTSup, 37 (Leiden: E. J. Brill, 1973), 108–9, argues, I think well, that by the concept of angel is expressed the latent and inactive presence of the Holy Spirit. Hence, when prayer was made to God and the answer was sent, the angel (the latent Spirit) disappeared and the active operation of the Spirit (prophecy) began. Reiling's interpretation parallels the account in Irenaeus, *Against Heresies*, 1.13.2, in which δαίμων πάρεδρος enabled Marcus to prophesy; cf. Reiling, *Hermas and Christian Prophecy*, 88–91. In this particular situation, however, the action of the angel who beat the woman's neck (with its wings?) is an indication that the idea of a literal angel, and not the latent Holy Spirit, is present and that the content of the saying itself speaks against its being an oracle of the Spirit.

40. Common in Tertullian's day was the idea that some angels had fallen when they fell in love with and married the daughters of men. This perception was the acceptable interpretation of Gen. 6:1–2; cf. Tertullian, *On the Veiling of Virgins*, 7.2–4.

41. Tertullian, *On the Veiling of Virgins*, 17.3: "*Elegantes, inquit, cervices et merito nudae! bonum est usque ad lumbos a capite reveleris, ne et tibi ista cervicum libertas non prosit*" (*Tertullian Opera*, 2:1226). See appendix F.

42. Tertullian, *On the Veiling of Virgins*, 17.4: "*Quantam autem castigationem merebuntur etiam illae*" (*Tertullian Opera*, 2:1226).

43. Tertullian, *On the Veiling of Virgins*, 17.3: "*Et utique quod uni dixeris, omnibus dixeris*" (*Tertullian Opera*, 2:1226).

CHAPTER ELEVEN

1. Tertullian, *On the Veiling of Virgins*, 1.4–5, 7.

2. Ibid., *On Monogamy*, 1.2.

3. Ibid., 4.1: "*Hoc ipsum demonstratur a nobis, neque novam neque extraneam esse monogamiae disciplinam, immo et antiquam et propriam Christianorum, ut Paracletum restitutorem potius sentias eius quam institutorem*" (*Tertullian Opera*, 2:1233).

4. Tertullian, *On Monogamy*, 2.2.

5. Tertullian, *On Monogamy*, 2.2; Ronald E. Heine, *The Montanist Oracles and Testimonia*, PMS, 14 (Macon, Ga.: Mercer University Press, 1989), 77; "*satis utique praetendit et docturum illum quae et nova existimari possint, ut nunquam retro edita, et aliquando onerosa, ut idcirco non edita*" (*Tertullian Opera*, 2:1230).

6. Tertullian, *On Monogamy*, 2.3: "*Adversarius enim spiritus ex diversitate praedicationis appareret, primo regulam adulterans fidei*" (*Tertullian Opera*, 2:1230).

7. Tertullian, *On Monogamy*, 2.3. James A. Sanders, "Adaptable for Life: The Nature and Function of Canon," in *Magnalia Dei: The Mighty Works of God: Essays on the Bible and Archeology in Memory of G. Ernest Wright*, ed. F. M. Cross et al. (Garden City, N.Y.: Doubleday, 1976), 537, notes that "a community's ethos issues from its muthos." See Cecil M. Robeck, Jr., "Canon, *Regulae Fidei*, and Continuing Revelation in the Early Church," in *Church, Word & Spirit: Historical and Theological Essays in Honor of Geoffrey W. Bromiley*, ed. James E. Bradley and Richard A. Muller (Grand Rapids: William B. Eerdmans, 1987), 79–80.

8. This seems to point to the idea that Tertullian was in some sense relying on 1 Cor. 12:3, "Therefore I want you to understand that no one speaking by the Spirit of God ever says, 'Let Jesus be cursed!' and no one can say 'Jesus is Lord' except by the Holy Spirit," as well as 1 John 4:2–3, "By this you know the Spirit of God: every spirit that confesses Jesus Christ has come in the flesh is from God, and every spirit that does not confess Jesus is not from God." These truths have been revealed in Scripture and are commonly held by the church. Those who adulterate these truths are not to be heard.

9. Tertullian, *On Monogamy*, 2.4: "*Paracletus . . . ipsum primo Christum contestabitur qualem credimus, cum toto ordine Dei creatoris, et ipsum glorificabit, et de*

ipso commemorabit, et sic de principali regula agnitus illa multa quae sunt disciplinarum revelabit" (*Tertullian Opera*, 2:1230). Tertullian obviously has in mind here the statements of Jesus found in John 15:26, as well as John 16:12–15 and John 14:26. "Just as the Paraclete guarded against the adulteration of the Christian '*regula fidei*', so it prevented the degeneration of Christian morals" (Timothy David Barnes, *Tertullian* [Oxford: The Clarendon Press, 1971], 139–40).

10. Tertullian, *On Monogamy*, 3.9.

11. Tertullian, *On Monogamy*, 4.4: "*Negat scriptura quod non notat*" (*Tertullian Opera*, 2:1233). In essence, this is the argument *ex silencio* that he also uses in his *Exhortation to Chastity*, 4.2–3; *Against Hermogenes*, 22.5; *The Chaplet*, 2.4. It has been noted by James L. Ash, "The Decline of Ecstatic Prophecy in the Early Church," *TS* 37 (1976): 243, that this statement points to the fact that Tertullian "was himself a champion of the emerging concept of canon."

12. Tertullian, *On Monogamy*, 14.4.

13. Ibid.; cf. *On Fasting*, 1.3, where Tertullian alluded to the idea that Montanus, Priscilla, and Maximilla taught a limitation on marriages. This may be the basis for Apollonius's charge that Montanus taught the dissolution of marriage and, hence, both Priscilla and Maximilla had abandoned their husbands, Priscilla joining an order of "virgins" (Eusebius, *Ecclesiastical History*, 5.18.2–3). Cf. John 16:12–14.

14. Tertullian, *On Monogamy*, 14.4.

15. Ibid., 14.6.

16. Ibid., 1.1: "*Haeretici nuptias auferunt, psychici ingerunt. Illi nec semel, isti non semel nubunt*" (*Tertullian Opera*, 2:1229); Heine, *Montanist Oracles and Testimonia*, 77. His reference to *psychici* is again an apparent reference to the Catholics, for he wrote in *On Monogamy*, 1.2, as a contrast to these persons, "But with us, who are justly called 'spiritual' [*spiritalis*] because we recognize spiritual gifts, continence is the more religious because the freedom to marry is diffident; . . . We recognize one marriage as we recognize one God." Likewise, in *On Monogamy*, 1.3, he remarked, "But the things which are of the Spirit are not pleasing to the psychics who do not receive the Spirit." It would seem that this last statement in particular equated the Spirit with the Paraclete of the New Prophecy and the Psychics with the Catholics. Cf. Johannes Quasten and Joseph C. Plumpe, eds., *Tertullian: Treatises on Marriage and Remarriage*, trans. William P. LeSaint, ACW, 13 (Westminster, Md.: Newman Press, 1951), 151, n. 2.

17. Tertullian, *On Monogamy*, 15.1–2. Christine Trevett, "Apocalypse, Ignatius, Montanism: Seeking the Seeds," *VC* 43(4) (1989): 322, observes that Tertullian "is not at odds with Paul or the Seer in suggesting that celibacy was esteemed above marriage (*de Monog*. iii.10; cf. *ad Uxor*. i.3.3; *de Exhort. Cast.* iii.9f; cf. 1 Cor. 7; Rev. 14:4) though Tertullian was against heretics who rejected entirely the idea of marriage."

18. This contention is based on Matt. 19:8, "He [Jesus] said to them [a group of Pharisees who came to test him asking, 'Is it lawful to divorce one's wife for any cause?'], 'It was because you were too hard hearted that Moses allowed you to divorce your wives, but from the beginning it was not so.'" Cf. Deut. 24:1–4.

19. It seems that Tertullian had as background here Paul's argument in 1 Cor. 7:39–40 that while second marriage was possible, it was better that it not take place. To show how strongly he believed this, he remarked that he thought he had the "Spirit of God." This seems to mean that he thought his judgment was in line with the desire or will of the Spirit. Cf. C. K. Barrett, *A Commentary on the First Epistle to the Corinthians*, HNTC (New York: Harper and Row, 1968), 186. Cf. too, 1 Cor. 7:25.

20. Tertullian, *On Monogamy*, 14.3.

21. Ibid., 1.2; 14.3–6.

22. I would suggest that a parenetic or prescriptive oracle could have been given in a pattern paralleling Matt. 19:8–9. It would appear as follows:

> Thus says the Spirit,
> "For your weakness of flesh Paul allowed you to remarry when widowed,
> but from the beginning it was not so.
> But I say to you:
> Whoever remarries
> is guilty of license."

This is a composite constructed from the arguments of Tertullian, *On Monogamy*, 1.2; 14.2–6. H. K. La Rondelle, *Perfection and Perfectionism* (Berrien Springs, Mich.: Andrews University Press, 1971), 282, notes that by this appeal he replaced the law and the prophets, thereby abrogating "what Paul or even Christ had still allowed, e.g., the second marriage."

23. Tertullian, *On Monogamy*, 2.1–2. The standard for judgment would seem to have included Matt. 11:29–30 as well as Gal. 1:9. Also, see 2 Thess. 2:15; 3:6.

24. Tertullian, *On Monogamy*, 1.3: "*Sed psychicis, non recipientibus spiritum, ea quae sunt spiritus non placent*" (*Tertullian Opera*, 2:1229).

25. Tertullian, *On Fasting*, 1.3. One might, by inference from this passage, assume that the subject of monogamy as opposed to digamy likewise had its origins in Montanus, Priscilla, and Maximilla, for Tertullian laments, "*propter hoc novae prophetiae recusantur . . . quod plane doceant* [Montanus, Priscilla, and Maximilla] *saepius ieiunare quam nubere*" (*Tertullian Opera*, 2:1257). Cf. Eusebius, *Ecclesiastical History*, 5.18.2, where Apollonius remarks that Montanus made laws regarding fasts.

26. This conclusion was reached since Tertullian was reacting to the charge that the discipline of fasting as manifest in the New Prophecy was apparently declared to be false prophecy by the church, Tertullian, *On Fasting*, 1.5; 14.2 and 4.

27. Ibid., 1.5; cf. 14.2.

28. Ibid., 1.4. The New Prophecy apparently kept certain fasts marked on the Jewish calendar (ibid., 2.1; 13.6) as well as the Wednesday and Friday fasts of the church; prolonged stations (official fasts), which normally ended about the ninth hour (3 P.M.) to a time late in the evening (ibid., 2.3; 10.8 and 13); observed xerophagies (periods when a dry diet was introduced, ibid., 15.5) for a period of two weeks excluding Sabbaths and Lord's Days (ibid., 2.4; 15.2); and

imposed certain dietary restrictions, including the exclusion of onions and garlic (ibid., 5.4), meats, wines, and vegetables (ibid., 15.3).

29. Ibid., 2.6; cf. Gal. 4:10.

30. See Jerome, *Epistle* 41:3, who wrote, "We, according to the apostolic tradition . . . fast through one Lent yearly; whereas they [the New Prophecy] keep three in the year as though three saviours had suffered. I do not mean, of course, that it is unlawful to fast at other times through the year—always excepting Pentecost—only that while in Lent it is a duty or obligation, at other seasons it is a matter of choice" (*NPNF*, 6:55–56); cf. Origen, *Principles*, 2.7.3.

31. Tertullian, *On Fasting*, 11.6; *Tertullian Opera*, 2:1270. The reference to *charismatibus* is clearly a reference to the Montanist expression of the gift of prophecy, and perhaps the gift of tongues. It would seem that the church, by this period (circa A.D. 210) was already attempting to eliminate the Montanist claim of being within the true prophetic tradition by limiting tongues and prophecy to a previous era ("*Sed rursus palos terminales figitis deo*"). Cf. R. P. C. Hanson, *Tradition in the Early Church* (London: SCM Press, 1962), 160.

32. Tertullian, *On the Veiling of Virgins*, 1.4–5.

CHAPTER TWELVE

1. Numerous references to, as well as some analysis of, Adolf von Harnack's article "Cyprian als Enthusiast," *ZNTW* 3 (1902): 177–91 will be made in the sections analyzing the various types of visions that appear in Cyprian's writings.

2. Celerinus in *Epistle* 39.1; Mappalicus in ibid. 10.4; and an unnamed bishop in *Treatise* 7:20 (*On Mortality*); the numeration of Cyprian's epistles will follow the Oxford scheme rather than that used in the *ANF* series. For a chart comparing these two numbering systems see appendix K. The translations and notes by G. W. Clarke, *The Letters of St. Cyprian of Carthage*, 4 vols., ACW, 43, 44, 46, and 47 (New York: Newman Press, 1984, 1986, 1989), will be used throughout.

3. Cyprian, *Epistles* 16.4; 76.1.

4. Ibid., 11.5–6; 40; 7; 58.1; 63.1; 66.10; and Pontius, *The Life and Passion of Cyprian, Bishop and Martyr*, 7, 12–13.

5. Michael M. Sage, *Cyprian*, PMS, 1 (Cambridge, Mass.: The Philadelphia Patristic Foundation, 1975), 204, remarks that "Visions were an enduring part of Cyprian's character and are a regular feature of contemporary Christianity."

6. Cyprian, *Epistle* 66.10.2; Clarke, *Letters*, 3:122. See here, Peter Hinchliff, *Cyprian of Carthage and the Unity of the Christian Church* (London: Geoffrey Chapman, 1974), 25.

7. Cyprian, *Epistle* 16.4.1. Cyprian's term was *in ecstasi.*

8. Cyprian, *Epistle* 16.4.1; Clarke, *Letters*, 1:95. "*impletur apud nos spiritu sancto puerorum innocens aetas, quae in ecstasi videt oculis et audit et loquitur ea quibus nos Dominus monere et instruere dignatur*" (Guilelmus Hartel, *S. Thasci Caecili Cypriani Opera Omnia*, CSEL [Vienna: C. Geroldi Filium Bibliopolam Academ-

iae, 1871], 3.2.520). Cf. *Epistle* 57.4 and M. Réveillaud, *"Note pour une Pneumatologie Cyprienne," SP* 6 (1962): 183–84.

9. Cyprian, *Epistles* 11.3; 10.4; 16.4; *Treatise* 7.19 (*On Mortality*).

10. Cyprian, *Epistles* 16.4; 39.1; 66.10.

11. See appendix G for a list of oracles quoted by Cyprian that were attributed to such visionary experiences.

12. These purposes were: to show (*ostendere*), *Epistles* 11.3; 11.4; 66.9; 66.10 (2x); to reveal (*revelare*), ibid. 11.3; 66.10; *Treatise* 7.20; to reproach (*exprobrare*), *Epistle* 11.5; to admonish (*admonere*), ibid. 11.6, 7 (2x); 39.1; 40.1; 57.5; 58.1; 66.9; to instruct (*instruere*), ibid. 11.7 (2x); 16.4; 40.1; 58.1; to guide (*regere*), ibid. 11.7; to warn (*monere*), ibid. 16.4; to make clear (*inlustrare*), ibid. 39.1; to adorn (*honestare*), ibid. 39.1; to exhort (*hortorari*), ibid. 39.1; to foretell (*praenuntare*), ibid. 57.5; to incite (*instigare*), ibid. 58.1; to honor (*honorare*), ibid. 66.5; to command (*praecipere*), ibid. 66.10; *Treatise* 7.20; to elect (*eligere*), *Epistle* 48.4; to appoint (*constituere*), ibid. 48.4. The last two were applied only and specifically to the use of divine revelations to appoint priests.

13. Cyprian, *Epistles* 11.5–7; 16.4; 39.1; 40.1; 57.5; 58.1; 66.9. In their negative form they encompassed Cyprian's use of *admonere* and *exprobrare*, and possibly *monere*.

14. Cyprian, ibid. 11.7; 16.4; 39.1; 40.1; 57.5; 58.1; 66.10, and *Treatise* 7.20. Their positive expressions might include *instruere, regere, inlustrare, hortorari, praenuntare, instigare,* and *praecipere*.

15. Cyprian, *Epistle* 73.15; Hartel, *S. Thasci Caecili Cypriani,* 3.2:789.

16. Cyprian, *Epistle* 73.17; Hartel, *S. Thasci Caecili Cypriani,* 3.2:790. Cyprian did not, however, include Hebrews, James, Jude, 2 John, 3 John, or 2 Peter. See, on Cyprian's New Testament, Edgar J. Goodspeed, *A History of Early Christian Literature* (Chicago: The University of Chicago Press, 1966), 178.

17. Cyprian, *Epistle* 73.13: "*sancto spiritu revelatum*" (Hartel, *S. Thasci Caecili Cypriani,* 3.2:787).

18. Cyprian, *Epistle* 73.13; Hartel, *S. Thasci Caecili Cypriani,* 3.2:787.

19. Cyprian, *Epistle* 73.13: "*post inspirationem vero et revelationem factam, qui in eo quod erraverat perseverat prudens et sciens, sine venia ignorantiae peccat*" (Hartel, *S. Thasci Caecili Cypriani,* 3.2:787). Cyprian's "understanding" of Scripture cannot always be said to be infallible, however. On this, see S. L. Greenslade, "Scripture and other Doctrinal Norms in Early Theories of Ministry," *JTS* 44 (1943): esp. 171–76.

20. Cyprian, *Epistle* 73.16; *Treatise,* 1.14–15.

21. Cyprian, *Epistle* 43.5.1; Clarke, *Letters,* 2.64; Hartel, *S. Thasci Caecili Cypriani,* 3.2:593. Cyprian here quotes from Jer. 23:16–17, and applies it to the contemporary situation. Cf. *Treatise* 1.11–12 (*On the Unity of the Church*).

22. Cyprian, *Epistle* 43.5; cf. Deut. 13.5.

23. Cyprian's analysis of Felicissimus's situation was founded on his belief that outside the church there could be no bishop. He wrote, "God is one and Christ is one; There is one Church and one chair founded, by the Lord's authority, upon Peter. It is not possible that another altar can be set up, or that a

new priesthood can be appointed, over and above this one altar and this one priesthood. Whoever gathers elsewhere, scatters. Whatever is so established by man in his madness that it violates what has been appointed by God is an obscene outrage, it is sacrilege" (Cyprian, *Epistle* 43.5.1; Clarke, *Letters*, 2:64). See also *Treatise* 1.5 and 1.13 (*On the Unity of the Church*).

24. Cyprian, *Epistle* 43.5. See Paul's contention that genuine prophecy edified in 1 Cor. 14:3.

25. Cyprian, *Treatise* 1.15.

26. Cyprian, *Epistle* 55.15.

27. Ibid. 55.6.1; Clarke, *Letters*, 3:35–36. "*in unum convenimus et scripturis [div] ex utraque parte prolatis temperamentum salubri moderatione libravimus*" (Hartel, *S. Thasci Caecili Cypriani*, 3.2:627). The Council appears to have taken place about A.D. 252 or 253 (Clarke, *Letters*, 3:213).

28. Cyprian, *Epistle* 57.5.1; Clarke, *Letters*, 3:59. "*placuit nobis sancto spiritu suggerente et Domino per visiones multas et manifestas admonerte, ut quia hostis nobis inminere praenuntiatur et ostenditur, colligere intra castra milites Christi et examinatis singulorum causis pacem lapsis dare, immo pugnaturis arma suggerere*" (Hartel, *S. Thasci Caecili Cypriani*, 3.2:655); ANF, 5:338.

29. Cyprian, *Epistle* 75.7, 10, 19. This epistle is part of the collection of Cyprian's correspondence file, but it is not penned by Cyprian. It is written by Firmilian, bishop of Caesarea in Cappadocia, about the year A.D. 256. Firmilian, no doubt, had had direct confrontations with certain of the Montanists of Asia Minor. Although Montanus, Prisc[ill]a, and Maximilla were long gone from the scene, the sect had continued, for he writes of an incident involving a woman "prophetess" in Asia Minor that had taken place twenty-two years before his writing the present letter. Firmilian's account will be ignored in this study since it describes events in Asia Minor and not North Africa.

30. Jerome, *Letter* 84.2, wrote, "The blessed Cyprian takes Tertullian for his master, as his writings prove; yet, delighted as he is with the ability of this learned and zealous writer, he does not join him in following Montanus and Maximilla" (NPNF, 6:176). It might be said, however, that Cyprian had "outflanked" Tertullian in that, while he never aligns himself with the sect of Montanism, he feels free to admit visions and revelations in the Montanist tradition. On this, see Hugo Koch, *Cyprianische Untersuchungen: Arbeiten zur Kirchengeschichte*, ed. Karl Hall and Hans Lietzmann (Bonn: A. Marcus and E. Weber's Verlag, 1926), 4:323, n. 1.

31. Cyprian, *Epistle* 55.6. See here W. H. C. Frend, *The Donatist Church* (Oxford: Clarendon Press, 1971), 137–38, who writes that at a meeting of bishops convened at Carthage by Cyprian in A.D. 256, each bishop was allowed to share his view on the subject to be discussed and all views were expressed in the form of "Scriptural text, backed by argument." Thus, scriptural text provided the precedent, and such things as visions and analyses of contemporary events provided the argumentation for conforming to the canonical norm. The work entitled *Concerning the Baptism of Heretics* (The Seventh Council of Carthage under Cyprian) (ANF, 5:565–72) provides many fascinating examples of this

style of argumentation, and it appears to be not unlike some of Tertullian's own argumentation.

32. Cyprian, *Epistle* 57.5.

33. Such passages as 1 Cor. 9.22; 10.33; 11.1; and 12.26 are mentioned in Cyprian, *Epistle* 55.15.

34. Cyprian, *Epistle* 55.18.

35. Ibid., 57.5.1; Clarke, *Letters*, 3:59.

36. Cyprian, *Epistle* 39.1.2, for instance, gives an example of an appointment, already made by Cyprian and others, that was confirmed in a vision or divine visitation to Celerinus. For a full discussion of this account, see chapter 13, section "The Case of Celerinus."

37. See Cyprian, *Epistle* 11.4.2, for such an example. His claim for the legitimacy of the vision experienced in this passage is a simple one: "And we see now fulfilled what was then revealed" (Clarke, *Letters*, 1:78). He evaluated the words of Mappalicus similarly in *Epistle* 10.4.1 (Clarke, *Letters*, 1:73). It is also fascinating to realize just how accurate Cyprian was in predicting the future in two other instances. In one, he received a vision in which an imminent end was predicted for the Decian persecution, an end that was fulfilled through the untimely death of Decius (*Epistle* 11.6.1). In a second one, he predicted his own death as a martyr on the basis of a vision (Pontius, *The Life and Passion of Cyprian, Bishop and Martyr*, 12 and 13).

38. Cyprian, *Epistles* 63.1; 81; *Treatise* 11.1 (*Exhortation to Martyrdom*). See also *Epistles* 1.4; 11.5–6; 40.7; 58; 66.10; etc.

39. Cyprian, *Epistle* 48.4. *Treatise* 11.1, addressed to Fortunatus on the subject of martyrdom, provides an excellent example of this fact. Fortunatus had apparently asked Bishop Cyprian for some treatise which would lay out various scriptural exhortations that could prepare and strengthen those about to be martyred. It was with the aid of divine inspiration ("*auxilio divinae inspirationis instructa*") that Cyprian succeeded in fulfilling the request.

40. Cyprian, *Epistle* 7; *Treatise* 7.19 (*On Mortality*).

41. Cyprian, *Epistle* 11 (*Carthage*); ibid. 58 (*Thibaris*).

42. Ibid. 6.

43. Ibid. 57.5.

44. Ibid. 11.7.1: "I had no right to keep these particular matters concealed or to confine knowledge of them to myself alone; for they can serve to govern and guide each one of us. In your term, 'he instructed,' you ought not to keep this letter concealed among yourselves but you should make it available to the brethren to read. To obstruct those things by which God has favoured us with admonishment and instruction is the action of someone who would not have his own brother receive admonishment and instruction" (Clarke, *Letters*, 1:79–80); *ANF* 5:287.

45. Cyprian, *Epistles* 40; 71.3.

46. Ibid. 71.3.

47. "Let two or three prophets speak, and let the others weigh what is said. If a revelation is made to another sitting by, let the first be silent."

48. Cyprian, *Epistle* 71.3.2: "*multa singulis in melius revelari et debere unum-quemque non pro eo quod semel inbiberat et tenebat pertinaciter congredi, sed si quid melius et utilius extiterit libenter amplecti*" (Hartel, *S. Thasci Caecili Cypriani*, 3.2:774); Clarke, *Letters*, 4:50–51; ANF, 5:378. Cf. *Epistles* 74.10 and esp. 75.4, which shows that Cyprian was not alone in this thinking.

49. Cyprian, *Epistle* 16.4; but see 14.1 and 20.1.

50. Ibid. 7.

CHAPTER THIRTEEN

1. Cyprian, *Epistles* 39.1, 4; 40; 48.4; 63.1; 66.5, 10; and 70.3.

2. Ibid. 39 and 40 (A.D. 251). I will assume the dates established by G. W. Clarke, *The Letters of St. Cyprian of Carthage*, ACW, 43, 44, 46, 47 (New York: Newman Press, 1984, 1986, 1989).

3. Cyprian, *Epistle* 66 (A.D. 254–255).

4. Ibid. 63 (A.D. 254–256).

5. Ibid. 48 (A.D. 251).

6. Ibid. 70 (A.D. 255).

7. Ibid. 63.1.1. The words he uses, "*episcopos plurimos ecclesiis dominicis in toto mundo divina dignatione,*" clearly imply that this was a widespread practice (Guilelmus Hartel, *S. Thasci Caecili Cypriani Opera Omnia*, CSEL [Vienna: C. Geroldi Filium Biliopolam Academiae, 1971], 3.2:701).

8. Cyprian, *Epistle* 66.5.

9. Ibid. 66.5.1; Clarke, *Letters*, 3:119. "*dum episcopus qui unus est et ecclesiae pracest superba quorundam praesumptione contemnitur et homo dignatione Dei honoratus indignus hominibus iudicatur*" (Hartel, *S. Thasci Caecili Cypriani*, 3.2.730).

10. What Cyprian may have in mind here is something like what we read in Acts 13:2: "While they were worshipping the Lord and fasting, the Holy Spirit said, 'Set apart for me Barnabas and Saul for the work to which I have called them.'" See my article on "The Gift of Prophecy in Acts and Paul, pt. 1," *SBT* 5(1) (1975): 31–33, for an analysis of this passage.

11. Cyprian, *Epistle* 48.4; Hartel, *S. Thasci Caecili Cypriani*, 3.2:608.

12. Cyprian, *Epistle* 70.3.3: "*quare qui cum Domino sumus et unitatem Domini tenemus et secundum eius dignationem sacerdotium eius in ecclesia administramus*" (Hartel, *S. Thasci Caecili Cypriani*, 3.2:770; ANF, 5:376).

13. Cyprian, *Epistle* 70.3: "*quare qui cum Domino sumus . . . quaecumque adversarii eius et antichristi faciunt repudiare et reicere et pro profanis habere debemus*" (Hartel, *S. Thasci Caecili Cypriani*, 3.2:770). Cf. *Epistle* 48.4, where Cyprian wrote: "*quod ut simul cum ceteris quoque collegis nostris stabiliter ac firmiter administremus adque [ut] catholicae ecclesiae concordi unanimitate teneamus, perficiet divina protectio*" (Hartel, *S. Thasci Caecili Cypriani*, 3.2:608).

14. Cyprian, *Epistle* 39.3.

15. Eusebius, *Ecclesiastical History*, 6.43.6; NPNF, 1:287.

16. Cyprian, *Epistle* 39.1.2; Clarke, *Letters*, 2:54.

17. Cyprian, *Epistle* 39.1.2; Hartel, *S. Thasci Caecili Cypriani*, 3.2:582;

Clarke, *Letters*, 2:54. Celerinus's elevation within the clergy was to the level of reader (*Epistle* 39.4.3).

18. Cyprian, *Epistle* 39.4.1.

19. Ibid. 39.1.2: "*ecclesiae ipsius admonitu et hortatu in visione per noctem conpulsus est ne negaret*" (Hartel, S. *Thasci Caecili Cypriani*, 3.2:582).

20. Cyprian, *Epistle* 39.1.2: "*quem sic Dominus honoravit caelestis gloriae dignitate*" (Hartel, S. *Thasci Caecili Cypriani*, 3.2:582).

21. Cyprian, *Epistle* 39.1.2: "*quia nec fas fuerat nec decebat sine honore ecclesiastico esse quem sic Dominus honoravit*" (Hartel, S. *Thasci Caecili Cypriani*, 3.2:582).

22. Cyprian, *Epistle* 39.1.

23. Adolf von Harnack, "Cyprian als Enthusiast," *ZNTW* 3 (1902): 179 and 183. One need not adopt such a cynical interpretation of Cyprian's motives, however. Patricia Cox Miller, "'A Dubious Twilight': Reflections on Dreams in Patristic Literature," *CH* 55 (June 1986): 164, suggests that "These voices [dream-speakers] testify to a way of thinking, lying dormant in the Western religious tradition, that has been largely neglected: that the language of the dream was an important religious language for early Christians, as it was for their cultural fellows."

24. Von Harnack, "Cyprian als Enthusiast," 183: "*Die Wahl des Saturus und Optatus kündigt er dem Clerus einfach an (weil sie, wie er behauptet, schon früher zu diesen Amtern designiert worden sein), die aber des Celerinus . . . und Numidicus . . . motiviert er unter Berufung auf göttliche Kundgebungen. . . . die Einsetzung des Celerinus wird durch eine Vision nachträglich von Gott bestätigt—Celerinus hat die Offenbarung gehabt.*"

25. Ibid.; see also Luc Duquenne, *Chronologie des lettres de S. Cyprien* (Brussels: Société des Bollandistes, 1972), 159.

26. Cyprian, *Epistle* 40.1: "*Carissimus ac desiderantissimus fratribus*" (Hartel, S. *Thasci Caecili Cypriani*, 3.2:585).

27. Cyprian, *Epistle* 40.1.1; Clarke, *Letters*, 2:57058; Hartel, S. *Thasci Caecili Cypriani*, 3.2.585; *ANF*, 5:314. See appendix H for an outline of the account regarding Celerinus beside that regarding Numidicus.

28. Von Harnack, "Cyprian als Enthusiast," 183: "*die Einsetzung des Celerinus wird durch eine Vision nachträgich von Gott bestätigt—Celerinus hat die Offenbarung gehabt—; die Einsetzung des Numidicus wird auf direkte göttliche Anweisung zurückgeführt.*"

29. Ibid., 184: "*Die Gemeinde soll sich mit der blossen Thatsache begnugen.*"

30. Cyprian, *Epistle* 66.8.1.

31. Ibid. 66.1.2.

32. Ibid. 66.10.1; Clarke, *Letters*, 3:122; Hartel, S. *Thasci Caecili Cypriani*, 3.2:734: "*Memini enim quid iam mihi sit ostensum, immo quid sit servo obsequenti et timenti de dominica et divina auctoritate praeceptum: qui inter cetera quae ostendere et revelare dignatus est et hoc addidit: 'itaque qui Christo non credit sacerdotem facienti postea credere incipiet sacerdotem vindicanti.'*"

33. It seems that Cyprian's word here is to be understood in much the same

way that Ignatius's was a century before. See Ignatius, *To the Philadelphians*, 7: "Do nothing without the bishop."

34. Cyprian, *Epistle* 66.10. A. d'Ales, "Le mysticisme de Saint Cyprien," *RAM* 2 (1921): 258, wrote: "*Tout de monde ne goûtait pas les visionnaires; Cyprien le savait mieux que personne. Sa correspondence nous fait connaître un certain Florentius, qui blâmait dan l'évêque diverses choses et notamment ses visions.*"

35. Von Harnack, "Cyprian als Enthusiast," 185: "*die Offenbarung, auf die sich Cyprian beruft, ist ihm selbst geschenkt worden, daher auch hier wieder, wie oben sub 1 (Schluss), der Ausdruck der Bescheidenheit.*"

36. Ibid.: "*Episkopalismus und Enthusiasmus haben sich in Cyprian enge verbunden.*" Translation mine. This fact is noted also by W. H. C. Frend, *The Donatist Church* (Oxford: Clarendon Press, 1971), 131. This point in particular is used by James L. Ash, "The Decline of Ecstatic Prophecy in the Early Church," *TS* 37 (1976): 250, to argue for the takeover of prophecy by the episcopate. For him, Cyprian is the epitome or culmination of those bishops who fought against the misuse of the prophetic gifts but who, in capturing these gifts, contributed to their demise within the congregation as genuine practical charismata.

37. Cyprian, *Epistle* 66.9: "*prius dominum meum consulam an tibi pacem dari et te ad communicationem ecclesiae suae admitti sua ostensione et admonitione permittat*" (Hartel, *S. Thasci Caecili Cypriani*, 3.2:733–34).

38. Von Harnack, "Cyprian als Enthusiast," 183.

39. Cyprian, *Epistle* 39.1.

40. E. A. Andrews, ed., *Harpers' Latin Dictionary: A New Latin Dictionary* (New York: American Book, 1907), 893–94.

41. Von Harnack, "Cyprian als Enthusiast," 190: "*Wie über Cyprian's 'Enthusiasmus' zu urteilen ist, überlasse ich dem Leser; aber ich darf ihn wohl davor warnen, den Bischof für einen 'heuchlerischen Pfaffen' zu eklären und unter dieses Urteil alles zu subsummieren. Gewiss hat es hier eine Linie gegeben, von welcher an der Enthusiasmus verschwand und die Politik eintrat; aber wo diese lag, hat Cyprian schwerlich selbst gewusst. Er hatte wie das un der Antike üblich, heilige Traüme; sie kamen öfters gerade dann, wenn er sie brauchte, und das übrige gab sich fast von selbst und noch einiges dazu.*"

42. Michael M. Sage, *Cyprian*, PMS, 1 (Cambridge, Mass.: Philadelphia Patristic Foundation, 1975), 204. Cf. Peter Brown, *The Making of Late Antiquity* (Cambridge, Mass.: Harvard University Press, 1978), 79–80, esp. 124, n. 99.

43. Clarke, *Letters*, 1:287–88.

44. However, Peter Hinchliff, *Cyprian of Carthage and the Unity of the Christian Church* (London: Geoffrey Chapman, 1974), 26, seems to accept von Harnack's position fully.

CHAPTER FOURTEEN

1. Cyprian, *Epistles* 10.4; 58.1; 78.1–2; and 6.1–3.

2. Ibid. 6. The date is that established by Luc Duquenne, *Chronologie des lettres de S. Cyprien* (Brussels: Société des Bollandistes, 1972), 159, and clearly

established by G. W. Clarke, *The Letters of St. Cyprian*, ACW, 43, 44, 46, 47 (New York: Newman Press, 1984, 1986, 1989), 1:190. It is held to be a possibility by Ernest Wallis in *ANF*, 5:406, n. 5, although he prefers a date near the end of Cyprian's final imprisonment, about A.D. 257, a date that may be preferred because Rogatianus is mentioned in *Epistles* 7; 12; 41; 42; and 43.

3. Cyprian, *Epistle* 6.1.2; Clarke, *Letters*, 1:63; Guilelmus Hartel, *S. Thasci Caecili Cypriani Opera Omnia*, CSEL (Vienna: C. Geroldi Filium Bibliopolam Academiae, 1871), 3.2:480; *ANF*, 5:406.

4. The passage to which Cyprian makes reference is Matt. 28:20b: "lo, I am with you always, to the close of the age." Gregory Dix, "The Ministry in the Early Church," in *The Apostolic Ministry: Essays on the History and the Doctrine of Episcopacy*, ed. Kenneth E. Kirk (London: Hodder and Stoughton, 1946), 224, writes, "In the later second century there had arisen a general belief (resting on Matthew x. 19–20 and Mark xiii. 11) that the martyrs and confessors endured their torments only by the aid of a special *charisma* of the Holy Spirit personally present with them." See also Joseph H. Fichter, *Saint Cecil Cyprian* (London: B. Herder, 1942), 180–81. This was also the conclusion of G. W. H. Lampe, "Martyrdom and Inspiration," in *Suffering and Martyrdom in the New Testament*, ed. William Horbury and Brian McNeil (Cambridge: Cambridge University Press, 1981), 118–35, which was also published in G. W. H. Lampe, *Explorations in Theology 8* (London: SCM Press, 1981), 71–88, and William C. Weinrich, *Spirit and Martyrdom* (Washington, D.C.: University Press of America, 1981), 277–78.

5. Cyprian, *Epistle* 6.2.1; Clarke, *Letters*, 1.64; Hartel, *S. Thasci Caecili Cypriani*, 3.2:481; *ANF*, 5:407.

6. John 14:26: "But the Advocate, the Holy Spirit whom the Father will send in my name, will teach you everything, and remind you of all that I have said to you."

7. According to Cyprian, such passages, include Ps. 51:19; John 12:25; Matt. 10:28, 28:20, Rom. 8:16–18, etc.

8. Cyprian, *Epistle* 6.3; Hartel, *S. Thasci Caecili Cypriani*, 3.2:483; *ANF*, 5:407.

9. Matt. 10:19–20. This theme is a popular one in the gospels; cf. Luke 12:11–12; 21:11–19; Mark 13:9–13. It was a promise made by Jesus himself, and it showed a close relationship between a legitimate use of the gift of prophecy and martyrdom. See also E. Earle Ellis, *The Gospel of Luke*, ed. H. H. Rowley and Matthew Black, NCB (Greenwood, S.C.: Attic Press, 1974), 243–44, on the parallel passage in Luke. I. Howard Marshall, *The Gospel of Luke*, NIGTC (Exeter: Paternoster Press, 1978), 520–21, 766–67, sees it as an impartation of divine wisdom.

10. What Cyprian seems to have in mind is something akin to Stephen's visionary experience at the moment of his martyrdom (Acts 7:55–56).

11. Cyprian, *Epistle* 10; *ANF*, 5:287.

12. In this case, Cyprian clearly relies on the Matt. 10:19–20 version of this saying.

13. Cyprian, *Epistle* 10.4.1; Clarke, *Letters*, 1:73; ANF, 5:288; Hartel, *S. Thasci Caecili Cypriani*, 3.2:492: "*Documentum rei praesens proelium praebuit. vox plena spiritu sancto de martyris ore prorupit, cum Mappalicus beatissimus inter cruciatus suos proconsuli diceret: 'videbis cras agonem.' et quod ille cum virtutis ac fidei testimonio dixit Dominus impleuit. agon caelestis exhibitus et Dei servus in agonis promissi certamine coronatus est.*"

14. For a clearer understanding of Cyprian's meaning here, one should refer to *Epistle* 81 in which he wrote clearly: "For whatever a confessor-bishop speaks at the very moment he confesses his faith he speaks under inspiration of God (*aspirante Deo*)"; Clarke, *Letters*, 4.105; ANF, 5:409; Hartel, *S. Thasci Caecili Cypriani*, 3.2:341.

15. Cf. Cyprian, *Epistle* 27.1, which speaks of Mappalicus's request that his mother and sister, both *lapsi*, be reinstated; also 22.2.

16. Ibid. 10.4; ANF, 5:288; Hartel, *S. Thasci Caecili Cypriani*, 3.2:492: "*vox plena spiritu sancto de martyris ore prorupit.*" A similar comment is made about Cyprian in *Epistle* 78.2.

17. The term *agon* was generally used in connection with a contest in the public games. In the case of Mappalicus, it may have been to face either gladiators or wild beasts. See E. A. Andrews, ed., *Harpers' Latin Dictionary: A New Latin Dictionary* (New York: American Book, 1907), 77.

18. The reference to a predictive word said by a voice "full of the Holy Spirit" and confessed with virtue and "faith" tends to underscore the belief that the gift of prophecy is in focus here. See Rom. 12:6.

19. Cyprian, *Epistle* 10.4; Hartel, *S. Thasci Caecili Cypriani*, 3.2:492: "*quod ille . . . dixit Domnus impleuit.*"

20. This test is an application of the guideline in Deut. 18:22: "If a prophet speaks in the name of the Lord, but the thing does not take place or prove true, it is a word that the Lord has not spoken. The prophet has spoken it presumptuously, you need not be frightened by it."

21. This is a primary function for a prophetic oracle according to Paul. Cf. 1 Cor. 14:3.

22. Cyprian, *Epistle* 58.1.2; Clarke, *Letters*, 3:60; Hartel, *S. Thasci Caecili Cypriani*, 3.2:656; ANF, 5:347.

23. Cyprian, *Epistle* 58.1.2; Clarke, *Letters*, 3:60; ANF, 5:347.

24. Cyprian, *Epistle* 58.1; Hartel, *S. Thasci Caecili Cypriani*, 3.2:656: "*pressurae diem super caput esse coepisse et occasum saeculi atque antichristi tempus adpropinquasse.*" Translation mine.

25. Cyprian seems to have had a thought in mind here that runs parallel to 1 John 2:18: "Children, it is the last hour! As you have heard that antichrist is coming, so now many antichrists have come. From this we know that it is the last hour." Cyprian's words require only an equation between John's "last hour" ($\dot{\epsilon}\sigma\chi\acute{\alpha}\tau\eta$ $\H{\omega}\rho\alpha$) and Cyprian's "end of the age" (*occasum saeculi*). Cf. 2 Thess. 2:1–12. See Edward White Benson, *Cyprian: His Life, His Times, His Work* (London: Macmillan, 1897), 258.

26. Cyprian, *Epistle* 58.1.2; Clarke, *Letters*, 3:60.

27. Cyprian, *Epistle* 58.1.2; Clarke, *Letters*, 3:60; ANF, 5:347.

28. Cyprian, *Epistle* 58.5.2; Clarke, *Letters*, 3:64; Hartel, *S. Thasci Caecili Cypriani*, 3.2:661: "*dixit quid loqui et respondere possimus dari nobis in illa hora divinitus et offerri, nec nos tunc esse qui loquimur, sed spiritum Dei patris: qui cum a confitentibus non discredit neque dividitur, ipse in nobis et loquitur et coronatur.*" See here, *Epistle* 81.2, and Tertullian, *On Modesty*, 22; note here, too, a great similarity to the position taken by the redactor of *The Passion of Perpetua and Felicitas* who recorded the words of Felicitas in *The Passion* 15.6: "What I am suffering now . . . I suffer by myself. But then [at the time of my martyrdom] another (*alius*) will be inside me (*in me*) who will suffer for me (*prop me*), just as I shall be suffering for him (*prop illo*)."

29. This conception of the gift of prophecy is generally similar to that conveyed in the oracle of Montanus, which is preserved by Epiphanius, *Panarion* 48:4 (Ronald E. Heine, *The Montanist Oracles and Testimonia*, PMS, 14 [Macon, Ga.: Mercer University Press, 1989], 3):

> Behold, man   is like a lyre
>   and I flit about like a a plectron;
>   man sleeps
>   and I awaken him;
> behold, it is the Lord who changes the hearts of men
>   and gives men a heart.

For further information on the *Christus in martyre* theme, see Clarke, *Letters*, 1:228, 235–36.

30. Cyprian, *Epistle* 78.2.

31. Ibid. 76.1; 77.3; 78.1; 79.

32. Undoubtedly *Epistle* 76 is the one which Cyprian wrote and to which Lucius refers, while *Epistles* 77, 78, and 79 included what was written to Cyprian in response to it. The correspondence seems to be dated while Cyprian was in exile at Curubis, about A.D. 257; cf. Duquenne, *Chronologie des lettres de S. Cyprien*, 161; Clarke, *Letters*, 4:277–78.

33. *Epistle* 78.1.1; Clarke, *Letters*, 4:102; "*recepimus in vinculis laxamentum, in pressura solacium et in necessitate praesidium*" (Hartel, *S. Thasci Caecili Cypriani*, 3.2:836); ANF, 5:405. The response from Bishops Nemesianus, Dativus, Felix, and Victor (*Epistle* 77.3) makes it clear that they too, as well as many others, received some measure of edification from Cyprian's words.

34. *Epistle* 78.1.2; Clarke, *Letters*, 4:102; "*excitati sumus et robustius animati ac si quid amplius fuerit poenarum*" (Hartel, *S. Thasci Caecili Cypriani*, 3.2:836); ANF, 5:405.

35. *Epistle* 78.2.2; Clarke, *Letters*, 4:102–3; I have marked the italicized portion for emphasis. It reads: "*ad prophetiam quam litteris tuis spiritu sancto plenus spopondisti*" (Hartel, *S. Thasci Caecili Cypriani*, 3.2:837); ANF, 5:406. While Nemesianus did not use the word "prophecy" to describe what Cyprian conveyed to the bishops in the mines, he did speak of the writing of Cyprian as laying bare "the hidden mysteries," which resulted in the captive bishops growing in faith,

and made it possible for men of the world to draw near to belief (*Epistle* 77.1); "*dum enim non desinis tractatibus tuis sacramenta occulta nudare, sic nos in fidem facis crescere et de saeculo homines ad credulitatem accedere*" (Hartel, *S. Thasci Caecili Cypriani*, 3.2:834). Nemesianus's use of the phrase "the hidden mysteries" (*sacramenta occulta*) parallels the recognition of Paul in Eph. 3:1–6 that prophecy consists at times in a mystery revealed by God.

36. *Epistle* 76.1.2; Clarke, *Letters*, 4:95; Hartel, *S. Thasci Caecili Cypriani*, 3.2:828; *ANF*, 5:402–3.

37. *Epistle* 76.7.3; Clarke, *Letters*, 4:99–100; Hartel, *S. Thasci Caecili Cypriani*, 3.2:833; *ANF*, 5:404.

38.

Matthew 10:19–20	Luke 21:14–15
When they deliver you up do not be anxious how you are to speak or what you are to say; for what you are to say will be given to you in that hour; for it is not you who speak but the Spirit of your father speaking through you.	Settle it there in your minds, not to meditate before how to answer; for I will give you a mouth and wisdom which none of your adversaries will be able to withstand or contradict.

The number of times in which these passages (especially Matthew's version) were cited and affirmed by Cyprian is staggering. Cf. *Epistles* 10.4; 57.4; 58.5; 76.5; 81.1; and *Treatises* 11.10; 12.3.16. Michael Andrew Fahey, *Cyprian and the Bible* (Tübingen: J. C. B. Mohr, 1971), 294, remarks that "This is one of the most frequently cited Biblical quotations in Cyprian's writings." Cf. Clarke, *Letters*, 1:233, who notes, "Cyprian obviously interprets the passage in a very literal sense: this indicates an essential feature of the current theology of martyrdom— martyrs were in a position of privileged access to the Holy Spirit . . . ; hence the dominant motif in the *Acta* tradition of an *apologia* by the martyr before the magistrate on the tribunal."

39. The passage to which he refers is Rom. 8:18, as cited in *Epistle* 76.7.2; Clarke, *Letters*, 4:99; *ANF*, 5:404.

40. *Epistle*, 78.2.2; Clarke, *Letters*, 4:103.

CHAPTER FIFTEEN

1. Luc Duquenne, *Chronologie des lettres de S. Cyprien* (Brussels: Société des Bollandistes, 1972), 159 (A.D. 250). See appendix I for a comparison of these four visions.

2. Cyprian, *Epistle* 11.1–2.

3. Ibid. 11.3; Guilelmus Hartel, *S. Thasci Caecili Cypriani Opera Omnia*, CSEL (Vienna: C. Geroldi Filium Bibliopolam Academiae, 1871), 3.2:497: "*scire debetis, sicut Dominus ostendere et revelare dignatur, dictum esse in visione: 'petite et inpetratis.'*"

4. The nature of prescriptive oracles is described in David E. Aune, *Prophecy in Early Christianity and the Ancient Mediterranean World* (Grand Rapids: William B. Eerdmans, 1983), 321–22.

5. To have emphasized the ability of the Carthaginian congregation to receive as opposed to the Lord's ability to give does not seem to violate the intent of Jesus' words in Matt. 7, but undoubtedly the two served slightly different purposes.

6. Adolf von Harnack, "Cyprian als Enthusiast," *ZNTW* 3 (1902): 180, also finds this passage not to be totally clear when he writes, "*Die Vision ist un-deutlich—wo hat sie angefangen, wo endigt sie?*" I will attempt to establish the limits of the vision itself, but the passage is obscure. G. W. Clarke, *The Letters of St. Cyprian*, ACW, 43, 44, 46, 47 (New York: Newman Press, 1984, 1986, 1989), 1:243, merely mentions its vagueness, which he suggests, "matches the generality of its message."

7. See Peter Hinchliff, *Cyprian of Carthage and the Unity of the Christian Church* (London: Geoffrey Chapman, 1974), 51.

8. Von Harnack, "Cyprian als Enthusiast," 180. Harnack's reconstruction again has some plausibility to it, but it does not fit all the facts in Cyprian's account.

9. Appeals were made to Ps. 118:6; Acts 4:32; John 15:2; and Matt. 18:19.

10. Cyprian, *Epistle* 11.3.

11. Ibid., 11.3.2; Clarke, *Letters*, 1:77; ANF, 5:286; Hartel, *S. Thasci Caecili Cypriani*, 3.2:498: "*immo vero nec venissent fratribus haec mala, si in unum frater-nitas fuisset animata.*"

12. The test of the fruit of the prophet (Matt. 7:15–20) is unusable since the text does not reveal who delivered the vision/prophecy. The test of fulfillment based on Deut. 18:22 does not seem to be applicable. There was division within the congregation, but the vision/prophecy is exhortative and not predictive in nature. The method of delivery is beyond recovery, and, therefore, beyond the realm of judgment within our contemporary setting. We can only rely on Cyprian's ability to judge such things as they took place in his presence. His judgment was that the vision/prophecy was from the Lord.

13. Cyprian, *Epistle* 11.4; ANF 5:286; Hartel, *S. Thasci Caecili Cypriani*, 3.2:498: "*Nam et illud ostensum est.*"

14. Von Harnack, "Cyprian als Enthusiast," 179, argued regarding the first two visions: "*Wer diese Vision erlebt hat, das sagt Cyprian nicht; die Ausleger nehmen hier und bei den gleich zu besprechenden beiden folgenden Visionen als selbstverständlich an, dass Cyprian selbst der Visionär sei.*"

15. On Figure 7, see Cyprian, *Epistle* 11.4; ANF, 5:286; von Harnack, "Cyprian als Enthusiast," 498.

16. See Acts 7:55–56 for the version of Jesus standing at the right hand of God at the moment of Stephen's martyrdom; *Shepherd of Hermas*, Vision 2:4, describes a young man of comely appearance who leads Hermas through several visions; cf. Visions 3.10–13; 5; etc. Cyprian, *Treatise* 7 (*On Mortality*, 19–20, records the vision of another priest while he lay on his deathbed) and Pontius, *The Life and Passion of Cyprian, Bishop and Martyr*, 12, undoubtedly meant it understood that the man is Jesus. See here, Gustave Bardy, *La vie spirituelle d'après les pères des trois premiers siècles* (Tournai, Belgium: Desclée et Cie, 1968), 2:200.

17. John 15:2; Cyprian, *Epistle* 11.3.1.

18. Paul, for instance, calls Satan "the Destroyer" in 1 Cor. 10:10.

19. Cyprian, *Epistle* 11.4.2; Clarke, *Letters*, 1:78; ANF, 5:286; von Harnack, "Cyprian als Enthusiast," 498. Hinchliff, *Cyprian of Carthage*, 42, writes: "In appealing for constant readiness and obedience Cyprian was simply echoing Tertullian's insistence that Christians must live at all times the kind of life that would enable them to stand firm whenever persecution might come." Cf. Tertullian, *On Flight in Persecution*, 9:1–4.

20. Cyprian, *Epistle* 11.4.1 and 11.3.1; Clarke, *Letters*, 1:77.

21. Cyprian, *Epistle* 11.4; von Harnack, "Cyprian als Enthusiast," 498: "*hoc prius longe ostensum est quam tempestas vastitatis huius oriretur. et videmus impletum quod fuerat ostensum.*"

22. Cyprian, *Epistle* 11.5.1; Clarke, *Letters*, 1:78; ANF, 5:286; von Harnack, "Cyprian als Enthusiast," 498.

23. It is interesting to note the Vulgate's related *gemitibus inerarrabilibus* in verse 26. Thus, while it is by no means certain, Cyprian may here be encouraging prayer in tongues if that is what Paul has in mind in Rom. 8:26–27. That, of course, is still a debatable issue. Cf. Ernst Käsemann, *Perspectives on Paul* (Philadelphia: Fortress Press, 1971), 122–37. See above, chapter 4, n. 6.

24. Cyprian here quotes from Heb. 12:6 or Prov. 3:12: "For the Lord disciplines who he loves."

25. Cyprian, *Epistle* 11.5.2; Clarke, *Letters*, 1:78–79.

26. Cyprian, *Epistle* 11.6.1; Clarke, *Letters*, 1:79; ANF, 5:287.

27. Cyprian, *Epistle* 11.6; Hartel, *S. Thasci Caecili Cypriani*, 3.2:500.

28. See von Harnack, "Cyprian als Enthusiast," 181.

29. Von Harnack, "Cyprian als Enthusiast," 181: "*Die Vision ist so zu denken, dass Gott einem Engel.*" It has been suggested that the messenger was the same young man who appeared in another vision in Cyprian's writings. See H. Carey, trans., *The Epistles of S. Cyprian: A Library of the Fathers* (Oxford: John Henry Parker, 1844), 27, n. i.

30. Aune, *Prophecy in Early Christianity*, 326.

31. Cyprian, *Epistle* 11.6; ANF, 5:287; Hartel, *S. Thasci Caecili Cypriani*, 3.2:500: "*dic, illi, . . . securus sit, quia pax ventura est, sed quod interim morula est, supersunt adhuc aliqui qui probentur.*"

32. Carey, *Epistles of S. Cyprian*, 27, n. k; cf. ANF, 5:287, n. 2.

33. Cyprian, *Epistle* 11:6–7; Hartel, *S. Thasci Caecili Cypriani*, 3.2:500.

34. Cyprian, *Epistle* 11.6; ANF, 5:287. Such argumentation is reminiscent of Tertullian's own words (*On Fasting*, 1.4).

CHAPTER SIXTEEN

1. Cyprian, *Epistles* 8.1; 16.4; 20.1.

2. Ibid. 20.1.

3. Cyprian, *Epistle* 8, raises the question and points to Crementius as the one who carried the news of Cyprian's retreat to Rome.

4. Ibid. 20.1.2; G. W. Clarke, *The Letters of St. Cyprian*, ACW 43, 44, 46, 47 (New York: Newman Press, 1984, 1986, 1989), 1:101. This entire epistle is a response to questions from the Roman clergy regarding his action. Clarke, 307–8, indicates that we are not here dealing with visions or prophecies but, rather, with "scriptural injunctions" such as those found in Matt. 10:23. He rightly suggests that Cyprian may also have in mind Isa. 52:11 and Rev. 18:4. He also notes that Cyprian does not mention the role which visions or prophetic promptings might have played in his retirement. Rather skeptically, Clarke asks, "did he sense the vulnerability of such an argument?" His question is well taken, for unlike his perception of his own congregation, Cyprian may have felt threatened by his Roman inquisitors.

5. Cyprian, *Epistle* 16.4: "*Dominus, qui ut secederem iussit*" (Guilelmus Hartel, *S. Thasci Caecili Cypriani Opera Omnia*, CSEL (Vienna: C. Geroldi Filium Bibliopolam Academiae, 1871), 3.2:520); ANF, 5:290.

6. Cyprian, *Epistle* 16.4.1; Clarke, *Letters*, 1:95; ANF, 5:290. Hartel, *S. Thasci Caecili Cypriani*, 3.2:520: "*praeter nocturnas visiones per dies quoque impletur apud nos spiritu sancto puerorum innocens aetas, quae in ecstasi videt oculis et audit et loquiter ea quibus nos Dominus monere et instruere dignatur. et audietis omnia quando me ad vos reducem fecerit Dominus, qui ut secederem iussit.*" This epistle dates from A.D. 250.

7. Cf. Cyprian, *Epistle* 20.1.2. Note the general nature of Cyprian's remarks in *Epistle* 20 and the more specific nature of his remarks in the present passage. Cf Clarke, *Letters*, 1:290. William Tabbernee, "Early Montanism and Voluntary Martyrdom," *Col* 17(2) (May 1985): 33, rightly observers that "Cyprian . . . defended his flight . . . by claiming that as God had not specifically directed him to be a martyr, he could serve the church better by remaining alive, if in hiding."

8. Cyprian, *Epistle* 7; circa A.D. 250, according to Luc Duquenne, *Chronologie des lettres de S. Cyprien* (Brussels: Société des Bollandistes, 1972), 159.

9. Cyprian, *Epistle* 7.1: "*quando ergo vos scripseritis rebus compositis me venire debere aut*" (Hartel, *S. Thasci Caecili Cypriani*, 3.2:485).

10. Cyprian, *Epistle* 7.1: "*si ante dignatus fuerit Dominus ostendere, tunc ad vos veniam*" (Hartel, *S. Thasci Caecili Cypriani*, 3.2:485).

11. Pontius, *The Life and Passion of Cyprian, Bishop and Martyr*, 7. From the language of Pontius, this work is of mixed value. On the one hand, it is clearly a hagiographic text written to satisfy Pontius's apologetic passion; cf. Aronen, "Indebtedness to Passio Perpetuae in Pontius' Vita Cypriani," VC 38 (1984): 67–76. The document does, however, contain some passages that reveal a more objective and, hence, reliable hand. One such passage is the account of Cyprian's vision in section 12.

12. Pontius, *Life and Passion of Cyprian, Bishop and Martyr*, 7; "*vultis sciere secessum illum non fuisse formidinem?*" (Hartel, *S. Thasci Caecili Cypriani*, 3.3:xcviii).

13. Pontius, *Life and Passion of Cyprian, Bishop and Martyr*, 7; ANF, 5:270; "*bene bene tunc et vere spiritaliter contigit, quod vir necessarius tam multis et tam bonis*

rebus a martyrii consummatione dilatus est" (Hartel, *S. Thasci Caecili Cypriani,* 3.3:xcviii).

14. Pontius, *Life and Passion of Cyprian, Bishop and Martyr,* 7, ANF, 5:270. Italics mine. The italicized portion reads: "*dicata enim in omnibus Deo mens et sic de divinis admonitionibus mancipata credidit se, nisi Domino latebram tunc iubenti parvisset, etiam ipsa passione peccare*" (Hartel, *S. Thasci Caecili Cypriani,* 3.3:xcviii).

15. Cyprian, *Epistles* 16.4; 39.1; and *Treatise* 7.19.

16. W. H. C. Frend, *The Early Church* (London: Hodder and Stoughton, 1965), 116. For a description of these events as recorded by Dionysius, see Eusebius, *Ecclesiastical History,* 7.10.1–9; NPNF, 1:298–99.

17. Eusebius, *Ecclesiastical History,* 7.11.6–11.

18. Pontius, *Life and Passion of Cyprian, Bishop and Martyr,* 11–12.

19. Cyprian became the first bishop-martyr of the African Church exactly one year after he was banished. This is known from the vision, which was said to have predicted a one-year imprisonment (Pontius, *Life and Passion of Cyprian, Bishop and Martyr,* 12–13, 15, 19). Cf. *The Acts of St. Cyprian,* 1.1–2.1, for an account of Cyprian's appearance before the proconsul Paternus. It is impossible to know whether the writer of *The Acts of St. Cyprian* made use of the actual court records, but Herbert Musurillo has rightly observed that "the document presents an impression of honesty and objectivity" (*The Acts of the Christian Martyrs,* OECT [Oxford: Clarendon Press, 1972], xxxi).

20. Pontius, *Life and Passion of Cyprian, Bishop and Martyr,* 12; ANF, 5:271–72. Edgar J. Goodspeed, *A History of Early Christian Literature* (Chicago: University of Chicago Press, 1966), 177, remarks of Pontius's work, "The *Life* by Pontius runs through the questions dealt with in the treatises so accurately that a collection of them, and probably of the letters, must have lain before the deacon when he wrote." Undoubtedly, the genuineness of this vision must bear equivalent value in any assessment of the thought of Cyprian on the subject.

21. Pontius, *Life and Passion of Cyprian, Bishop and Martyr,* 12.

22. Peter Hinchliff, *Cyprian of Carthage and the Unity of the Christian Church* (London: Geoffrey Chapman, 1974), 123.

23. See also Edward White Benson, *Cyprian: His Life, His Times, His Work* (London: Macmillan, 1897), 470, who wrote, "His candour about the fright it gave him shows a trustworthy witness to a really remarkable dream."

24. Pontius, *Life and Passion of Cyprian, Bishop and Martyr,* 12–13. The words are "God's wonderful visitation" (*admirabilem visitationem Dei*); an appearance (*apparvit mihi . . . nondum somni quieto sopito*); a revelation (*revelatione manifestius*); a condescension (*dignatione felicius*); and a vision (*visionem*) (Hartel, *S. Thasci Caecili Cypriani,* 3.3:cii–civ).

25. One could argue without too much difficulty that the term which best describes such an altered state of consciousness is none other than *ecstasis*. Cf. Tertullian, *Against Marcion,* 4.22.4; 5.8.12; *On the Soul,* 21.2 and esp. 45.3.

26. See above, chapter 15, note 16.

27. The use of prophetic symbolism is nothing new here, for it is a consistent

pattern in both Old and New Testament prophecy. Cf. 1 Kings 11:29–40; Isa. 20:2–6; Jer. 13:1–11; 28:10–11; Ezek. 4:1–3; and Acts 21:11.

28. Pontius, *Life and Passion of Cyprian, Bishop and Martyr*, 13.

29. Ibid., 12.

30. Ibid., 13.

31. Ibid.; *ANF*, 5:272.

32. Pontius, *Life and Passion of Cyprian, Bishop and Martyr*, 13; *ANF*, 5:272.

33. Pontius, *Life and Passion of Cyprian, Bishop and Martyr*, 13; *ANF*, 5:272. The incident to which he referred is found in Luke 1:63 and relates to the priest Zacharias.

34. Pontius, *Life and Passion of Cyprian, Bishop and Martyr*, 13.

35. Frend, *Early Church*, 117, cf. Eusebius, *Ecclesiastical History*, 7.10–11.

36. Pontius, *Life and Passion of Cyprian, Bishop and Martyr*, 13; cf. Cyprian, *Epistles* 77.3; 78.3; 79; and 6.1–4.

37. Cyprian, *Epistle* 81.2.

CHAPTER SEVENTEEN

1. An intense debate on the actual date of its emergence has raged for years, due largely to the apparent disagreement among certain of the few early sources that speak about it. Eusebius, *Ecclesiastical History*, 4.27; 5.17.4, appears to set it about A.D. 172. Epiphanius in his *Panarion*, 48.1.2, seems to put it about A.D. 157. I have chosen the later date as the more probable, having followed the arguments set forth by Timothy D. Barnes, "The Chronology of Montanism," *JTS*, n.s., 21 (1970): 403–8, and D. Powell, "Tertullianists and Cataphrygians," *VC* 29 (1975): 41, although, as Barnes has pointed out, final resolution of the problem must await further conclusive evidence.

2. Eusebius, *Ecclesiastical History*, 5.16.4, 10, 22; 5.18.13; 5.19.3.

3. Tertullian, *Against Praxeas*, 1.5.

4. Jerome, *Letter* 84.2: "The blessed Cyprian takes Tertullian for his master as his writings prove; yet, delighted as he is with the ability of this learned and zealous writer, he does not join him in following Montanus and Maximilla." Cf. Jerome, *Lives of Illustrious Men*, 53.

5. To argue that Cyprian should be understood as post-New Prophecy does not mean that the New Prophecy, or as it would later be called, Montanism, was dead by his day. It was very much alive as is evidenced by Jerome's *Letter* 41, which he addressed from Rome about A.D. 385 to a woman, Marcella, who had faced an effort to convert her in his own day to Montanism. It means merely that Cyprian had most probably moved the congregation away from the excesses of that movement while maintaining the legitimacy of an enthusiastic form of Spirit inspiration in the form of condescensions.

6. William C. Weinrich, *Spirit and Martyrdom* (Washington, D.C.: University Press of America, 1981), 276–77.

7. G. W. H. Lampe, "Martyrdom and Inspiration," in *Suffering and Martyr-*

dom in the New Testament, ed. William Horbury and Brian McNeil (Cambridge: Cambridge University Press, 1981), 122; cf. 135.

8. James L. Ash, "The Decline of Ecstatic Prophecy in the Early Church," TS 37 (1976): 252.

9. Benjamin B. Warfield, Counterfeit Miracles (London: Banner of Truth Trust, 1972), 23–24.

ARTICLES

Aland, Kurt. "Bemerkungen zum Montanismus und zur frühchristlichen Eschatologie." In *Kirchen geschichtliche Entwürfe: Alte Kirche, Reformation und Luthertum, Pietismus und Erweckungsbewegung,* edited by Kurt Aland, 105–48. Gütersloh: Verlagshaus Gerd Mohn, 1960.

Alden, Robert L. "Ecstasy and the Prophets." *Journal of the Evangelical Theological Society* 9 (1966): 149–56.

d'Ales, A. "L'auteur de la passio Perpetuae." *Revue d'histoire ecclésiastique* 8 (1907): 5–18.

———. "Le mysticisme de Saint Cyprien." *Revue d'ascétique et de mystique* 2 (1921): 256–67.

Anderson, H. "4 Maccabees." In *The Old Testament Pseudepigrapha,* edited by James H. Charlesworth, 2:531–64. Garden City: Doubleday, 1985.

Aronen, Jaakko. "Indebtedness to Passio Perpetuae in Pontius' Vita Cypriani," *Vigiliae Christianae* 38 (1984): 67–76.

Ash, James L. "The Decline of Ecstatic Prophecy in the Early Church." *Theological Studies* 37 (1976): 227–52.

Atkinson, P. C. "The Montanist Interpretation of Joel 2:28, 29 (LXX 3:1, 2)." Texte und Untersuchungen, 126. *Studia Evangelica* 7 (1982): 11–15.

Aune, David E. "*Herm. Man.* 11.2: Christian False Prophets Who Say What People Wish to Hear." *Journal of Biblical Literature* 97(1) (1978): 103–4.

———. "The Odes of Solomon and Early Christian Prophecy," *New Testament Studies* 28 (1981/82): 435–60.

Bardy, Gustav. "Les martyrs de Carthage." In his *La vie spirituelle d'après les pères des trois premiers siècles.* Tournai, Belgium: Desclée et Cie, 1968, 1:216–24.

Barnes, Timothy D. "Pre-Decian *Acta Martyrum.*" *Journal of Theological Studies,* n.s., 19(2) (October 1968): 509–31.

———. "The Chronology of Montanism." *Journal of Theological Studies,* n.s., 21 (1970): 403–8.

Bastiaensen, A. A. R. "Tertullian's Reference to the *Passio Perpetuae* in *De Anima* 55, 4." *Studia Patristica* 17(2) (1982): 790–95.

Bender, Wolfgang. "Der Montanismus in Tertullians Lehre über den Heiligen Geist." In *Die Lehre über den Heiligen Geist bei Tertullian,* edited by Joseph Pascher and Klaus Morsdorf, 150–69. Münchener Theologische Studien. II Systematische Abteilung, vol. 19. Munich: Max Hueber Verlag, 1961.

Bonwetsch, N. "Montanus, Montanism." In *The New Schaff-Herzog Encyclopedia of Religious Knowledge,* edited by Samuel McCauley Jackson, 7:485–87. New York: Funk & Wagnalls, 1910.

Boring, M. Eugene. "The Apocalypse as Early Christian Prophecy: A Discussion of the Issues Raised by the Book of Revelation for the Study of Early Christian Prophecy." In *Society of Biblical Literature 1974 Seminar Papers,* edited by George Macrae. Cambridge: Society of Biblical Literature, 1974.

Braune, R. "Séance du 26 Mars 1955." *Revue des études Latines* 33 (1955): 78–81.

Cadbury, Henry J. "The Odor of the Spirit at Pentecost." *Journal of Biblical Literature* 47 (1928): 237–56.

Calder, W. M. "Philadelphia and Montanism." *Bulletin of the John Rylands Library* 7(3) (August 1923): 329.

Campos, Julio. "El autor de la 'Passio SS. Perpetua et Felicitatis'," *Helmantica* 10 (1959): 357–81.

Corsini, Eugenio. "Proposte per una Lettura della 'Passio Perpetua'." In *Forma Futuri: Studi in Onore del Cardinale Michele Pellegrino*, 481–541. Torino: Bottega d'Frasmo, 1975.

Cothenet, E. "Prophetisme Dans Le Nouveau Testament." In *Supplément au dictionarie de la Bible*. Fasc. 46–47, cols. 1222–1337. Paris: Letouzey & Ané, 1971, 1972.

Countryman, L. Wm. "Tertullian and the Regula Fidei." *The Second Century* 2(4) (Winter 1984): 208–27.

Davies, J. G. "Tertullian, 'De Resurrectione Carnis LXIII': A Note on the Origins of Montanism." *Journal of Theological Studies* 6 (1955): 90–94.

Dix, Gregory. "The Ministry in the Early Church." In *The Apostolic Ministry: Essays on the History and the Doctrine of Episcopacy*, edited by Kenneth E. Kirk, 183–303. London: Hodder and Stoughton, 1946.

Dodd, C. H. "The Appearances of the Risen Christ: An Essay in Form-Criticism of the Gospels." In *Studies in the Gospels: Essays in Memory of R. H. Lightfoot*, edited by D. E. Nineham, 9–35. Oxford: Basil Blackwell, 1955.

Dölger, F. J. "Antike Parallelen zum leidenden Dinocrates in der Passio Perpetuae," *Antike und Christentum* 2 (1930): 1–40.

———. "Gladiatorenblut und Martyrerblut: Eine Szene der Passio Perpetuae in Kultur- und religionsgeschichtlicher Beleuchtung." *Vörtrage der Bibliothek Warburg* (1923/1924): 196–214.

———. "ΘΕΟΥ ΦΩΝΗ: Die 'Gottes-Stimme' bei Ignatius von Antiochien, ειλσος und Origenes." *Antike und Christentum* 5 (1936): 218–23.

———. "Der Kampf mit dem Ägypter in der Perpetua-Vision: Das Martyrium als Kampf mit dem Teufel." *Antike und Christentum* 3 (1932): 177–88.

Fontaine, Jacques. "Tendances et difficultés d'une prose Chrétienne naissante": L'esthétique composite de la *Passio Perpetuae*." In his *Aspects et problèmes de la prose d'art Latin au IIIe siècle: La genèse des styles Latins Chretiens*. Torino: Bottega d'Erasmo, 1968.

Frend, William H. C. "Blandina and Perpetua: Two Early Christian Heroines." In *Les Martyrs de Lyon (177)*. Vol. 575, 167–77. Paris: Éditions du Centre National de la Recherche Scientifique, 1978.

———. "Open Questions Concerning the Christians and the Roman Empire in the Age of the Severi." *Journal of Theological Studies*, n.s., 25 (1974): 333–51.

———. "The *Memoriae Apostolorum* in Roman North Africa," *Journal of Roman Studies* 30 (1940): 32–49. Reprinted in W. H. C. Frend, *Town and Country in the Early Christian Centuries*. Vol. 18:32–49. London: Variorum Reprints, 1980.

――――. "A Severan Persecution? Evidence of the 'Historia Augusta.'" In *Forma Futuri: Studi in Onore Del Cardinale Michele Pellegrino*, 470–80. Torino: Bottega d'Erasmo, 1975.

――――. "Montanism: Research and Problems." *Revista di Storia e Letteratura Religiosa* 30 (1984): 521–37.

――――. "Montanism: A Movement of Prophecy and Regional Identity in the Early Church." *Bulletin of the John Rylands University Library of Manchester* 70(3) (Autumn 1988): 25–34.

Froehlich, Karlfried. "Montanism and Gnosis." In *The Heritage of the Early Christian Church*, edited by David Neiman and Margaret Schatkins, 91–111. Orientalia Christian Analecta, 195. Rome: Pont. Institutum Studiorum Orientalium, 1973.

Grant, Robert M. "Gnostic Spirituality." In *Christian Spirituality: Origins to the Twelfth Century*, edited by Bernard McGinn and John Meyendorff in collaboration with Jean Leclercq. World Spirituality: An Encyclopedic History of the Religious Quest, vol. 17. New York: Crossroad, 1985.

Greenslade, S. L. "Scripture and Other Doctrinal Norms in Early Theories of Ministry." *The Journal of Theological Studies* 44 (1943): 162–76.

Groh, Dennis E. "Utterance and Exegesis: Biblical Interpretation in the Montanist Crisis." In *The Living Text: Essays in Honor of Ernest W. Saunders*, edited by Dennis E. Groh and Robert Jewett, 73–95. Lanham: University Press of America, 1985.

Hanson, R. P. C. "Notes on Tertullian's Interpretation of Scripture." *Journal of Theological Studies*, n.s., 12 (1961): 273–79.

von Harnack, Adolf. "Cyprian als Enthusiast." *Zeitschrift für die neue testamentliche Wissenschaft* 3 (1902): 177–91.

Heine, Ronald E. "The Role of the Gospel of John in the Montanist Controversy." *The Second Century* 6(1) (Spring 1987–88): 1–19.

Jeremias, Joachim. "Ἀμήν." In *Theological Dictionary of the New Testament*, edited by Gerhard Kittel, translated and edited by Geoffrey W. Bromiley, 1:146–49. Grand Rapids: Wm. B. Eerdmans, 1946.

Johnson, T. A. "The Passion of SS. Perpetua and Felicitas." *Month* 153 (1929): 216–22.

Käsemann, Ernst. "An Apology for Primitive Christian Eschatology." In *Essays on New Testament Themes*, translated by W. J. Montague, 169–95. Philadelphia: Fortress Press, 1982.

Kee, Howard Clark. Review of *New Testament Prophecy* by David Hill. *Journal of the American Academy of Religion* 49 (1981): 677.

Klawiter, Frederick C. "The Role of Martyrdom and Persecution in Developing the Priestly Authority of Women in Early Christianity: A Case Study of Montanism." *Church History* 49 (1980): 251–61.

Klein, Johannes. "Tertullians theologische Ethik des Martyriums als Kommentar zur Passio Perpetuae." In *Tertullian: Christliches Bewusstsein und sittliche Forderungen*, edited by Fritz Tillmann, 274–313. Abhandlungen aus Ethik und

Moral, 15. Düsseldorf: Mosella-Verlag, 1940; republished, Hildescheim: H. A. Gerstenberg, 1975.

Kraft, Heinrich. "Vom Ende urchristlichen Prophetie." In *Prophetic Vocation in the New Testament and Today*, edited by J. Panagopoulos, 162–85. Novum Testamentum Supplement, 45. Leiden: E. J. Brill, 1977.

Kraft, Heinz. "Die altkirchliche Prophetie und die Entstehung des Montanismus." *Theologische Zeitschrift*, 11 (1955): 249–71.

Labriolle, Pierre de. "Les premières phases de l'évolution de Tertullien vers le Montanisme." In his *La Crise Montaniste*, 338–53. Paris: Ernest Leroux, 1913.

Lambdin, Thomas O., trans. "The Gospel of Thomas." In *The Nag Hammadi Library*, edited by James Robinson, 117–30. San Francisco: Harper & Row, 1981.

Lampe, G. W. H. "Martyrdom and Inspiration." In *Suffering and Martyrdom in the New Testament*, edited by William Horbury and Brian McNeil, 118–35. Cambridge: Cambridge University Press, 1981.

Lawlor, H. J. "The Heresy of the Phrygians." *The Journal of Theological Studies* 9 (1908): 481–99.

Lefkowitz, Mary R. "The Motivations for St. Perpetua's Martyrdom." *Journal of the American Academy of Religion* 44(3) (1976): 417–21.

Lomanto, Valeria. "Rapporti fra la 'Passio Perpetuae' e 'Passiones' Africane." In *Forma Futuri: Studi in Onore Del Cardinale Michele Pellegrino*, 566–86. Torino: Bottega d'Erasmo, 1975.

Long, Burke O. "Prophetic Call Traditions and Reports of Visions." *Zeitschrift für Alttestamentliche Wissenschaft* 84 (1972): 494–500.

McDonnell, Kilian. "Communion Ecclesiology and Baptism in the Spirit: Tertullian and the Early Church." *Theological Studies* 49 (1988): 671–93.

Maurer, Christian. "Apocalypse of Peter." In *New Testament Apocrypha*, edited by Edgar Hennecke, edited by Wilhelm Schneemelcher and translated by R. McL. Wilson, 2:663–83. Philadelphia: Westminster Press, 1965.

Mazzucco, Clementina. "Il Significato Cristiano della 'Libertas' Proclamata dai Martiri della 'Passio Perpetuae'." In *Forma Futuri: Studi in Onore Del Cardinale Michele Pellegrino*, 542–65. Torino: Bottega d'Erasmo, 1975.

Meslin, Michal. "Vases sacrés et boissons d'éternité dans les visions des martyrs africains." In *Ipektasis: Mélanges patristiques offerts au Cardinal Jean Daniélou*, edited by Jacques Fontaine and Charles Kannengieser, 139–52. Paris: Beauchesne, 1972.

Miles, Margaret R. "Patriarchy as Political Theology: The Establishment of North African Christianity." In *Civil Religion and Political Theology*, edited by Leroy S. Rouner, 169–86. Notre Dame, Ind.: University of Notre Dame Press, 1986.

Miller, Patricia Cox. "'A Dubious Twilight': Reflections on Dreams in Patristic Literature," *Church History* 55(2) (June 1986): 153–64.

Oepke, Albrecht. "ἐξίστημι." In *Theological Dictionary of the New Testament*, edited by Gerhard Kittel, translated and edited by Geoffrey W. Bromiley, 2:460. Grand Rapids: Wm. B. Eerdmans, 1964.

Owen, H. P. "Stephen's Vision in Acts VII. 55–6." *New Testament Studies* 1 (1955): 224–26.

Paciorkowski, A. "L'héroïsme religieux d'après la Passion des saintes Perpétue et Félicité." *Revue des études augustiniennes* 5 (1959): 367–89.

Pagels, Elaine H. "Visions, Appearances, and Apostolic Authority: Gnostic and Orthodox Traditions." In *Gnosis: Festschrift für Hans Jonas*, edited by Barbara Aland, 415–30. Göttingen: Vandenhoeck & Ruprecht, 1978.

Panagopoulos, John [Παναγοπούλου, Ἰωάννου]. Ἡ Ἐκκλησία τῶν Προφητῶν. Το Προφητικόν Χάρισμα ἐν τῇ Ἐκκλησίᾳ τῶν δύο Πρώτων Αἰώνων. Αθηναι: ΙΣΤΟΡΙΚΕΣ ΕΚΔΟΣΕΙΣ ΣΤ; ΒΑΣΙΛΟΠΟΓΛΟΣ, 1979.

———. Review of *New Testament Prophecy* by David Hill. *Journal for the Study of the New Testament* 10 (1981): 61–65.

Parrott, Douglas, ed. "The Gospel of Mary." In *The Nag Hammadi Library*, edited by James Robinson, 471–74. San Francisco: Harper & Row, 1981.

Pelikan, Jaroslav. "Montanism and Its Trinitarian Significance." *Church History* 25 (1956): 99–109.

Petraglio, R. "Des influences de l'Apocalypse dans la 'Passio Perpetuae' 11–13." In *L'Apocalypse de Jean: Traditions exégétiques et iconographiques IIIᵉ–XIIIᵉ siècles*, edited by R. Petraglio et al., 15–29. Vol. 11, *Études et documents publíes par la Section d'Histoire de La Facultédes Lettres de l'Universitéde Genéve*. Geneva: Librairie Droz, 1979.

Petterson, Alvyn. "Perpetua—Prisoner of Conscience." *Vigiliae Christianae* 41 (1987): 139–53.

Pizzolato, Luigi F. "Note alla 'Passio Perpetuae et Felicitatis.' " *Vigiliae Christianae* 34(2) (1980): 105–19.

Poirier, M. "Note sur la *Passio Sanetarum Perpetuae et Felicitatis*: Félicité était-elle vraiment l'esclave de Perpétue?" *Studia Patristica* 10 (1970): 306–9.

Powell, D. "Tertullianists and Cataphrygians." *Vigiliae Christianae* 29 (1975): 33–54.

Quasten, Johannes. "A Coptic Counterpart to a Vision in Acts of Perpetua and Felicitas." *Byzantion* 15 (1940/41): 1–9.

———. "A Roman Law of Egyptian Origin in the 'Passio SS Perpetuae et Felicitatis.' " *The Jurist* 1(3) (1941): 193–98.

Rader, Rosemary. "The *Martyrdom of Perpetua*: A Protest Account of Third Century Christianity," with a translation of the *Martyrdom of Perpetua*. In *A Lost Tradition: Women Writers of the Early Church*, edited by Patricia Wilson-Kastner, G. Ronald Kastner, Ann Millin, Rosemary Rader, Jeremiah Reedy, 1–32. Washington, D.C.: University Press of America, 1981.

Reiling, J. "The Use of Ψευδοπροφήτης" in the Septuagint, Philo, and Josephus." *Novum Testamentum* 13 (1971): 147–56.

Réveillaud, M. "Note pour une Pneumatologie Cyprienne." *Studia Patristica* 6 (1962): 181–87.

Robeck, Jr., Cecil M. "The Gift of Prophecy in Acts and Paul." 2 parts. *Studia Biblica et Theologica* 5 (1) (1975): 15–38; 5(2) (1975): 37–54.

———. "Origen, Celsus, and Prophetic Utterance." *Paraclete* 11(1) (Winter 1976): 19–23.

———. "Written Prophecies: A Question of Authority." *Pneuma: The Journal of the Society for Pentecostal Studies* 2(2) (Fall 1980): 26–45.

———. "Montanism: A Problematic Spirit Movement." *Paraclete* 15(3) (Summer 1981): 24–29.

———. "Visions and Prophecy in the Writings of Cyprian," *Paraclete* 16(3) (Summer 1982): 21–25.

———. "Hippolytus on the Gift of Prophecy." *Paraclete* 17(3) (Summer 1983): 22–27.

———. "The Prophet in the *Didache*." *Paraclete* 18(1) (Winter 1984): 16–19.

———. "Prophecy in the *Shepherd of Hermas*." *Paraclete* 18(2) (Spring 1984): 12–17.

———. "Tertullian and Prophetic Gifts." *Paraclete* 18(3) (Summer 1984): 16–21.

———. "Irenaeus and 'Prophetic Gifts.'" In *Essays on Apostolic Themes: Studies in Honor of Howard M. Erven*, edited by Paul Elbert, 104–14. Peabody, Mass.: Hendrickson Publishers, 1985.

———. "Canon, *Regulae Fidei*, and Continuing Revelation in the Early Church." In *Church, Word, & Spirit: Historical and Theological Essays in Honor of Geoffrey W. Bromiley*, edited by James E. Bradley and Richard A. Muller, 65–91. Grand Rapids: William B. Eerdmans, 1987.

———. "Prophecy, Gift of." In *Dictionary of Pentecostal and Charismatic Movements*, edited by Stanley M. Burgess and Gary B. McGee. Grand Rapids: Regency Reference Library/Zondervan Publishing House, 1988.

Ruble, Richard L. "The Doctrine of Dreams." *Bibliotheca Sacra* 125 (1968): 360–64.

Rupprecht, Ernst. "Bermerkungen zur Passio SS Perpetuae et Felicitatis." *Rheinisches Museum für Philologie*, n.s., 90(3) (1941): 178–92.

Sanders, E. P. "Testament of Abraham." In *The Old Testament Pseudepigrapha*, edited by James H. Charlesworth, 1:871–902. Garden City, N.Y.: Doubleday & Company, 1983.

Sanders, James A. "Adaptable for Life: The Nature and Function of Canon." In *Magnalia Dei: The Mighty Works of God: Essays on the Bible and Archeology in Memory of G. Ernest Wright*, edited by F. M. Cross et al., 531–60. Garden City, N.Y.: Doubleday, 1976.

Schlier, Heinrich. "Ἀμήν." In *Theological Dictionary of the New Testament*, edited by Gerhard Kittel, translated and edited by Geoffrey W. Bromiley, 1:335–38. Grand Rapids: Wm. B. Eerdmans, 1964.

Scholer, David M. "'And I Was a Man': The Power and Problem of Perpetua." *Daughters of Sarah* 15 (September–October 1989): 10–14.

Schöllgen, Georg. "'Tempus in Collecto Est': Tertullian, der Frühe Montanismus und die Naherwartung ihrer Zeit." *Jahrbuch für Antike und Christentum* 27/28 (1984/1985): 74–96.

Scott, R. B. Y. "Is Prophecy Preaching?" *Canadian Journal of Theology* 1 (1955): 11–18.

Shewring, W. H. "En Marge de la *Passio des Saintes Perpétue et Félicité.*" *La revue benedictine* 43(1) (January 1931): 15–22.

———. "Prose Rhythm in the *Passio S. Perpetuae.*" *Journal of Theological Studies* 20 (1929): 56–57.

Smith, R. Gregor. "Tertullian and Montanism." *Theology* 46 (1943): 127–36.

Soyres, John de. "Passio SS Perpetuae et Felicitatis cum Sociis Earum." In his *Montanism and the Primitive Church*, 138–41. Cambridge: Deighton, Bell, 1879; reprint, Lexington, Ky.: The American Theological Library Association, 1965.

Spittler, Russell P. "The Limits of Ecstasy: An Exegesis of 2 Corinthians 12:1–10." In *Current Issues in Biblical and Patristic Interpretation*, edited by Gerald F. Hawthorne, 259–66. Grand Rapids: William B. Eerdmans, 1975.

Stam, John E. "Charismatic Theology in the *Apostolic Tradition* of Hippolytus." In *Current Issues in Biblical and Patristic Interpretation*, edited by Gerald F. Hawthorne, 267–76. Grand Rapids: William B. Eerdmans, 1975.

Tabbernee, William. "Early Montanism and Voluntary Martyrdom." *Colloquium: The Australian and New Zealand Theological Review* 17(2) (May 1985): 33–44.

———. "Dissenting Spiritualities in History." *The Way: A Review of Contemporary Christian Spirituality* 28 (April 1988): 138–46.

Townes, W. Sibley. "On Calling People 'Prophets' in 1970." *Interpretation* 24 (1970): 492–509.

Trevett, Christine. "Apocalypse, Ignatius, Montanism: Seeking the Seeds." *Vigiliae Christianae* 43(4) (1989): 313–38.

———. "The Use of Scripture in the Montanist Controversy." Texte und Untersuchungen, 103. *Studia Evangelica*, 5 (1968): 317–20.

Trigg, J. W. "Martyrs and Churchmen in Third-Century North Africa." *Studia Patristica* 15 (1984): 242–46.

Vokes, F. E. "Penitential Discipline in Montanism." *Studia Patristica* 14 (1976): 62–76.

———. "The Use of Scripture in the Montanist Controversy." Texte und Untersuchungen, 103. *Studia Evangelica*, 5 (1968): 317–20.

von Franz, Marie-Louise. "Die Passio Perpetuae." In *Aion: Untersuchungen zur Symbolgeschichte*, edited by C. G. Jung, 389–496. Psychologische Abhandlungen, 7. Zurich: Racher Verlag, 1951.

Waal, A. de. "Der leidende Dinocrates in der Vision der heil. Perpetua." *Rhomische Quartalschrift für christliche Altertumskunde und Kirchengeschichte* 17 (1903): 339–47.

Wallis, R. E. "The Martyrdom of Perpetua and Felicitas." In *Ante-Nicene Fathers*, edited by Alexander Roberts and James Donaldson, 3:699–706. Reprint, Grand Rapids: Wm. B. Eerdmans, 1973.

Walls, A. F. "The Montanist 'Catholic Epistle' and Its New Testament Prototype." *Studia Evangelica* 3(2) (1964): 437–46.

Waszink, J. H. "Tertullians' Principles and Methods of Exegesis." In *Early Christian Literature and the Classical Intellectual Tradition: In Honorem Robert M. Grant*, edited by William R. Schoedel and Robert L. Wilkens, 17–31. Théologie Historique, 53. Paris: Éditions Beauchesne, 1979.

Weinrich, William C. "Passion of Perpetua and Felicitas." In *Spirit and Martyrdom*, 223–51. Washington, D.C.: University Press of America, 1981.

Whale, John S. "Montanus." *The Expository Times* 45 (1934): 496–500.

Williams, Cyril G. "Ecstaticism in Hebrew Prophecy and Christian Glossolalia." *Studies in Religion/Sciences Religieuses* 3 (1974): 320–38.

Williams, D. H. "The Origins of the Montanist Movement: A Sociological Analysis." *Religion* 19 (1989): 331–51.

Williams, George H., and Waldvogel, Edith. "A History of Speaking in Tongues and Related Gifts." In *The Charismatic Movement*, edited by Michael P. Hamilton, 61–113. Grand Rapids: William B. Eerdmans, 1975.

Wilson, J. W. "The Career of the Prophet Hermas." *Harvard Theological Review* 20 (1927): 21–61.

Wood, Leon J. "Ecstasy and Israel's Early Prophets." *Journal of the Evangelical Theological Society* 9 (1966): 125–37.

Wright, David F. "Montanism: A Movement of Spiritual Renewal?" *Theological Renewal* 22 (November 1982): 19–29.

———. "Why Were the Montanists Condemned?" *Themelios* 2(1) (September 1976): 15–22.

BOOKS

Aune, David E. *Prophecy in Early Christianity and the Ancient Mediterranean World.* Grand Rapids: William B. Eerdmans, 1983.

Bardy, Gustav. *La question des langues dans l'Église ancienne.* Études de théologie historique, 1. Paris: Beauchesne et Ses Fils, 1958.

———. *La Vie spirituelle d'après les pères des trois premiers siècles.* 2 vols. Tournai, Belgium: Desclée et Cie, 1968.

Barker, Ethel Ross. *Rome of the Pilgrims and Martyrs.* London: Methuen, 1913.

Barnes, Timothy David. *Tertullian: A Historical and Literary Study.* Oxford: Clarendon Press, 1971.

Barnett, Maurice. *The Living Flame.* London: Epworth Press, 1953.

Barrett, C. K. *A Commentary on the First Epistle to the Corinthians.* Harper's New Testament Commentaries. New York: Harper and Row, 1968.

Benson, Edward White. *Cyprian: His Life, His Times, His Work.* London: Macmillan, 1897.

Berger, Klaus. *Die Amen-Worte Jesu.* Beiheft zur Zeitschrift für die neutestamentliche Wissenschaft und die Kunde der alteren Kirche, 39. Berlin: Walter de Gruyter, 1970.

Bittlinger, Arnold. *Gifts and Graces: A Commentary on I Corinthians 12–14*, translated by Herbert Klassen. Reprint, Grand Rapids: William B. Eerdmans, 1976.

Bonwetsch, D. Nathanael. *Texte zur Geschichte des Montanismus*. Kleine Texte für Vorlesungen und Ubungen, 129. Bonn: A. Marcus und E. Weber's Verlag, 1914.

Bonwetsch, Nathanael. *Die Geschichte des Montanismus*. Erlangen: Andreas Deichert, 1881.

Boring, M. Eugene. *Sayings of the Risen Christ: Christian Prophecy in the Synoptic Tradition*. Society for New Testament Studies, Monograph 46. Cambridge: Cambridge University Press, 1982.

Bray, Gerald Lewis. *Holiness and the Will of God: Perspectives on the Theology of Tertullian*. New Foundations Theological Library. Atlanta: John Knox Press, 1979.

Brown, Peter. *The Making of Late Antiquity*. Cambridge, Mass.: Harvard University Press, 1978.

Bury, R. G., trans. *Plato: Timaeus*. Rev. ed. Vol. 7. Loeb Classical Library. Cambridge: Harvard University Press, 1952.

Cameron, Ron. ed. *The Other Gospels: Non-Canonical Gospel Texts*. Philadelphia: Westminster Press, 1982.

von Campenhausen, Hans. *Ecclesiastical Authority and Spiritual Power*, translated by J. A. Baker. Stanford: Stanford University Press, 1969.

Carey, H., trans. *The Epistles of S. Cyprian: A Library of the Fathers*. Oxford: John Henry Parker, 1844.

Charles, R. H. *The Apocrypha and Pseudepigrapha of the Old Testament in English*. 2 vols. Oxford: Clarendon Press, 1913.

———. *The Book of Enoch*. Oxford: Clarendon Press, 1893.

Church, Alfred J., in collaboration with Arthur Gilman. *Carthage of the Empire of Africa*. Reprint, Freeport, N.Y.: Books for Libraries Press, 1971.

Clarke, G. W. *The Letters of St. Cyprian* (1–27). Vol. 1. Ancient Christian Writers, 43; New York: Newman Press, 1984.

———. *The Letters of St. Cyprian* (28–54). Vol. 2 Ancient Christian Writers, 44; New York: Newman Press, 1984.

———. *The Letters of St. Cyprian* (55–66). Vol. 3. Ancient Christian Writers, 46; New York: Newman Press, 1986.

———. *The Letters of St. Cyprian* (67–82). Vol. 4. Ancient Christian Writers, 47; New York: Newman Press, 1989.

Colson, F. H. *Philo*, translated by G. H. Whitaker. Vol. 5. Loeb Classical Library. Cambridge, Mass.: Harvard University Press, 1949.

Crone, T. M. *Early Christian Prophecy: A Study of Its Origin and Function*. Baltimore: St. Mary's University Press, 1973.

Cullmann, Oscar. *Early Christian Worship*, translated by A. Stewart Todd and James B. Torrance. Studies in Biblical Theology, 1st ser., 10. London: SCM Press, 1969.

Cumont, Franz. *After Life in Roman Paganism*. Reprint, New York: Dover Publications, 1959.

Daniélou, Jean. *The Angels and Their Mission*, translated by David Hiemann. Westminster, Md.: Christian Classics, 1976.

————. *The Origins of Latin Christianity: A History of Early Christian Doctrine before the Council of Nicaea.* 3 vols. Philadelphia: Westminster Press, 1977.

Dautzenberg, Gerhard. *Urchristliche Prophetie.* Beitrage zur Wissenschaft vom Alten und Neuen Testament, 4. Stuttgart: W. Kohlhammer, 1975.

Dodd, C. H. *The Interpretation of the Fourth Gospel.* Cambridge: University Press, 1968.

Dodds, E. R. *Pagan and Christian in an Age of Anxiety.* Cambridge: University Press, 1965.

Dronke, Peter. *Women Writers of the Middle Ages: A Critical Study of Texts from Perpetua (+ 203) to Marguerite Porete (+1310).* Cambridge: Cambridge University Press, 1986.

Duchesne, Louis. *Early History of the Christian Church.* London: John Murray, 1909.

Duquenne, Luc. *Chronologie des lettres de S. Cyprien: Le dossier de la persécution de Dèce.* Brussels: Société des Bollandistes, 1972.

Ellis, E. Earle. *The Gospel of Luke,* edited by H. H. Rowley and Matthew Black. New Century Bible. Rev. ed. Greenwood, S.C.: Attic Press, 1974.

————. *Prophecy and Hermeneutic in Early Christianity.* Grand Rapids: William B. Eerdmans, 1980.

Evans, Ernest, ed. and trans. *Tertullian Adversus Marcionem.* Oxford: Clarendon Press, 1972.

————. *Tertullian's Tract on the Prayer.* London: SPCK, 1953.

————. *Tertullian's Treatise Against Praxeas.* London: SPCK, 1948.

Evelyn-White, Hugh G., trans. *Hesiod, The Homeric Hymns and Homerica.* Loeb Classical Library. Cambridge: Harvard University Press, 1936.

Fahey, Michael Andrew. *Cyprian and the Bible: A Study in Third-Century Exegesis.* Tübingen: J. C. B. Mohr, 1971.

Fairclough, H. Rushton, trans. *Virgil: Ecologues, Georgics, Aeneid I–VI.* Rev. ed. Vol. 1. Loeb Classical Library. Cambridge: Harvard University Press, 1953.

Fee, Gordon D. *The First Epistle to the Corinthians.* The New International Commentary of the New Testament. Grand Rapids: Wm. B. Eerdmans, 1987.

Fichter, Joseph H. *Saint Cecil Cyprian: Early Defender of the Faith.* London: B. Herder, 1942.

Forma Futuri: Studi in Onore Del Cardinale Michele Pelligrino. Torino: Bottega d'Erasmo, 1975.

Frend, W. H. C. *The Donatist Church: A Movement of Protest in Roman North Africa.* Oxford: Clarendon Press, 1971.

————. *The Early Church.* London: Hodder and Stoughton, 1965.

Fridh, Åke. *Le problème de la Passion des Saintes Perpétue et Félicité.* Studia Graeca et Latina Gothoburgensia, 26. Göteborg: Acta Universitatis Gothoburgensis, 1968.

Gee, Donald. *Concerning Spiritual Gifts.* Rev. ed. Springfield, Mo.: Gospel Publishing House, 1980.

Goodspeed, Edgar J. *A History of Early Christian Literature.* Revised and enlarged by Robert M. Grant. Chicago: University of Chicago Press, 1966.

Grant, Robert M. *The Apostolic Fathers: An Introduction.* New York: Thomas Nelson & Sons, 1964.

————. *Second Century Christianity: A Collection of Fragments.* Translations of Christian Literature, series 6. London: SPCK, 1957.

————, and David Noel Freedman. *The Secret Sayings of Jesus.* Garden City: Doubleday & Company, 1960.

Grudem, Wayne A. *The Gift of Prophecy in I Corinthians.* Washington, D.C.: University Press of America, 1982.

————. *The Gift of Prophecy in the New Testament and Today.* Westchester, Ill.: Crossway Books, 1988.

Hanson, R. P. C. *Tradition in the Early Church.* London: SCM Press, 1962.

von Harnack, Adolf. *History of Dogma,* translated by Neil Buchanan. 5 vols. Reprint, New York: Dover Publications, 1961.

Harris, J. Rendel, and Seth K. Gifford. *The Acts of the Martyrdom of Perpetua and Felicitas.* London: C. J. Clay and Sons, 1890.

Heine, Ronald E. *The Montanist Oracles and Testimonia.* Patristic Monograph Series, 14. Macon, Ga.: Mercer University Press, 1989.

Helmbold, W. H. S. *Plutarch: Moralia.* Vol. 9. Loeb Classical Library. Cambridge: Harvard University Press, 1961.

Hennecke, Edgar, ed. *New Testament Apocrypha,* edited by Wilhelm Schneemelcher, translated by R. McL. Wilson. 2 vols. Philadelphia: The Westminster Press, 1963–65.

Héring, Jean. *The Second Epistle of Saint Paul to the Corinthians,* translated by A. W. Heathcote and P. J. Allcock. London: Epworth Press, 1967.

Hill, David. *New Testament Prophecy.* Marshall's Theological Library. London: Marshall, Morgan & Scott, 1979. Also New Foundations Theological Library. Atlanta: John Knox Press, 1979.

Hinchliff, Peter. *Cyprian of Carthage and the Unity of the Christian Church.* London: Geoffrey Chapman, 1974.

Holme, L. R. *The Extinction of the Christian Churches in North Africa.* Reprint, New York: Burt Franklin, 1969.

Hölscher, Gustav. *Die Profeten: Untersuchungen zur Religionsgeschichte Israel.* Leipzig: J. C. Hinrichs'sche Buchhandlung, 1914.

Horton, Harold. *The Gifts of the Spirit.* Reprint, Nottingham: Assemblies of God Publishing House, 1971.

Jacob, Edmond. *The Theology of the Old Testament,* translated by Arthur W. Heathcote and Phillip J. Allcock. New York: Harper & Row, 1958.

Joly, Robert. *Le Pasteur.* Sources Chrétiennes, 53. Paris: Éditions du Cerf, 1958.

Jones, W. H. S., trans. *Hippocrates: Aphorisms.* Vol. 4. Loeb Classical Library. Cambridge: Harvard University Press, 1953.

Kaiser, Otto. *Isaiah 13–39: A Commentary,* translated by R. A. Wilson. Old Testament Library. Philadelphia: Westminster Press, 1974.

Käsemann, Ernst. *Perspectives on Paul.* Philadelphia: Fortress Press, 1971.

Kennedy, H. A. A. *Sources of New Testament Greek.* Edinburgh: T. & T. Clark, 1895.

Knox, R. A. *Enthusiasm.* Oxford: Clarendon Press, 1950.

Koch, Hugo. *Cyprianische Untersuchungen: Arbeiten zur Kirchengeschichte,* edited by Karl Hall and Hans Lietzmann. Bonn: A. Marcus und E. Weber's Verlag, 1926.

Kraft, Robert A. *Barnabas and the Didache.* The Apostolic Fathers, vol. 3. New York: Thomas Nelson & Sons, 1965.

Kydd, Ronald Alfred Narfi. "Charismata to 320 A.D.: A Study of the Overt Pneumatic Experience of the Early Church." Ph.D. diss., University of St. Andrews, 1972.

Labriolle, Pierre de. *La Crise Montaniste.* Paris: Ernest Leroux, 1913.

————. *Les sources de l'histoire du Montanisme Collectanea Friburgensia.* New series. Fasc. 15 [24 in the collection]. Fribourg: Librairie de l'Université; Paris: Ernest Leroux, 1913.

————. *History and Literature of Christianity, from Tertullian to Boethius,* translated by Herbert Wilson. New York: Alfred A. Knopf, 1924.

Lampe, G. W. H. *Explorations in Theology 8.* London: SCM Press, 1981.

La Rondelle, H. K. *Perfection and Perfectionism: A Dogmatic-Ethical Study of Biblical Perfectionism and Phenomenal Perfectionism.* Berrien Springs, Mich.: Andrews University Press, 1971.

Leclercq, Dom H. *L'afrique Chrétienne.* Bibliothèque de l'enseignement de l'histoire ecclésiastique. 2 vols. Paris: Librairie Victor Lecoffre, 1904.

Lewis, Naphtali. *Life in Egypt under Roman Rule.* Oxford: Clarendon Press, 1983.

Lietzmann, Hans. *The Beginnings of the Christian Church.* New York: Charles Scribner's Sons, 1938.

Lindblom, Johannes. *Gesichte und Offenbarungen: Vorstellungen von göttlichen Weisungen und übernatürlichen Erscheinungen im ältesten Christentum.* Aeta Reg. Societatis Humaniorum Litteratum Lundensis. Lund: Gleerup, 1968.

————. *Prophecy in Ancient Israel.* Philadelphia: Fortress Press, 1973.

Luther, Martin. *Lectures on the Minor Prophets,* edited by Hilton C. Oswald. Luther's Works, vols. 18 and 20. St. Louis: Concordia Publishing House, 1973, 1975.

MacDonald, Dennis Ronald. *The Legend and the Apostle: The Battle for Paul in Story and Canon.* Philadelphia: Westminster Press, 1983.

MacKenzie, Donald A. *Egyptian Myth and Legend.* Reprint, Portland, Maine: Longwood Press, 1976.

MacKenzie, Ross, trans. *The Epistles of Paul the Apostle to the Romans and to the Thessalonians.* Calvin's Commentaries. Grand Rapids: Wm. B. Eerdmans, 1960.

Marshall, I. Howard, *The Gospel of Luke.* New International Greek Testament Commentary. Exeter: Paternoster Press, 1978.

Metzger, Bruce M. *The Text of the New Testament: Its Transmission, Corruption, and Restoration.* 2d ed. New York: Oxford University Press, 1968.

Monceaux, Paul. *Histoire littéraire de l'afrique Chrétienne depuis les origines jusqu'a l'invasion Arabe.* 7 vols. in 3. Paris: Ernest Leroux, 1901–1905.

Müller, Ulrich B. *Prophetie und Predigt im Neuen Testament*. Studien zum Neuen Testament, 10. Gütersloh: Verlagshaus [Gerd Mohn], 1975.

Muncey, R. Waterville. *The Passion of S. Perpetua*. London: J. M. Dent & Sons, 1927.

Murray, A. T. trans. *Homer: The Odyssey*. Loeb Classical Library. London: William Heinemann, 1930.

Musurillo, Herbert. *The Acts of the Christian Martyrs*. Oxford Early Christian Texts. Oxford: Clarendon Press, 1972.

O'Malley, T. P. *Tertullian and the Bible*. Latinitas Christianorum Primaeva. Utrecht: Dekker and VandeVegt N. V. Nijmegen, 1967.

Ombres, Robert. *The Theology of Purgatory*. Theology Today Series, vol. 24. Butler, Wis.: Clergy Book Service, 1978.

Pagels, Elaine. *The Gnostic Gospels*. New York: Vintage Books/Random House, 1981.

Panagopoulos, John, ed. *Prophetic Vocation in the New Testament and Today*. Novun Testamentum Supplement, 45. Leiden: E. J. Brill, 1977.

Pelikan, Jaroslav. *The Emergence of the Catholic Tradition (100–600): The Christian Tradition*. Chicago: University of Chicago Press, 1971.

Perrin, Bernadotte, trans. *Plutarch: Solon*. Vol. 1. Loeb Classical Library. Cambridge, Mass.: Harvard University Press, 1948.

Petroff, Elizabeth Alvilda. *Medieval Women's Visionary Literature*. New York: Oxford University Press, 1986.

Plummer, Alfred. *Second Epistle of St. Paul to the Corinthians*. International Critical Commentary. Edinburgh: T. & T. Clark, 1970.

Pridie, J. R. *The Spiritual Gifts*. London: Robert Scott, 1921.

Quasten, Johannes. *Patrology*. 3 vols. Utrecht-Antwerp: Spectrum Publishers, 1975.

————, and Joseph C. Plumpe, eds. *Tertullian: Treatises on Marriage and Remarriage*, translated by William P. LeSaint. Ancient Christian Writers, vol. 13. Westminster, Md.: Newman Press, 1951.

Rahner, Karl. *Visions and Prophecies*. Questiones Disputatae, 10. New York: Herder and Herder, 1983.

Reiling, J. *Hermas and Christian Prophecy: A Study of the Eleventh Mandate*. Novum Testamentum Supplement, 37. Leiden: E. J. Brill, 1973.

Robinson, J. Armitage, ed. "The Passion of S. Perpetua." In *Texts and Studies* 1(2). Cambridge: University Press, 1891; reprint, Nendeln/Liechtenstein: Kraus Reprint, 1967.

Robinson, James, ed. *The Nag Hammadi Library*. San Francisco: Harper & Row, 1981.

Robinson, Theodore H. *Prophecy and the Prophets in Ancient Israel*. 2d ed. London: Gerald Duckworth & Co., 1967.

Rowland, Christopher. *The Open Heaven: A Study of Apocalyptic in Judaism and Early Christianity*. New York: Crossroad, 1982.

Rowley, H. H. *The Servant of the Lord*. 2d rev. ed. Oxford: Basil Blackwell, 1965.

Russell, D. S. *Between the Testaments*. Rev. ed. Philadelphia: Fortress Press, 1965.

————. *The Method and Message of Jewish Apocalyptic*. Old Testament Library. Philadelphia: Westminster Press, 1964.

Sage, Michael M. *Cyprian*. Patristic Monograph Series, 1. Cambridge, Mass.: Philadelphia Patristic Foundation, 1975.

Schaff, Phillip. *Teaching of the Twelve Apostles*. New York: Funk & Wagnalls, 1885.

————. *History of the Christian Church: Ante-Nicene Christianity*. 8 vols. Reprint, Grand Rapids: William B. Eerdmans, 1970.

Shewring, W. H. *The Passion of S. S. Perpetua and Felicity MM, Together with The Sermons of S. Augustine on these Saints*. London: Sheed and Ward, 1931.

Soyres, John de. *Montanism and the Primitive Church*. Cambridge: Deighton, Bell, 1878; reprint, Lexington, Ky.: The American Theological Library Association, 1965.

Tabernee, William. "Opposition to Montanism from Church and State: A Study of the History and Theology of the Montanist Movement as shown by the Writings and Legislation on the Orthodox Opponents of Montanism." 2 vols. Unpub. thesis, University of Melbourne, 1978.

Tasker, R. V. G. *The Second Epistle of Paul to the Corinthians*. Tyndale New Testament Commentaries. Grand Rapids: Wm. B. Eerdmans, 1958.

Terrien, Samuel. *The Elusive Presence: Toward a New Biblical Theology*. New York: Harper & Row, 1978.

Warfield, Benjamin B. *Counterfeit Miracles*. Reprint, London: Banner of Truth Trust, 1972.

Waszink, J. H. *Quinti Septimi Florentis Tertulliani De Anima*. Amsterdam: J. M. Meulenhoff, 1947.

Weinrich, William C. *Spirit and Martyrdom: A Study of the Work of the Holy Spirit in Contexts of Persecution and Martyrdom in the New Testament and Early Christian Literature*. Washington, D.C.: University Press of America, 1981.

Withington, E. T., trans. *Hippocrates: ΠΕΡΙ' ΑΡΘΡΟΝ*. Vol. 3. Loeb Classical Library. Cambridge, Mass.: Harvard University Press, 1948.

Wood, Leon J. *The Holy Spirit in the Old Testament*. Grand Rapids: Zondervan Publishing, 1976.

Woodward, G. R., and H. Mattingly, trans. *Barlaam and Iosaph*, by St. John Damascene. LCL. Cambridge, Mass.: Harvard University Press, 1953.

Yocum, Bruce. *Prophecy: Exercising the Prophetic Gifts of the Spirit in the Church Today*. Ann Arbor, Mich.: Word of Life, 1976.

REFERENCE WORKS

Abbott-Smith, G. *A Manual Greek Lexicon of the New Testament*. 3d ed. Edinburgh: T. & T. Clark, 1964.

Andrews, E. A., ed. *Harpers' Latin Dictionary: A New Latin Dictionary*. Revised and enlarged ed. by Charlton T. Lewis and Charles Short. New York: American Book, 1907.

Arndt, William F., and F. Wilbur Gingrich. *A Greek-English Lexicon of the New*

Testament and Other Early Christian Literature, edited by Walter Bauer. Rev. ed. Chicago: University of Chicago Press, 1957.

van Beek, Cornelis I. M. I. *Passio Sanctarum Perpetuae et Felicitatis.* Florilegium Patristicum, 43. Bonn: Petri Hanstein, 1938.

Hartel, Guilelmus. *S. Thasci Caecili Cypriani Opera Omnia.* 3 vols. Corpus Scriptorum Ecclesiasticorum Latinorum. Vienna: C. Geroldi Filium Bibliopolam Academiae, 1868–1871.

Kittel, Gerhard, ed. *Theological Dictionary of the New Testament,* translated and edited by Geoffrey W. Bromiley. 10 vols. Grand Rapids: William B. Eerdmans, 1964–1976.

Lampe, G. W. H., ed. *A Patristic Greek Lexicon.* Oxford: Clarendon Press, 1961.

Migne, J. P., ed. *Patrilogiae Graecae.* 168 vols. Reprint, Turnholti, Belgium: Typographi Brepols, 1978. (Referred to throughout notes as *PG.*)

Roberts, Alexander, and James Donaldson, eds. *The Ante-Nicene Fathers.* Rev. ed. by A. Cleveland Coxe. 10 vols. Grand Rapids: William B. Eerdmans, 1971–79. (Referred to throughout notes as *ANF.*)

Schaff, Philip, and Henry Wace. *A Select Library of Nicene and Post-Nicene Fathers of the Christian Church.* 2d series. 14 vols. Grand Rapids: Wm. B. Eerdmans, 1971. (Referred to throughout notes as *NPNF.*)

Simpson, D. P., ed. *Cassell's New Compact Latin-English, English-Latin Dictionary.* New York: Funk & Wagnalls, 1963.

Tertullian. *Tertullian Opera: Corpus Christianorum Series Latina.* 2 vols. Turnholti, Belgium: Typographi Brepols; Rome: Editores Pontificii, 1954. (Referred to throughout notes as *Tertullian Opera.*)

Author Index

Ancient Texts Index